ADLERTAG

ADLERTAG

THE BATTLE OF BRITAIN INTENSIFIES
11–13 AUGUST 1940

PATRICK G. ERIKSSON

AMBERLEY

First published 2025

Amberley Publishing
The Hill, Stroud
Gloucestershire, GL5 4EP

www.amberley-books.com

Copyright © Patrick G. Eriksson, 2025

The right of Patrick G. Eriksson to be identified as the Author of this work has been asserted in accordance with the Copyright, Designs and Patents Act 1988.

All rights reserved. No part of this book may be reprinted or reproduced or utilised in any form or by any electronic, mechanical or other means, now known or hereafter invented, including photocopying and recording, or in any information storage or retrieval system, without the permission in writing from the Publishers.

British Library Cataloguing in Publication Data.
A catalogue record for this book is available from the British Library.

ISBN 978 1 3981 1738 9 (hardback)
ISBN 978 1 3981 1739 6 (ebook)

1 2 3 4 5 6 7 8 9 10

Typeset in 10.5pt on 13.5pt Sabon.
Typesetting by SJmagic DESIGN SERVICES, India.
Printed in the UK.

Appointed GPSR EU Representative: Easy Access System Europe Oü, 16879218
Address: Mustamäe tee 50, 10621, Tallinn, Estonia
Contact Details: gpsr.requests@easproject.com, +358 40 500 3575

Contents

Dedication	6
Acknowledgements	7
Preface	9
A Brief Explanation of German *Luftwaffe* Terminology	18
1 The First Major Raid, Portland: 11 August 1940	21
2 Second Major Raid, Portsmouth, Radar Stations and Forward Airfields Attacked: 12 August 1940	78
3 Eagle Day: 13 August 1940	149
4 Conclusions	251
Notes	260
Bibliography	331
Maps	340
Index	342

Dedication

To my parents. George Eriksson who had to leave school and get a job at age 15, at the height of the Great Depression. He worked himself up from office boy to admitted attorney, studying exclusively through nighttime classes. Adelheid Eriksson, who had to leave school at age 16, to work as a hotel chef, due to an unexpected death in the family. They ensured their three children had easy and comfortable access to superior education.

To my father-in-law. Major Willem Smit, badly wounded with the South African 6th Armoured Division in Italy in 1944, who never got over war-induced stress as a consequence. They were part of that *Greatest Generation*, as were all those, both named and un-named, who wrote the three days of history analysed in this book, which is dedicated to all their memories. We will not see their like again.

To Rob Buchanan NCO in the Rhodesian Army and Lieutenant in the South African Army. To him and all my comrades in the Memorable Order of Tin Hats, South Africa, past and present: veterans of five wars over the past ninety-seven years. Particularly members of the Atomic Shellhole, Hilton.

Fortis et fides

Acknowledgements

I am greatly privileged to have had contact with RAF veterans of the Battle of Britain; my correspondence with them provided critical insights into the fighting of the late summer and autumn of 1940. I gratefully acknowledge the support and interest offered by the following. Sir Douglas Bader, Air Commodore Alan Deere, who also sent me a signed copy of his autobiography *Nine Lives*, Air Commodore James Coward, Wing Commander Michael Crossley, Group Captain David Haysom and his compatriot, Air Commodore Edward 'Teddy' Morris. From the *Luftwaffe*, *Oberst* Hanns Trűbenbach, a true old-world gentleman and wise warrior.

I have received enormous support and very generous help over many years, especially in the form of documents relating to the Battle from several outstanding aerial historians and authors: Nigel Parker and Robert Forsyth (UK), Juha Vaittinen (Finland), and Lothair Vanoverbeke (Belgium). I owe them all a significant debt of gratitude, for friendship, advice and copious quantities of original wartime material. Peter Arnot, Andreas Baumann, Antonio Argudo and Markus Polleichtner all played critical roles in unravelling *Gefreiter* Hans-Helmut Habermehl's history within *1/JG 54* in 1940. Shaun Barrington of Amberley Publishing has long provided inspiration, encouragement, support and ongoing enthusiasm and has made this book possible, although only the author is to blame for any inherent faults therein. Philip Dean at Amberley has also been a great support. Kerry Pentz of Penzil Advertising is acknowledged for her drafting skills.

My heartfelt gratitude is owed to my wife, Mariánne, herself a very successful writer and illustrator of her own series of children's books, for her love and support, and for allowing me to bury myself in my study for extended periods. My brother, Dr Andrew Eriksson, remains a great help in many ways: storing back-ups, reading several chapters, and chipping away at my ignorance of computers. A final thanks to my parents who gave me flying lessons in my youth and helped to build up a critical and growing World War Two library from an early age.

Preface

Adlertag or 'Eagle Day' was 13 August 1940. The chosen time-period covered here of 11 August to 13 August 1940 fits in after the early convoy battles and attacks on coastal targets which dominated July and the first few days of August. Hitler's *Führer* Directive No. 17 of 1 August 1940 had let the reins off the *Luftwaffe* in its attacks against the United Kingdom and its surrounding seas; *Adlertag* was to open the great offensive after the warm-up of July, and was planned initially for 5 August, depending on air force readiness and the weather.[1] However, after a first postponement to 8 August, when the weather once again was judged not to be good enough to open the grand aerial assault, the dispatch of a British convoy down-Channel from east to west allowed the Germans to carry out their first really large-scale set of shipping assaults, by the Stuka dive-bombers of *Luftflotte 3*. After further delays to the launch of *Adlertag*, largely weather-related, planned for 10 August and then the next day, Eagle Day was finally launched on the 13th. Once again, the weather disrupted the complex planning inherent in this opening attack; something of a fiasco ensued as the fog of war descended, with raids launched then cancelled, but some still carried out.

In the event, the massive aerial attack against the British was finally to take place on 15 August, which would begin the anticipated short assault on the RAF which *Reichsmarschall* Göring, the commander of the German *Luftwaffe*, and the vast majority of his men were sure would suffice to destroy their opponents within a few days. This, the effective raising of the German curtain on 15 August saw the participation of much of the strength of all three *Luftflotten* (air fleets) ranged against the British Isles, Numbers 2 (stationed in Belgium and northern France), 3 (Normandy and north-western France) and *Luftflotte 5* (Norway and Denmark). This widespread set of attacks also included for the first time raids on inland Fighter Command sector stations as targets, which would continue for much of the rest of the month. Having recently overwhelmed Poland, Denmark, Norway, the Low Countries and France, having sent the British Army back across the Channel from Dunkirk, and having beaten all their opposing air forces other than the RAF, the Germans and the *Luftwaffe* in particular were dangerously over-confident. The restraint, strategic vision and the subtle and functional integrated aerial defence system set up under Air Chief Marshal Sir Hugh Dowding's leadership, and tactically mastered by the 11 Group commander, Air Vice Marshal Keith Park, his 10 Group colleague Air Vice Marshal Sir Quintin Brand and their sector commanders, stands in stark contrast to the bombast of *Reichsmarschall* Göring of the *Luftwaffe*. That air force was not well prepared for the battle of attrition carefully planned by Dowding and Park, a strategy carried out close to perfection by them.

The three days in the Battle of Britain from 11–13 August 1940 can be seen as something of a watershed, separating the skirmishing of July and early August and its focus on convoy attacks culminating in the 8 August shipping assault from the heavy raids starting on 15 August. While large raids against southern England were carried out on 11, 12 and 13 August, they did not yet reach the full force of the assaults to follow from 15 August onwards. Raids on 12 August, which targeted the radar stations as well as several forward fighter bases in Kent and Sussex, were necessary precursors to any 'Eagle Day' opening assault on the RAF and engagements beyond.

What really characterizes the 11–13 August period is the distinct contrast in the strategy and tactics applied by the two main German units, *Luftflotte 2* under Field Marshal Albert Kesselring and *Luftflotte 3* of Field Marshal Hugo Sperrle. Each of the field marshals also used very specific forces from those available to them: Kesselring, with a single exception, used only one of his bomber *Geschwadern*, supported by his two Ju 87 'Stuka' dive-bomber *Gruppen* and his sole fighter-bomber outfit (all from his *Fliegerkorps II*), covered by all of his considerable fighters. Sperrle on the other hand, used multiple conventional bomber *Geschwadern*, but largely those equipped with the modern Ju 88 aircraft, and a range of his considerable Stukas, from across three *Fliegerkorps*, again covered by his (lesser) fighter resources. The strategy and tactics adopted by these two German leaders in these three days formed the basis of their fighting philosophies and would extend across the entire daylight bombing Battle until its effective conclusion on 15 September 1940. While their boss, *Reichsmarschall* Hermann Göring often sent out streams of instructions and orders to his *Luftflotte* commanders and also to subordinate units, he had no consolidated and reasoned strategic

Preface

policy for the Battle about to begin in earnest on 11 August 1940. Unless unavoidable, most high *Luftwaffe* commanders tended to ignore the *Reichsmarschsall's* edicts, often emanating from his luxury German country estate far from the Channel front.

While Kesselring thus in a way husbanded his bombing attack resources and shepherded them with massive fighter support, Sperrle was immediately rather profligate with his best bombing units, despite lacking large fighter resources. These rather divergent German strategies and tactics provided the crucible within which the RAF won the Battle, during which the achievements of the controllers (at Fighter Command, Group and sector station levels) and the tactical leadership in the air of squadron leaders and flight lieutenants leading small British fighter formations into combat, provided the necessary sharp blade of the sword forged by the Dowding – Park high command and its organised and prepared defensive system. Only once the incoming German formations were sighted by the frontline RAF unit leaders, could the tactical situation be assessed, and necessarily rapidly so: what were the enemy numbers, formations, escorts and their relative placements vis-a-vis bombers? And how were the British placed to attack, assessing whether there was time to get at bombers before escorts intervened, and which attack method(s) were realistically possible. These decisions were equally critical in winning the Battle of Britain as the 'Dowding system' and its commanders were.

Kesselring's raids during the 11–13 August period were carried out almost exclusively by only a part of one of the two main *Fliegerkorps* (*FlK*) in his *Luftflotte*, namely *FlK II*: with three full bomber *Geschwadern* in this *Korps*, only *KG 2* was used, as well as the two *Stukagruppen* in the *Korps* (*II/StG 1* and *IV/LG 1*) and its specialised fighter-bomber unit, *Erprobungsgruppe 210*. *KG 2* was led by the inimitable *Oberst* Johannes Fink who had been the *Kanalkampfführer* (Channel battle leader) since early July 1940. It was the most experienced bomber unit on the Channel and had one of the *Luftwaffe*'s best formation leaders. Kesselring, using essentially only one of his five available bomber *Geschwadern* but all of his limited Stukas and his only fighter-bomber *Gruppe*, utilised all of his Me 109 single engine fighters, comprising the equivalent of five full *Geschwadern*, and most of his Me 110 twin-engine machines.

His fighter leader (*Jagdfliegerführer*, abbreviated to *Jafü*) was *Generalmajor* (Air Commodore equivalent) Theo Osterkamp, a famous World War 1 ace, the German navy's top scorer in that conflict and holder of the *Pour le Mérite* for his thirty-two recognised aerial victories. As the long-time commander of the *Luftwaffe*'s premier fighter school pre-war, and having led *Jagdgeschwader 51* over France in May–June 1940 and

Adlertag

over south-east England during July, he was an expert in his chosen field, an excellent leader, a man predisposed to speak his mind to authority, and he had the full confidence of Kesselring.[2] He saw the defeat of the RAF as being achieved largely by fighter versus fighter combat between what he considered the superior Me 109 and Fighter Command's Hurricanes and Spitfires, espousing the need to apply all possible stratagems to surprise British fighters and bounce them from above, in pursuit of what he held to be an implicitly necessary kill ratio of 5 to 1.

For Osterkamp, and also for his boss Kesselring, the bombing attack by conventional bombers, dive-bombers and fighter-bombers on RAF fighter airfields (and on British naval and merchant shipping and ports) served as a framework within which the fighters could do their deadly work. During the three days 11–13 August, the fighter-rich raids sent into south-east England by Kesselring (which began from 12 August) were typically multi-pronged bombing assaults carried out simultaneously by *Gruppen*-sized formations and covered by advance fighter sweeps, direct and indirect escorts and outgoing sweeps, all intended to achieve the basic aim of downing the British fighters. This strategy and its concomitant tactics would continue to dominate the aerial warfare practised by Kesselring in the Battle of Britain; from late August 1940 he would control almost all of the German single-engine fighters stationed in the Pas de Calais area, hitting Fighter Command intensely until the switch to bombing London from 7 September.

By 15 September, when the bombing assault was essentially defeated and after which it was largely discontinued at least by day, the numbers of Me 109s had shrunk, allowing effective escort only of a limited number of bombers, whose ranks were anyway similarly diminished. Osterkamp's 5 to 1 ratio was never maintained and in the end it was the Me 109s who lost the battle of attrition, so expertly planned and carried out by Air Chief Marshal Sir Hugh Dowding of Fighter Command and his principal subordinate, Air Vice Marshal Keith Park of 11 Group in south-east England. It was thus a losing German strategy adopted by *Luftflotte 2*, and it was first demonstrated with great clarity in the period 11–13 August 1940, when using only the Do 17s of *Oberst* Fink's *KG 2* and three further *Gruppen* of dive- and fighter-bombers.

In the same three days, *Feldmarschall* Sperrle took a somewhat different approach. Having a total of five conventional bomber *Geschwadern* plus the majority of the available Stukas, but only three Me 109 *Geschwadern* plus the equivalent of two more *Geschwadern* of Me 110s, Sperrle used several of his Stuka units (*FlK VIII*) between 11 and 13 August, plus conventional bombers from both his other *Fliegerkorps* (*IV* and *V*) and all of his fighters. However, he did apply one significant filter to his conventional bombers: he used mostly only the Ju 88-equipped *Geschwadern* (*KG 51, 54* and *LG1*). All the Do 17 bombers were with Kesselring's *Luftflotte 2*, and both Field Marshals also possessed two He 111-equipped *Geschwadern* (Keselring had only limited Ju 88s) but these were not favoured. While both Dorniers and Heinkels were by 1940 rather old and slated in the longer term to be replaced by the new Junkers 88 bombers, the He 111s had suffered disproportionately over France during that campaign and were used more for night bombing in the Battle of Britain.

While a new machine and a much better aircraft, the Ju 88 was still suffering teething troubles in August 1940, due largely to being placed within combat units rather too soon; this is all too often a resort of high command in war. The main problem with the fast and manoeuvrable Ju 88 was that its airframe had been stressed for dive-bombing thus increasing its weight significantly, and that most of the bombload was carried on external pylons rather than internal bomb bays as on the older Do 17s and He 111s.[3] The old Do 17 had air-cooled engines, giving it greater survivability in combat and these units were thus fated to fight throughout the Battle of Britain, climaxing on 15 September with the final heavy losses of these venerable aircraft and their enduring crews.

Sperrle thus from the word go used all three *Geschwadern* of his best aircraft, the Ju 88s, and two of them, *KG 51* and *KG 54*, suffered significant losses and dents in morale in the three days of 11–13 August. By 15 August, when the massive *Luftwaffe* assault was finally launched against the United Kingdom, Sperrle's third Ju 88 *Geschwader LG 1* had to be employed in strength and it suffered significant casualties on that day, forcing him to send in his Heinkels on the next, 16 August. Sperrle thus understood little of the need to fight a battle of attrition, no doubt believing that the *Luftwaffe* would easily smash the RAF and specifically Fighter Command within a few days, a fantasy enthusiastically entertained by his boss, Göring. As the days passed, Sperrle's attack potential weakened and his Stukas, perforce having to take a major part of the attack load, were hammered on 16 and 18 August 1940, to be withdrawn from the Battle after that. Sperrle's more limited numbers of Me 109s, who also had a much longer sea crossing to reach the English south coast in the general Portland-Isle of Wight target region, were not able to apply the Theo Osterkamp method of assumed fighter predominance in the overall strategy, and by late August were largely transferred to Kesselring in the Pas de Calais, where they, too, fell under the baton of *Jagdfliegerführer* Theo Osterkamp.

In the event, Sperrle failed totally to understand the Dowding-Park strategy of fighting the Battle of Britain as one of attrition, and Göring

Adlertag

was equally unappreciative of this. Kesselring and his fighter expert Osterkamp seemingly did understand it well enough, but they greatly overestimated the capabilities of their fighter aircraft and their pilots. Once victory did not eventuate as expected by a generally over-confident *Luftwaffe* within a matter of days or even a couple of weeks, with the Germans using all their available fighters continuously, battle fatigue set in, fighter unit effectiveness decreased and losses climbed, leaving them no longer capable of escorting enough bombers to make the difference, this reality climaxing on 15 September 1940. The Me 110s were of little assistance, being too unmanoeuvrable to survive in the longer term. The three days were also marked by rapid and significant evolution in Me 110 escort and bomber support tactics. In addition, there was another interesting tactical innovation made in the use of Me 109s to escort the slow and vulnerable Stukas.

The true genius of Hugh Dowding (aided by the loyal Park and Brand) in fighting the Battle as one of attrition, limiting intercepting British fighter formations to squadron strength (and later two squadrons), trying to intercept all incoming bomber raids before they struck their targets (but not always succeeding) worked because tired units and later tired pilots from squadrons kept in the front line were relieved in good enough time and fresh men provided. The Germans were not able to emulate this. The three days ushered in the beginning of the intense part of the Battle of Britain when the German leaders almost immediately displayed and applied their chosen strategies and tactics but did not see the errors of their choices.

11–13 August also marks a strangely specialised yet intense struggle involving only part of the forces available to a single *Fliegerkorps* in Kesselring's *Luftflotte 2* (but all his fighters); in contrast, Sperrle his *Luftflotte 3* counterpart further west along the Channel coast almost immediately began to fritter away his best bombers in his Ju 88 units in the firm belief that a few days of combat would suffice. From 15 August onwards, the Germans changed course and began to use the full forces available to them, but that is a different story for another day.

The Battle of Britain has spawned so many books that a very valid question is why another one? The detailed research in this volume has revealed three days fraught with interest, not least involving the human element. In addition to the policies of the high commanders detailed above, at the level of the ordinary participants and witnesses to the Battle, there are fascinating details to be found. Wolfgang Edelstein, a twelve-year-old Jewish schoolboy extracted from a lethal German homeland just before war broke out through the Quaker-organised *Kindertransport* scheme, finds himself conflicted between patriotic feeling

Preface

for his *Luftwaffe* countrymen flying overhead of his German refugee-run boarding school near Haslemere, Surrey, on 13 August 1940 (in fact, members of *KG 54*) and the knowledge that their defeat by the RAF would preserve his own life. Secret evesdropping on *Luftwaffe* prisoners of war from *KG 2* shot down by Fighter Command on the same date by RAF Intelligence reveals the unpopularity of their *Staffelkapitän* in secretly recorded crew conversations, as well as their rather shocking Nazi-inspired views on organised religion.

Just like the *Luftwaffe*, RAF fighter squadrons also suffered from discord and infighting; the case of S/L Hill Harkness of 257 Squadron, an Irishman who enjoyed little support from many of his squadron colleagues, on the ground and much worse in the air, is discussed, concerning a combat over Spithead on 12 August. Me 110 tactics show a radical change from 11 and 12 August, when recourse was had to large, high altitude circles of Me 110s, supported by higher Me 109s, used to distract RAF fighters and protect German bombers leaving target areas, to 13 August, when these twin-engined fighters were used in a more conventional fighter escort role, and employed dive and zoom-climb tactics much more suited to this aircraft when British fighters attacked their charges. Eagle Day on 13 August also saw the Me 109s of *I/LG 2*, flying in to strafe Detling airfield from low level as a prelude to the attack by the Ju 87 Stukas they were escorting minutes later; Hanns Trübenbach, the *Gruppenkommandeur* of the Me 109s, was one of the few German fighter leaders to deliberately use his aircraft in this very dangerous way.

A second German innovation, also on Eagle Day and applied by both *Luftflotten* 2 and 3, was to use Me 109 fighter sweeps ahead of Stuka raids, which flew shallow penetrations of British coastal airspace before deliberately exiting the southern English coast at the places where the incoming dive bombers crossed the same coast on their way in. This obviated the Me 109s trying to keep pace with the slow Ju 87s, yet provided cover as the latter overflew enemy territory.

Following a self-imposed requirement to examine all available data for the Battle during 11–13 August, the various RAF records held by the National Archives, UK, were critical: the Fighter Command Squadron Operational Record Books, the Intelligence Patrol Reports/Fighter Command Combat Reports, the Combat Reports for individual pilots, and finally, the RAF Casualty Files. The latter give insight into the terrible price paid by the RAF pilots, and the anguish of their loved ones. War is certainly a terrible human failing, and should not ever be glorified, but nor should it be trivialised either. This volume attempts to provide an accurate account of the aerial fighting over the United Kingdom and adjacent seas for the chosen three-day time period, as a small tribute to those who endured it.

Access to such records was supported by the generosity of Nigel Parker, noted Battle historian, particularly through his well-known *Luftwaffe Crash Archive* book series. Other air historians who have supported and encouraged me greatly are thanked in the acknowledgements. I owe them all a great debt of gratitude for copious quantities of original material. My approach has been to study all available records for each raid and action to analyse what transpired in some detail; it took several months to cover a single day in the Battle.

Additional valuable records, especially for aerial actions over the sea, include naval and merchant marine records as well as those of the lifeboat services, particularly the Royal National Lifeboat Institution. Obviously, I have not in any way done a better job than the many other students of the Battle, but I have possibly researched deeply. The many books written on the Battle by my peers have provided a much-valued secondary source of data and opinions. The journey through very large numbers of reports, action intelligence summaries and squadron records has been one of unending fascination and satisfaction; very often, the canvas thus broadened has proven to be a real eye-opener and has revealed numerous amazing experiences and ordeals experienced by the participants. Though perhaps the detail provided in the current volume may be tedious to some, I hope the book will provide a modicum of the interest and satisfaction which I have experienced in its creation to readers.

Documents alone are not enough and I have been extremely fortunate to have corresponded with several RAF veterans of the Battle in past decades (alas, they have now all passed on). Some are thantked in the acknowledgements. Group Captain David Haysom, who led a flight in 79 Squadron and Air Commodore Edward 'Teddy' Morris, flying officer in 79 Squadron, were both South Africans. These men provided me with critical insights into the realities of the fighting over the UK during the late summer and autumn of that fateful year, 1940. I also corresponded with a number of *Luftwaffe* veterans of this fighting and was very greatly assisted by one in particular cited in the acknowledgments, *Oberst* Hanns Trűbenbach, *Kommandeur* of I/LG 2, and subsequently *Kommodore* of *JG 52* during the Battle, who gave me a completely honest viewpoint of fighter leadership at *Gruppen* and *Geschwader* levels on the German side. Additionally, he provided me with his personal copies of several books long out of print, perhaps the most critical being *Generalleutnant* Theo Osterkamp's autobiography, *Durch Hohen und Tiefen jagd ein Herz*.[4] Osterkamp was from late July the *Jagdfliegerfűhrer* (*Jafű*, or

Preface

fighter leader) for *Luftflotte 2*. Being exposed to the German side of the Battle of Britain, even though they tend to deny any such discrete battle actually occurred (!), has enabled me to give perhaps a more balanced appreciation of the various raids and engagements.

Finally, I have been positively influenced by having taken flying lessons from the age of fifteen, due to parental generosity, and have thus some small comprehension of what it is like flying a small aeroplane at a young age. Being poor pilot material, I only soloed when I was seventeen and no air force was ever disadvantaged by allowing me near their aircraft. Although in no way comparable to a Hurricane or Spitfire, my time in a variety of Cessnas including a first instructor of World War 2 vintage with a rather gung-ho approach to flight training, my first lesson being spins and stalls, gave me a small exposure to the excitement and occasional dread inherent in aviation.

A Brief Explanation of German *Luftwaffe* Terminology

No attempt is made in this volume to apply English language terminology from either the US Air Force or RAF usage to German air force (*Luftwaffe*) ranks and unit designations. The reasons for this are simple: there are no real equivalents for unit designations, and *Luftwaffe* ranks generally carried greater responsibility and concomitant command sizes than in either British or American air forces. Rank terms are shown below (with commonly used abbreviations):

Enlisted grades: *Flieger (Flg) – Gefreiter (Gefr) – Obergefreiter (Ogefr)*

NCOs: *Unteroffizier (Uffz)*, a rank requiring completion of a training course, and in some ways equivalent to US-RAF sergeants. In the *Luftwaffe*, their 'real sergeants' (cf. senior NCOs) began with *Feldwebel (Fw) – Oberfeldwebel (Ofw)* (RAF flight sergeant) – *Stabsfeldwebel (Stabsfw)* (staff sergeant) – *Hauptfeldwebel (Hauptfw)* (warrant officer; in the German forces, the holder of this rank was known colloquially as a *Spiess* and avoided by all enlisted personnel).

Officers: *Leutnant (Lt)* (Pilot Officer) – *Oberleutnant (Oblt)* (Flying Officer) – *Hauptmann (Hpt)* (Flight Lieutenant) – *Major (Maj)* (Squadron Leader) – *Oberstleutnant (Obstlt)* (Wing Commander) – *Oberst* (Group Captain) – *Generalmajor* (Air Commodore) – *Generalleutnant* (Air Vice Marshal) – *General* (Air Marshal) – *Generaloberst* (Air Chief Marshal) – *Generalfeldmarschall* (often an operational post in active command, as opposed to Marshal of the RAF, which is an essentially honorary rank and

A Brief Explanation of German Luftwaffe Terminology

non-operational). Finally, there was the *Reichsmarschall* for Hermann Göring, literally Marshal of the Empire and unavoidably carrying some element of comic opera, at least to insubordinate outsiders, not that Nazism offered much to laugh at.

While in the RAF a squadron leader commanded a squadron of some twelve operational machines and usually four to eight reserve aircraft in Fighter Command in 1940, in the *Luftwaffe*, a *Major* commanded either a *Gruppe* of about thirty operational aircraft or even a *Geschwader* of three *Gruppen* and a staff flight (*Stabsschwarm*), at least in single-engined or twin-engined fighters. For bombers and larger machines, the ranks of *Oberstleutnant* or *Oberst* were generally pertinent at *Geschwader* level. German air force units formally comprised *Geschwader* (c. 120 machines, including reserves), made up mostly of three component *Gruppen*, in turn containing three *Staffeln* (addition of an 'n' to these three unit designations, provides the plural).

At the outbreak of the war many fighter units flew in sub-formations of three-machine vics (*Ketten*), and then an operational *Staffel* comprised twelve aircraft in the air. Towards the Battle of Britain, the 'finger four' formation of two pairs, arranged like the fingers on a hand, became predominant amongst German fighters, and an operational *Staffel* more typically flew as two such formations (viz eight machines) rather than three, especially once casualties became endemic. The German pair was termed a *Rotte* and two such as a *Schwarm*. Formal leaders of each unit, from large to small, were called Geschwaderkommodore (cf, *Kommodore*), Gruppenkommandeur (*Kommandeur* etc), and *Staffelkapitän*, while *Schwarmführer* and *Rottenführer* were of informal usage. The German term *Führer* has many applications, basically meaning a leader, varying in importance from *der Führer* (Hitler) down to *Staffelführer*. Just to complicate things, a not uncommon feature of German linguistics, there were specific usages of '*Führer*' as well: *Jagdfliegerführer* (abbreviated commonly to *Jafü*) for the fighter commander for all such aircraft in an entire *Luftflotte*, or the even more tongue-twisting *Kanalkampfführer*, clumsily translated as Channel Battle Commander, as fulfilled by Oberst Johannes Fink, *Kommodore* of the bomber *Geschwader KG 2* along the eastern Channel coast in July 1940 during the early days of the Battle.

The *Luftwaffe* in the Battle of Britain was divided into three *Luftflotten*, 2 (north-east France, Belgium and Holland), 3 (north-west France) and 5 (Denmark and Norway). Each *Luftflotte* numbered multiple *Geschwadern* of all aerial specialisations: thus *Jagdgeschwadern* (abbreviation JG, single-engined fighters), *Zerstörergeschwadern* (ZG, 'destroyers',

Adlertag

twin-engined Me 110 heavy fighters), *Kampfgeschwadern* (*KG*, twin-engined bombers), *Stukageschwadern* (*StG*, Ju 87 dive-bombers) as well as *Aufklärergruppen* and *–staffeln* (*Aufkl. Gr.*, reconnaissance units; although the larger *Geschwader* did exist to a degree, they normally operated independently as smaller formations). The German word *Stuka*, short for *Sturzkampfflugzeug* or dive-bomber has become so much a part of English aviation historical literature that it is not treated as an exotic German term here.

All of the above unit terms could also be applied down the subordinate units, thus: *Jagdgruppe* or *Jagdstaffel* etc. There were also two *Lehrgeschwadern* (LG, mixed units, formed originally from training formations) involved in the Battle: *LG 1* contained three bomber *Gruppen* (I/LG 1, II/LG 1, III/LG 1), one of Stukas (*IV/LG 1*) and finally another of Me 110s (*V/LG 1*). Just as the subordinate *Gruppen* were designated by Roman numerals as shown for *LG 1*, the nine *Staffeln* typically making up a full Geschwader, and three each to a *Gruppe*, were numbered from '1' to '9' using Arabic numerals, thus for example: 8/StG 2 is the eighth *Staffel* (part of 3rd *Gruppe, III/StG 2*) of *Stukageschwader* 2. A single *Gruppe* of the second *Lehrgeschwader, II/LG 2* operated over the UK as an independent fighter-bomber (*Jagdbomber* or *Jabo*) unit; just to complicate things (and very un-Germanic at that), *I/LG 2* was also an independent *Jagdgruppe* falling within *Jagdgeschwader 77* (*JG 77*), whose other two *Gruppen* were *II* and *III/JG 77*. However, there was logic behind this, *I/LG 2* having been the pre-war aerobatic flight of the German air force. *I/LG 2* was subordinated to *JG 52* during the Battle, whose *Kommodore* happened to be their pre-war and pre-Battle *Kommandeur, Major* Hanns Trübenbach.

While *Luftflotten* (*LFl* abbreviation) typically consisted of about ten *Geschwadern* plus a few independent *Gruppen* or even *Staffeln* (generally of a specialised function), they were subdivided into either *Fliegerkorps* (*FlK*) or smaller *Fliegerdivisionen*, these comprising up to around five *Geschwadern* and perhaps some smaller units. An example of a specialised unit attached to *Fliegerkorps II* of *Luftflotte 2* was *Erprobungsgruppe 210*, an experimental fighter-bomber unit flying Me 110s and Me 109s. Each *Geschwader* and *Gruppe* also had a staff flight (*Schwarm*) or, for some bomber units, a staff *Staffel* or *Stabstaffel*. Finally, there were the German air-sea rescue services, the *Seenotdienst*, better equipped than the equivalent RAF service, with He 59 floatplanes, high speed boats and a number of rescue platforms anchored in mid-Channel providing shelter, food, water and basic communication by radio.

1

The First Major Raid, Portland: 11 August 1940

This was to be a day of major air combat, with two earlier incursions over Dover pitting RAF and *Luftwaffe* fighters against each other before a massive raid on Portland at about 10h00–11h00, encompassing a large Me 110/Me 109 circle, which distracted many British fighters as intended, but the Ju 88 raid on Portland itself was seriously disrupted by a well-led beam attack by 213 Squadron. For the squadrons involved against the circling Me 110s this was a new experience and their tactical response soon crystallised around the wisdom and advantage of deflection attacks from the outside of the circles. A complex set of actions occurred as the various parts of the raid, bombers, circling Me 110s and Me 109s and escorting Me 109 formations, retreated back across the Channel, harassed by Spitfires and Hurricanes. Losses on both sides were to be high as the action was essentially over the sea. Within the following three hours, there were three sizeable raids on convoys off the East coast and shipping off North Foreland, involving Stukas and a large Dornier formation, but little damage was done to the vessels involved.

Early morning raid on Dover harbour; combat versus supporting Me 109s, *c.* 07h37–08h10

RAF radar picked up two formations at 15,000 ft, together made up of thirty or more German machines rapidly approaching South Foreland, a few miles east-north-east of Dover, at 07h35. Four Spitfires of 64 Squadron already airborne were directed towards Dover, 32 Squadron scrambled twelve Hurricanes from their forward base at Hawkinge at 07h42 who were instructed to patrol the airfield at 15,000 ft, while thirteen Spitfires of 74 Squadron scrambled from

Adlertag

Manston two minutes later were ordered to intercept the enemy.[1] However, all these moves by the 11 Group controller were too late, as the raiders were over their target of Dover harbour two minutes after the first detection by radar.[2] The raid itself was made up of Me 109s from *3/EGr 210*, who went for the Dover balloons, shooting down three of them, followed by the *Gruppe*'s Me 110s, which bombed the harbour; they were not molested by the British fighters.[3] Elements of *JG 51* provided the escort to *EGr 210* as well as to some Dorniers from *KG 2* who also attacked Dover.[4] As was common for raids by this fighter-bomber Gruppe, *EGr 210* came in very fast and were thus difficult for controllers to counter effectively.

In the meantime the two RAF squadrons were climbing towards their allocated altitudes, but while doing so further *Luftwaffe* formations were detected over the Straits of Dover, one about ten miles north-east of North Foreland and proceeding southwards, and the second situated in the centre of the Straits and approaching Dover directly from the east.[5] F/Lt Crossley flying as Red 1 and leading 32 Squadron had climbed up to 20,000 ft, and just after 08h00 when they were between Deal and Dover, Crossley observed nine Me 109s coming straight towards them, at the same level.[6] In fact, one went just beneath him and another just above him and he only got off a short burst without any obvious result.[7] Simultaneously, three more Me 109s were seen diving on them from behind; P/O Barton, Red 3, who was already in a right-handed turn saw these three machines diving past to his left and seeing as they were all going in the same direction opened fire on the last one, observing large pieces apparently flying off before looking around quickly for his two pals, and when he looked again his victim had vanished.[8] Two searchlight sites near Deal later confirmed seeing an aircraft go into the sea off that town, one reporting it was an Me 109, and Barton's claim was confirmed.[9] However, what they had in fact seen was a Spitfire of 74 Squadron which plunged into the sea a mile off Deal, as observed by its pilot dangling on his parachute, P/O Stevenson;[10] thus does blameless over-claiming occur. Stevenson was lucky to survive, having been dragged underwater by his parachute and almost drowned, and having landed in the water eleven miles out to sea had to stay afloat for one and a half hours before an MTB appeared. He managed to attract its attention through firing off two loads from his soaked revolver.[11]

74 Squadron led by the redoubtable 'Sailor' Malan, newly promoted to command the squadron on 8 August 1940, had been placed in an excellent tactical position by their leader to surprise another dozen or so Me 109s approaching Dover from the east. Malan's tactics are described admirably in his combat report:[12]

The First Major Raid, Portland: 11 August 1940

I was Dysoe Leader when the Squadron set off to intercept bandits approaching Dover at a reported height of 13,000ft. I climbed on an east-north-east course to 20,000ft. and then turned down-sun towards Dover. I ordered the Squadron to attack. Some of the enemy adopted the usual German fighter evasive tactics, i.e. quick half-roll and dive. On this occasion, as the air seemed clear above us, I followed one down and overtook him after he had dived 2,000ft., opening fire at 200 yards' range with deflection. He levelled out at about 12,000ft. when I gave him two two-second bursts, when he suddenly burst into flames and was obscured by heavy smoke. This was at 4,000ft., one mile north of Cap Gris Nez. I did not watch him go in, but flew back as fast as I could. I did not see the engagements of the rest of the Squadron. N.B. Normally I have strongly advised all pilots in the Squadron not to follow 109s on the half-roll and dive because in most cases we are outnumbered, and generally at least one layer of enemy fighters is some thousands of feet above. It was found that even at high altitude there was no difficulty in overtaking E/A on diving apart from the physical strain imposed on the body when pulling out. [Dysoe = 74 Squadron radio call sign]

Malan's leadership placed his men in an excellent tactical attacking position; their only casualty, P/O Stevenson's Spitfire, resulted from this pilot remaining in the battle area and making repeated attacks on Me 109s;[13] rather inevitably, he was surprised from behind and below, typical Me 109 bounce tactics, diving down and beneath the tail of an unsuspecting opponent. The rest of 74 Squadron experienced little danger in their surprise attacks on the dozen Me 109s, claiming six destroyed unconfirmed and three damaged.[14] Malan's combat report is very interesting in that it provides sober comment on the relative performance of the Spitfire against the Me 109, and also provides strongly felt tactical advice against following enemies down; this not only gave him gravitas as an active Fighter Command combat leader amongst the higher echelons, but also provided valuable material for them and fellow active fighter pilots in the RAF. The influence of such leadership was much more significant in the ongoing battle of attrition than the activities of a victory-conscious 'fighter ace'.

'Sailor' was quite correct in his expressed concerns about larger numbers of Me 109s, and at higher altitude; a number of small formations up to about *Staffel*-strength arrived during 74 Squadron's action, between 18,000 and 23,000 ft, sweeping in from France, overflying Dover briefly and then retiring again.[15] It was almost certainly one of these that dispatched Stevenson's Spitfire. Despite all 74 Squadron's claims, including also S/L Malan's rather convincing claim in his combat report, no relevant *Luftwaffe* losses of Me 109s can be traced; equally over-optimistic were the German claims. *I/JG51* claimed three Spitfires, and *II/JG 51* another two, all in the Dover area and between 08h03 and 08h10 for four of them.[16] Lt Segatz of *5/JG 51*'s claim was made over Deal,[17] but of course, more than one Me 109 pilot may have attacked or even hit Stevenson's Spitfire.

Both sides thus made equally highly inflated claims of success in this engagement. Regarding the apparent lack of any German victims, it was quite common practice in the listing of *Luftwaffe* casualties to include only machines that were 100% destroyed, and to exclude damaged aircraft that made it back to base or even friendly territory. 'Sailor' Malan's rather convincing claim of serious damage to his unconfirmed Me 109 may thus have damaged its engine enough to require an engine change after a successful forced-landing at a fighter base near Calais. If the Messerschmitt had been close to an engine change already, this may then not have been listed as a combat-damaged machine in loss returns. The famous German ace from *JG 2*, Helmut Wick, generally flew in combat at full throttle and this obviously led to reduced engine life[18] and interestingly, Malan himself was also known for this.[19] In 1940, fighter pilots experiencing combat emergencies would have often resorted to using maximum engine boost, as is for example revealed by study of multiple combat reports from Fighter Command.

High sweep over Dover and lower Me 109s attack balloons there, *c.* 09h50–10h30

There was a lull in *Luftwaffe* incursions over the English south-east coast from about 08h30–09h00, and then British radar detected German aircraft which remained over mid-Channel in the Dover Straits; at about 09h40, a force of thirty or more German machines was detected approximately ten miles east of Dover, roughly coincident with the first detections over the Baie de la Seine of the building raid to come, on Portland in the central-western Channel.[20] The plan to distract with their eastern Channel manoeuvres was clear.[21] The 11 Group controller reacted by sending up 64 Squadron, nine Spitfires strong from Kenley at 09h32; twelve Spitfires from 74 Squadron from forward base at Manston at 09h50; and 32 Squadron from Biggin Hill at 10h05.[22]

All were directed towards Dover, 64 Squadron being first to arrive there by *c.* 09h51[23] and flying at aroundt 15,000 ft saw about a *Gruppe* of Me 109s some 10,000 ft higher heading north from the

The First Major Raid, Portland: 11 August 1940

town.²⁴ S/L MacDonell led his men in a climb for altitude and at about 20,000 ft saw the Me 109s now heading westwards and then out over the Channel for home at about 10h00; MacDonell and two other pilots from 64 Squadron chased the Me 109s towards France, but other small Me 109 formations attacked two of them from behind in turn. The squadron leader managed to get behind the last one of these, pursued it to the French coast and left it smoking heavily and lagging behind its pals.²⁵ The third pilot similarly claimed to have hit a Me 109, leaving it in a dive for the coast near Cap Gris Nez.²⁶ On the strength of ground observers from Dover reporting two Me 109s down in the sea, S/L MacDonell and P/O King were awarded confirmed victories, while P/O O'Meara claimed one damaged.²⁷ No *Luftwaffe* Me 109s went down in the sea at around this time.²⁸

One of 64 Squadron's Spitfires was damaged by Me 109s in this engagement, landing wheels up at base as the undercarriage would not lower.²⁹ One of the 64 Squadron pilots may well have hit the Me 109 of *Oblt* Keller, the *Staffelkapitän* of *1/JG 3* who reported being struck by bullets in an engagement with Spitfires; *JG 3* appears to have put up all three *Gruppen* to escort a Me 110 reconnaissance machine over Dover and southern England, with *I/JG 3* taking off at 09h13 and landing again, including Keller with his lightly damaged aircraft, by 10h25.³⁰ Timings suggest that *I/JG 3* probably had its minor encounter with 64 Squadron rather than 74 Squadron.

That highly accomplished tactician and leader of 74 Squadron, S/L 'Sailor' Malan had led his men after taking off from Manston, first away from Dover to the north-east, and once they had reached 24,000 ft he turned them back and brought them out of the sun over Dover, coming in from the north-east, over the sea, an unexpected direction.³¹ Over mid-Channel they saw small groups of Me 109s heading back for France; 'Sailor' came in too fast on a pair over mid-Channel at about 25,000 ft and overshot, thereafter having various short fights with retreating Me 109s and claiming one damaged.³² Interestingly, 74 Squadron pilots carried *c.* 2,700 rounds of ammunition, three hundred above the norm.³³ P/O Freeborn was flying behind Malan and recorded the following combat report, claiming a Me 109 unconfirmed at 10h15:³⁴

> I was flying as Yellow Leader with No. 74 Squadron at 25,000 feet, we were flying towards Dover, when we sighted two M.E. 109's. Dysoe Leader attacked the first 109 and I attacked the 2nd. The E/A half rolled and dived towards Cape (sic) Griz (sic) Nez. I dived after it and fired several short bursts at 300 yards range, closing to 150 yards range. The E/A then began to break up. Pieces seemed to break off the fuselage and

wings as my bullets entered the E/A. The E/A then went into a vertical dive with glycol coming from his radiator. I then returned to my base. (E/A = enemy aircraft)

One other pilot from 74 Squadron claimed a probable and a damaged Me 109 in this engagement.[35]

Lt Bűrschgens of 7/JG 26 had his Me 109 damaged in combat on this mission but managed to make it back to France where he belly-landed in a field near his base at Caffiers at about 10h30; his aircraft was a write-off (80%) and he was wounded.[36] P/O Freeborn was the likely victor in this engagement. Sweeps by multiple small formations of Me 109s at relatively high altitude over the Dover Straits generally created dangerous conditions for intercepting RAF fighters; however, S/L Malan's canny tactical manoeuvres, first heading away from the location indicated by the controller as they gained height, and then once at altitude turning onto the reciprocal course and coming at the enemy from the sun and from over the sea, placed 74 Squadron in a highly advantageous position. A score of only one victory under such conditions is still a positive result, and even more so when there are no casualties to their own numbers.

32 Squadron were the last to arrive over Dover and found no enemy there, and thus flew back towards Biggin Hill.[37] On the way back, F/O Gardner who had earlier become separated from the squadron, spotted five Me 109s over Dungeness at about 10h30, flying just above clouds at 4,000 ft, and attacked one, hitting it and seeing it shed pieces, claiming a damaged enemy.[38] Under cover of these myriad small sweeps, apparently by *III/JG 26*,[39] a small formation of Me 109s lower down, attacked the Dover balloon barrage half-heartedly, but the anti-aircraft guns prevented them gaining any success.[40] Elements from *JG 54* were also involved in one or more of these engagements, with two pilots from *4/JG 54* each claiming a Spitfire at about 20,000 ft at 10h00-10h05 in the Dover area;[41] a pilot from *1/JG 54* also recorded a mission across the Channel between 09h29 and 10h55.[42] They may have been engaged with some of the 64 Squadron Spitfires, one of which was damaged.

German plans and dispositions, and RAF controllers' reactions: Portland raid, *c.* 10h00–11h00

German weather reconnaissance by *Luftflotte 3* over the Channel indicated isolated cloud accumulations but with Portland clear, while to the south of it there was a thin layer of cloud at *c.* 6,500 ft; visibility was about eighteen and a half miles, and there was a light haze to the

The First Major Raid, Portland: 11 August 1940

west.⁴³ Weather conditions were thus ideal for a large raid on Portland. British radar picked up the first evidence of this incursion at about 09h10 with thirty-plus aircraft detected in the Baie de la Seine (off Le Havre; most likely, *Stab* and *II/ZG 2*) on a course towards Portland; initial moves by the 11 and 10 Group controllers were to scramble 145 Squadron from Westhampnett (thirteen Hurricanes), 1 Squadron (nine Hurricanes) was diverted from a flight to North Weald to patrol off Tangmere, and 609 Squadron's twelve Spitfires (Middle Wallop) sent to cover Warmwell.⁴⁴ By 10h05–10h09 radar plots had grown to encompass fifty-plus aircraft (*I* and *II/KG 54* and *c.* a *Gruppe* of *JG 27* Me 109 escorts) about fifteen miles north of Cherbourg, with the thirty-plus aircraft (*Stab* and *II/ZG 2*) from the Baie de la Seine some miles to their right, and about nine aircraft (Me 109 remote bomber escort, effectively a sweep ahead, probably from *JG 27*)⁴⁵ twenty six miles north-west of Cherbourg.⁴⁶ As this picture developed, more squadrons were ordered up between 10h00 and 10h15: 601 (12 aircraft from Tangmere), 152 (4 aircraft diverted from flight to Warmwell forward base), 213 (12 aircraft) and 87 (7 machines) Squadrons from Exeter, and 238 Squadron (12 aircraft) from Middle Wallop,⁴⁷ all Hurricanes with the exception of 152's machines.

At the same time, 1 Squadron was vectored out over the Channel towards the south-west, 609 sent south of Swanage and 145 also diverted there.⁴⁸ Examination of German victory claim times⁴⁹ suggests that I and III/JG 27 were first into action, and thus likely provided a *Gruppe* as direct bomber escorts for *KG 54*, and another *Gruppe* for a sweep ahead. Claim times⁵⁰ for *JG 53* and *II/JG 27* were mostly a little later than most of those by *JG 2*, suggesting *JG 53* and *II/JG 27* went in last, providing fighter cover for the other withdrawing units returning south, bombers, Me 110s and Me 109s. II and III/JG 53 took off from Guernsey, and I/JG 53 from Cherbourg East, from which area *II/JG 27* also lifted off; the Guernsey-based *Gruppen* took off some minutes after *JG 2*⁵¹ and had further to fly than those taking off from the Cherbourg region.

Stab and *II/ZG 2*, detected by RAF radar as thirty-plus north-east of Le Havre and heading towards Portland, advanced to a position over the Channel about twenty miles south-south-west of Swanage, placing them about fifteen miles south-east of Portland.⁵² They reached there approximately at 10h09 and formed holding circles between about 20,000 and 25,000 ft.⁵³ The 10 Group controllers had pushed a section of 213 Squadron forwards from Portland to this approximate position, and at *c.* 10h19 they duly intercepted a large formation of Me 110s, estimated as fifty-sixty, between 10,000 and 15,000 ft and just starting to form circles.⁵⁴ *I/ZG 2*, based at Amiens Glissy⁵⁵ on the Somme River, would logically have flown a different route; the shortest Channel crossing for them, about perpendicular to the French coastline at the mouth of the Somme, would have taken them towards the Beachy Head-Brighton area, where the 11 Group controllers had placed two sections of 145 Squadron, soon after vectored parallel to the coast back towards the Isle of Wight.[56]

One section of 145 Squadron sighted a formation of Me 110s while they were flying over the Bembridge area on the east of the Isle of Wight and were vectored westwards, engaging them approximately over the Needles on the western tip of the Isle.[57] A second section of 145 Squadron met them soon after towards the south-west of the Isle, followed by B Flight of the squadron.[58] I/ZG 2 thus approached the Isle of Wight from the east and after passing over it flew south-westwards to join the rest of ZG 2 to form a massive combined circle of c. sixty Me 110s, about fifteen to twenty miles south-east of Portland over the Channel. The whole of JG 2 had moved forward to the Cherbourg area from where they took off[59] to provide the top cover for the Me 110 circles. With most of I/JG 2's claims being earlier than the rest of the *Geschwader*[60] they probably engaged 145 and 609 Squadrons, whose losses largely overlap with those times, while II and III/JG 2's claims fit with them having engaged 238, 87 and possibly also 601 Squadrons.[61]

I/JG 2 thus probably flew directly from Cherbourg towards the south-west of the Isle of Wight to join I/ZG 2's initial circles there, with 145 Squadron reporting an increase in the presence of Me 109s as the engagement with the German fighter circles ensued. *Oblt* Paul Temme, Adjutant of I/JG 2,[62] reported that they had strict instructions to tie down the RAF fighters in combat for thirty five minutes;[63] this was a very long time for dogfighting, but claim times for the *Gruppe* suggest they kept at it for a full half hour.[64] The other two JG 2 *Gruppen* flew to the south-east of Portland where the *Stab* and II/ZG 2 circles had formed. As is clear from the combat reports from 145, 609 and 238 Squadrons, all discussed below, the I/ZG 2 circles steadily moved south-west away from the Isle of Wight and joined the *Stab-II/ZG 2* circles about twenty-five miles south-east of Portland, thereby amalgamating Me 110s of ZG 2 and the Me 109s of JG 2.

Based on the above, the overall German plan appears to have been rather complex and relied on good timing and attention to detail by all units. The Me 110s of ZG 2 approached their chosen location for holding circles some fifteen to twenty five miles south-east of Portland from two directions, *Stab* and II/ZG 2 flying in from the Le Havre area directly to that location, while I/ZG 2, based much further away on the Somme River at Amiens, were directed to fly to the Brighton area and

The First Major Raid, Portland: 11 August 1940

then down the coast towards the Isle of Wight before diverting to the south-west thereof to join their colleagues in a massive circling group of aircraft over the Channel. This was not a set of defensive circles, but an intended distraction to suck in as many British fighters as possible. The Me 109s of *JG 2* were tasked with providing the top cover to these Me 110s, which they did while they were still in two groups and after they joined up. With the Me 110 circles first in place, followed by their top cover, the Ju 88s of *I and II/KG 54* flew north from Cherbourg, with their two attendant Me 109 *Gruppen, I and III/JG 27*, the one as direct escort and the other, the indirect escort, sweeping ahead.

As they reached a position to the east of the *Stab-II/ZG 2* circle south-east of Portland, the bombers and escort turned westwards to pass beneath the protective circle, emerging on its western side, turned north for their targets at Portland, one *Gruppe* of *JG 27* Me 109s above and behind them, the other forging ahead. The intention was that the Ju 88s would turn away from Portland after bombing and fly south-east, passing beneath the now amalgamated circles of fighters, still south-east of Portland, thus giving them protection against fighter attack on the way out. Finally, the three *Gruppen* of *JG 53* and *II/JG 27* would fly out from Guernsey (*II and III/JG 53*) and Cherbourg (*I/JG 53, II/JG 27*), to meet the returning Ju 88s, Me 110s and Me 109s, now short of fuel, some damaged, and low to empty on ammunition.

The German plan was rather successful. Blue Section from 213 Squadron sent towards the south-east of Portland as an advance reaction was first to meet the Germans, engaging the Me 110s of *Stab and II/ZG 2* as they started to form their circles at about 10h19; none of the section made it home, only one pilot surviving, slightly wounded. The other part of the Me 110 circles, *I/ZG 2*, swept along the south coast from Brighton towards the Isle of Wight, similarly being first engaged by a single section, this time Yellow Section of 145 Squadron over the Needles and soon after by Red Section of the same squadron further south-westwards from the Isle. Very soon after, B Flight of 145 Squadron followed and then 609 Squadron, again slightly further south-westwards, and some of them saw several of 145 Squadron's Hurricanes in action. B Flight of 238 Squadron were the next to be sucked in by the Me 110s and soon after 601 Squadron, the two *Zerstörer* formations and their top covers by now amalgamated, south-east of Portland.

The distraction was thus successful in achieving its purpose and keeping many RAF fighters busy as the bombers did their work. The latter were, however, to be partially thwarted by a very successful attack by the remainder of 213 Squadron as they approached Portland, and they were attacked on their way out along with various Me 109 units

Adlertag

by flights of 87 Squadron and 238 Squadron (A Flight). As action moved further offshore, elements of 1 and 152 Squadron had some final encounters. There were thus almost two parallel battles, one revolving round the escorted bombers and their retreat, and the other against the stacked Me 110/Me 109 circles. Overall, casualties to both sides were high, particularly as almost the entire engagement took place over the unforgiving waters of the Channel.

213 Squadron, Blue Section, first in action against an Me 110 circle, south-east of Portland, c. 10h20

The only surviving witness to this first engagement of the entire action was Sgt Ernest Snowden, who submitted the combat report[65] cited below, having met the enemy at 10h19, stepped up from 10,000–15,000 ft.

> I was forming Blue Section, No. 213 Squadron, with F/Lt. Wight and Sgt. Butterfield when we intercepted a large formation of M.E. 110's 15 miles S.E. of Portland. We individually attacked the centre of the formation, which executed a gentle left-hand turn with the apparent intention of forming a circle. I took a deflection shot on an M.E. 110 which turned on its side after the second burst and went down. I obtained deflection shots on two others, silencing the rear gunners. I had used up all my ammunition by now, and received a cannon shell in my engine from underneath, setting me on fire and bursting an oil pipe. I spiralled down and the flames went out, and I forced landed at Lulworth Tank Ranges. Soldiers there told me that they saw 4 M.E. 110's crash in the sea.

F/Lt R. D. G. Wight DFC and Sgt Samuel Butterfield DFM were both experienced and decorated fighter pilots, Wight also being the senior flight commander in 213 Squadron; both were missing after this engagement, and Wight's body was washed up and buried in France at Cayeux-sur-Mer,[66] close to the mouth of the Somme River. Sgt Butterfield's body washed up on Plage Bellevue in France on 22 September 1940 and he lies in Boulogne Eastern Cemetery; his Hurricane was found on the seabed off Lulworth by divers.[67] Samuel Butterfield thus likely managed to break away from the fight with *Stab* and *II/ZG 2* and head north for the coast near Lulworth, but he was not as lucky as Sgt Snowden.

While *Stab* and *II/ZG 2* claimed three Hurricanes and three Spitfires shot down in this raid,[68] no ZG 2 claims are given in official *Luftwaffe* victory lists,[69] so how many of these six claims were confirmed in the

The First Major Raid, Portland: 11 August 1940

Luftwaffe system is unknown. While it is perfectly possible that *Stab* and *II/ZG 2* did shoot down all three Hurricanes from Blue Section, 213 Squadron, they may also have fallen victim to Me 109s. Some of the claim times for *JG 27* (two at 10h20, one at 10h27, all south of Portland)[70] closely match this section's engagement, which began at 10h19;[71] Snowden's combat report suggests that the three 213 Squadron Hurricanes made essentially deflection attacks on the Me 110s, without becoming embroiled in a chaotic charge into the middle of a large enemy formation.

This is the kind of cool leadership one might expect from an experienced combat leader such as F/Lt Wight. If there is any truth in this suggestion, then *JG 27* Me 109s may have surprised the three Hurricanes while they were concentrating on attacking the Me 110s; Sgt Snowden records being hit in the engine from beneath, a typical attack method for many Me 109 pilots, to dive down below an opponent and pull up to fire, thus lessening the likelihood of being seen. Two of these earliest claims by *JG 27* were made by *III Gruppe*, inferred to have been flying as indirect escort ahead of the bombers, thought to have been escorted directly by *I/JG 27*, which made the third early claim.

With the engagement between Blue Section 213 Squadron having begun about 10h19, the sweep ahead by *III/JG 27* would have passed by close to the forming *Stab-II/ZG 2* circle to the south only some minutes thereafter, and not far behind would have followed *KG 54* and its inferred escort of *I/JG 27*. Possibly one of those pilots broke away to attack a Hurricane already damaged in the *ZG 2* fight; perhaps Sgt Butterfield made for the coast neat Lulworth some minutes after the beginning of their action.

There is no way to determine if *Stab* and *II/ZG 2* suffered any casualties during their action with Blue Section, 213 Squadron; their losses during the entire raid comprised one Me 110 of *Stab/ZG 2* close to Cherbourg, with *II/ZG 2* having one machine damaged 10% and returned to base, and *4/ZG 2* losing a Me 110 and crew missing from operations over the Channel.[72] While the first casualty does not fit the engagement with 213 Squadron south-east of Portland, that suffered by *4/ZG 2* does. Sgt Snowden claimed one Me 110 probable and two more damaged.[73]

145 Squadron, second in action against an Me 110 circle, Isle of Wight and south-westwards, *c.* 10h30

The controller at Tangmere sent up A Flight of 145 Squadron (seven Hurricanes) at 09h36 from Westhampnett, then B Flight's six machines

Adlertag

twelve minutes later.[74] F/Lt Dutton leading Red Section of A Flight was first directed towards Beachy Head, but as they passed over Brighton his section was detached and ordered to patrol Brighton at 15,000 ft.[75] Later they were directed back westwards and told to patrol base. Yellow Section, meanwhile, led by S/L Peel, were sent further eastwards, with orders to patrol Beachy Head at 15,000 ft; they were then redirected back westwards once more and instructed to fly a new patrol over Bembridge on the eastern tip of the Isle of Wight, at 20,000 ft.[76] B Flight, led by F/Lt Boyd, had been kept on patrol above the Tangmere area, protecting the main sector base.[77] Clearly, there must have been radar indications of German aircraft approaching towards the Brighton-Beachy Head area initially, which then presumably turned westwards before reaching the coast, leading the Tangmere controller to make these dispositions.

The three Yellow Section Hurricanes patrolling over Bembridge saw a large number of Me 110s to the east of them and at a higher altitude of *c.* 27,000-30,000 ft, and were then vectored towards the Needles on the opposite western end of the Isle of Wight, with orders to patrol to seawards (south) thereof, at 20,000 ft.[78] Climbing as they went, they made for these enemy machines, contact being joined at about 10h30; P/O Parrott, Yellow 2 noticed four Me 110s passing above them trying to get on their tails as they attacked, and he broke away so steeply that he spun down.[79] P/O Harrison, Yellow 3, lost his section and attacked one of five circling Me 110s.[80] As Parrott pulled out of his spin, he saw the enemy machines above him, now in a circle and climbed back up, putting a short burst into each Messerschmitt as they passed before attacking the tail end Charlie from astern; however, he was driven off by three more Me 110s and could only evade them by spinning down for a second time.[81] His attempts to get back into the fight were foiled by German fighters.

Harrison, meanwhile, fortunately survived a head-on attack from a Me 110 with only a single bullet in his wing and managed to outmanoeuvre it, but his fire had no visible effect; he then attacked a Me 109 after also outmanoeuvring it and getting on its tail but ran out of ammunition, so broke off.[82] Being almost out of fuel after all their pre-combat perambulations, he had to refuel at nearby Gosport naval air base. Yellow Section leader, S/L Peel appears to have dropped out of the fight early, his machine damaged, but he managed to crash-land on the Isle of Wight at about 10h30, his Hurricane repairable and himself lightly wounded, just south of Mottistone Manor, about six miles east-south-east of the Needles.[83]

From the above combat reports and the squadron IPR,[84] Yellow Section appears to have been the first part of 145 Squadron to make

The First Major Raid, Portland: 11 August 1940

contact with the enemy, in the vicinity of the western part of the Isle of Wight. The Me 110s were clearly seen coming in from the east, and a few Me 109s only were apparent during the section's actions. The Me 110s also seem to have been starting to form their circles, and at a high altitude of *c.* 27,000-30,000 ft. Red Section's four Hurricanes led by F/Lt Dutton, orbiting base, had been told to rejoin Yellow Section and proceed to the south of Swanage; unable to locate the other section, Dutton and his small formation were at 25,000 ft and about six miles south-east of Swanage, flying towards the south-west, when he spotted a smoke trail above and to the south of his position.[85] He immediately made for the trail and very soon saw a dogfight just starting (presumably Yellow Section?), and climbed up to 27,000 ft and up-sun, a prescient tactical move; however, they were attacked from above by some Me 109s, which were engaged by Red 2, Sgt. Kwiecinski.[86] The latter's report, however, makes clear that the attackers were actually Me 110s, which might explain why Dutton basically ignored them. Kwiecinski turned and claimed to have shot down one of the Me 110 attackers, pursuing it right down to about 5,000 ft where he dispatched it into the sea.[87]

F/Lt Dutton had launched himself right into a mass of Me 110s, and his rapid tactical innovation in reaction to a rather chaotic situation is best spelled out with an excerpt from his combat report.[88]

> I attacked and was attacked from all angles. I decided however it was best to wait outside the defensive circles of the 110's and attacked from underneath while they were banked vertically. I attacked two Me 110s in this manner and each in their turn first gave off white smoke from the engines, then fell into a dive, shedding their tail units on the way into the sea. Amongst others I fired at hastily, two gave off white smoke from the engines – I did not see any final result. On one occasion, nearing the end of the fight, I noticed about 4 Me 110's trailing white smoke from both engines and obviously in trouble. I also noticed at various times at least 10 E/A fall in sea. (E/A = enemy aircraft)

Dutton broke away and south of Swanage saw a pilot bail out of a flaming Hurricane, which he reported;[89] may this have been F/O Branch (see below) of his squadron? This was F/Lt Dutton's first experience of massed Me 110s flying in circles and after a fearless yet somewhat unwise start he rapidly devised an effective tactic for making efficient attacks on what were rather difficult formations to engage. As will be seen, various other squadrons which engaged with the same massive circling formation of Me 110s (and Me 109s) came up with their own approaches to this problem. Red Section of 145 Squadron, consisting of

Adlertag

four Hurricanes, was using a box formation of a vic of three machines with the fourth behind them; while Dutton and Kwiecinski were battling the Me 110s, Red 4 F/O Urbanowicz chased three Me 109s approaching the section from the beam as they first went in to attack against the German fighters.[90] Then he noticed a smoking Me 109 followed by a second Me 109, apparently undamaged, and followed them southwards; finding himself then beneath fifteen-odd Me 109s retreating across the Channel, he had to bide his time before shooting the rearmost of the two Me 109s into the sea.[91] Red 3, F/O Ostowicz, disappeared, being shot down into the sea somewhere south of the Needles.[92]

B Flight of 145 Squadron had been patrolling base until ordered to tackle enemy aircraft south of Swanage; F/Lt Boyd led them in a dive onto five Me 109s at about 10h35 but his windscreen became obscured by oil and he had to break off his attack.[93] The squadron IPR describes both flights having been vectored to the Swanage area where they met 100 to 200 Me 110s, mainly flying in large line astern formations from 30,000 ft and downwards, with Me 109s lower down, flying in vic formation.[94] Yellow Section of the squadron had seen the Me 110s approaching from the east when still over the Isle of Wight and engaged them approximately over the Needles, with Red Section intercepting further to the south-west, to the south of Swanage, as already outlined above.

While Yellow reported contact with one Me 109 (but note there is no report surviving for S/L Peel who, though likely shot down by a Me 110, may have fallen victim to a Me 109), Red Section reported more extensive action against Me 109s and sighted many more of them; B Flight seems to have mainly engaged Me 109s. This suggests that an initial incursion of Me 110s from the east of the Isle of Wight was met to the south-west of the island (i.e. south of Swanage) by an Me 109 contingent that appears to have grown in numbers as the fighting with 145 Squadron proceeded. B Flight reported that the enemy formation was already fighting RAF opponents (presumably Yellow/Red Sections) when they arrived.[95] Due to range constraints, the Me 109s could not have accompanied the Me 110s on a more lengthy approach from east of the Isle of Wight but must have taken a course directly from Cherbourg to south-west of the Isle. The Me 110s would logically have been from *I/ZG 2*, based at Amiens Glissy on the Somme River, as opposed to *Stab* and *II/ZG 2*, based in the Guyancourt area in the south-western outskirts of Paris.[96] Presumably, *I/ZG 2*, taking the shortest route from their location across the Channel, flying basically at right angles to the French coast at the mouth of the Somme, would have approached the English coast near Beachy Head, in the area where the Tangmere controller had dispatched Red and Yellow Sections of 145 Squadron.

The First Major Raid, Portland: 11 August 1940

P/O Dunning-White, Blue 3 in B Flight of 145 Squadron, after firing ineffectively at a Me 109, climbed up again and, avoiding the many circling aircraft, tackled a lone Me 109 diving onto a Hurricane and shot it down into the sea.[97] Green 3, Sgt. Forde, who was forced to much lower levels by a missing panel on his machine allowing freezing air into the cockpit where he was flying without gloves, engaged several Me 109s at about 5,000 ft who were attacking a lone Hurricane, and after fighting in and out of cloud fired at a Me 109 climbing up at him at about 2,500 ft and shot its hood off before losing it again.[98] Overall, however, B Flight did not do too well against the rather numerous Me 109s; P/O Storrar flying in the Green 2 position saw his leader shot down into the sea and despite circling over him and guiding a life boat to within about 50-100 yards, F/O Branch was not sighted in the water and was lost.[99] Blue 2, P/O Weir's Hurricane was damaged in combat and he crashed at Walkford in the north-eastern outskirts of Christchurch; his machine was repairable.[100] In total, 145 Squadron claimed unconfirmed victories over three Me 110s, two Me 109s, damaging two more Me 110s and one Me 109.[101] However, having gone into battle against vastly superior numbers of Me 110s and 109s, about 60 of them, in three separate small formations of Hurricanes, they paid the price of two missing pilots and two more Hurricanes brought down, damaged.[102]

As already inferred, *I/JG 2* are thought to have provided the Me 109s that flew directly from the Cherbourg area to the western Isle of Wight and then provided single-engine fighter cover for the *I/ZG 2* Me 110 circle moving steadily south-west from the Isle. This Me 109 *Gruppe* made nine claims between 10h25 and 10h55 in the area from the Isle of Wight to east of Weymouth, and these times coincide reasonably well with casualties suffered by 145 and 609 Squadrons.[103] *I/ZG 2*'s provisional claims of seven Hurricanes and four Spitfires for the entire raid,[104] bearing in mind that none appear in the confirmed claims list,[105] must obviously also be taken account of for losses to both 145 and 609 Squadrons (and also for 601 Squadron), but there is no way to differentiate the relative merits of the claims by Me 110s and Me 109s. The same applies in reverse to German losses and RAF claims for them: British fighters claimed a total of seven confirmed, eleven unconfirmed, three probable and eight damaged Me 110s in the entire set of actions related to the Portland raid,[106] as against a total of four lost with their crews from *I/ZG 2*, plus four damaged, and from *II/ZG 2*, one lost with crew and one damaged, with *Stab/ZG 2* losing one Me 110, pilot wounded, gunner dead.[107] To determine which claims from any particular RAF squadron involved can be confirmed is an impossibility.

I/JG 2 lost two Me 109s from *2nd Staffel*, one pilot being killed, the other wounded but rescued by the *Seenotdienst*.[108] While these might have fallen to 145 Squadron, once again RAF claims against Me 109s on the raid exceed German losses. There is an account by *Lt* Bethke of *2/JG* 2 on the Portland raid.[109] He remembers them encountering a group of Hurricanes near the coast (which coast is unknown: Dorset, Hampshire or Isle of Wight?) at about 13,000 ft flying in a tight formation, from which he and a colleague claimed to have shot down two before the enemy formation split apart. Claim times for these two Hurricanes were 10h25 and 10h37; Bethke claimed a second Hurricane some seven minutes later from which the pilot jumped, but that was south-east of Portland,[110] probably once the two fighter circles, Me 110s and Me 109s, had joined up or were about to do so.

Fw Leipelt of *2/JG* 2 had also claimed an earlier Hurricane at 10h37, south-east of Portsmouth and thus probably near the Isle of Wight, but had his own Me 109 badly damaged, and in flying south across the Channel had to bail out some thirty miles from France and was rescued north of Cherbourg; *Uffz* Sass of his *Staffel* was killed near Portland.[111] While three earlier claims by *3/JG* 2 at 10h25-10h34[112] may have been in combat with Yellow Section, 145 Squadron, Bethke's *2/JG* 2 may have engaged Red Section while it was still in formation; such possibilities remain speculative.

Balance of 213 Squadron: effective attack on KG 54's bombers in Portland area, *c.* 10h25–10h35

The KG 54 formation with direct escort from *I/JG* 27 appears to have flown in as the large protective fighter circle formed south-east of Portland and then passed westwards from having flown underneath the circle to attack Portland from the south, turning north from their original course soon before attacking the naval base.[113] The raid was met by 213 Squadron before they bombed, and one flight each of 238 and 87 Squadrons as they retreated, also in very quick succession and with overlap between their attacks.[114] After some vectoring about by the controller, 213 Squadron was positioned over Portland at 10,000 ft, prior to the arrival of the German raid; the controllers had done their job expertly as the squadron was perfectly placed and at the exact same height as that of the bombers soon to arrive.[115] Being thus at the same height as the bombers they were able to attack them as they came in before their Me 109 escort could intervene, as it was about 5,000 ft higher and behind.[116] The leader of 213 Squadron did exactly the right thing as

The First Major Raid, Portland: 11 August 1940

well, ensuring that this unit's attack significantly disrupted the bombers' planned raid on Portland harbour, which was little damaged,[117] while the squadron itself was hardly troubled at all by the escorting Me 109s. S/L McGregor had expertly got his Hurricanes at the bomber formations and attacked successfully before the escort could intervene. There were thirty-eight Ju 88s from *I* and *II/KG 54* with two He 111s (from *KG 27*) which acted as lookout aircraft to spot crew members needing rescue;[118] the direct escort was made up of *I/JG 27*, with *III/JG 27* flying ahead as indirect escort or sweep.

213 Squadron had planned to scramble eleven Hurricanes comprising Yellow, Red, Blue Sections of three each, with the two Green Section machines no doubt intended to form the tail-end-Charlie guard pair; in the event, Green 2 was late taking off, only getting off the ground at Exeter as the action against the Ju 88s started.[119] S/L McGregor had joined the leading section, Yellow, for the take-off, and actually made the first attack on the Ju 88s; it is not known what formation the resultant four Hurricanes in Yellow Section flew on their way to the interception.[120] Squadron leaders led very busy lives, with an entire squadron of ground personnel, lots of equipment, transport, in addition to pilots to look after, and much administrative work also, and often could not join specific sections for a planned mission. However, when indications of a major raid came into the base, many of them such as S/L McGregor latched onto the 'formal' squadron formation. Blue Section had been detached to the south-east of Portland where it engaged the forming Me 110 circle there just prior to the bombing formation's appearance (discussed above), leaving eight Hurricanes (Green 2 took-off late) to meet the onslaught over Portland itself.

F/O Strickland leading the three Hurricanes of Yellow Section provides the best description[121] of the early attacks on the incoming Ju 88 formation of *II/KG 54*, which *Gruppe* was flying in front of *I/KG 54*; his attack was preceded slightly by that of S/L McGregor, from the opposite flank of the leading vic of bombers.

> I was ordered to patrol Portland Bill at 10,000 ft. I sighted about 70 enemy aircraft in waves approaching Portland from the east. I called my section together and climbed to the seaward side of the enemy. We attacked the leading section of JU88s, who immediately started to dive and break formation, dropping their bombs wide of Portland. I picked out one 88 and gave him 2 short bursts on the way down, his port engine started to smoke quite a bit. He went down to about 2,000 ft and I gave him two more bursts coming in on a quarter attack. The rear gunner ceased firing, and the starboard engine looked as if it

Adlertag

was U/S. Aircraft then losing height rapidly and I gave him two more short bursts and then followed him right down. He forced landed on Portland Bill with undercarriage up. I saw 3 airmen get out and were captured by the Army. I then flew away and tried to find some more enemy aircraft, but by that time they had all gone. I saw several enemy aircraft falling in flames. The only evasion action used by the E/A was to throttle right back and use diving brakes and turning towards me. It was quite effective and caused me a certain amount of trouble because I was apt to overshoot. (U/S = unserviceable)

When the JU 88s were still flying in from the east, their port flank was to seaward, but once they turned north to bomb Portland, their starboard flank was on the eastern side of the formation; it was from this side that S/L McGregor attacked, slightly ahead of Yellow Section's three machines, his combat report[122] very briefly detailing his experiences: 'Attacked JU88 in leading Section from beam and gave two second burst and rear gunner stopped firing. Put a second burst into starboard engine which caught fire, and aircraft crashed in flames on west side of Portland Bill. Attacked No.2. of "A" section of 3 J.U.88s and saw petrol streaming from aircraft, but as No. 3. of section was about to drop his bombs, diverted my attack on to that aircraft; but ammunition ran out before any result was observed.'

Clearly, both Strickland and McGregor attacked the leading vic of three Ju 88s from opposite sides in beam attacks, although the former's target rapidly dived away as this vic broke up and recourse was had by Strickland to attacks from astern and quarter thereafter. That McGregor was able to make two beam attacks denotes not only considerable skill in deflection shooting but also in positioning himself twice to attack from the beam; this would also have required a couple of minutes to achieve and would not have been possible once the machines were diving. As can be seen from the two combat reports, McGregor and Strickland attacked the same aircraft, the squadron leader detaching it from the Ju 88 formation, and Yellow leader finishing it off; together the two 213 Squadron pilots made five attacks on this bomber, once again underlining that multiple attacks by more than one fighter and large expenditure of ammunition were normally required to down these larger aircraft. S/L McGregor had also hit the *II/KG 54* formation at the perfect time, just before they started their dives onto the targets at Portland Bill and Portland harbour.

While Strickland went for the bomber already hit by McGregor and saw the front vic break up and the Ju 88s begin their dives, his two wingmen made their attacks on Ju 88s already in their dives. Sgt Croskell, Yellow

The First Major Raid, Portland: 11 August 1940

2, made two attacks on one of several Junkers dive-bombing Portland Bill and saw it catch fire and the crew bail out; he then attacked another, which gave off smoke and shed some large pieces.[123] The third member of the section, Sgt Llewellyn, attacked the Ju 88 nearest to him from astern and it exploded and caught fire; nobody got out.[124] He attacked a second bomber from astern and observed a red glow at its starboard wing root and large pieces falling off, before another Hurricane engaged it from the starboard beam and he last saw this Ju 88 burning furiously.

Red Section of 213 Squadron was not far behind Yellow, and also engaged diving Ju 88s. Their leader, P/O Philippart, made an astern attack on the leader of the formation and overshot when the bomber put out its dive brakes, but he came back and engaged again as the bomber tried to escape at low level, set the starboard engine on fire and saw it crash into the sea.[125] His two wingmen both set the port engine of their victims on fire; P/O Osmand had to break off when attacked by a Me 109, and P/O Buchin saw his enemy going down in a large circle, burning.[126] They may have attacked the same machine. Between them, these seven Hurricanes had accounted for the three Ju 88s in the leading vic of the bomber formation, all from *Stab II/KG 54*. McGregor's and Strickland's shared victim, piloted by *Oblt* Wette who was seriously wounded, managed to put down in a field near Blacknore Fort on Portland Head at about 10h40, the undercarriage collapsing soon after touching down and the machine sliding backwards to a halt, the other three crew members being unharmed.[127] The second bomber lost crashed into the sea at about 10h50 at West Bay, off the northwest coast of Portland Bill; two of the crew managed to bail out but only one survived, *Uffz* Klatte telling RAF interrogators that they had been attacked by five Hurricanes, and they had carried four 250 kg bombs (also reported by the crew from the previous Junkers brought down).[128] The third Ju 88 from *Stab II/KG 54* was missing after fighter attack over the Channel off Portland, the *Gruppenkommandeur Major* Leonardi and his crew all being lost.[129]

To assign either of the other two *Stab II/KG 54* Ju 88s to specific pilots of 213 Squadron is impossible; Sgt Croskell saw crew members bailing out from one of the bombers he attacked and was presumably involved in the destruction of Klatte's machine. The latter reported being attacked by a total of five Hurricanes which again stresses what it normally took to bring down a larger aircraft using rifle calibre machine guns. While S/L McGregor had damaged a second Ju 88 after detaching the first from the leading vic, Yellow 2 and 3, Sgts Croskell and Llewellyn each made effective attacks on two bombers, and all three members of Red Section had each attacked one bomber. What mattered was that the six pilots of

Adlertag

Yellow and Red Sections, 213 Squadron and their leader S/L McGregor had destroyed the leading vic, including the *Gruppekommandeur's* aircraft, thereby badly disrupting their bombing of targets on Portland Bill, damage there and to the harbour being minor.[130] These few Hurricanes had inflicted a loss rate of close to 16% on *II/KG 54*, about three times what could typically be borne by any aerial unit in long-term action.

Yellow and Red Sections of 213 Squadron each had one Hurricane damaged by return fire by a Ju 88, P/O Philippart flying as Red 1 being hit by seven bullets from his claimed victim, hitting the oil tank, engine and wings, but made it back to base.[131] P/O Osmand of Philippart's section was attacked by a Me 109 from astern which damaged his hydraulics and controls and he crash-landed at Exeter as a result, but his Hurricane was repairable.[132] There is a victory claim for *III/JG 27* timed at 10h37, south of Portland[133] that could fit this damage to Osmand's Hurricane. Sgt Croskell (Yellow 2) was forced to break off his attack on a second Ju 88, which he damaged, by five attacking Me 109s; he claimed one shot down into the sea and managed to evade the other four successfully, who left him once he crossed the coast, his machine being undamaged.[134] *I/JG 27*, assumed to have been the Ju 88 escort, lost one Me 109 in the Channel to RAF fighters, its pilot bailing out and being rescued later by the *Seenotdienst*; *III/JG 27* had an Me 109 and pilot go missing over the Channel.[135] One of these two Me 109s may well have fallen victim to Sgt Croskell; the other likely fell to either 87 or 238 Squadron, who engaged outgoing Ju 88s and Me 109s from the Portland raid (see below).

The bombers' escort thus achieved little, and S/L McGregor had timed his attack by Yellow and Red Sections to perfection as they managed to disrupt *II/KG 54* and cause them serious losses before the Me 109 escort played any role. Possibly both *Gruppen* of JG 27, *I* and *III*, close and advance free chase escorts, became marginally involved against 213 Squadron; the sweep ahead, presumably *III/JG 27*, could by this stage have already turned around on their way home and made some minor attacks on Yellow and Red Sections of the squadron. Disruption to the bombing by 213 Squadron dispatching the leading section of *II/KG 54*'s Ju 88s no doubt played a role in the rather poor bombing results; at least seventy bombs appear to have been dropped on Portland by this *Gruppe* between c. 10h25 and 10h35.[136] Bearing in mind each bomber, there being about 19 of them, carried four 250 kg bombs and four much smaller 50 kg bombs,[137] almost all the aircraft except for one or two thus got to drop their main ordinance, but rather poorly aimed and scattered.[138]

The First Major Raid, Portland: 11 August 1940

Both sides experienced a relatively insoluble dilemma in the Battle of Britain related to attacks on German bomber formations. If the German escorts were closer to the bombers, they would be flying too slow to react promptly to most RAF fighter attacks and were then also vulnerable to being shot down themselves; if they were further away they could maintain effective speed but then left a gap through which an able RAF leader could make an effective if brief assault on the bomber formations before trouble arrived. The dilemma also applied to the attacking British fighters, as so often such a brief attack under the risk of counter-attack by the higher-flying German escort would often mean that some members of a flight would almost inevitably be attacked in their turn by a faster enemy descending from greater altitude. The judgement of timing and placement of your units within a rapidly changing three-dimensional space was always a challenge for both squadron and *Staffel* leaders to finesse and perfect. Those that could, would be effective, often surviving and scoring victories, while leaders that could not do this well would see little success and often suffer casualties to their own comrades or become casualties themselves.

Getting back to 213 Squadron's action over Portland, Sub Lt Jeram as Green 1, flying alone as his number two had only just taken off as the action against the Ju 88 formations began,[139] saw a large number of Ju 88s, most likely still in formation, one mile south of Portland Bill at 10,000 ft.[140] This was most likely the remaining *Gruppe* of *KG 54*, namely *I/KG 54* flying behind *II/KG 54*, which was attacked just before by A Flight, which had then pursued them into their dives on the target as well. Jeram very bravely attacked what appears to have been an as yet undisturbed formation, opening fire on one bomber from astern and silenced the gunner, and saw how it dove, petrol, oil and smoke coming out of it.[141] He attacked another Ju 88 and the starboard engine caught fire, and he last saw it diving towards Chesil Beach west-north-west of Portland harbour. Despite Jeram claiming one conclusive and one inconclusive victory over Ju 88s, he probably only damaged them, and they were most likely finished off by aircraft from 238 and 87 Squadrons who attacked the outgoing raid's Ju 88s and Me 109s as they headed back over the Channel. Their actions will be examined in detail below, but before that 609 Squadron's engagement with the one Me 110-Me 109 circle, *I/ZG 2–I/JG 2* south of Swanage and south-west of the Isle of Wight will be dealt with, as it was approximately coeval with 213 Squadron's engagement with *II/KG 54* and elements of *I* and *III/JG 27*. 213 Squadron overall claimed seven Ju 88 and one Me 109 conclusive victories and two inconclusive Me 109s in this engagement against *KG 54* and escorts.[142]

Adlertag

609 Squadron takes on Me 110-Me 109 circle south of Swanage *c.* 10h30-10h35, while elements of 145 Squadron were still engaging

609 Squadron was already in the air at 09h45.[143] An excerpt from S/L Darley's combat report below describes well their early moves and then several different methods he applied to tackle the circling Me 110 formation encountered. It is assumed that 609 Squadron engaged the I/ZG1 – I/JG 2 circle south-south-west of Swanage and south-west of the Isle of Wight. The squadron was using an experimental formation based on their past experience: the leading flight of six Spitfires was in line astern, and the two remaining sections were placed on either flank of the central flight and about 1,500 feet higher, thereby providing an upper guard to each side of the initial six aircraft.[144] Initial experience with this setup resulted in the two upper sections easily becoming detached when the whole formation made a turn or flew towards the sun; the solution to this problem would in time be found through bringing the two flanking sections down to the same level as the central six line astern machines.[145]

This time round, Blue Section with Darley at their head, followed by Green Section, in line astern, had Red and Yellow Sections disposed above and at the sides.[146] As Darley led 609 Squadron towards the enemy on this Sunday morning, a sharp turn combined with a steep climb sunwards led to Yellow and Red Sections losing the other flight; the latter section did not come into action at all, while Yellow 1, F/O John Dundas, found himself at 24,000 ft and about 10 miles south-west of the Isle of Wight in splendid three-man isolation.[147] The initial attack on the German formation was thus made by the six Spitfires of B Flight, Blue and Green Sections, with S/L Darley in the lead; part of his account appears below.[148]

> Squadron ordered to patrol Warmwell 18,000ft. After reaching 18,000ft saw smoke trails out to sea 25 miles S.S.E. of Swanage. Reported to controller received reply, that bandits reported still in that direction but did not appear to be doing anything definite. Squadron afterwards ordered to intercept these bandits. Flew about 15 to 20 miles S.S.E. of Swanage. Saw nothing and turned West. Saw single smoke trail 25,000ft about 6 miles ahead of me. Then intercepted very large number of A/C ranging from 30,000ft to 15,000ft comprising of Me 110s and Me 109s turning in left hand tight turns. I flew straight into the general scrimmage, tried to join in one of the circles with about 12 A/C init (sic) and fired short burst at one of them. Then I attempted to join in circle in opposite direction in order to break them up, but

The First Major Raid, Portland: 11 August 1940

found it rather impossible. I then flew across the circle and had a quick snapshot at a Me 110 going across my bows. Attack then developed into short attacks, breaking away quickly. I went into a steep diving turn to evade A/C behind me, when I found I could not get out of dive and lost 5,000ft. Then I went back again and found A/C then flying South with exception of some 30,000ft above me.

The controller's reply that the enemy formation was still in the same area and apparently not 'doing anything definite', while certainly concomitant with a circling mass of fighters, was not quite what the pilots tackling it would have felt. The smoke trails seen suggests the circles were already in action and this likely was elements of 145 Squadron, as described above. The left-hand tight turns being maintained by the Me 110s refers to anti-clockwise circles. The circling mass of German fighters was estimated by 609 Squadron as a hundred-plus in number, with Me 109s far above the Me 110s.[149] S/L Darley's observation when he climbed back up into the fight to find that the mass of the enemy were flying south most likely indicates this circle moving to join up with the *Stab* and *II/ZG 2* circle located south-east of Portland (against which Blue Section of 213 Squadron fought their early, lone battle), thereby forming a giant combined circle of ZG 2's Me 110s and most of *JG 2*'s Me 109s.

S/L Darley had tried various tactics to engage the circling Me 110s: initially he had tried to join a circle, which was really dangerous as that was the intention of the circling Messerschmitts, with the one behind shooting at any enemy that tried to join the circle and attack a Me 110 flying head of it, from astern. Next, he circled the rotating Me 110s in the opposite direction but found this too difficult; other pilots would perform a similar attack this day and find it quite effective; it must also have been extremely bad for German morale. Finally, Darley settled for what were essentially full deflection attacks on the circling Me 110s from outside of the circles. Once they had seen their leader perform his lone attack and successfully harry the circling enemy without himself being dispatched in short order, his fellow pilots joined in as well, essentially each on his own and applying different approaches to what was a very sticky tactical problem.[150]

Darley's courageous fight came to an end when he carried out a steep diving turn to evade a German aircraft; his combat report does not detail what type, but presumably a Me 110, as the Me 109s were reported to have mostly stayed higher up leaving their heavier twin-engine colleagues largely to their fate. There was some wisdom in this too, as once the Me 109s did come down, their fuel state would not easily have allowed them to climb up again and repeat their bounce. Dogfighting also ate up

Adlertag

fuel and once they entered the fray they would soon have had to depart back across the Channel, which was much wider here than in the Straits of Dover. Having watched his squadron leader show the way, Blue 2 of 609 Squadron, P/O Noel Agazarian, tried his best to emulate him, diving straight in and opening fire with full deflection.[151] Finding like his leader that this did not produce tangible results, he climbed back up, all the way to 30,000 ft and into the sun, observing Me 109s still well above him, where they remained, providing a continuous deterrent.[152] Agazarian came roaring down back into the fight and as he approached the Me 110s saw that two of them were separated (possibly due to Darley's efforts) and attacked, missing the first one but hitting the second fair and square, setting its port engine and adjacent fuselage alight.[153] He was not able to observe its fate. The third member of Blue Section submitted no combat report and presumably did not involve himself very closely in the action.

It thus fell to Green Section to take up the unequal fight and Green 1, F/Lt James McArthur, on only his second operational mission, demonstrated tactical wisdom in leading his section into action, as detailed below in his combat report.[154]

> I was following Blue Section West, when I saw many bandits circling around anti-clockwise high up. There seemed to be many 110s at 27,000ft and more lower down at about 20,000ft. My section was then at 24,000ft. Above the 110s at over 30,000ft I saw 4 or 5 Me 109s. I turned slightly left, and climbed into the sun and started to make a wide circle outside the Me 110s in a clockwise direction. At just over 27,000ft I decided to cut across the lower 110s. I fired a short burst of about 5 seconds at one and saw his glass roof come off and he turned over and dived. I could not follow him down, as other Me 110s were all around me, and while doing evasive action, I spun down for about 15,000ft and then had trouble getting my motor to start again. Estimate number of machines at least 100. I saw many machines falling down in flames and 2 parachutists, could distinguish nothing as was feeling unwell by this time.

A spin of 15,000 ft would make anyone feel unwell. P/O John Bisdee, Green 2, followed his section leader, saw the latter make his attack, and himself took on a Me 110 circling in the opposite direction to its fellows:[155] just a confused German inadvertently disobeying orders or a brave man trying to counter enemies flying diametrically opposing courses? Bisdee gave his target a short burst from immediately above and saw it roll over to the right; then as bullets passed over the top of his own wing, he turned sharply to the left, seeing an attacking Me 109

The First Major Raid, Portland: 11 August 1940

overshoot.[156] In his turn trying to get on the 109's tail, John Bisdee spun down to about 12,000 ft; thereafter he had several more skirmishes with Me 109s.[157]

Like Green 2, P/O David Crook (Green 3) climbed up behind F/Lt McArthur but lost contact with the rest of his section. After the initial sighting of the enemy formation when the Squadron was still patrolling over Warmwell and as they were climbing towards the enemy formation sighted out to sea, Crook had noted that some Hurricanes were already in action with the circling Me 110s.[158] Logically, these would have been from 145 Squadron. David Crook clearly saw Hurricanes engaging the Me 110s at about 25,000 ft, before 609 Squadron's B Flight attacked. Despite the time given in the 609 Squadron combat reports[159] for this action, of *c.* 10h15, the evidence that Hurricanes preceded them into the fight means they could only have been from 145 Squadron and suggests that 609 in fact engaged the circle at about 10h30-10h35. The 10h15 time could perhaps rather reflect when 609 Squadron first sighted smoke trails to the south-south-west of them. P/O Crook, the last pilot of 609 Squadron's B Flight to enter the fray against the large stack of circling Me 110s and 109s, climbed well above the melee and dived down on a Me 110 he had noticed flying directly below him and separated from its brothers.[160] However he had come down too fast and his first burst missed, so he came round on the twin-engined fighter's tail and fired from such close range that he almost collided with it, and as it vanished from his vision saw that its port engine was pouring out black smoke.[161] The last he saw of it was an apparent stall after a sharp right turn and then it turned over on its back and vanished.

Heading southwards leading Yellow Section of 609 Squadron in the hope of catching up with B Flight and his leader, F/O John Dundas spied nine Hurricanes flying south-westwards below him, about halfway across the Channel. This was in fact 1 Squadron, of which more later. Realising his mistake, Dundas turned his little band northwards and after some time saw the smoke trails marking the ongoing aerial battle and began a wide climbing turn to join the action.[162] Going in to the attack but unaware that he had become separated from the rest of his section, Yellow 1 attacked the circling Me 110s from above.[163] Having fired at one from very close range but without any visible result, Dundas, who was enduring considerable return fire from the circling *Zerstörer* rear-gunners, took his time making a second assault from a climbing turn and using full deflection, closing in from 250 to 100 yards; both engines appeared to catch fire, the enemy machine seemed to stagger in the air and fell over to the left.[164]

As Yellow 1 broke away his Spitfire was hit and seriously damaged in left wing and rudder, so he had to rapidly pull the plug and disappear.[165]

Neither of John Dundas' wingmen followed him into the mass of Me 110s; Yellow 3, P/O Miller, instead chose to climb up to attack the high flying Me 109s above 30,000 ft, but finding his aircraft struggling to gain height he was himself attacked by a diving Me 110 and turned to meet it, giving a short burst of fire, before turning away as he considered himself outnumbered.[166] Yellow 2 submitted no report so presumably did not seriously engage the German fighter formation.

Only a few of the high-flying Me 109s came down during the various attacks made by the 609 Squadron sections. However, their mere presence well above the fighting against the Me 110s provided an ongoing deterrent; at *c.* 25,000 ft the Me 110s appeared to have better performance[167] and it thus made sense that these circling *Zerstörer* chose to fight at these heights, with the added security of Me 109 top cover. While Blue and Green Sections, 609 Squadron, claimed four confirmed victories[168] from the documentation consulted, they appear to have seriously damaged three Me 110s, two of which were detached with engines almost certainly knocked out and one had its long glasshouse-like canopy shot off; P/O Bisdee's account does not provide definite indications of damage from his fire.[169] None of these aircraft appears to have survived to reach France damaged, but most if not all of them were likely finished off by pilots from other squadrons, most probably 601 and 1 Squadrons, detailed below. F/O John Dundas leading Yellow Section also claimed a Me 110 confirmed; he probably also detached and significantly damaged one of the Me 110s, later finished off by others. By attacking in small driblets and even as solo aircraft, Darley and his men from 609 Squadron also avoided serious disruption from the higher flying Me 109s, few of which came down to disrupt the attacks of such small RAF packets.

Several of the Me 110s that were attacked by both 609 and soon after by 601 Squadron were seen to have engines smoking or burning, and Darley had also seen one towards the end of the entire 609 Squadron engagement.[170] None of the five damaged *ZG 2* Messerschmitt 110s that made it back to France reported a damage state above 10-15%,[171] and replacement of an engine with attendant systems would normally reflect a damage state of 40-45%.[172] This suggests that the several Me 110s seen to have one or even two burning engines by several different pilots from three different squadrons, 145, 609 and 601, engaged against the massive circling German fighter formation, did not make it home, and this also implies that it often took a second attack on a Me 110 (at least, possibly more in some cases) to ensure the destruction of one of these relatively large twin-engine aircraft.

This of course goes a long way to explaining the greater number of claims made by the British fighter pilots as against known losses from the

The First Major Raid, Portland: 11 August 1940

German side. Any attempts to tie specific claims and pilots with specific losses of their opponents thus becomes almost impossible. In the whirling, fast-paced three-dimensional reality that was a Second World War aerial battle this was really the norm. Things happened within seconds, any individual pilot only saw a part of what did, and many aircraft would have been attacked and hit from different directions at virtually the same moment. This reality would have applied not just in the examples detailed here but also in a generic way in the majority of encounters. It is thus a rather futile practice to try and tie specific losses with specific victory claimants from either side; and such inferences must by definition be fraught with potential errors, especially when made long after the time by historians and other non-participants, never mind by excited pilots giving reports to an over-taxed intelligence officer after landing back at base.

238 Squadron in two separate actions: A Flight two miles east of Weymouth, B Flight five miles south of Swanage, c. 10h35

This squadron had an unfortunate leadership situation in the first half of August 1940. S/L Harold Fenton had been appointed to command on 15 July 1940 but was shot down and wounded when ditching in the Channel on 8 August; he did not rejoin the squadron until almost mid-September.[173] The two flight commanders in a unit that had only been reactivated in mid-May 1940 were both substantive Flying Officers and Acting Flight Lieutenants, David Hughes and Stuart Walch: the former had joined the RAF in February 1936 and the latter the RAAF (later moving to the RAF) in July of the same year.[174] While Walch had joined the unit on its reconstitution in May and Hughes only on 4 August,[175] the latter would have had five months seniority on his colleague.

Unfortunately, in the absence of their C/O, no system had been worked out whereby one of them (or both alternately) led the squadron in the air, and an acting squadron commander, F/Lt Blake, was only appointed on 16 August to do just that.[176] As a result, on 11 August 1940, six aircraft of each flight lifted off from Middle Wallop, A Flight of Red and Yellow Sections being led off by Hughes at 10h14, and two minutes behind them was B Flight (Blue and Green) with Walch at their head.[177] There is no documentary evidence of one of them being in charge of the squadron as a whole, and despite both flights being given exactly the same instructions by the controller to patrol Portland at 20,000 ft, the two flights operated independently under their own flight commanders and became engaged in different combats.[178]

Adlertag

Hughes led his six Hurricanes to their ordered destination and altitude where his rear section (Yellow) observed Portland Head being dive-bombed, the bombers descending from about 10,000 ft to *c.* 6,000 ft where they released their ordinance.[179] Very shortly after this observation, which shows that 238 Squadron's arrival coincided with the bombing and the ongoing action of 213 Squadron over the Portland area, flight commander David Hughes saw aircraft milling around at about 6,000 ft in and out of broken cloud, circled round to be able to attack down-sun, and instructing Yellow Section to ensure no enemy machines followed them down, led his three Hurricanes of Red Section into a steep dive and at the same time ordering line astern.[180] The milling machines proved to be Me 109s, presumably of the *I/JG 27* direct escort to *KG 54* and/or of the *III/JG 27* sweep ahead, now possibly returning south again; all three pilots of Red Section engaged them, but only Hughes managed to claim one, seeing it burst into flames and the pilot bail out into the sea about six miles east of Portland Bill.[181]

These *JG 27* units lost three Me 109s in this raid, as already discussed when describing 213 Squadron's engagement with *II/KG 54*. Clearly, the Me 109s of the escort had now intervened, too late to hinder 213 Squadron's effective attack on the bombers but in time to come down to the defence of the Ju 88s as they came out of their dives over the targets when they were at their most vulnerable, and also kept Red Section of 238 Squadron from taking on any of the retreating bombers.

Yellow Section, meanwhile, having watched Red Section dive down, obeyed the order to ensure no 109s followed them down, and seeing no enemy aircraft at their level or above, Sgt Marsh their leader ordered his section into line astern and led them down from *c.* 20,000 ft to attack what Marsh estimated as forty-plus enemy aircraft, described as Me 109s, He 111s and some Do 17s.[182] With A Flight of 238 Squadron engaging the enemy roughly two miles east of Weymouth,[183] these aircraft were probably those of *I/KG 54* and escorts, which had flown from south of Portland Bill (where Sub Lt Jeram of 213 Squadron had attacked them) and turned north-west and then to the north-east, flying over Chesil Beach and over Portland Naval Base along the same track, with Weymouth just to the north-north-east.

As they exited over the naval base and turned back towards France, the Ju 88s would have been placed east of Weymouth. Sgt Marsh saw one 'He 111', really a Ju 88, separated by about 200 yards from the other enemy aircraft and attacked it with many short bursts from 300 yards down to point blank range from slightly above and astern.[184] With a final burst of about four seconds, Marsh last saw the bomber's port engine smoking and it turned in the same direction; he then had to take on three Me 109s,

The First Major Raid, Portland: 11 August 1940

which he managed to evade despite an aileron damaged by return fire from the bomber.[185] Sgt Bann (Yellow 3) attacked the same bomber, as detailed in his combat report, below (report not corrected grammatically).[186] The German bomber was claimed as a shared victory by the two NCOs.[187]

> I was yellow three and "A" Flight was ordered to patrol Portland at 20,000 ft. Yellow 1 gave line astern and he made the first attack on a He. 111 at 6,000 and I observed smoke coming from port engine of E/A. I made number two attack and fired fairly long burst of about 3 secs. from 150 yds. closing in a vertical attack. The E/A exploded and fell into the water. I found two Me's 109 on my tail and broke away and did a steep turn to evade them. After then (sic) I found myself out numbered and it took all my time doing evasive tactics. I eventually gained height and proceeded towards Portland and patrolled as ordered and eventually was ordered to land. Landed at Middle Wallop 1135. No. of rounds fired. 480. (Number two attack = from rear quarter)

Yellow 2, Sgt. Domagala, meanwhile had broken away from his two section mates as they had dived down, to fend off an Me 109; he had just opened fire from very close range when a Hurricane suddenly appeared between him and his target and received the tail end of his fortunately very short burst in its left wing.[188] The suddenly intruding Hurricane was already smoking and Domagala saw the pilot bail out and watched him go down, before climbing back up and having a successful dogfight with another Me 109, which he saw fall in the sea.[189] This might have been one of the two Me 109s which *III/JG 27* lost.[190] He then returned to base, rearmed rapidly and took off again and engaged some enemy stragglers; the Poles were not backward in coming forward in engaging the enemy.[191] Domagala had seen the Hurricane pilot bale out over Chesil Beach, south of Chickerell;[192] this was quite clearly P/O John Cock of 87 Squadron who survived being shot down and immersion in the cold sea, with relatively minor injuries.[193] This incident demonstrates that 87 Squadron's arrival over Portland overlapped with the ongoing action of 238 Squadron against the same German raiders.

The actions of all three RAF units, 213, 238 and 87 Squadrons, thus took place sequentially, but with overlaps, within a short time period.[194] Interestingly, while P/O Cock landed in the sea close to Chesil Beach, Red and Yellow Sections of 238 Squadron were in actions mostly at about two miles east of Weymouth;[195] with combat proceeding at speeds in excess of 300 mph things happened very fast and the location of overlapping actions soon spread over a wide area. It would appear that Sergeants Marsh and Bann of 238 Squadron likely dispatched a Ju 88 of

I/KG 54 which was missing with all its crew after this raid.[196] It was seen to explode and fall into the sea.[197]

The actions and experiences of the unfortunate B Flight of 238 Squadron, about 5 miles south of Swanage over the sea,[198] can be gleaned from the combat report of Green 1, P/O Urwin-Mann.[199] B Flight, with orders to patrol Portland at 20,000 ft, on crossing the coast in the Swanage area at 16,000 ft saw about 100 enemy aircraft directly in front of them and 5,000 ft higher. This was the stepped-up circling fighters from ZG 2 and JG 2, by now probably amalgamated from their initial separate circles into one very large mass. 145 and 609 Squadrons had become spread out from south of Swanage to south-east of Portland. B Flight of 238 Squadron were unlucky suddenly to be confronted with this large formation right ahead of them and high above.

With great courage but rather unwisely, B Flight immediately began to climb into the sun to get into a favourable attack position against these many enemy machines, ranging up in height to well above 30,000 ft. Before Green 1, whose section was flying above and to the left of Blue Section at the time,[200] could give the climb order to his section, it was surprised from above by Me 109s.[201] Green 1 saw his number two get shot down by an Me 109 diving from above who kept going downwards after his successful attack; P/O Cawse was killed when he crashed into the sea off Weymouth and his body washed up in France later.[202] Urwin-Mann immediately dived down after the victor and dispatched him, seeing him dive into the sea in his turn.[203] This pilot soon after saw what appeared to be a Spitfire dive vertically into the sea;[204] this was possibly a Hurricane from either 238 Squadron or 601 Squadron. Blue Section of 238 Squadron were all missing:[205] F/Lt Walch, F/O Steborowski and Sgt Gledhill; only Gledhill's body was found, on the French coast.[206] Gledhill was only nineteen and on his first operation, but even F/Lt Walch who was flying on his fifty fifth mission[207] had little chance, trying to climb right underneath such a large body of enemy fighters.

Green 3, Sgt Pidd, was also attacked and badly shot up in the initial bounce of that section and landed slightly wounded at Warmwell; despite his machine being seriously damaged and himself wounded, he turned on his attackers, claiming a Me 109 unconfirmed which appeared to be out of control.[208] His combat report[209] demonstrates his determination to get at the enemy despite his aircraft being badly hit; the Battle would never have been won without widespread and oft-repeated demonstrations of this fighting spirit.

> I was Green 3 and the section was ordered with rest of Flight B to patrol Portland angels 20. When I was approx. S of Swanage I was

The First Major Raid, Portland: 11 August 1940

attacked by Me. 109 at 16,000 ft. who was accompanied by a number of other E/A. I sustained a heavy burst of machine gun and shell gun fire which shot practically all starboard rudder away, caused considerable damage to starboard wing and I received numerous other perforations and damage to engine, including glycol feed and liquid gushed into cockpit. I pulled into a steep turn and got inside one E/A and fired a quarter deflection shot at about 300 yds. (2 secs. burst) and I could see tracer going straight along the fuselage and cockpit. The E/A immediately went over into a left hand spin and disappeared from my vision, spinning continuously down vertically. I did not see it hit the sea but it appeared to be out of control. I made straight for the shore owing to the damaged condition of A/C but was later attacked near coast by a single Me. 109 at which I was able to fire a very short one sec. burst deflection at about 2,000 (sic, 200) yds. in order to scare him away, as my engine was smoking. The aircraft was almost uncontrollable and the cockpit full of oil and smoke. This E/A turned to right and dived down, and I fell into a spin straight after that. I lost 7,000 ft. in recovery but eventually landed at Warmwell. Number of rounds fired:- approx. 360 rounds. (Angels 20 = 20,000 ft)

Quite logically, his initial German attacker no doubt claimed his Hurricane as shot down, and his second Me 109 attacker as he neared the coast was surely also convinced of *his* victory if he saw Pidd's subsequent spin; thus does over-claiming occur.

238 Squadron B Flight almost certainly fought against Me 109s from *JG* 2, the three *Gruppen* claimed ten victories between 10h41 and 10h50, including two near the Isle of Wight and two near Bournemouth, which could have been related geographically to a battle fought south of Swanage.[210] *JG* 2 lost a total of nine Me 109s shot down in this raid[211] and one may have fallen to P/O Urwin-Mann. Total claims of 238 Squadron were for a He 111 shared between Sergeants Marsh and Bann, one Me 109 each for F/O Hughes, P/O Urwin-Mann and Sgt Domagala; all of these claims were confirmed, while Sgt Pidd claimed a Me 109 unconfirmed.[212]

87 Squadron versus probably outgoing aircraft of I/*KG 54* raid and Me 109s, *c.* 10h45–10h50

87 Squadron arrived in the Portland area while A Flight of 238 Squadron were still in action a couple of miles to the east-south-east of the Weymouth-Portland area. They could see the dive-bombers of *KG* 54 at

about 7,000 ft and their escort at about 10,000-15,000 ft as the bombers cleared the Portland-Weymouth area and flew out over Weymouth Bay; the seven Hurricanes of 87 Squadron fought their action 10 miles south-east of Portland Bill, a few also to the south-west of the Bill.[213] Whereas 238 Squadron's A Flight faced the same retreating enemy about two miles east-south-east of the target, it took only two or three minutes for the German machines to reach the position ten miles to the south-east where 87 Squadron caught up with them.[214] By the time 87 Squadron got stuck in, they could see Ju 88s spread over a wide area as they lost some altitude and flew away at increasing speed.[215] They mainly fought against the escorting Me 109s, presumably from *JG 2* breaking away from the large fighter circle south-east of Portland, and some straggling bombers separated from the mass of outgoing Ju 88s,[216] most likely from *I/KG 54*; they probably also engaged the two Ju 88s damaged by Sub Lt Jeram of 213 Squadron which, having been hit, fell behind the protection afforded by other aircraft.

Led by F/Lt Voase-Jeff, the seven Hurricanes of 87 Squadron were put in line astern to attack the Ju 88s first as they turned away from Portland, but before anyone except Voase-Jeff could do so, a group of Me 109s dived through the Hurricanes, breaking up their line astern formation and apparently dispatching F/Lt Voase-Jeff who was already diving down; he was last seen by a member of his flight diving steeply at a level too low to have been able to bail out, and must have gone straight into the sea.[217]

Most of the remaining pilots became involved with the Me 109s now present in numbers; F/Sgt Badger, Blue Section, followed the lead Me 109 which had broken them up and damaged it, then shot another into the sea.[218] P/O McLure, Green 2, out-turned one of the attacking Messerschmitts and sent it spinning into the sea, only to be set upon by several more who wounded him in the leg and shot up his machine, wrecking his instrument panel and covering him with oil; he managed to get away and make for the shore but was then attacked again by several more. He hit one whose oil now covered his windscreen while they were only about 30 ft over the sea.[219] Despite being pursued by his now no doubt vengeful adversaries, McClure managed to make it to the coast and force-land near Warmwell. P/O John Cock engaged two enemy aircraft before himself being shot down, lightly wounded in one arm, as detailed in his C/O's report in the relevant casualty file.[220]

P/O Cock took off from Exeter Aerodrome at approx. 1015 hours. Enemy aircraft were encountered 10 miles S.E. of Portland at approx. 1030 hours. The aircraft was attacked from below by an enemy aircraft whilst the pilot was attacking a JU.88, and owing to the damaged state of the aircraft the pilot was compelled to abandon the aircraft at approximately 20,000 feet. The pilot turned the aircraft onto its back and baled out, from the upside position, the pack of the parachute caught up with the hood of the aircraft, but by kicking the control column forward was, eventually, thrown out. The aircraft burst into flames immediately afterwards and the pilot executed a delayed drop and the parachute opened without incident and descended into the sea near West Bay. The pilot was wounded in the arm but managed to swim to the beach where he was rescued and admitted to Portway Hospital suffering from slight injuries to the right arm.

He claimed the Ju 88 as conclusive and the Me 109 first attacked as inconclusive, before his own machine was hit.[221] Just before abandoning his Hurricane, Cock must also have been hit in the wing by Sgt Domagala as discussed earlier, but in view of what was going on in his immediate vicinity at the time, he probably did not even notice this friendly fire incident. P/O Dennis David also engaged both an Me 109 and a Ju 88:[222]

(1) We sighted several Ju88 and I went into attack, but was attacked by 2 me (sic) 109s. I at once went into a steep turn and after 2 or 3 turns the me came into my sights, he then climbed steeply and I followed him putting my Airscrew into fine and quickly came into near range, after two short bursts the me stalled and just dived straight into the Sea near Portland Bill. This scrap started at about 10,000' and finished at 5,000'.
(2) After having had a fight with a ME 109 I then saw some JU 88s going away from the harbour having just completed their dive bombing. I then singled one out that appeared to be falling back from the rest and got into close range (the rear gunner opened fire miles away) and after 3 bursts his right wing caught on fire and the Ju spiraled (sic) down into the sea. (Fine = fine pitch)

P/Os Cock and David had thus each attacked and destroyed lone Ju 88s separated from their formations, and likely already damaged earlier by 213 Squadron, most probably by Sub Lt Jeram.[223] Both bombers almost certainly belonged to *I/KG 54*, one crew having a lone survivor who was taken prisoner, and the other crew, much more fortunate, surviving to be rescued later by the *Seenotdienst*.[224] Another Ju 88 of *I/KG 54* was 35% damaged by RAF fighters in this raid;[225] it is possible this was hit by F/Lt Voase-Jeff before he was shot down and lost, as he was seen to dive on a Ju 88 at the start of the engagement.[226] 87 Squadron claimed three Me 109s conclusively destroyed, two inconclusive and two Ju 88s shot down, conclusive.[227] Their own losses encompassed two

Adlertag

Hurricanes lost, F/Lt Voase-Jeff missing and P/O Cock slightly wounded, and one Hurricane force-landed by its wounded pilot but the machine repairable.[228] 87 Squadron probably fought against Me 109s from JG 2, which formed the upper part of the large fighter circle south-east of Portland; the three *Gruppen* claimed ten victories between 10h41 and 10h50, including six in the Portland area or south-south-east from there,[229] which may be related to 87 Squadron's losses. JG 2 lost a total of nine Me 109s[230] and one or more may have fallen to 87 Squadron.

601 Squadron, last to engage Me 110 circles, *c.* 20 miles south of Swanage, and Me 109 outgoing sweeps by JG 53 and II/JG 27, *c.* 10h45–10h55

601 Squadron on take-off from Tangmere was ordered by the controller to patrol St Catherine's Point, the southern-most point of the Isle of Wight, at 20,000 ft, but once airborne this was changed to Swanage at 19,000 ft.[231] They observed large numbers of enemy aircraft about twenty miles south of Swanage and about ten miles south of their position, stacked up from about 15,000 ft to 25,000 ft and consisting of circles of three–five Me 109s and circles of about six–nine Me 110s; the German fighters were seen to be milling about with British fighters[232] – probably those of B Flight 238 Squadron. The location of the stacked circles was south-east of Portland and about a third of the way across the Channel to Cherbourg. Once the enemy was sighted, the squadron turned south and climbed to attack.[233] They were flying in a formation with Blue Section in the middle, with Red to the left and Green to the right, while Yellow section brought up the rear and was one or two thousand feet higher.[234]

601 Squadron had reached about 22,000 ft when they went in to attack, led by F/Lt Rhodes-Moorhouse as Blue 1.[235] He led them in towards the circling Me 110s but had forgotten to switch from his gravity tank to the main fuel tanks and had his engine stop and his aircraft plunge down just at the critical moment; he engaged various Me 109s lower down and, having climbed back up to *c.* 25,000 ft, claimed two to have crashed into the sea.[236] He also observed many of the *Luftwaffe*'s green dye markers in the sea where German aircraft had obviously gone in during the raid.[237] As F/Lt Rhodes-Moorhouse fell away he told his squadron to carry on, and the next man behind him, P/O 'Billy' Fiske, Blue 3, took over leadership immediately, ordering line astern over the R/T and went full speed into the attack closely followed by Blue 2.[238]

Fiske bravely made a total of five attacks on Me 110 circles; he first attacked a machine in a circle from above and slightly astern and as he

The First Major Raid, Portland: 11 August 1940

closed with the circle another Messerschmitt presented itself, crossing him from right to left, so he fired at this one and almost collided with it.[239] By then he found himself flying from the centre of the circle outwards, and once free of it climbed briefly for a third attack, from the quarter, and saw the Me 110 smoke from one engine and drop out of the formation. A fourth attack was made from slightly below and head-on to another Me 110, which he just missed as he passed narrowly beneath it and saw it plunge downwards; his fifth and final attack on a circling Me 110 was, as he put it, a 'bad deflection shot' as he was plagued by one of its pals on his own tail.[240]

As he climbed up after getting rid of this Me 110, all of the enemy aircraft had disappeared. Blue 2, Sgt Hawkings, followed Fiske in and managed to separate a Me 110 from its circle with astern and beam attacks, setting its port engine alight and then foolishly, as he admitted in his combat report, followed it down and fired some more before realising his error; as he climbed back up to the combat, the enemy machines had all disappeared.[241] Blue 2 and 3 fought exclusively against Me 110s.

Red Section leader F/O Carl Davis used a spectacular tactic few pilots would have considered, as described in his combat report.[242] As described earlier, S/L Darley of 609 Squadron had attempted to circle against the rotation of the Me 110s but found it too difficult and did not persist with this method.

> I was Red 1; my section was on the left of Wepon leader. When flying to Portland at 20000' where enemy were bombing we saw a very large dogfight to the south. We were then over Swanage and turned south in line astern to attack. A general dogfight developed. Enemy were flying in circles of 6-12 machines, circles flying above each other from 20000-30000. We were at 20000'. I attacked circle against rotation and did head on attacks on 110s. My first burst blew in the windscreen and took off the glasshouse. I then attacked another. Port engine stopped, the port tank started to smoke and my bullets went through windscreen. I had to pull up sharply to avoid collision. Both these aircraft went down completely out of control, but I was too busy to follow them down. I fired a half deflection shot from behind and below at a third 110 and his starboard engine started to emit white smoke. My ammunition was then exhausted and I returned to base, landing at 1102 hrs. During the course of the engagement I saw 5 Me 110s hit the sea. (Wepon = squadron radio call sign)

The determination to get at their enemy and to cause his destruction come what may was a hallmark of this entire action by 601 Squadron,[243] but it came at a high cost. Carl Davis's two wingmen were killed in this engagement, between *c.* 10h45 and 10h50.[244] P/O Julian Smithers' body was washed ashore near Le Havre.[245] Richard Demetriadi was William Rhodes-Moorhouse's brother-in-law and his remains were washed ashore and buried near Le Treport in France.[246] He was last seen by a fellow Squadron member twenty miles out to sea south of Swanage in hot pursuit of an enemy machine, but with petrol leaking from his damaged port fuel tank;[247] clearly his blood was up and he realised there was no way to get back.

As with Blue 2 and 3, F/O Davis only engaged Me 110s; there seemed to be far fewer Me 109s at the top of the circling formation, suggesting that *JG 2* had departed back across the Channel by this stage. The *Geschwader* did, however, make two late victory claims at 10h53-10h55 and may have been marginally involved with a few of 601 Squadron.[248] It is thought that by this stage in the raid that sweeps by *JG 53* and *II/ JG 27* were coming across the Channel to shepherd earlier *Luftwaffe* combatants back to safety, and that some members of 601 Squadron engaged them. F/Lt Rhodes-Moorhouse, after losing height when his engine cut out and engaging some Me 109s lower down, climbed up to about 25,000 ft where he found circling Me 109s above the main German Me 110 formation, and claimed two of them.[249] F/O Doulton leading Green Section also saw some Me 109s above the Me 110 circles probably belonging to these sweeps.[250]

Green Section was next to attack, but seeing that the central layers of the circling Me 110s were hotly engaged by his colleagues, F/O Doulton climbed up several thousand feet to attack the top two Me 110 circles; as he did so he noted the lack of clouds seawards and excellent visibility of thirty to forty miles.[251] (Michael Doulton was reputed to be the tallest fighter pilot of his day in the RAF.) Doulton also noted several Me 109s flying outside the Me 110 circles and about 1,000 ft higher. Ignoring the danger they posed, he piled into the circling Me 110s and attacked four, damaging at least two of them but constantly losing height,[252] as is typical for steeply banked aircraft when circling and turning tightly. He noted several aircraft wrecks and green patches in the sea, as well as some Hurricanes on the tails of enemy machines. He could not make out who they were but his two wingmen, Green 2 and 3, F/O Gillan and P/O Dickie, did not answer his calls nor those of Tangmere control[253] and were not seen again. Quite possibly, those higher-flying Me 109s were responsible for their loss.

JG 53 claimed three confirmed victories, all by *III Gruppe* and at 10h40, 10h53 and 10h55, as well as five probables on this raid, but suffered no losses themselves; Hpt *v*on Maltzahn, *Gruppenkommandeur*

The First Major Raid, Portland: 11 August 1940

II/JG 53 who had turned back with engine trouble, experienced a single brief attack by a Hurricane but suffered no damage.[254] II/JG 27 claimed two RAF fighters, both as Spitfires, one off the Cotentin Peninsula, the other west of Portland, timed at 10h40 and 10h50.[255] In return, they lost a Messerschmitt 109 from 5/JG 27, missing with its pilot from combat over the Channel.[256] These sweep-out units most likely also engaged Spitfires from 152 Squadron and Hurricanes from 1 Squadron, detailed below.

Yellow Section of 601 Squadron was the last to attack, led in by F/O Gordon Cleaver who also climbed up with his section before making his attack; he noted in his combat report that the enemy was so thick that they presented an almost permanent target. He fired at a *Zerstörer* that appeared right in front and slightly below him at very close range and thought he had blown it apart.[257] He followed this up with shooting down a Me 109 which might have been damaged already, watching it catch fire and its pilot bail out. Yellow 2, P/O John McGrath saw a Me 109 going down and a British fighter in flames, and surprised one Me 110, which he saw dive into the sea without anyone getting out, and then had a dogfight with a second, easily outmanoeuvring it and sending it down similarly to the first one.[258] His final encounter was with an already smoking Me 109 heading for home, but his burst appeared to have no further effect than increasing the smoke. This may have been a JG 2 machine already mortally hit. At some time during his battle McGrath also saw a Spitfire apparently out of control.[259] The third member of the section, Sgt Guy claimed two Me 110 probables and one damaged.[260] In total, 601 Squadron claimed seven Me 110s and three Me 109s destroyed unconfirmed, as well as two Me 110 probables and four damaged.[261]

152 Squadron skirmishes with outgoing Me 109s, probably from JG 2 and sweep-out formations of II/JG 27 and JG 53, c. 10h45–11h00

This squadron had taken to flying in pairs, but seemingly without the close cooperation that applied to pairs and the concomitant four-fighter formations as used by the *Luftwaffe*. On this day as the Portland raid developed, four Spitfires of 152 Squadron, en route from Middle Wallop sector station to their forward base at Warmwell, were diverted and ordered to patrol Portland at 14,000 ft.[262] The Squadron Leader Peter Devitt was Blue 1 and led the four aircraft over the middle of Weymouth Bay, about ten to fifteen miles off the coast, and there they saw ten Me 109s dogfighting.[263] The time, location and the fact that they also

Adlertag

engaged a lone Ju 88, would fit with them having seen 238 Squadron A Flight and/or 87 Squadron fighting against the last of the retreating *KG 54* bombers and likely a few of the outgoing Me 109s from *JG 2*, now leaving the circles to get home, low on fuel.

Two of the ten Me 109s broke away and climbed, and the second Spitfire pair, Black Section of 152 Squadron led by P/O Wildblood seeing them positioning themselves to attack the Spitfires, climbed up, outmanoeuvred them and then chased them, Black 1 shooting one down into the sea in flames, while both pilots attacked the other which dived seawards issuing black smoke from its engine.[264] It was claimed as either damaged or destroyed unconfirmed as its fate was not seen.[265] Black 2, P/O Shipley had spotted a lone Ju 88 below this second Me 109 and deviated away to attack it, but after running out of ammunition saw no result of his attack. The remaining eight Me 109s had taken off back to France, hotly pursued by S/L Devitt and his wingman of Blue Section (pair). Despite following them almost to the French coast, they were not able to close into effective range.[266]

About half an hour later F/Lt Boitell-Gill, Yellow 1 led off another two pairs of Spitfires of Red and Yellow Sections. Red Section saw no action, but Yellow 1 climbed up after a couple of Me 109s and opened fire, but then saw his number 2 going down and bailing out into the sea; P/O John Jones did not survive.[267] This later action was probably against elements of *JG 53* or *II/JG 27* flying the outgoing covering sweep as the other raiding units straggled back to France.[268]

1 Squadron skirmishes with outgoing *ZG 2* Me 110s, and with Me 109s probably from the sweep-out formations of *II/JG 27* and *JG 53, c.* 10h50–11h10

Nine Hurricanes of 1 Squadron from Northolt had been ordered off, originally to fly to North Weald, but these instructions were changed to an orbit off Tangmere on the south coast at 16,000 ft and they were then vectored south-south-west over the Channel towards Cherbourg.[269] On the way over the Channel they were sighted by Yellow Section of 609 Squadron[270] and after going further out over the Channel, past the midpoint, they observed a melee of Me 109s and Hurricanes above them.[271] Two of the fighters from this affray dived towards 1 Squadron, which broke up in reaction and thereafter reformed but without two Hurricanes which had oxygen problems and turned for home; on their reforming two 'strange' Hurricanes joined them.[272] These two Hurricanes, followed soon after by two from 1 Squadron, P/Os Chetham

The First Major Raid, Portland: 11 August 1940

and Goodman, respectively Yellow 3 and Blue 3, broke away from the north-flying squadron by now heading back towards the Isle of Wight, to pursue a lone Me 110 seen to the south.[273] The Me 110 was diving gently from 17,000 ft and turning left and right; the two 'guest' Hurricanes closed to within about 400 yards of the Me 110 without firing and it dived to sea level, the two 1 Squadron machines diving behind at about 400 mph, and observing the enemy pull gently out of its dive and continue on to France just above the water.[274] When only six to eight miles off the French coast, Chetham closed and made three astern to quarter attacks, setting the starboard engine afire and observing a drone being released by the Me 110; P/O Goodman followed up with an astern attack setting the port engine on fire and the Me 110 crashed into the sea, breaking up. No survivors were seen.[275]

As is seldom possible, this Me 110 claim can be tied to a specific *Luftwaffe* loss with some confidence, that of a Me 110 belonging to *Stab/ZG 2* and flown by the *Geschwader* Adjutant, *Oblt* Schäfer who was shot down, wounded in the shoulder and got into his dinghy, released his green dye bag and was eventually rescued, but his luckless gunner was killed.[276] However, what is missing from the account that *Oblt* Schäfer gave to his interrogators later, when taken prisoner in September 1940, is that the gunner was in fact *ZG 2*'s intelligence officer, *Oblt* Günther Hensel.[277] Obviously, neither crew member was expecting much trouble on this mission, an attitude likely to have changed by the next operation of this *Geschwader* after their experiences on 11 August 1940. To risk capture of the *Geschwader's* intelligence officer was not the best of decisions.

The rest of the squadron heading north met another lone Me 110 about twenty miles south of St Catherine's Point at approximately 18,000 ft, which the 1 Squadron leader, F/Lt Brown followed in a shallow dive, firing three bursts from 250 down to 50 yards, and the enemy dove into the sea on fire at about 10h50; there had been neither return fire nor evasive action,[278] suggesting an already damaged Me 110. P/O Shaw reported being attacked by a Hurricane which slightly damaged his machine.[279] As Brown returned towards the Isle of Wight he saw one of his Hurricanes flown by P/O Davey which was streaming glycol, and all attempts to communicate with it, by formatting on it, by R/T calls, were in vain and the pilot was quite possibly wounded.[280] Flames were then seen from the engine and the pilot tried a wheels down forced-landing in a very inappropriate space on Sandown golf course on the Isle; his machine turned over several times and burst into flames, killing the unfortunate pilot. It is unclear who had attacked him to cause the damage resulting in the crash, but it was probably a roving Me 109 from the sweep-out units, *JG 53* and *II/JG 27*. Poor John Davey had only recently joined the squadron and had a mere 224 hours flying time to his name.[281] The Me 110s engaged by 1 Squadron were from ZG 2, and the Hurricanes encountered most likely from 601 Squadron, bearing in mind the time of F/Lt Brown's claim, 10h50. 1 Squadron claimed two Me 110s shot down, confirmed, one misidentified as a Do 17.[282]

Summary of tactics and numbers for the Portland engagements, c. 10h20–11h10

The German tactic of using large circling formations of Me 110s with Me 109s circling higher up, in this instance starting off with two separate circles which later amalgamated into one, was successful. It drew off a significant proportion of the intercepting RAF fighters: one section of 213 Squadron, 145 Squadron, 609 Squadron, one flight of 238 Squadron and 601 Squadron. However, four Hurricanes of 213 Squadron made a superb beam attack on the leading vic of Ju 88s coming in to attack Portland harbour, led by S/L McGregor and F/O Strickland, which disorganised the formation of the leading bomber *Gruppe* and enabled succeeding attacks largely from astern on diving Ju 88s by Red Section of 213 Squadron, with a lone pilot from Green Section attacking the second *Gruppe* formation from astern and knocking two Ju 88s out of formation. Follow-up attacks on outgoing Ju 88s, now largely split up, by a flight each of 87 and 238 Squadrons added to the casualties. These amounted to six Ju 88s shot down, one damaged, with five full crews lost, a loss rate of almost 16%, three times the acceptable norm of about 5% losses per mission for a unit planning to sustain operations in the longer term.

Those fighter units distracted by the fighter circles and engaged against them applied a wide range of different tactics, in what for them was a new challenge: how best to attack mutually defending masses of circling Me 110s. F/Lt Roy Dutton of 145 Squadron, after first charging into the melee flew out again and applied full deflection attacks from outside the circle successfully against two vertically banked Me 110s. S/L Darley leading 609 Squadron tried first to join a Me 110 circle from behind, then flew an attack from inside a circle and against its rotation but found this too difficult to maintain; thereafter he made full deflection attacks flying across the circles, a tactic also employed by F/Lt McArthur and F/O Dundas, section leaders in his squadron.

601 Squadron pilots made fierce and repeated attacks on the Me 110 circles, P/O Fiske making five attacks and F/O Doulton, four;

The First Major Raid, Portland: 11 August 1940

Fiske tried attacking from above, across the circle, from the quarter of circling Messerschmitts, from head-on and finally from a full deflection approach. F/O Davis of 601 Squadron performed two spectacular and successful head-on attacks while flying inside the Me 110 circles and against their rotation; this method, while definitely effective, was only for an exceptionally skilled and aggressive pilot. Overall, the full deflection attack into the underside of vertically banked and circling Me 110s was probably the best overall method for the average Fighter Command pilot. 1 Squadron, having been vectored out over the Channel towards Cherbourg by the Northolt controller, were lucky not to have been massacred by the many German fighters involved in this raid, and managed to pick off two Me 110s, very likely already damaged by others. Overall, ZG 2 lost six Me 110s, five more were damaged, while five full crews were lost in the sea, including that of the *Gruppenkommandeur I/ZG 1, Major* Ott,[283] a sixth crew losing one member, the other rescued wounded. Once again, high losses, amounting to about 10% of those dispatched on the mission.

RAF losses of fighters totalled twelve destroyed, three force-landed and two damaged, with twelve pilots killed and two wounded, in action against the Me 110-Me 109 circles. In contrast, fighters lost in action against the German bombers and Me 109s trying to protect them were limited to two fighters destroyed, one force-landed and three damaged, one pilot killed and two wounded. In small actions between RAF fighters and Me 109s a single Spitfire and its pilot were lost, while engagements between RAF fighters and small numbers of outgoing Me 110s and Me 109s no longer in circles and possibly also including the German sweep-out fighters, amounted to one aircraft lost and one damaged, one pilot being killed. The German fighter circles thus did attract a large component of the defending British fighters and also apparently accounted for most of their casualties. Of course, as with any generalisation as in these figures ascribed to specific engagements, overlap between different types of fighter action would almost certainly have occurred – thus, for example, some of the circle-related Me 109s almost certainly engaged RAF fighters tackling outgoing bombers.

Me 109 losses overall for this complex raid for *JG* 2 came to nine aircraft, with five pilots killed and four rescued by the *Seenotdienst*, three of whom were wounded.[284] *JG* 27 lost another two aircraft and both pilots.[285] Losses of Me 110s and Me 109s and personnel from the circle formations and those of their RAF attackers were essentially equal. RAF pilot losses were excessively high for this day, due largely to much of the fighting being quite far out over the sea, and the limited resources of the RAF rescue arrangements at this stage. For the entire engagement,

Adlertag

German claims amounted to twenty-five confirmed, twelve probables and one rejected,[286] to be balanced against RAF losses of sixteen aircraft, four more force-landed and six damaged.

The RAF squadrons claimed twenty-five confirmed, sixteen unconfirmed and seven probable victories plus ten damaged German machines, as detailed above, to be balanced against twenty-three machines lost and six damaged. German personnel losses encompassed seven Me 109 pilots dead and three wounded, five and a half Me 110 crews dead, one crewman wounded, and the bombers lost five complete crews. The acknowledged claims list[287] for the *Luftwaffe* excludes seventeen claims by ZG 2, and two by KG 54.[288] This does not necessarily imply that all ZG 2's claims were rejected by the *Luftwaffe* claims adjudication procedures; Me 110 unit claims are quite often incomplete in the claims list for the Battle of Britain period. While German claims were reasonably close to RAF losses, RAF claims exceeded German losses by a factor not far short of two.

An unsuccessful German seaplane rescue mission

Twelve Spitfires of 610 Squadron led by S/L Ellis took off from Hawkinge at 10h46 to patrol the Channel at 26,000 ft; in mid-Channel a seaplane was observed on the water, presumably a German air-sea rescue machine, and Red Section led by F/Lt Smith was sent down to investigate.[289] Smith was an experienced and canny leader, taking his section down low over the Channel off Calais and thus heading north from enemy territory to tackle the camouflaged He 59 seaplane, now airborne low over the water; he gave it a couple of short bursts, saw his rounds apparently hitting it and overshot due to excessive speed, claiming a damaged He 59.[290] Shortly after that he sighted and briefly attacked another seaplane, this one wearing red cross markings, but without apparent result.[291] It would appear that the two other Spitfires of Red Section were still there when Smith overshot the first seaplane, but they never returned and their pilots were posted missing; Sgt Neville, on only his second operational flight, was never found, but Sgt Tanner's body washed ashore near Calais only a few hours later, and he was initially buried there.[292]

F/Lt Smith had in fact seen *Luftwaffe* fighters over the French coast as he began his run-in on the first He 59.[293] Neither Smith nor the other nine Spitfires of 610 Squadron providing cover high above saw their demise. While F/Lt Smith displayed tactical acumen in his low approach from the German shore towards the first He 59, he failed to keep a sharp lookout for enemy Me 109s he had already seen; the 610 Squadron top cover was

The First Major Raid, Portland: 11 August 1940

just too high, either to see properly what was happening at sea level, or to have been able to intervene in time if they had.

German official loss records list two He 59 rescue seaplanes lost in operations over the Channel for this day, without noting any crew casualties.[294] However, another source details casualties to both; *Seenotzentrale Cherbourg* recorded the two losses, one crew suffering one wounded while the other crew was missing.[295] One of these is credited to Spitfires while rescuing the crew of three from a Blenheim supposedly in turn shot down by *Hpt* Wiggers of *I/JG 51*.[296] However, no such claim by Wiggers exists in the *Luftwaffe* claims records, but *Ofw* Grosse of *I/JG 52* did make such a claim, at about 10h50.[297] There is no recorded Blenheim loss to Fighter Command, and only one to Bomber Command, and that far to the west (see below). 53 Squadron, Coastal Command, operating from Detling, lost one Blenheim from a patrol that day, which had taken off at 10h24, the crew being lost.[298] Although it was unusual that a He 59 normally stationed in Cherbourg would be flying a mission in the Straits of Dover, it is quite possible if there was a shortage of aircraft there at the time.

Lt Ulrich Steinhilper of *I/JG 52* records flying as part of a *Schwarm* of four Me 109s that intercepted a Blenheim while flying as top cover to the red cross-marked He 59, and that it was shot down rapidly by three of them, but as was the German system, it was credited to the pilot considered to have done the most damage.[299] The crew is recorded as having survived, and was apparently rescued by a He 59 which was attacked by Spitfires, two of them being shot down by 1/JG 52 at 11h23-11h25;[300] presumably the rescued crew was lost with that rescue machine, inferred to be the one shot up by F/Lt Smith of 610 Squadron.

Convoy attack south-east/east of Orfordness, *c.* 11h40–12h15

Two East Coast convoys, sailing on opposite courses, were located south-east of Orfordness when at about 11h30 British radar picked up concentrations of *Luftwaffe* aircraft between Calais and Dunkirk.[301] The northbound convoy, FN 249 was very large, with over fifty ships.[302] A section of 85 Squadron was on convoy patrol at the time, and by 11h40 when it was obvious that the Germans were targeting the convoys the 11 Group controller launched eleven 74 Squadron Spitfires from Manston who lifted off at 11h45, and a flight of 17 Squadron from Martlesham Heath five minutes later.[303] With some German forces still being picked up on the eastern side of the Dover Straits, as a precaution

Adlertag

eight Spitfires of 64 Squadron were ordered up from Hawkinge to patrol that airfield.[304] The German incursion making for the northbound convoy was made up of nineteen Me 110s of *EGr 210*, accompanied by that unit's *3rd Staffel* of Me 109s.[305] At the same approximate time, small numbers of Dornier 17s from *KG 2* were tasked with nuisance raids across the Channel and against the northbound convoy, and possibly also aimed at shipping in the Thames Estuary, always a busy sea road.[306]

A German account of the convoy raid survived in the diary of an *EGr 210* pilot shot down and killed four days later in a raid on Croydon, and was soon in the hands of RAF intelligence as a result.[307] Most of the *Gruppe*'s aircraft took part, escorted by Me 110s from *ZG 26*; the bombers lifted off at 11h20 from Calais Mark, and were to join their escort over Gravelines at 1,500 ft before climbing together to 11,000 ft to head for the convoy.[308] However, it is in the nature of war to disrupt carefully laid plans, and under the leadership of *Hpt* Hans Kogler, *Staffelkapitän* of *1/ZG 26* in the absence of the *Gruppenkommandeur*, *I/ZG 26* were a few minutes late arriving over the rendezvous where there was no sign of their charges, who had presumably already flown on towards the convoy.[309]

I/ZG 26 do not seem to have caught up with their comrades from *EGr 210* and the escorting Me 110s were intercepted before reaching the convoy, to the south-east thereof. A widespread cloud bank with its base at 4,000 ft enabled *EGr 210* to approach the convoy without being seen by the convoy patrol section of 85 Squadron, and the fighter bombers were thus able to attack the ships without fighter interference.[310] While claiming to have sunk an 8,000-ton ship, *EGr 210* actually badly damaged a 3,800 ton merchant vessel and an empty oil tanker of 5,550 tons, but both ships were saved.[311]

S/L Peter Townsend was leading the section from 85 Squadron patrolling the convoy, which initially comprised only a pair as Yellow 2, Sgt Allgood, had difficulty starting his engine and arrived over the convoy some minutes late.[312] When he first arrived over the convoy at about 11h40, Townsend sighted an unidentified aircraft a couple of miles away and turned towards it but lost it in the heavy, broken clouds; ten minutes later, he saw it again about three miles east of the ships and got in two astern attacks as the Do 17 dodged in and out of the clouds, last seeing it with black smoke coming from the starboard engine.[313] He continued to search east of the convoy and came across about twenty Me 110s circling at 4,000 ft thirty miles east of the ships; after trying to follow them in the clouds as they turned away eastwards for a while, he turned back towards the convoy.[314] These Me 110s were probably those of *I/ZG 26*, discussed further below, related to 74 Squadron's engagement. Yellow 3, Sgt Hampshire of 85 Squadron

The First Major Raid, Portland: 11 August 1940

initially followed his leader towards the lone Dornier, but having lost his squadron leader in the clouds, which he experienced as several layers varying in height from 1,500–5,000 ft, he returned to the convoy where he found Yellow 2 below the lowest cloud base.[315]

A highly complex engagement followed between the two sergeants of 85 Squadron and the flight from 17 Squadron, and a set of Me 110s and a few Me 109s. The two 85 Squadron pilots were patrolling at the southern end of the convoy, when they observed bombs being dropped approximately north-east of the convoy, and simultaneously received an order to climb to 5,000 ft where some twenty enemy aircraft were to be engaged.[316] Sgt Allgood, 85 Squadron, saw about seven Me 110s climbing for the clouds.[317] As they were leaving the coast behind, several pilots of 17 Squadron, two from the leading Red Section and one from Yellow Section, also saw the convoy being bombed.[318] F/Lt Harper leading the 17 Squadron Flight as Red 1 saw the last two of a number of Me 109s complete their bombing and led his section after one of them.[319]

Yellow Section of 17 Squadron meanwhile, led by P/O Manger, had broken from Red Section and made off to starboard, in pursuit of about six to eight Me 110 Jaguars, Manger disappearing into cloud behind them never to be seen again.[320] So both 85 and 17 Squadron machines, having seen bombing taking place and one pilot having observed enemy fighter-bombers climbing away, had engaged *EGr 210*, whose two Me 110 and one Me 109 *Staffeln* had attacked the shipping. *EGr 210* lost two of their Me 110s in this engagement, both Me 110 C-6 models armed with the heavy 30 mm cannon,[321] which were even more clumsy than their twin-engined brethren, thus having enhanced vulnerability.

By studying the IPRs from 85 and 17 Squadrons, and the relevant combat reports[322] some sense can be made of the highly complex set of engagements. P/O Stevens (Red 3) in his report says that there were two different Me 110s shot down, one at a lower level in whose demise he was involved, and the other higher up which he saw shot down by two Hurricanes from his lower height of about 1,000 ft, they were 1,500 ft higher. Sgt Hampshire of 85 Squadron also saw two Hurricanes shoot down a Me 110 into the sea as he climbed up again. Hampshire saw this at *c.* 12h10 and 20 miles east of the convoy. The upper Me 110 appears to have been attacked first by P/O Pitman and Sgt Griffiths of Yellow Section, 17 Squadron, and while they were still attacking it, F/O Hanson from Red Section also attacked it several times – it was given as close to the clouds (at about 4,000 ft) for Hanson and at *c.* 3,000 ft for the other two.

As Yellow Section had broken away from Red Section early on, it was thus logical that Pitman-Griffiths attacked the high Me 110 first, Hanson joining in soon after. This Me 110 had lots of black smoke issuing from the starboard engine from the Pitman-Griffiths efforts, and when Hanson attacked this engine was seen to be out of action and smoking. When P/O Stevens flying as Red 3, 17 Squadron, first attacked the low Me 110, two other Hurricanes, those of Sgts Allgood and Hampshire of 85 Squadron, were already attacking it; the times in the combat reports fit, Allgood reporting engagement at 11h50 and Stevens at 11h55. This Me 110 was seen to give off white fumes from the port engine and white smoke from the starboard engine. Sgt Allgood saw three fighters join in from the south and later thought they might have been Spitfires; however, it was probably the arrival of the three Hurricanes of 17 Squadron, flown by Stevens, Pitman and Griffiths. No 74 Squadron pilot reported seeing Hurricanes engaging Me 110s.[323]

If the above suggestions have merit, then each Me 110 was shot down by three Hurricanes, a not atypical result, as the larger, twin-engined *Luftwaffe* machines generally needed multiple fighter attacks to dispatch them.[324] In excess of fourteen individual attacks were made by the six Hurricanes, two from 85 Squadron and four from 17 Squadron; eight of these attacks were from quarter-astern, astern and from a quarter, with three beam and three head-on attacks.[325] Sgts Allgood and Hampshire executed a series of well-coordinated alternating attacks on the lower Me 110. The two section leaders of 17 Squadron, F/Lt Harper and P/O Manger led their units straight at the enemy in both cases. While both Me 110s lost did show some fight, the *EGr 210* Messerschmitts fought alone and there was no attempt by any of the others to aid those under heavy attack. After the higher Me 110 had already been attacked several times and had lost its starboard engine, it still managed to slow down suddenly as F/O Hanson attacked it for the third time, hitting his Hurricane as it overshot the Me 110 and starting a cockpit fire; Hanson managed to put this out by side-slipping.[326] For the two *EGr 210 Zerstörer* shot down, 85 Squadron claimed two Me 110s unconfirmed, while 17 Squadron claimed one confirmed, another unconfirmed as well as a damaged Me 110, and a damaged Me 109.[327]

Me 109s of *3/EGr 210* put in two claims for Spitfires shot down, both of which were assessed by the *Luftwaffe* system as probables,[328] and presumably shot down the missing P/O Manger of 17 Squadron. The *EGr 210* Me 110s seem to have been responsible for the damaged Hurricanes of Sgt Allgood, 85 Squadron, and those of P/O Stevens and F/O Hanson of 17 Squadron, which all returned to their bases.[329]

Returning to the escorting Me 110s of *I/ZG 26*, led by *Hpt* Kogler, the *Staffelkapitän* of their *1st Staffel*, who had missed their rendezvous with *EGr 210* over the French coast, they were east-south-east of the convoy when spotted by S/L Townsend of 85 Squadron, as already discussed. Not long afterwards, they were sighted by the eleven Spitfires of 74 Squadron, led by P/O Freeborn:[330]

> I was leading Squadron when it took off from Manston at 1145hours to patrol a convoy off Clacton. While on patrol I sighted a formation of 40 Me. 110's in vics of 3 and 4 approaching the convoy below the clouds (8/10 heavy cumulus at 4,000 feet). I led the Squadron in a diving attack into the defensive circle which the E/A formed. On the dive and climb which followed I fired at 3 E/A, and in each case saw my De Wilde ammunition registering hits. The combat then developed into a dog-fight.

Sgt Kirk flying as Red 4 in Freeborn's section recalled their attacking the Me 110s from dead ahead.[331] The initial tactics adopted by the 74 Squadron leader Freeborn were detailed with much greater clarity by P/O H. M. Stephen, who describes the Me 110s as forming a large circle with 74 Squadron diving into the middle of the circle, then pulling up and flying around inside the circle in the opposite direction, leading to the Me 110s breaking up and scattering in all directions within only a few seconds.[332]

The circle comprising an entire Me 110 *Gruppe* would have had a large diameter, enabling 74 Squadron's eleven Spitfires to dive into the space in the middle and then pull up and around, until they were themselves circling around within the larger Me 110 circle, but in the opposite direction. Unsurprisingly, this almost immediately broke up the German circle. In the earlier morning raid on Portland over the western Channel, it may be recalled how S/L Darley of 609 Squadron tried to perform a similar manoeuvre against ZG 2's circling Me 110s but found it too difficult. On 10 July 1940, 74 Squadron had attacked a *III/ZG 26* Me 110 circle near Dover, using a spiral dive into their midst under the leadership of F/Lt Measures.[333] It is very likely in a squadron containing a leading tactician like 'Sailor' Malan, that a determination to come up with a more suitable method was worked out before 74 Squadron again encountered such a Me 110 formation; Freeborn's leadership in the action against the circle off Harwich is thus unlikely to have been merely an unrehearsed tactic, as the squadron happily followed his lead and obviously knew what complex manoeuvres were implicit in the chosen method.

74 Squadron was also already flying in sections of four aircraft, comprising two pairs, who were to fight as such also once action ensued. The relevant formation was detailed by W/O Mayne in his combat report from the Harwich action:[334] 'I was Blue 2 when 74 Squadron was

ordered to intercept e/a which were on their way to attack a convoy. The Squadron flew in a formation of three fours and the understanding was 1 and 3, 2 and 4 to fight together.' Such was the tactical innovation of S/L Malan of 74 Squadron who had only taken command of the unit three days previously.[335] For the sake of clarification, 74 Squadron's formations of fours comprised a normal, tight Fighter Command style vic of three Spitfires, with the fourth one being tucked in the box behind and below the vic leader; the next four were below them etc.[336] It is most important to realise that this formation was only used for gaining height or a good tactical position as a squadron, but not for fighting,[337] which was done using the designated pairs of aircraft.

After the Me 110 circle broke up following 74 Squadron's initial attack into the middle of the circle and then around within it, a series of dogfights ensued. Seven of the eleven pilots reported successful attacks, claiming one Me 110 confirmed, eight unconfirmed, and five damaged.[338] Two pilots, flying as a pair, Yellow 1 and 3, were missing from the engagement, P/O Cobden and P/O Smith[339] and must have been surprised by tactically well managed Me 110s or overwhelmed by superior numbers. No one saw them shot down due to the typically rapid dispersal of aircraft in aerial engagements. *I/ZG 26* claimed nine victories, none of them apparently confirmed.[340] The nine claims for destroyed Me 110s made by 74 Squadron must be assessed against two Me 110s actually lost from *1/ZG 26* with one crew missing and one wounded, and two Me 110s damaged from *2/ZG 26* without any crew casualties, but one of them was written off with 70% damage in France.[341] One crew, that of *Hpt* Kogler and gunner from *1/ZG 26* was rescued from their dinghy three days later.[342]

Three actual losses for nine claims conforms to most larger, twin-engined German machines requiring multiple attacks and attackers to bring them down. It is impossible to detail which British pilots attacked any specific German casualty; some seeing their targets dive or spiral towards the sea (as claimed by many) were convinced they had plunged into the water as well, which may not always have happened. Sgt Kirk of 74 Squadron gave a ten-second burst from 300 yards down to 100 yards, saw pieces breaking off and the Me 110 then made a climbing turn, rolled onto its back and dived at a shallow angle into the sea still inverted.[343] While making a convincing case for the Me 110's destruction, it may well have been attacked by other Spitfires prior to his assault. Analogously, three pilots, F/O Mungo-Park, W/O Mayne and Sgt Skinner each saw their victims with a port engine on fire, two observing further that it dived into the sea, and F/O Nelson, who claimed the only confirmed (i.e. witnessed, by W/O Mayne) victory, saw his victim dive into the sea

The First Major Raid, Portland: 11 August 1940

from 3,500 ft and burn on the water.[344] Possibly these all related to a single aircraft.

S/L Peter Townsend, leader of the 85 Squadron section originally on convoy patrol who had been investigating further east of the convoy, came upon *I/ZG 26* as 74 Squadron's engagement with them came to an end. Not having encountered an Me 110 circle before, he struggled unsuccessfully to attack, thereby demonstrating how effective such a circle could be to an inexperienced attacker. Soon, however, the very able and tactically innovative Townsend would become a leading exponent of the head-on attack on German bomber formations, in late August 1940. An excerpt from Townsend's combat report on his experiences with *I/ZG 26* makes for interesting reading.[345]

> ...came upon 20 plus ME 110 again. Waited above in cloud cover and picking what seemed to be an isolated one some 200' below, dived steeply head on and took snap shot, bullets appeared to enter right wing of ME. but no result observed. Immediately on breaking upwards saw I was being attacked head on by ME. 110; we passed each other pretty close, and I withdrew at high speed towards nearest cloud. (ME's were circling and it was a matter of extreme difficulty to select an outsider without getting involved in circle). Emerged from cloud again and selected another prospective victim. Dived from above and behind but was immediately attacked by another from behind. After short burst – inaccurate – hurried into cloud again pursued by my attacker. Spitfire only other British A/C seen, attacked him and he immediately turned down towards "circle" again. Turned on him to attack as he went down, but he rejoined "circle" before I could get a good lead on him. Spitfire seen deploying into cloud. As petrol was low and my attempts to isolate a single ME. were not being very profitable, I withdrew to the W. and landed at Martlesham Heath.

The raid on the convoy off Orfordness-Harwich appears to have also included a few Dorniers, single Dornier bombers being engaged by S/L Townsend of 85 Squadron[346] and very briefly by P/O Stevens of 17 Squadron.[347] These possibly were from *I/KG 2*; their *3rd Staffel* suffered a combat-damaged machine which crashed at St Inglevert airfield, being written off, the crew all wounded.[348] This may have been S/L Townsend's victim.

When the enemy incursions began, the 11 Group controller had left eight Spitfires of 64 Squadron led by S/L MacDonell on patrol over Hawkinge, as described above. They were later ordered to a position about twelve miles north-east of North Foreland at 15,000 ft shortly before midday, in order to intercept German machines returning from the main convoy raid.[349] This was an astute move by the controller, such returning machines being short of fuel and ammunition and thus not keen on a fight. Having arrived at their assigned position, the rear section sighted around fifteen Me 109s above and behind at 20,000 ft, the enemy being observed circling and diving in line astern from the sun.[350] It was an ideal ambush position, but having been sighted in time, the ambush was bound to be less successful; in fact it was a disaster. The Me 109s managed only to overshoot 64 Squadron, all then circling away right-handed, and the Spitfires broke up and engaged them[351] enthusiastically. S/L MacDonell and three other pilots latched onto the tails of four individual Me 109s and saw them all dive away into clouds below; one Spitfire was damaged in the engagement, but P/O Andreae landed safely at base.[352]

Sgt Mann who had made one of the initial astern attacks on the fleeing Me 109s later met a lone Messerschmitt at about 10,000 ft south-east of Dover:[353] 'A ME.109 appeared below me over our Coast and heading for France. I dived and positioned myself on its tail and opened fire with a 5 sec burst at 250, then dived and came up beneath him and gave a long burst, finally coming up onto its tail again at 50 and still firing. E/A lost speed and I climbed to watch effect of fire. A thick trail of black smoke appeared together with flashes of flame. E/A dived in a spiral turn and disappeared through cloud heading for English Coast. I did not see it crash but assume it must have hit the sea about 8-10 miles N of Cap Griz (sic) Nez.' His victim may have been a missing Me 109 and pilot of 5/JG 51 lost over the Channel after an engagement which began off the Thames Estuary; though no time was noted for this loss.[354] 5/JG 51 made three probable victory claims, two over the Thames Estuary and one east of Calais this day, again no times being noted;[355] the one east of Calais may have related to this engagement with 64 Squadron, damaging the machine of P/O Andreae. The other two probable claims may reflect a later engagement with 111 Squadron at *c.* 14h00, discussed below.

Convoy attack east of Clacton, *c.* 12h45–13h00 and another unsuccessful German seaplane rescue

This incursion and another that followed about three quarters of an hour later are difficult to analyse as the radar track charts are no longer extant and pilot reports are somewhat confusing.[356] At least two German formations and possibly three, each comprising bombers and fighters, crossed the sea at the northern entrance to the Dover Straits between about 12h45 and 13h00, one of which reached the southbound

The First Major Raid, Portland: 11 August 1940

convoy near Clacton at *c.* 12h50 at pretty much the same time as three Hurricanes of 151 Squadron arrived to take over the convoy patrol.[357] Unit documents make clear that the 151 Squadron trio led by S/L Gordon were already in place when approximately twenty-five Ju 87s escorted by some twenty Me 109s were seen to be bombing a single escort vessel a mile or two east of the convoy.[358] Making directly for them, the Hurricane section were convinced they had put them to flight and claimed damage to one each of the bombers and fighters;[359] however, in all probability the German machines were just heading home and worried about their fuel. The escort vessel suffered only slight damage and the merchant ships in the convoy itself were not attacked at all.[360] *IV/LG 1* lost a Stuka and crew to fighter attack over the Thames Estuary this day[361] and this was probably the victim of 151 Squadron, S/L Gordon possibly being more successful than he surmised.

The 151 Squadron section had relieved a flight of 56 Squadron patrolling this convoy shortly before the former unit saw action. 56 Squadron had lost one of their number due to unexplained circumstances:[362] 'Whilst on convoy patrol Sgt Baker was seen to dive down into the sea with glycol pouring out at approximately 1245 hours on the 11/8/40 12-15 miles S.E. of Walton-on-Naze.' The location is a few miles north-east of Clacton. His flight leader F/Lt Weaver lost his two wingmen, one of whom was Baker, flying through cloud and after emerging beneath it, observed a Hurricane trailing a white plume descending seawards and the pilot jumping about six miles east of the convoy, but there was a large rent in the one parachute panel.[363] An escorting destroyer was not able to go immediately and directly to his aid due to treacherous shoals, and a motorboat struggled to find him despite being directed by two of 56 Squadron's aircraft; by the time he was finally hauled aboard the destroyer it was too late and he had perished.[364] It is unclear whether this was an accident due to a mechanical problem with the aircraft or whether Sgt Baker had been attacked by German fighters flying in advance of the raid intercepted by 151 Squadron. The commanding officer of the destroyer did report having seen an engagement between British fighters and unidentified aircraft.[365] Any potential German claimant is unknown.

A second rescue mission, this time in the central-western Channel and at about 13h35 involved a He 59, one of the two from *Seenotzentrale Cherbourg* already mentioned, which was found landed on the sea some thirty miles off Cherbourg; the two Blenheims from 604 Squadron sent out to intercept this machine were escorted by a section from 152 Squadron.[366] While the Spitfires kept six protecting Me 109s busy, the Blenheims, piloted by S/L Anderson and P/O Crew set the seaplane on fire and destroyed it.[367]

Adlertag

Shipping attack and air engagements off Margate/ North Foreland, *c.* 13h30–14h15

There were two separate German formations, each with Me 109 escort, involved in this phase, and each was engaged within the same general area and time period. Some forty-five to fifty Do 17s of *KG 2*, protected by Me 109s from *JG 51* were intercepted by 111 Squadron off North Foreland and out to sea to the east for about thirty miles; they were flying east and thus on their way home and the bombers being still in close formation had most likely not been successful in locating their target in the cloudy conditions over the Thames Estuary at the time.[368] Presumably the Dorniers' target was shipping in the mouth of the estuary. The second German formation was made up of about thirty Ju 87s of *II/StG 1*, with a direct escort from *I* and *II/JG 3*, and encountered 74 Squadron.[369] As F/Lt Connors, positioned at the rear of the one 111 Squadron flight in cloudy conditions, flew off Margate towards the Dornier formation further out to sea to the east, his Green Section was engaged by Me 109s at *c.* 13h40, and on diving through the clouds Connors observed a destroyer being attacked by a Ju 87.[370] P/O Freeborn of 74 Squadron similarly engaged with Me 109s (but a different unit to Connors' opponents) off Margate, also passed through the clouds during the combat and saw a destroyer being attacked by a Ju 87.[371] That the Dorniers being tackled by 111 Squadron were already on their way home while the Ju 87s were actively bombing shipping suggests that the Dornier formation had come into the Thames Estuary ahead of the Ju 87s; despite this, 74 Squadron seems to have tackled the Ju 87 formation and more particularly their Me 109 escorts prior to 111 Squadron catching up with their Dorniers.

The very first event appears to have been the majority of the Stukas ganging up on two naval minesweeper trawlers, *HMTs Edwardian* and *Peter Carey* anchored near Hope Buoy; at about 13h30 the two trawlers were attacked by a large number of German bombers which came in from 1,500–2,000 ft, then formed a line astern formation and dived down towards the ships, releasing their bombs at 300 ft about five seconds apart. Each Stuka followed up with machine gun fire.[372] Both trawlers replied with their twelve pounders and Lewis guns, and sailors aboard both vessels observed six aircraft fall into the sea; the first appeared to be shot down by the destroyer HMS *Windsor*, presumably the vessel observed by the two pilots, Connors and Freeborn, while the second was claimed by HMT *Edwardian*.[373]

Who got the next three aircraft seen to fall was unclear, with the two trawlers firing at them as well as RAF fighters which had just arrived; the sixth aircraft seen to fall into sea came down some two miles east of them.³⁷⁴ The *Edwardian* had been holed by the bombing and lost three crew killed and three wounded; she was towed towards shore by her fellow trawler, also damaged, and with her assistance and that of a drifter, *Edwardian* was beached just below the North Foreland lighthouse.³⁷⁵ She was later salvaged. The six aircraft seen to fall into the water by the sailors may reflect the two Me 109s and four Hurricanes shot down in the fighting off Margate. A Ju 87 of *II/StG 1* and its crew were shot down, apparently by RAF fighters into the Thames Estuary.³⁷⁶ It may however, have fallen to naval gunfire, as seen by the trawler sailors.

The Stukas were protected on this mission by *I/JG 3*, flying direct escort as well as by *II/JG 3*, most likely flying as top cover as they did not become involved in the subsequent engagement; *I/JG 3* had only recently arrived on the Channel coast on 1 August 1940 and this mission on 11 August was only their second one since arriving.³⁷⁷ Their inexperience is underlined by the orders the *Gruppe* had, to keep the Ju 87s company as they dived down to attack in order to protect them.³⁷⁸ Eight Spitfires of 74 Squadron from Hornchurch were initially sent to patrol Hawkinge at 15,000 ft before being vectored to the north-east of Margate where they observed ten Stukas in the distance passing through the clouds, with about twenty Me 109s seen above them at c. 10,000 ft.³⁷⁹ *I/JG 3* were pounced on by the experienced 74 Squadron pilots led by S/L Malan, with altitude advantage, and for no losses they claimed four Me 109s destroyed and one damaged.³⁸⁰ *I/JG 3*, while losing two aircraft and pilots for no claims in return, adjudged the mission a success, as the Stukas were not seen to be attacked.³⁸¹

In the meantime a second RAF squadron, twelve Hurricanes from 111 Squadron at Croydon had also been sent forward to Hawkinge at 12h45; they were almost immediately vectored to a position off the North Foreland, at about 17,000 ft, but encountering heavy cloud on the way, two pilots became detached and returned early to land at Hawkinge: P/Os Hardman, Green 3 and A. Fisher, Yellow 2.³⁸² As 111 Squadron was near the North Foreland, with Green Section led by F/Lt Connors behind Blue Section, which was the leading trio of the squadron, led by S/L Thompson, Me 109s struck at the former;³⁸³ A Flight comprising Red and Yellow Sections was close by but not directly behind B Flight. What happened next is best described by F/Lt Connors himself,³⁸⁴ leading a now depleted section of only two Hurricanes due to the third member having been detached in cloud earlier:

> Whilst on patrol with No. 111 Sqdn. at 17000′ I noticed 15 M.E. 109 pass over the formation 3000′ above they disappeared into the sun, and a few moments later I noticed one M.E. 109 climbing up behind

Adlertag

> Green 3. I turned towards E/A which immediately dived for cloud cover. I followed him down through a gap in the clouds, and found a destroyer being attacked by J.U. 87. I noticed a number of M.E. 109 below cloud base and attacked the nearest to me with a 2 sec. burst dead astern and followed him down until he crashed into the sea and caught fire. Immediately after this I noticed Green 3 spin slowly into the sea. I then attacked another M.E. 109 with a 1 sec. burst, and short burst at a J.U. 87, but as my windscreen was completely obscured by oil from e/a I had brought down I landed Manston without observing subsequent result.

Green 3 in Connors' report was actually Green 2, P/O Copeman who was posted missing.[385] It would appear that Green Section had been bounced from behind by elements of *JG 51*, who claimed three confirmed victories over British fighters in the Thames Estuary area at about 13h45–13h50 by *4* and *5/JG 51*; two more probables were claimed by *5/JG 51* in the same area with no times given,[386] possibly also in this engagement. *1/JG 51* made a single, confirmed claim about twenty minutes later.[387] 111 Squadron were to lose five aircraft and four pilots on this mission,[388] as further described below. Green 2 had the misfortune to meet highly experienced pilots from *II/JG 51* who had been flying regularly across the Channel since the beginning of July.

Employing typical *Jagdflieger* tactics, they had dived down and approached their victim from behind and below, as observed by F/Lt Connors. From F/Lt Connors' combat report quoted above, it is likely that when he went below the cloud and engaged the Me 109 which he claimed destroyed (confirmed), that he had become involved in the combat between *I/JG 3* and 74 Squadron, presumably then contributing to the destruction of one of the two Me 109s lost by *I/JG 3*. This would have been a distinct engagement from that which occurred between *II/JG 51* and P/O Copeman, above the clouds. What happened to Blue Section flying ahead of Connors' depleted Green Section of 111 Squadron is evident from S/L Thompson's combat report,[389] which describes their engagement with a large Dornier formation some thirty miles east of North Foreland.

> Squadron took off to proceed to Hawkinge, on arrival at Hawkinge we were ordered to patrol at 15000'. Clouds were 10/10ths. and we maintained position by "pip-squeak". We were then sent to Deal and from there to Ramsgate. From here we were given a vector of 330° and after six minutes told to orbit. After about 20 minutes we were told to return and patrol forward base at 5000'. By this time

The First Major Raid, Portland: 11 August 1940

we had been in the air for approx. 1 hour 15 minutes, and Green section had become detached. On the way back on a vector of 180° we encountered about 45-50 D.O. 215s. The D.O. 215s were flying at about 200′ above the top of the clouds on an Easterly course. They were divided into 3 large formations about 100 yards between each, and each formation consisted of about 5 sections of three aircraft, each section about 20 yards apart. I immediately ordered an attack by sections. I got my section into line astern and closed up on the E/A from astern. During this period I flew just in the top of the clouds until I was approx. 400 yards astern, when I ordered my section into echelon right, and pulled up underneath the rear left e/a. I fired a burst of approx. 5 secs. and when about 100 yards away raked the complete rear of the formation. I observed a very bright glow in the fuselage of the left e/a. During this attack I experienced a considerable amount of fire from practically all the lower guns of the rear formation. I broke away straight downwards into the clouds followed by Blue 2. I then pulled up out of the clouds with the intention of carrying out another attack, but on the way noticed that Blue 2, who was with me when I commenced my approach, had disappeared. I looked round and saw a M.E. 109 behind me. I turned to engage this e/a but he dived into the clouds. I think this e/a must have shot down Blue 2. By this time the D.O. 215s were too far away to carry out another attack so I returned to base (Hawkinge). In the meantime Red section had endeavoured to get ahead of the bombers and execute a head-on attack, but owing to the Dorniers' speed and their own shortage of petrol were eventually compelled to carry out a quarter attack.

There are a number of interesting aspects to this combat report. The reported Do 215s were, of course, Do 17s. S/L Thompson showed considerable tactical skill in leading his section in the tops of the clouds until popping up to open fire on the bombers, having then also put his section into echelon right, i.e. spread out abreast, to his right. However, the Me 109s of *JG 51* were active and dangerous; they shot down Blue 2, P/O J. W. McKenzie, who was posted missing, while Blue 3 Sgt H. S. Newton became detached from the section after his first attack, lost his bearings in the cloud and finally picked up the coast far to the north, where he crash-landed unhurt in a field near Orfordness after running out of fuel as he neared the coastline.[390] Red Section of 111 Squadron had evidently broken away from Thomson's squadron formation intending to perform a head-on attack, implying that the squadron had given some thought to methods of tackling tight bomber formations since their last experience on 10 July 1940.[391] It is also likely that the debacle of

Adlertag

111 Squadron's operations on this mission would have reinforced their intent to use the head-on method, as would be practised noticeably by this squadron in the next week or so, and thereafter. Yellow Section numbering only two machines due to an early return mentioned above, was missing.[392]

The other interesting comment in S/L Thompson's combat report is that they maintained their allocated patrol position above clouds by 'pip-squeak'. This was a system built into at least two aircraft per squadron, where they already possessed the new TR9D radio; it regularly keyed the aircraft's radio to transmit and emit a signal lasting fourteen seconds in every minute.[393] This allowed three ground direction-finding stations to take bearings from the signal and by triangulation obtain the position of the squadron leader's aircraft, and thus of the squadron more generally.[394] This earlier system was later superseded by the IFF or 'identification friend or foe' system once radar coverage of the UK extended inland from the coastal zone.[395] At the end of the day, triggering the system in the air was one more duty performed by the RAF formation leader, one more thing to remember and to perform in addition to his many other concerns and duties.

In the overall engagement of all the 111 Squadron sections, one confirmed Me 109 by F/Lt Connors as well as several damaged Dorniers were claimed.[396] In the general Thames Estuary area *KG 2* suffered two damaged Do 17s from *4/KG 2*, one of which was written off, with three wounded crew members between the two aircraft, resulting from combat over the Channel; three more were damaged from *9/KG 2* by RAF fighters between Ostend and Calais, three more crew being wounded and one killed.[397] The entire crew of another damaged machine from *3/KG 2* were wounded and it was written off after crashing at St Inglevert airfield, already ascribed possibly to attacks by S/L Townsend of 85 Squadron in a preceding engagement. While three of *KG 2*'s damaged aircraft have been related to actions during 'nuisance' raids[398] and the other three to action off the French coast during a later engagement,[399] the five from *4th* and *9th Staffeln* can also logically fit the attacks on the tight *KG 2* Dornier formation by 111 Squadron.

This forty-five to fifty-strong formation strongly suggests two *Gruppen* flying together, and S/L Thompson's Blue Section damaged at least one Dornier badly (possibly the written-off one from *4/KG 2*) and likely a second less severely, while Red Section's beam attack[400] possibly hit three from *9/KG 2*, which suffered only slight damage, amounting to five per cent in two cases and eight per cent in the other.[401] With a beam attack, crew casualties were more likely as there was no real armour protection along the sides of the Dorniers, and this *Staffel* suffered three wounded and one killed in the engagement.

The First Major Raid, Portland: 11 August 1940

Final combat of the day: reconnaissance aircraft shot down, North Yorkshire, c. 19h10–19h20

The final aerial combat of the day was when Green Section of 41 Squadron intercepted a lone Ju 88 reconnaissance aircraft of *1(F)/121* at about 17,000 ft over Thirsk in North Yorkshire; the Junkers dived very fast into cloud cover at about 10,000 ft.[402] F/O Wallens, Green 1, led his three Spitfires in hot pursuit, engaging twelve boost to catch the steeply diving machine.[403] Green 2, F/O Boyle, got in the first attack from astern expending 2,400 rounds of ammunition, with Wallens following up with two quarter-astern attacks, using 1,000 rounds.[404] Sgt Darling flying as Green 3 expended all his ammunition, 2,695 rounds, in a series of attacks from astern, beam and quarter, and the machine crashed near Whitby on the coast, 30-odd miles to the north-east of the initial interception.[405] Once more, the commonly experienced reality that it took three fighters and several thousand rounds of ammunition to bring down a lone bomber, pertained. Interestingly, 41 Squadron were carrying more than the standard 2,400 rounds of ammunition.[406]

2

Second Major Raid, Portsmouth, Radar Stations and Forward Airfields Attacked: 12 August 1940

Small raid on Lympne, heavily escorted, feint towards North Foreland, *c.* 08h10–08h40

What at first appears as a rather minor and straightforward pair of actions involving only two RAF units, 610 Squadron over Romney Marshes and Dungeness and a little later 54 Squadron over the Dover area, concerning a heavily escorted small German bomber raid on Lympne airfield, is in fact more complex. Radar picked up early activity at approximately 07h20: 6+ enemy machines behind Cap Gris Nez aimed at Dungeness, and 3+ aircraft in the central Dover Straits; however, both *Luftwaffe* formations were waiting for reinforcements and did not cross the Kent coast.[1] Just before 07h45, radar detected twenty or so hostiles near Guines and a similar formation behind Cap Gris Nez; the 11 Group controller had already reacted shortly after 07h30 by scrambling 610 Squadron from their advanced base at Hawkinge and vectoring them towards the Dungeness-bound raiders, putting 54 Squadron on patrol over their own forward base at Manston, and sending up a second squadron, 111 from Hawkinge to patrol that airfield.[2]

While 54 Squadron's ordered height is not recorded, the other two units were at 10,000 ft,[3] too low for 111 Squadron to see any action, and placing 610 Squadron at a distinct height disadvantage to the German incursion over New Romney.[4] F/Lt Alan Deere, leading the 54 Squadron contingent, when they were vectored forward towards Dover soon after, was too experienced to place his men under a similar tactical handicap, and proceeded south-westwards at 25,000-27,000 ft.[5] The 610 Squadron engagement will be dealt with first as it preceded that of 54 Squadron, but an element of overlap also appears to have occurred.

German dispositions were much more numerous and complex: nine Do 17s of *I/KG 2* were to bomb Lympne, with a close escort provided by *I/JG 26*, *III/JG 54* also being part of the escort, probably more indirect, and the other two *Gruppen* of this *Geschwader* were also aloft, also part of the same indirect escort; *I/JG 52* flew a sweep between Dungeness and Beachy Head, their compatriots in *II Gruppe* another, between Hastings and Eastbourne, and finally, *III/JG 26* also performed an early morning sweep.[6] *I/JG 52* and *III/JG 26* did not see any action, and the latter may have been part of the possibly diversionary German formation of bombers and fighters seen by 54 Squadron near the North Foreland.[7] Large numbers of German fighters were out and about, sweeping from Beachy Head to Dungeness, as well as an apparent diversion over North Foreland, threatening the Manston forward base, and there was the excessively heavily escorted small raid in the centre on Lympne, a minor RAF airfield.

Looked at in retrospect, this would all appear to have been intended to clear the air of British fighters from their advanced bases in eastern Kent before the radar station raids to follow within the hour. The radar station attacks were to be an unpleasant surprise to Fighter Command and could not have been foreseen by the Command or 11 Group controllers from the previous activity spread from approximately Eastbourne in the west-south-west to Manston in the east-north-east. Hindsight history is much easier than martial reality. It was 610 Squadron's fate for its twelve Spitfires to become engaged with elements of all three of JGs 26, 52 and 54.[8] Thanks to it having become well experienced during the previous few months, 610 Squadron came through the ordeal very well.

The nine Dorniers of *I/KG 2* flew west-south-westwards from Cap Gris Nez towards Dungeness and then turned north to cross the coast at Romney Marshes at 08h12, flying at 16,000 ft.[9] What happened next is best described by S/L John Ellis, Blue 1, leading 610 Squadron:[10]

> I was leading 610 Sqdn. which was detailed to intercept raid approaching Dungeness. Nine enemy bombers were sighted at 16,000 ft. over New Romney in very tight vic formation in sections of three, Sections were also in vic. The presence of the bombers was first noticed after a stick of bombs was seen to fall just out to sea off New Romney. Our height at the time was 10,000ft. We climbed to attack the bombers which were flying towards Rye. When we were 1,000ft below them and about

1000 yds behind, twelve escorting Me 109s came diving down out of the sun on to our tails. We were forced to break off our attack on the bombers and a general dog fight ensued with the enemy fighters.

Ellis's reference to the bombers flying towards Rye would appear to be an error, it being in the opposite direction to their target at Lympne; Sgt Chandler, flying Red 2 in A Flight behind Ellis' B Flight of Blue and Green Sections, clearly states in his combat report that the Dorniers were 'heading east at 200 mph'.[11]

Ellis's B Flight's engagement soon moved over the sea towards the east, the obvious direction of retreat for Me 109s short of fuel, and he and Green 3 engaged single Me 109s in a number of combats.[12] In contrast, A Flight of 610 Squadron comprising Red and Yellow Sections led by F/Lt Smith, appears to have been attacked from superior altitude by much larger numbers of Me 109s than the twelve reported by S/L Ellis; Sgt Chandler in Red Section reported forty of them and P/O Rees in Yellow Section fifty to sixty Messerschmitts descending on them.[13] Similar to B Flight, the engagement rapidly moved eastwards over the Channel, but combats tended to be much more confused and rapid due to the numbers of enemies involved.[14]

A dozen Me 109s from *II/JG 52* were most likely the first in action, diving onto the head of 610 Squadron (B Flight) as they climbed for the bombers; they were not, however, part of the formal escort but rather had flown a free chase from further west along the coast.[15] The *Gruppe* were on their first mission over England and lost *Lt* Gelhaar of *4th Staffel* over New Romney, who was taken prisoner soon after 08h00, while his colleague *Uffz* Kern from *5th Staffel* perished in the Channel; they claimed three Spitfires and a Hurricane on this mission and an evening engagement, but none appear to have been confirmed in the *Luftwaffe* victory list, the claims thus lacking times and locations.[16] B Flight did have at least two and possibly three Spitfires damaged in the general engagement over Romney Marsh and environs,[17] so *II/JG 52* may have performed better than surmised. Their losses, if indeed to B Flight of the Squadron, can be ascribed to S/L Ellis and Sgt Gardner who both made multiple claims for Me 109s, with serious visible damage and/or observed demise.[18]

The larger numbers of Me 109s which dived down onto A Flight of 610 Squadron, possibly somewhat separated from the leading B Flight during the steep climb made to intercept the bombers seen initially, may have belonged, logically, to either *I/JG 26* or to elements from *JG 54*. *I/JG 26*, being the allocated close escort[19] would be the more likely candidate. The *3rd Staffel* of this *Gruppe* also claimed two Spitfires south of Folkestone,[20] an area just eastwards and thus seawards of

New Romney, which fits their having engaged 610 Squadron and likely their A Flight. This flight also lost the Spitfire of F/Lt Smith leading the flight, who was rescued wounded from the Channel eight miles from shore and about midway between Dungeness and Dover,[21] placing him approximately south of Folkestone. There is thus reasonable evidence to link A Flight, 610 Squadron and *I/JG 26* in an engagement seawards of New Romney; in addition to Smith, one and possibly two more members of the flight had their Spitfires damaged in combat.[22] *I/JG 26* suffered the loss of *Oblt* Butterweck who was killed in the Ashford area at about 08h30;[23] Smith in contrast was shot down somewhat earlier in the general action.[24]

The engagements between 610 Squadron and the Me 109s of *II/JG 52* and *I/JG 26* began near Dungeness over New Romney and then moved eastwards over the sea, but some fighters from both sides also flew northeastwards, following the Dornier bombers from *I/KG 2* to their target at Lympne; Sgt Gardner of B Flight and Sgt Chandler of A Flight reported engaging Me 109s near Lympne.[25] Another A Flight pilot, P/O Pegge, had an engagement near Hawkinge about fifteen minutes after the initial combat near New Romney:[26]

> On the 12.8.40 I was No.3 of Yellow Section of 'A' Flight 610 Sqdn. At about 08.10, after a fight with Me 109s, in which I did not fire, I got detached from the rest of the Squadron so I climbed up to 23,000 feet. At 08.15 I saw 6 Me 109s going round in a circle about 3000 feet below me. I came down & from a range of about 100 yds I gave one a burst of 1-2 secs. Smoke & flame came from it & it went down slightly inland & I climbed back to 23,000 again.

Only one Me 109 came down inland from the Hawkinge-Dover area, that of *I/JG 26* flown by *Oblt* Butterweck which exploded near Elham, the pilot bailing out but not surviving, his body being found about six miles from the wreck of the Messerschmitt, which came down about a mile east of Elham.[27] People on the ground at Elham, including a local diarist, observed Lympne being bombed at 08h16 and four minutes later they saw an abandoned Me 109 flying in circles over the village with its wheels down and being pursued by several Spitfires before crashing into the ground.[28]

It thus appears as if several Spitfires were firing at the already doomed and abandoned Me 109 of *Oblt* Butterweck, and as was rather common and understandable, each pilot was convinced his fire had done the fatal damage to the enemy machine. As already detailed in the previous paragraph, at least three 610 Squadron Spitfires reported engaging

Adlertag

Me 109s in the Lympne-Hawkinge area, and one them, P/O Pegge, described a circle of six Me 109s below him; he might have seen a circling Me 109 in front being pursued by several Spitfires, bearing in mind the speed of aerial combat and the fleeting glimpses obtained of any detailed scene. The combat was also a few minutes after the bombers had attacked their target at Lympne, not far to the west, and having some of the direct escort Me 109s of *I/JG 26* passing to the east of it soon after is hardly surprising.

The situation is made more complex by Spitfires of 54 Squadron also engaging Me 109s in the general area to the north-west of Dover-Hawkinge. F/Lt Deere has just been described as leading eight 54 Squadron Spitfires from the Manston area towards Dover, at 25,000-27,000 ft; Deere observed a large Do 17 formation and escort off North Foreland and, instructing his men to follow, turned back in that direction where he and his wingman chased a few enemy aircraft ineffectively.[29] However, two of his sections with six of his eight fighters did not hear the order and observing Me 109s well below them instinctively took the opportunity to bounce them from above, as described by Blue Section leader, P/O Colin Gray in his combat report.[30]

> Sighted Squadron of enemy aircraft at 20,000 feet over Dover, dived down from 27,000 feet and engaged. Fired 3 second burst at one Me. 109 which smoked, caught fire and then commenced to spin in flames. Fired short burst at a second Me. 109 from 50 yds and observed glycol streaming from port radiator. I chased the enemy aircraft back to French Coast in a dive, firing all the time until ammunition ran out and pursued the enemy aircraft over Cape (sic) Gris Nez and observed him force land on the beach with his wheels up. Enemy aircraft written off.

Gray claimed two Me 109s, unconfirmed as he lacked witnesses to their apparent destruction. Did Gray fatally damage Butterweck's Me 109 at altitude, which the pilot then abandoned, and the pilotless machine subsequently flew on in circles over Elham, hotly pursued by several other Spitfires including some from 610 Squadron? It is certainly possible. His second claimed Me 109, seen to force-land on the beach at Cap Gris Nez, is a problem to identify in German loss records, as are a confirmed and a probable Me 109 claimed by P/O Matthews of Yellow Section, 54 Squadron, the other section which attacked the Me 109s from superior altitude along with Gray and his Blue Section.[31] Matthews did not see his probable claim crash, and his confirmed claim was reported as crashing into the sea approximately ten miles north-west of Dover.[32] Obviously, this is in error, as ten miles north-west of Dover is not that

Second Major Raid, Portsmouth, Radar Stations

far from Elham village where Butterweck perished. No meaningful interpretation of Matthews' claims is thus possible.

54 Squadron suffered two damaged Spitfires in this engagement, that of P/O Turley-George belly-landing on Newlands Farm, Denton, the pilot having bullet-shrapnel wounds to his head; Denton lies almost exactly ten miles north-west of Dover, and about four and a half miles from Elham,[33] thereby firmly placing 54 Squadron geographically close to I/JG 26's lost Me 109 at Elham. P/O Kemp from 54 Squadron was able to force-land his Spitfire at Lympne with only slight injury.[34] This also suggests that both 54 and 610 Squadrons engaged the enemy in the vicinity of Lympne; Kemp would only have landed there in dire emergency as the airfield had clearly just been bombed. 54 Squadron's actions were at about 08h30–08h40.[35]

P/O Gray's second claim, that observed by him to force-land with undercarriage up on the beach at Cap Gris Nez, may possibly relate to a Me 109 of I/JG 54 which German records indicate crash-landed at Campagne, the *Gruppe's* base.[36] It is possible that this Me 109 did indeed force-land on this beach, which was close to the *Luftwaffe* landing ground at Wissant,[37] and the aircraft could probably have been moved there easily enough where preliminary repairs were made to enable the short flight to Campagne-les-Guines, less than twenty kilometres away. It would appear likely that it was *JG 54* which principally engaged with 54 Squadron (and possibly also with a few of 610 Squadron flying over the Lympne area), as 4/JG 54 claimed one Spitfire confirmed and another probable at 08h35 in the Dover-Lympne area at about 21,000 ft, with 7/JG 54 claiming two more confirmed at the same approximate time, but with no location noted.[38] The three confirmed claims could well relate to the two Spitfire casualties of 54 Squadron, and perhaps to one of 610 Squadron's damaged machines. *JG 54* was flying escort to the bombers,[39] presumably fulfilling the role of the remote escort in contrast to I/JG 26's close escort,[40] and due to their claim times being consistently later that those of I/JG 26[41] and indeed overlapping with action times from 54 Squadron,[42] all support their flying in that role behind the main formation of Dorniers and its close escort.

Based on the preceding information and examining squadron leadership in this early set of actions from Dungeness to Dover on 12 August 1940, clearly 610 Squadron was caught on the climb towards a small but very heavily escorted bomber formation, but both S/L Ellis leading B Flight in front and F/Lt Smith leading A Flight behind turned away and faced the descending Me 109s, respectively of II/JG 52 (about a dozen) and what appears to have been the entire *Gruppe* of I/JG 26. The two 610 Squadron leaders were thus not caught by surprise, but

Adlertag

they fought the subsequent engagements at a distinct disadvantage. The squadron lost one Spitfire with four more damaged, one pilot wounded, another lightly so; in return they dispatched two *II/JG 52* machines and their pilots, and they may have contributed to the Me 109 and pilot lost by *I/JG 26*.

With hindsight and from an armchair perspective, the experienced 610 Squadron might have done even better had S/L Ellis first gone for altitude by climbing away from the bombers rather than close beneath them. F/Lt Deere, leading the 54 Squadron formation towards Dover from Manston, also faced a dilemma: with significant superior altitude to Me 109s spotted near Dover, there was a great temptation to bounce them, which indeed was carried out by two of the three sections available, led in the first instance by P/O Gray who claimed not to have heard the order from Deere. Deere, in contrast with only two Spitfires, turned back for Manston, having spotted a large Dornier formation and escort off the North Foreland, which he ordered to be engaged by the squadron. While this decision by Deere cannot be faulted, the North Foreland formation was a decoy intended to distract RAF fighters away from the Lympne raid coming in from Dungeness to the south-west, and in the event no engagement resulted off North Foreland, perhaps fortuitously so, bearing in mind that Deere only mustered two Spitfires.

Gray and his colleagues who bounced the Me 109s near Dover appear to have seriously damaged one Me 109 (*Oblt* Butterweck of *I/JG 26* killed, almost certainly also attacked by 610 Squadron pilots) and possibly put another (*JG 54*) on the beach at Cap Gris Nez, albeit repairable. In a way, both Deere and Gray made good decisions in the few moments granted to a Battle of Britain pilot. Overall, bearing in mind the vastly superior German fighter numbers engaged, 130 to 140 Me 109s to only twenty Spitfires, both British squadrons had done valiant and effective work. For a total of one Spitfire lost, six damaged (one force-landed off base), two pilots wounded, two more lightly so, they had cost Göring three Messerschmitts destroyed along with the three pilots lost, and another damaged (and force-landed). German fighter claims numbered five Spitfires confirmed and a probable; RAF fighter claims were three confirmed, eight unconfirmed, three probable and one damaged Me 109.

The small Dornier formation from *I/KG 2* got through to its target at Lympne, hardly surprising in view of the massive escort, where they dropped ninety 110 lb SC50 bombs, which damaged a hangar and cratered the landing field.[43] While one authoritative source lists another RAF loss, with P/O Edsall force-landing his 54 Squadron Spitfire at Dartford at about 08h45 after an engagement with an Me 109,[44] this is not mentioned in either the relevant IPR or the ORB Form 541.[45]

The relevant Form 541 only lists one flight for Edsall on this day, from 14h35-14h45, when S/L Leathart led his squadron up from Hornchurc,h but there was no engagement and most landed again soon afterwards; Dartford lies a few miles south of Hornchurch. It is therefore thought that Edsall's force-landing was not combat-related and occurred later at about 14h40.

Surprise attack on radar stations at Dover (Swingate), Rye, Pevensey and Dunkirk, c. 09h30–09h45

This attack on four radar stations was carried out by *EGr 210*, using eight Me 109s of *3rd Staffel* which tackled Swingate, six Me 110s of *1st Staffel*, four Me 110s of *2nd Staffel* and four Me 110s of the *Stab/ EGr 210*.[46] *Hpt* Rubensdörffer, the *Gruppenkommandeur* led the Me 110s up from their forward base at Calais-Marck and was to attack Dunkirk radar station in northern Kent with his *Stabschwarm*, while the two Me 110 *Staffeln* tackled Rye and Pevensey on the southern English coast, in East Sussex.[47] While most sources describe *1/EGr 210* attacking Pevensey and *2/EGr 210* bombing Rye, copies of pilot logbooks in the unit history[48] clearly show that *1st Staffel* attacked Rye and thus *2nd* by default must have bombed Pevensey. The same logbooks show that the Me 110 units took off from Calais-Marck about 09h15 with the faster Me 109s of *3rd Staffel* lifting off about fifteen minutes later. With a much shorter distance to fly to Dover they reached their target at Swingate at almost exactly the same time as Rye was bombed, as reported by a witness on the ground.[49]

Rubensdörffer led the Me 110s west-south-westwards down the Channel, flying basically parallel to the south coast,[50] until they turned in towards the coast past Dungeness where the two *Staffeln* separated for their respective targets,[51] Rye close by and Pevensey further westwards along the coast, just outside Eastbourne. An escort from *III/JG 54* had joined up above the Me 110s en route down the Channel.[52] The route of the Me 110s down the Channel parallel to the coast was reminiscent of the Lympne raid and escorts track earlier that morning, a measure no doubt intended to confuse the defenders. Meanwhile, Rubensdörffer led his four Me 110s north-north-eastwards, towards his target at Dunkirk radar station near Faversham. Pevensey and Dunkirk would have been bombed about the same time, about a quarter of an hour later than Swingate and Rye.

The German *Gruppe* suffered no losses on this mission, surprise being achieved everywhere, but none of the radar stations was off the air for more than a few hours;⁵³ Dunkirk remained operational despite two destroyed huts and a 1,000lb bomb shifting the concrete transmitting block several inches.⁵⁴ While the aerial towers at Swingate were slightly damaged, these targets were essentially invulnerable to the explosions; even more importantly these tall towers deflected lower level bomber attacks generally by their mere presence, thereby protecting the vitally important operational rooms underneath.⁵⁵ In spite of all the huts being destroyed at Rye, the critical transmitting and receiving blocks and the watch office were undamaged, a standby diesel engine enabling the station to get back on air by noon.⁵⁶ The main damage at Pevensey was a cut in the electricity mains.⁵⁷ Overall, within six hours all four of the stations were reporting once more⁵⁸ and the relevant radar emissions were picked up by the German signals specialists,⁵⁹ thereby discouraging further attacks.

Stuka raid on shipping in the Thames Estuary, c. 11h15–11h30

As was often the case, radar observed German formations behind Cap Gris Nez at about 10h50, and the 11 Group controller had elements of 65, 111 and 615 Squadrons patrolling the Dover Straits, with those from 65 and 111 due to land quite soon; to balance this out, another flight of 65 Squadron was sent up from Manston with orders to patrol Hawkinge, and 501 Squadron took off from Hawkinge to patrol off the North Foreland.⁶⁰ Concurrently, there was one coastal convoy about twelves miles east of Foulness; another convoy to the east of Clacton, further north, had a patrol of a section of 151 Squadron.⁶¹ As German formations plotted in the Calais region grew in size, a radar plot of 50+ emerged into the eastern entrance to the Dover Straits just prior to 11h10 and proceeded past North Foreland, carrying on further northwards halfway across the Thames Estuary, where it began manoeuvring from east to west; it was joined by a faster 12+ radar plot which passed North Foreland some five minutes later.⁶² At 11h15, the Margate lifeboat was launched,⁶³ obviously anticipating forthcoming maritime trouble. The 11 Group controller, suspecting an imminent attack on the two convoys, ordered 65 and 501 Squadrons northwards, while maintaining protection of Manston and Hawkinge by, respectively, 54 and 111 Squadrons.⁶⁴ Spitfires of 65 Squadron were vectored by the controllers to intercept higher flying escorts and 501 Squadron Hurricanes were sent in at a lower altitude towards the inferred bombers, an oft striven-for combination which, this time, worked to perfection.⁶⁵

Second Major Raid, Portsmouth, Radar Stations

The German force comprised twenty two Ju 87s from *IV/LG 1*, with escort provided by all three *Gruppen* of *JG 26*, as indicated by all three making claims.[66] *III/JG 26* is identified as having flown a sweep,[67] presumably in advance of the dive bombers, leaving *I* and *II/JG 26* to fulfil the roles of close escort and top cover or remote escort. As envisaged by the 11 Group controller, 65 Squadron Spitfires engaged the top cover Me 109s, with 501 Squadron intercepting the Ju 87s.[68] 501 Squadron records indicate intense action against the Ju 87s and only limited contact with an escort some 6,000 ft higher,[69] while 65 Squadron's records show an engagement starting for them from a superior altitude of 2,000-4,000 ft above high flying Me 109s at 24,000 ft, which they caught unawares.[70] As *I/JG 26* suffered the only Me 109 lost on this raid, and also claimed three victories, two of which were relegated to probables and the other rejected, this suggests they were the top cover which had been surprised; *II/JG 26*, making only a single claim for a British fighter,[71] was most likely the Stukas' close escort. 501 Squadron had one Hurricane force-land following the engagement while 65 Squadron had no casualties.[72]

The three Hurricanes of 151 Squadron were furthest north and appear to have been engaged first by the *III/JG 26* sweep, but only a few minutes before the other two *JG 26 Gruppen* combats began.[73] The 151 Squadron Hurricanes sighted about thirty Me 109s at 12,000 ft over the Thames Estuary, and F/O Tucker ordered line astern and led his pitifully small force into a climb towards the sun before attacking the enemy formation.[74] P/O Beley disappeared after the first encounter and although picked up from the sea off Manston, died soon afterwards, F/O Tucker suffered multiple cannon strikes, bailed out wounded about eight miles north of Margate at *c.* 10,000 ft and survived, despite only being picked up about five hours later; P/O Debenham put his badly damaged machine down at Rochford, unhurt.[75] *III/JG 26* claimed three confirmed Hurricanes north-west of Margate over the Thames Estuary at 11h15–11h20, with *Gruppenkommandeur* Adolf Galland claiming a probable in the same area some twenty minutes later.[76]

65 Squadron's two flights had scrambled half an hour apart, F/Lt Olive leading A Flight up from Manston at 10h30, with B Flight taking off under F/Lt Saunders at 11h00; despite this they managed to join up, Saunders leading Blue and Green Sections in the interception ahead of Red and Yellow Sections from A Flight.[77] As 65 Squadron crossed the coast between Dover and Deal they sighted twenty to thirty Me 109s to the north of them; they were not in pairs but in vics of five to seven aircraft.[78] B Flight, attacking first and achieving surprise, was able to claim two destroyed and two probable Me 109s, A Flight attacking second, only one destroyed and a probable; Yellow Section at the rear scored

nothing as the Me 109s were by then alerted and evading successfully.[79] Five of the six claimants reported Me 109s attacked and apparently hit, diving away pouring out black or grey smoke.[80] This more often reflected the favoured tactic of Me 109 pilots when attacked: a steep dive away, trailing black smoke as the throttle was shoved to emergency power.

F/Lt Saunders had done a good job leading his men successfully to surprise a *Gruppe*-sized Me 109 formation which put up little resistance; however, 65 Squadron did greatly over-estimate their successes, only one Me 109 apparently falling victim to them: *Oblt* Regenauer of 2/JG 26 who was shot down into the sea off Folkestone, bailed out and was rescued, becoming a POW.[81] His claim for a Spitfire was disallowed by the *Luftwaffe* authorities, who also ruled two others by his *First Gruppe* colleagues as only probables; these claims were made at 11h20–11h25;[82] 65 Squadron had no losses.[83] I/JG 26 did get one confirmed victory, awarded to a pilot claiming a Morane; ironically, this most likely relates to a Skua out on a sea search mission for downed RAF pilots, which avoided the attack and was not hit at all.[84]

Last into action, but only a few minutes after the engagements of 151 and 65 Squadrons, were twelve Hurricanes of 501 Squadron led by S/L Holland who was vectored towards Margate at about 7,000 ft and sighted what he thought was about thirty or forty (actually only twenty-two) Ju 87s stepped up between 4,000 and 5,000 ft over the Thames Estuary.[85] The Stukas were observed to be flying south-west and apparently ignored the two convoys to the north to attack some minesweeping trawlers about ten miles north-east of Margate near the North East Spit Buoy. As 501 Squadron approached them, the Ju 87s were observed to be bombing some ships and once they had done so to be making off at low level eastwards.[86] Their close escort of II/JG 26 flying several thousand feet higher did not come down to their aid, and many of the Ju 87s jettisoned their bombs and then scattered[87] at low level, obviously in some alarm.[88] While 501 Squadron claimed one confirmed and five unconfirmed destroyed Stukas in this rather wild melee at low level above the sea, no losses are recorded.[89]

One possible explanation for so many claims yet no known losses could lie in the Stukas jettisoning bombs in the sea at low level, the resultant explosions of these already armed bombs producing rather spectacular pillars of foaming seawater as well as flames and smoke, easily misinterpreted as a Ju 87 crashing and exploding as it hit the water. Sgt Lacey of 501 Squadron, for one, described just such a scene which he took to be one of the Stukas he had fired at.[90]

However, not all the Stukas jettisoned their bombs, some sinking two Royal Navy minesweeping trawlers near the North East Spit Buoy,

Second Major Raid, Portsmouth, Radar Stations

Pyrope suffering a direct hit and losing six men at 11h20, while *Tamarisk* also went down, seven of her crew lost.[91] The Margate lifeboat launched five minutes prior to this rescued twenty-seven men.[92] S/L Holland, who was flying as a supernumerary squadron leader in 501 Squadron to gain experience,[93] had led the squadron expertly, right into the Ju 87s, and he avoided the attention of the close escort; in fact, he was the only member of the squadron to engage them at all.[94] Following an abortive attack on a Ju 87, he climbed to about 10,000 ft where he engaged a dozen Me 109s, claiming a probable but enduring multiple attacks on his own Hurricane, eventually escaping by turning onto his back and diving steeply for the sea, pulling out at low level.[95] No doubt his *Luftwaffe* opponents thought they had shot him down, *II/JG 26* making one claim for a Spitfire near Margate at 11h25,[96] once more exhibiting their well-established 'Spitfire snobbery'. S/L Holland had his engine cut just north of Dover on his way back to Hawkinge forward base, no doubt due to an unlucky hit in the fighting, but managed to put his aircraft down with only slight damage.[97]

Trying to understand the German tactics with this Stuka shipping raid is challenging. A *Gruppe* of dive bombers escorted by an entire Me 109 *Geschwader* had apparently ignored two convoys in the northern reaches of the Thames Estuary, only to attack some minesweeping trawlers in the south. While German losses were minimal at one Me 109 and a pilot POW, an advance sweep by *III/JG 26* did massacre the 151 Squadron convoy patrol section, and *II/JG 26* damaged a single Hurricane of 501 Squadron, which force-landed. However, the Stuka close escort of *II/JG 26* performed dismally, the Stukas seemed to have panicked when attacked by 501 Squadron, well led by S/L Holland, while 65 Squadron, again well led by F/Lt Saunders, was able to bounce the high cover *Gruppe* of *I/JG 26*. Perhaps the entire operation was to distract attention and fighter resources away from the major raid on Portsmouth and Ventnor radar station to the West? If so, then the *Luftwaffe* demonstrated once again a poor understanding of the structure and operational application of Fighter Command, with groups and their subordinate sector stations dedicated to the defence of specific regions. The really wasteful use of fighter resources was by the Germans over Kent.

Major raids on Portsmouth and Ventnor radar station, *c.* 12h00–12h50

British radar picked up two formations of 30+ near the Cherbourg peninsula at 11h28, with two smaller forces moving to and fro off

Adlertag

Cherbourg; hostile formations were thus already seen assembling with smaller protecting formations offshore.[98] Fighter Command was thereby alerted to the likelihood of an incursion in the central-western Channel; this was indeed realised at 11h40, when the presumed protective formations disappeared from the screens and two large formations began to move northwards over the Channel.[99] The radar picture enabled distinction between an eastern formation, indicated as about 30+, heading for Selsey Bill, and a larger western formation, perhaps up to 150+, making for the Isle of Wight.[100]

Obvious targets to be considered by the RAF, apart from their own bases at Tangmere, Warmwell and Middle Wallop, would have been the major naval bases of Portland, west of the Isle of Wight, or Portsmouth north of the island, and in view of earlier raids this day in the eastern Channel, radar stations, in particular the key Ventnor site so ideally sighted. German plans were indeed to bomb Ventnor, and Portsmouth harbour and dockyard, employing sixty-three Ju 88s of *KG 51*, with fighter support from all *Zerstörer* (ZG 2, ZG 76) and Me 109 (*JG's 2, 27* and *53*) units available to *Luftflotte 3*.[101] Fifteen of the bombers were to attack Ventnor,[102] the balance assigned to Portsmouth. Average bombloads per Ju 88, calculated from total bombs carried by each formation,[103] indicate that the Ventnor raiders carried double the load of explosives compared to the Portsmouth attackers, *c.* 3,520 lbs and 1,787 lbs respectively.

As the British could not yet know the chosen targets, initial dispositions had to be made to cover a range of possibilities. Firstly, 11 Group diverted 257 Squadron (12 Hurricanes) which had just taken off from their base at Northolt at 11h40, en route to North Weald, and ordered them to patrol Tangmere; barely minutes later, at 11h45, 266 Squadron (12 Spitfires) lifted off from the latter airfield on local patrol.[104] This took care of the Selsey Bill-bound German formation (eastern plot, above) initially, while 152 Squadron (12 Spitfires) were scrambled by 10 Group at 11h48 from Warmwell and vectored towards the Isle of Wight,[105] thereby providing a first reaction to the western radar plot aimed at that isle. However, only two minutes later the radar plots had become clear, the Isle of Wight and surrounds being the obvious target area, and 257 and 266 Squadrons were also directed there.[106]

257 Squadron should have covered the distance to Tangmere by about 11h50 but would have needed about another five minutes at cruising speed to get to the island. At noon, the 10 Group controllers scrambled two more squadrons, 609 (12 Spitfires) from Warmwell and 213 Squadron (13 Hurricanes) from Exeter.[107] While 609 Squadron was relatively close to the Isle of Wight, Exeter was about 25 minutes flying

time away from the island and 213 Squadron would arrive quite late in the overall battle. Final British reinforcements, scrambled by 11 Group from Tangmere sector, encompassed Hurricanes from 43 Squadron (7 machines, up 12h15) and 145 Squadron (10 aircraft, up 12h10), both close to the targets, but both units necessarily saw the latter part of the engagement.[108]

What of the *Luftwaffe*'s formations and plans, pitted against the just-described RAF dispositions? Detailed information on escort assignments between the two *Luftwaffe* formations approaching the UK is limited. Of the three Me 109 *Geschwadern* involved, *JG 53* was definitely assigned a widespread free chase role for all three *Gruppen*, with take-offs from French forward bases from about 11h30.[109] Claim times for this unit stretch from 12h20 to 12h50, most being between 12h20 and 12h25.[110] Due to the distance across the Channel being much larger in the central-western region than at the Dover Straits, allied to the well-known limited fuel endurance of the Me 109, most Me 109 *Geschwadern* tended to stagger the times of their *Gruppen* take offs to enable a longer period of fighter cover over the coast in the Portland-Brighton region. To what extent *JG 53* applied this common principle on this mission is unknown, but as the three *Gruppen* are clearly stated to have lifted off at about 11h30,[111] the same time as the Ju 88 bomber *Gruppen* did so, and as both aircraft types were capable of flying at about 250 mph without undue difficulty,[112] the plan was probably to saturate briefly the area above Portsmouth and the Isle of Wight just ahead of the bombers' arrival and for about a quarter of an hour thereafter.

In a way, thus *JG 53* flew a sweep just ahead and then over the attacking Ju 88s during the first part of the engagement. The geographic placement of *JG 2* bases (south-east of Le Havre, their forward base) and *JG 27* (east-south-east of Cherbourg, forward base),[113] suggests that *JG 2* accompanied the eastern *Luftwaffe* formation spotted by British radar, and *JG 27* the western one. Le Havre was the rendezvous point for *KG 51*'s sixty-three bombers,[114] logically tying their formation to a high cover from *JG 2*. *ZG 2*'s one Me 110 *Gruppe* and its *Stab* were stationed around Paris, as were *KG 51*'s Ju 88s, its other Me 110 *Gruppe* being normally at Amiens to the north;[115] again a logical association with *KG 51* can be made. As *KG 51* in the majority of sources is described as approaching the UK coast east of the intended targets, essentially towards the Selsey Bill-Brighton area, the so-called eastern German formation plotted by RAF radar most likely encompassed *KG 51*'s Ju 88s, covered by *ZG 2*'s Me 110s and top cover provided by *JG 2*.

As regards the western German formation radar plot, *V/LG 1*'s Me 110s, which formed part of *ZG 76* at the time, were sent from their base of Rocquancourt near Caen, westwards to a forward base at Lessay on the west coast of the Cherbourg peninsula, for this mission, which was to cover bombers into the area of the Isle of Wight for the Portsmouth raid.[116] It is reasonable to assume that *II* and *III/ZG 76*, based south-south-east of the Cherbourg peninsula[117] accompanied them, as well as *JG 27* as top cover, their forward base being at Cherbourg anyway. The RAF's 'western' radar plot can thus be seen as, most likely, made up of the three *ZG 76 Zerstörergruppen,* and *JG 27*.

The *Luftwaffe* plan was typically complex, and relied on good timing by all air formations; this time it succeeded in this intention, as the *KG 51-ZG2-JG 2* (eastern) formation approached the Isle of Wight from the east, having turned west off the coast from the Brighton-Selsey Bill area, and the (western) formation of *ZG 76-JG 27* came in from the south-west. The latter was flying higher than the fighters accompanying *KG 51* and each set of fighters (Me 110s and Me 109s) formed its own circle, *ZG 76-JG 27* about three miles off Portsmouth and *ZG 2-JG 2* about ten miles south of Portsmouth. The various combat reports for 609 Squadron, discussed below, make it quite clear there were two Me 110-109 circles, that about ten miles out being east-south-east of the Isle of Wight and between about 12,000 and 20,000 ft, while the circle only three miles out was directly south of Portsmouth in the south-eastern reaches of the Spithead roadstead, and at about 22,000–27,000 ft.[118]

KG 51 and accompanying fighters initially flew almost directly north for Brighton, being picked up by the Poling RDF station just over ten miles to the west of that seaside town at about 11h45 and tracked for about five minutes maintaining that heading, before turning sharply to the west some fifteen miles off the coast; coastal Observer Corps posts soon began reporting them at long distance as they made for the Isle of Wight.[119] As *Oberst* Fisser's *KG 51* and escorts approached the eastern tip of the Isle of Wight, the Ju 88s swung half to starboard and proceeded up the Solent Estuary and, once over the Spithead roadstead, the bomber formation split: forty-eight Ju 88s of *I* and *III/KG 51* turned north and passed through the gap in the Portsmouth balloon barrage formed by the harbour entrance to attack Portsmouth harbour and naval dockyard; the remaining fifteen Ju 88s of *Stab* and *II/KG 51* turned in the opposite direction to the south, starting to dive towards Ventnor radar station over the middle of the Isle of Wight.[120] At the same time, *KG 51*'s Me 110/Me 109 cover had turned away, forming a massive circle above the Nab to the east of the Isle of Wight.[121] Such a circle is reported in several sources forming above the *KG 51* formation,[122] and equates to the *ZG 2-JG 2* circle off the east-south-east of the island, ten miles south of Portsmouth. A second Me 110/109 circle was formed about three miles south of Portsmouth and thus close above the *KG 51* bombers as they split over Spithead, but this one comprised *ZG 76-JG 27* and had attained their position by having flown in from the south-west ('western' German force plotted by British radar).

As the RAF fighter squadrons entered the arena, most of *KG 51*'s bombers were just reaching Portsmouth harbour, their colleagues were diving on Ventnor RDF station, and two large Me 110-Me 109 circles were in place, one just south of Portsmouth over Spithead at about 22,000-27,000 ft (*ZG 76 – JG 27*) and the other off the east-south-east of the Isle of Wight at about 12,000-20,000 ft over the Nab (*ZG 2-JG 2*). The time was 12h10 approximately.[123] 266 Squadron, being much closer to the scene of the action above Tangmere, should have been first to arrive, having taken off from there at 11h45, but appear to have been just preceded by 152 Squadron, based much further away, having scrambled from Warmwell to the west at 11h48. Possibly, 266 Squadron was instructed to make for Portsmouth without realising the urgency of getting there fast, they were after all inexperienced and on their first major action of the Battle of Britain. 152 Squadron, if scrambled under urgent instructions may have made for the Isle of Wight at full speed. In the event the two squadrons of Spitfires essentially arrived about the same time.

152 Squadron were vectored to St Catherine's Point on the southern coast of the Isle of Wight and on arriving there at 15,000 ft, observed about twelve Ju 88s 2,000–3,000 ft below them, heading south-eastwards and about to bomb the Ventnor RDF station.[124] F/Lt Thomas, leading the squadron, which already flew into action in pairs, led his men into a steep dive as the Ju 88s went down over Ventnor, and at least two pilots (Thomas himself, Blue 1 and F/O Hogg, Green 1) attacked bombers in their dives, and another fired at one as it pulled up out of its dive (Blue 2, F/Lt Boitel-Gill).[125] Thomas' rapid reaction ensured at least some of the Ju 88s were disturbed as they dive-bombed Ventnor, no doubt putting them off their aim, and of seventy-four bombs dropped, only fifteen were direct hits.[126] 152 Squadron's Spitfires were carrying 400 rounds of ammunition above the norm of 2,400 rounds.[127]

Oberst Dr Fisser had led *KG 51* to a point over the Spithead roadstead directly south of Portsmouth and ordered his *I* and *III Gruppen* northwards through the gap in the balloons and over Portsmouth harbour, while his own formation of twelve Ju 88s from *II/KG 51* made off over the Isle of Wight to attack Ventnor.[128] Fisser himself, being am astute commander, flew a circle, watching his larger formation in a very long line astern snake into the entrance and circle over Portsmouth dockyards.[129] No doubt he kept his *Stabskette* of three Ju 88s together while circling, which explains why 152 Squadron mostly reported meeting twelve bombers initially.[130] Thereafter Fisser led his *Kette* (vic of three) south-westwards over the Isle of Wight, speeding up rapidly as he carried out a shallow dive attack of his own on the radar station.[131] While the Ju 88s pulled up after bombing and climbed all out to the south and over the Channel to get away as ordered by their leader, and were chased by many of 152 Squadron's Spitfires, Fisser himself once again chose to be a conscientious commander, and this time it would cost him his life. Fisser turned away from Ventor, circling to the north, no doubt to see all was going according to plan at Ventnor and Portsmouth, but was attacked by RAF fighters and killed at the controls, with his crew managing a semi-controlled crash-landing at Godshill Park, Isle of Wight, at about 12h25.[132]

Fisser's small formation of fifteen Ju 88s lost another aircraft, of *6th Staffel* which disappeared into the channel with its crew;[133] 152 Squadron claimed two Ju 88s confirmed, another brace unconfirmed, with three probables and five damaged, while Ventnor's anti-aircraft defences claimed two.[134] No doubt there were multiple claims against the same aircraft amongst these, *Oberst* Fisser's machine, for example, being attacked by no fewer than three of 152's Spitfires.[135] This Ventnor raid suffered a loss rate in excess of 13%. As the rest of the squadron dived down on the Ju 88s bombing Ventnor, Black Section of 152 Squadron, P/O Shepley and his number two, P/O Wildblood, noticed fifteen to twenty Me 109s above and bravely turned to engage. Wildblood wisely broke off after a brief combat with the Me 109s, and later made a lone attack on a Ju 88 over Portsmouth, but Shepley was last seen diving towards the sea.[136] The squadron suffered one more loss, F/Lt Withall, who was last seen chasing a Me 109 south across the Channel was also posted missing.[137] The Me 109s concerned in these actions possibly belonged to *III/JG 53* who made two early, confirmed Spitfire claims in the engagements by *9th Staffel* on a free chase over the Isle of Wight.[138]

When *Oberst* Fisser had turned away to the south to attack Ventnor, his other two Ju 88 *Gruppen* were passing through the barrage balloon gap into the airspace above the Portsmouth naval dockyards, including those immediately on the western side of the entrance in the Gosport area, and the more extensive naval docks on the eastern side and further to the north. It would appear from survivors' accounts and from details of Ju 88 losses that *I/KG 51* went for the Gosport-side docks and *III/KG 51* for the more extensive naval dockyard on the eastern side, the *I Gruppe*'s dive-bombing apparently slightly preceding that of their colleagues in *III Gruppe*.[139]

Second Major Raid, Portsmouth, Radar Stations

One Ju 88 of *3/KG 51* reported being attacked by a Spitfire and losing control, all the crew bailing out, three of them wounded (one died later), and landing at Haslar just south-west of Gosport.[140] This might relate to P/O Wildblood's claim of a bomber shot down over Portsmouth and last seen spiralling down almost inverted and smoking.[141] The anti-aircraft fire over Portsmouth was very heavy, involving some eighty guns plus gunfire from naval vessels which included a Royal Navy cruiser, a monitor, an old French battleship and several destroyers from both navies.[142] The gunners at the Portsmouth naval base, land- and ship-based, sent just short of 400 rounds skywards between 12h04 and 12h20, claiming five enemy aircraft shot down,[143] while probably accounting for two.[144] Two *I Gruppe* bombers appear to have fallen to anti-aircraft fire over the harbour.[145] Of course many bombers were hit by shrapnel, and some afterwards further damaged or destroyed by RAF fighters.

The bombing took about fifteen minutes altogether as the various *Staffeln* circled the harbour and city, diving down to make their attacks in *Ketten* of three at a time, before exiting the harbour via the same balloon gap through which they had entered. Casualties on the ground were heavy at ninety-six.[146] The individual Ju 88s dive-bombed from about 12,000 ft, released their bombs at *c.* 4,000 ft; the bomb release button also triggered an automatic pull-out control which took some time, the heavy aircraft only coming out at about 2,300 ft, well below balloon height of some 6,000 ft.[147]

I and *III/KG 51*'s Ju 88s thus circled Portsmouth harbour, diving down one after the other in *Ketten* of three machines onto their targets and then rapidly exiting the target area via the southern gap in the balloon barrage, and climbing frantically for height as they overflew the Solent and the Spithead roadstead. This is where 266 Squadron's Spitfires met them at about 12h10 as they exited the harbour in irregular, small formations which tried to join up as they flew out over the sea, as recorded by P/O W. S. Williams, Green Section leader, in an excerpt from his Combat Report:[148] 'I sighted the enemy over Portsmouth – enemy not in formation until nine e/a were observed in tight formation 10 miles out to sea. Speed of e/a 250 M.P.H. increasing, travelling on southerly course.' The Spitfires engaged from a location a couple of miles south of the harbour mouth, and further to the south-east past Bembridge, Isle of Wight and over the Channel south of Selsey Bill.[149] This emergence of small, disorganised groups of bombers leaving Portsmouth and flying over the Channel would continue for about 15-20 minutes, as the bombing proceeded, *Kette* by *Kette* over the harbour. 266 Squadron was thus the first of several RAF units to intercept and engage *KG 51*'s Ju 88s, at various distances from the shore.

Adlertag

Meeting disorganised and small formations of bombers, S/L Wilkinson leading 266 Squadron ordered the individual sections to each tackle their targets and a spread-out, southward-verging series of small engagements followed.[150] By this time the bombers had regained some height, and average altitude of the interceptions was about 8,000 ft.[151] Wilkinson's own engagement with a bomber had a tragic ending, as detailed in his Combat Report;[152] he himself would only survive for another four days.

> Enemy aircraft sighted 1215 travelling south at 250 m.p.h. No particular markings were observed and the enemy did not manoeuvre. Attacked 2 aircraft from astern unsuccessfully and was driven off each time by other enemy aircraft coming up astern. Attacked third who was alone twice from astern and once from the beam and ran out of ammunition. Enemy aircraft was then losing height in a spiral and the port engine was on fire. One member of the crew tried to jump but caught up in the tail and enemy aircraft hit the sea vertically and a large pool of flame spread across the water.

S/L Wilkinson's men carried extra ammunition, 2,700 rounds in total.[153] The Ju 88s of *KG 51* relied on their speed to escape rather than using any avoiding manoeuvres, as noted above by S/L Wilkinson. 266 Squadron claimed two Ju 88s confirmed, another probable and six damaged, also claiming a Do 17 unconfirmed, an Me 110 unconfirmed, another probably destroyed and three damaged.[154] This was 266 Squadron's first major engagement of the Battle, and as appears from several of the relevant combat reports, the Do 17 and the Me 110 claims most probably included several Ju 88s attacked, though a few Me 110s may have descended from one of the two German fighter circles and become involved in the combats. Two of the Spitfires sustained minor damage, and P/O D. G. Ashton was missing; Ashton's body, headless and badly decomposed, was found at sea seven miles south of the Nab lighthouse early in September 1940.[155] P/O Bowen of 266 Squadron was probably a witness to his demise, according to his combat report:[156] 'I saw a Spitfire catch fire and dive into the sea. I circled round it for three or four minutes but nothing appeared again.' At the end of Bowen's report, where his signature is lacking, a poignant handwritten note gives evidence of another tragedy: 'P/O. Bowen has since been killed. 16/8/40'. P/O Williams was much more fortunate on 12 August; his Spitfire was set on fire by return fire from a Ju 88 but he managed to land safely at Bembridge airport, Isle of Wight, uninjured, but his aircraft burnt out.[157]

Eleven Spitfires of 609 Squadron led by F/Lt Howell flying as Red 1 scrambled from Warmwell at 12h00; the twelfth pilot, P/O Crook (Blue

1, in the rearmost section) had radio trouble and was late joining in the subsequent engagement.[158] Soon after take-off Howell had trouble with his machine and returned to Warmwell by 12h10, where nothing loath, he climbed into another Spitfire and was off again five minutes later; arriving late, he did not have any success in the engagement.[159] When he broke away initially, he assigned leadership of his A Flight to P/O Overton who was flying as Yellow 2 but then moved up to the head of Red Section. Approaching the Isle of Wight from an initial vector towards Swanage and climbing steadily to 17,000 ft, Overton led his five Spitfires towards Bembridge, noting very heavy anti-aircraft fire over Portsmouth and sighting an enormous Me 110 circle about ten miles south-west of Selsey Bill, located off the east coast of the Isle of Wight.[160]

F/Lt McArthur who was leading B Flight behind them, observed three dive-bombers attacking Ventnor which was already on fire, and tried to dive after them with his section but lost them against the ground view.[161] P/O Crook, Blue 1 of the last section, behind McArthur, arriving late still saw anti-aircraft fire over Portsmouth, though he could not find any bombers there anymore.[162] These observed occurrences constrain the time period of 609 Squadron's arrival over the Isle of Wight to the interval 12h05–12h20 when Portsmouth bombing was almost continuous. The three dive bombers seen attacking Ventnor by McArthur could conceivably have been *Oberst* Fisser with his *Kette* of three Ju 88s attacking at the end of that raid.

In the event, P/O Overton led the five Spitfires of A Flight almost straight into the circling Me 110s off the east of the Isle of Wight (the ZG 2-JG 2 circle), and his first attack was made in an anti-clockwise direction, head on against the rotating Me 110s.[163] Seeing no results from this brave start, he climbed away and twice made diving beam attacks from outside the circle, noting the advantage thereby of there being no return fire from them.[164] He followed this up with another head-on venture against the Me 110 circling stream, hitting one of them in the wing, and finally made a full deflection beam attack on a lone, detached Me 110. The beam attack from outside the circle was probably the best tactic against rotating Me 110 formations as already demonstrated repeatedly on the previous day off Portland, as also determined there by his own C/O, S/L Darley; the head-on attacks were much harder to perform but could be effective, but they were not for the average pilot.

This was aptly demonstrated by Overton's number 2, F/O Goodwin; he lost his leader against the sun while distracted by a couple of foreign Spitfires approaching them from astern and then climbed high above the circle and saw it extended from about 20,000 ft down to *c.* 12,000 ft.[165] Goodwin first made a quarter–head on attack on the circling Me 110s, but soon changed this to a beam attack, from outside the circle; he fired at the first one that came into his sights from about 600 yards, then at the next at about 300 yards and by the time the third Me 110 circled round and into his sights he was closing in to point blank range, and observed pieces of aircraft flying about.[166] This was an extension of Darley's attack method from the beam and outside the circle, whereby full deflection shooting was applied to several successive circling Me 110s.

Breaking away, Goodwin noticed a lone *Zerstörer* some 6,000 ft lower down and dived onto it from almost vertically above, opening fire at *c*. 400 and ceasing at about 200 yards range; wisely he kept on in his own dive but was able to see his victim diving vertically down, its fuselage glowing bright red.[167] The third member of Red Section, P/O Staples, attacked some circling Me 110s from below but then turned with their rotation and easily turning his Spitfire inside an Me 110, fired from 250 to 25 yards range and saw it dive away flaming from its nose.[168] Another effective tactic against the circling Messerschmitts was thus applied, but it had the inherent danger of attack from other Me 110s circling behind the one attacked.

The two remaining Spitfires of A Flight, Yellow 1 F/O Dundas and Yellow 3, followed Red Section in line astern, Dundas making two beam attacks and a head-on attack on the circles before waiting outside for a gap in a circle, and when one appeared inserting himself and firing a five-second burst at a *Zerstörer* from astern and leaving both engines smoking copiously, before being driven off by his *kameraden* coming up behind him.[169] Dundas thus demonstrated yet another tactic against the circles, similar to that applied by P/O Staples, but one that carried greater risk than a beam attack from outside. Yellow 3 claimed a Me 109.[170]

F/Lt McArthur (Green 1), leading the five Spitfires of B Flight, 609 Squadron, after losing sight of the last Ventnor attackers climbed and headed for Portsmouth, where the anti-aircraft fire must still have been fierce; about three miles off Portsmouth he found a large circle of Me 110s (ZG 76–JG 27 circle), and climbed up outside of them to 30,000 ft, which was about 3,000 ft above the top of the circling Me 110s.[171] He waited a few minutes for his flight to join him before diving down and using all his ammunition in one long deflection burst at a Me 110 which he claimed damaged.[172] Green 2, P/O Newbery, joined his flight leader at 30,000 ft but then lost sight of him and noted Me 109s circling 2,000 ft higher up, and he positioned himself to attack them but was outmanoeuvred and broke away.[173] After this disappointment he observed small numbers of Ju 88s making for France and dived down on them far below, and attacked one without allowing enough deflection before attacking another with the correct deflection at only 50 yards,

Second Major Raid, Portsmouth, Radar Stations

but could not hold the turn and only claimed it damaged.[174] P/O Miller, the third member of Green Section was flying an older Spitfire and could not climb with his two wingmen, but getting himself above the topmost Me 110s dived down and made a beam attack on one which he considered shot down; after climbing again and coming down to make a second attack on some circling Me 110s, he was forced to break away by two Me 109s[175] which had come down to help their more clumsy twin-engined counterparts.

By this time the combat had moved some fifteen to twenty miles offshore. The two remaining members of Blue Section had followed Green Section in their climb and went for the circling *Zerstörer* beneath them; P/O Agazarian (Blue 2) had a fight with a lone Me 110 and hit it well and truly.[176] Climbing once more he spotted two Spitfires and approaching them found them to be Me 109s, but their aircraft recognition was no better than his own, and they obligingly turned right in front of his gunsight and he gave them both the works; he claimed the earlier Me 110 and both Me 109s as having been shot down.[177]

The final member of B Flight, P/O Crook (Blue 1) who was delayed taking off with radio trouble, arrived late over the Isle of Wight area, spotted anti-aircraft fire over Portsmouth before sighting three layers of Me 110s in a large set of circles between 22,000 and 26,000 ft just south of Portsmouth.[178] Diving steeply down he made a beam attack on his selected victim, closing right in and just avoiding a collision, and then dived away again before pulling out, to see a flaming Messerschmitt going straight down within 200 yards of himself; he claimed this as his victim and destroyed.[179]

Altogether 609 Squadron claimed six Me 110s, with another two probables and three damaged, three Me 109s shot down and a Ju 88 damaged.[180] Three of their Spitfires were damaged but all got back to base, their pilots unhurt: P/Os Goodwin's and Agazarian's machines were hit by German fighters, while F/O Newbery's Spitfire had badly strained wings following his vertical dive onto a Ju 88 over the Channel.[181] While 609 had no doubt contributed to a lack of response by the high cover Me 110s and their uppermost Me 109 guardians against the RAF squadrons (152 and 266 Squadrons as described above) busy dispatching their Ju 88 comrades below, there also appears to have been some reluctance on the part of the German fighters themselves to come down.[182] This is understandable as the fighter circles were supposed to be maintained to draw in RAF fighters while the bombers did their work, and also to act as a shield for the retreating bombers on their way home with vengeful British fighters in hot pursuit. With the two fighter circles, a higher one just south of Portsmouth (ZG 76 and JG 27, 22,000–27,000 ft versus B Flight of 609 Squadron) and the other off the eastern end of the Isle of Wight at a lower altitude (ZG 2 – JG 2, 12,000–20,000 ft versus A Flight of 609 Squadron), there was thus a double application of the fighter circle dogma. 609 Squadron had attacked each one with a separate flight, and it was the small size of the RAF intercepting formations of a flight or squadron in strength which discouraged the *Luftwaffe* fighters from coming down and interceding on behalf of the Ju 88s. With the much wider Channel off the Isle of Wight, fighter fuel reserves were very limited and once the fighters came down, their protective cover role was over and after a brief engagement they would have to depart for France once more.

S/L Hill Harkness led the twelve Hurricanes of 257 Squadron who had been patrolling over Tangmere towards Portsmouth at about 11,000 ft, while large numbers of *KG 51*'s Ju 88s were still exiting the harbour mouth and making off southwards, with Me 110 fighters still above them over the Spithead area. Harkness recorded his engagement during which he claimed a probable Do 17, in his combat report.[183]

> After being vectored south of Tangmere at about 11,000 feet at 12h30, as I was leading the squadron towards Spithead, we saw about 500 enemy aircraft. I encountered several He 111's in line astern and made a quarter attack on the last one with no noticeable result. I then came across one Dornier 17 flying south. After two Hurricanes in front of me had made a head-on attack, I also gave a three-second burst attack from head-on. Breaking away and turning, I lost the e/a. I then encountered a Do. 17 turning in front of me. I gave it a three-second burst and saw it spiral-turn downwards with another Hurricane on its tail. I consider that I probably destroyed this aeroplane. I then noticed three Me 110's diving towards me and I did a quick steep turn, seeing cannon and machine gun fire pass by me. By this time I had got well out to sea. On attempting to re-form with my squadron, I found that the sky had cleared of enemy aircraft. (For He 111 read Ju 88, and for Do 17, read Me 110)

The squadron soon broke up into sections and even individual Hurricanes, which tackled either small groups of retreating Ju 88s or engaged their top cover of Me 110s. As the combat began over Spithead and as one of the 257 Squadron pilots broke off an engagement with a damaged Ju 88 diving away as he found himself too close to the Portsmouth balloon barrage,[184] it can be surmised that 257, in addition to intercepting fleeing bombers exiting the harbour, engaged the Me 110 circle just south of Portsmouth (*ZG 76-JG 27*), rather than that further south, to the east of the Isle of Wight. Sgt Hulbert, Green 3 in the squadron leader's section observed a dozen Me 110s flying over him about 3,000 ft higher and attacked a straggler, leaving its starboard engine pouring smoke.[185] F/Lt Beresford, leading Red Section behind S/L Harkness's section, first saw the enemy when he was seven miles east of Portsmouth, observing a lot of Ju 88s circling round at about 14,000 ft (presumably over Portland harbour); he then noted about sixty Me 110s above and climbed to engage them, but on the way up saw two Me 110s approaching him and gave one a short burst from head on.[186] About five Me 110s then broke away into the sun from the large formation above and dived onto his tail but he turned sharply and got behind one of them, firing as it dived away and expending his ammunition, claiming a probable victory.[187]

P/O Gundry, Red 2, had his Hurricane hit by two bullets when the Me 110s attacked, but easily outmanoeuvred them and gave one two deflection bursts and saw it dive away; following this, a Me 109 made a wild dive at and past him, firing away but missed him completely.[188] The third member of Red Section, Sgt Girdwood hit a *Zerstörer* in a head-on combat, but then turned too sharply and spun down.[189] Presumably, the two head-on attacks on Me 110s carried out by Red Section were those reported by S/L Harkness in his combat report, above.

P/O the Hon. David Coke led Yellow Section in to attack a vic of Ju 88s with a fourth in the box behind, which was the target; he damaged it before being hit in the hand and having his Hurricane damaged by return fire, and he broke off and landed at Thorney Island, being hospitalised; Yellow 2 P/O Cochrane followed him in and silenced the rear gunner and saw the bomber half roll and dive away pouring smoke. Yellow 3, P/O Chomley, was missing from this engagement.[190] Blue Section was about a mile behind the rest of the squadron on their being vectored towards the enemy, and saw the Me 110 formation above just outside Portsmouth and dived on a single aircraft going south, which Blue 1 pulled away from at the last minute, thinking it was a British Blenheim and Blue 3 gave it some ineffective fire.[191] Blue 2, P/O Capon, became separated from his two wingmen and attacked a lone Ju 88 from astern, silencing the rear gunner, setting the port engine on fire and having his own aircraft covered in his enemy's oil. He did not follow, wisely, when it dived away and was satisfied to claim a probable.[192] Prior to this, Capon had spotted some Spitfires attacking outgoing Ju 88s over Spithead,[193] which may have been from 266 Squadron. In the 257 Squadron engagement off Portsmouth, P/Os Coke and Cochrane each claimed damaged bombers (but attacked the same aircraft) in addition to Capon's probable, while S/L Harkness and F/Lt Beresford each claimed a Me 110 probable;[194] perhaps the latter two claims involved the same aircraft.

Adlertag

257 Squadron was an unhappy unit in the Battle of Britain; much of this revolved around the change in leadership on 22 July 1940, when S/L Hill Harkness, a supernumerary since 6 July, took over from his predecessor.[195] Harkness was born in Belfast on 28 March 1911 and was thus already old for a fighter pilot at 29, during the Battle of Britain; he had joined the RAF in December 1930, and served for seven years before joining the Reserve of Air Force Officers, and was recalled to the colours in October 1939.[196] His personality, leadership style and even his personal courage have been harshly treated in several publications.[197] Apart from replacing a popular leader, his Catholic Irish background probably did him little good, the refusal of the Irish Republic to aid Great Britain in the war probably also affected his role in the Squadron. His most outspoken critics were firstly the Squadron intelligence officer, P/O Geoffrey Myers, whose diaries formed the basis of much of the criticism levelled in print,[198] and supposedly the senior flight commander, F/Lt Beresford, a brave man who conquered his own fears (as did most Battle of Britain pilots) every mission, and was killed on 7 September 1940.[199]

Beresford's apparent attitudes and actions are all second-hand as reported by Myers, and certainly on 12 August 1940 Beresford led his section up close behind that of his squadron leader to attack a mass of Me 110s above them.[200] Myers' diaries are actually a set of letters written for his wife and two children, at the time trapped in occupied France, and were not ever sent nor meant to be either; they are not chronologically ordered and were begun on 8 September 1940, the day after Beresford was killed.[201] Trying to resolve the truth about S/L Harkness and the loyalty of F/Lt Beresford here will be attempted only by accessing official records. Amongst many other criticisms levelled at Harkness is that he avoided operations, and didn't even fly boring convoy patrols.[202] This is patently untrue, as revealed by 257 Squadron's own records: between 8 August and 11 September 1940, he flew twenty-five operational sorties, including at least three convoy patrols, and saw action five times.[203] He is criticised for following controllers' instructions to the letter,[204] surely a rather unfair comment as many other leaders did, too, and if there had been a general neglect to do so, the 'Dowding System' would not have worked very well. On 3 and 7 September 1940, he led head-on attacks on German bomber formations – but enjoyed little support from his squadron in following him in on these.[205] Harkness leading his squadron into head-on attacks on bomber formations must be seen as the act of a courageous man.[206]

P/O the Hon. David Coke's report of the 12 August engagement[207] is an example of a possibly deliberately biased account of Harkness's

Second Major Raid, Portsmouth, Radar Stations

leadership. He had been leading Yellow Section of 257 Squadron behind S/L Harkness' Green Section, flying above and to the left; an excerpt will suffice to illustrate this assertion:

> ...I heard Alert Leader (Harkness) ordered to climb to 17,000 feet and he started a climbing turn to the left – Yellow Section well on the inside of the turn, I could not maintain position so completed a much steeper turn. I momentarily lost sight of Alert Leader, but on completing the turn I found slightly below and behind Section, which I think was Blue Section. When heading South again at 15,000 feet, I saw bandits above us, I warned Alert Leader by R/T, but he still continued climbing to the left away from them. I then told Alert Leader that Yellow Section would show him the direction, and try to intercept. The nearest bandits were 5 Ju. 88's in vic. I put Yellow Section into line astern and intended to get above and to the south of them, and do quarter attacks from out of the sun. I found however, that even with full throttle and the plug pulled I had not enough margin of speed, and the attack developed into an astern chase on the right hand bandit which was lagging behind.

There is an element of contempt in this report – that a section leader will show his squadron leader where the enemy are and will intercept them. Harkness was climbing up towards the Me 110s, presumably as instructed by the controller, and these were the very enemy aircraft which Coke was apparently trying to draw to his attention. By climbing for altitude away from the Me 110s above initially was wise tactics (avoiding climbing up directly beneath them) by Harkness and not an attempt to avoid engaging them. In the end, P/O Coke did not himself climb to attack this reported enemy but went for a small formation of outgoing Ju 88s close by, possibly a less dangerous enemy to tackle, even though he was to be wounded by their return fire. The opinions expressed here are not intended to take sides in a sad debate but do serve to support a more balanced appreciation of S/L Harkness's actions in combat.

Ten Hurricanes of 145 Squadron led by F/Lt Dutton scrambled from Westhampnett at 12h10 and engaged many Ju 88s and Me 110s about five minutes later.[208] Dutton was leading Red Section and was ordered to patrol Selsey-Bembridge at 18,000 ft, and on taking off immediately noticed anti-aircraft fire over Portsmouth, and put his flight into line astern and climbed to attack; the Ju 88s were not in any order and were making east from Portsmouth towards Tangmere and were then observed to turn south over the Channel just north of Selsey Bill.[209] Dutton led his men in at c. 7,000 ft, about six miles south of Selsey Bill, into the starboard flank of a large gaggle of Ju 88s, as Spitfires attacked their rear; he fired a long burst from astern and below and saw the bomber slow down, with smoke coming from both engines and break away downwards.[210] He was himself hit and broke away for home but his number two saw the Ju 88 dive vertically into the sea.[211]

Red 2 attacked another, lone Ju 88 at only 1,700 feet, which had probably been damaged already by anti-aircraft fire as it was flying slowly and giving off some smoke; F/O Urbanowicz made a beam attack and saw it dive vertically into the sea also.[212] Urbanowicz also noted that his victim had appeared to attack a small coaster before its demise, and it can be postulated that having been already damaged over Portsmouth, it was unable to unload all or some of its bombload there; Dutton also noted some bombs being jettisoned by several Ju 88s.[213] Red 3, like F/Lt Dutton his section leader, saw a Spitfire firing at an isolated Ju 88 and then break for home, the bomber appearing undamaged except for silent rear gunners; P/O Parrott then chased it out over the Channel at about 3,000 ft and it finally went into the drink about fifteen to twenty miles south of Selsey Bill.[214] He observed two survivors from the bomber and on the way back saw a British pilot parachute into the sea about a mile east of the Nab lighthouse and managed to guide a minesweeper to him and was gratified to see him picked up. It is likely that the Spitfires seen by both Dutton and Parrott were from 266 Squadron. No RAF pilot was rescued from the sea in this large engagement but nine were posted missing; it is just possible that Parrott saw one of them land in the sea, and when the minesweeper picked him up only to find he was dead, the crew consigned him to the waves once more.

F/Lt Boyd led the four Hurricanes of B Flight, 145 Squadron behind Dutton's flight, and just off Selsey Bill observed the many outgoing Ju 88s, as had the others, but also noted about sixty Me 110s above them and climbed to attack them.[215] This certainly helped his colleagues in A Flight by distracting the Me 110s and was a brave step to take with only four Hurricanes. While still climbing, Boyd was attacked from the beam by what he thought was a Spitfire and his engine set on fire, forcing an immediate return to base, which was fortunately close by, where the engine burnt out; he was able to see the rest of his flight attack the Me 110s and one of them, F/Lt Pankratz did not return, and he also observed an enemy machine hit the sea four miles south-west of Selsey Bill.[216]

Blue 4 in Boyd's section, P/O Storrar, had followed him up in his climb into the Me 110s reaching some 26,000 ft before two Me 110s peeled off the circle and came down onto his tail; he had no trouble turning tightly inside his one opponent and gave him a burst which he thought went into the top of the cockpit, following which the *Zerstörer* plunged seawards.[217] His attention was then taken up by several more Me 110s before he could observe a green dye patch in the sea below; this and F/Lt Boyd's report of seeing an enemy fall in the sea a few miles off Selsey Bill led Storrar to claim a probable victory, which the squadron recorded as an unconfirmed Me 110.[218] The engagement of Blue Section with an Me 110 circle is thought to have been against that of *ZG 76-JG 27*, due to the location of the action just south of Selsey Bill and thus close to Portsmouth, and due to the height reported by P/O Storrar of 26,000 ft (and downwards). The alternative, the *ZG 2- JG 2* circle off Bembridge, was both further south and at lower altitude, *c.* 20,000 ft and below as reported by others. This circle is postulated to have been engaged by F/O Rowley's section at about 6,000–7,000 ft some twenty to thirty miles south of St Catherine's Point, Isle of Wight; these German fighters were was also seen to be moving southwards while still circling.

F/O Rowley, leading Yellow Section of 145 Squadron behind F/Lt Dutton of A Flight was the only member of his section to return, and recorded the following combat report.[219]

> As 'yellow one' I took off with my Section to patrol Selsey-Bembridge. A flight led by Red one. Soon after take off I saw a number of Ju 88's which proceeded South over Selsey Bill on sighting us. I ordered my Section into line astern and climbed towards the Enemy. I saw Messerschmitts circling high above me moving at the same time in a Southerly direction. Some 20-30 miles South of the I.O.W. I climbed and saw a Dornier 17 approaching me. I attacked it & broke away to see both engines flaming & was immediately attacked by 3 Me 109. During the fight I observed the rest of my Section also engaged by Messerschmitts. After one minute's fight the Messerschmitts broke away in a Southerly direction. Noticing that my oil pressure gauge was reading 'zero' I returned to base. (I.O.W. = Isle of Wight; for Dornier 17, read Me 110)

He claimed a 'Do 17' probable. His two wingmen, P/O Harrison and Sgt Kwiecinski, were posted missing south of the Isle of Wight at about 12h30.[220]

There is a German account which possibly matches this combat.[221] In his combat report, *Hpt* Mayer leader of *1/JG 53* who was flying a free chase over the Isle of Wight area at about 28,000 ft describes noticing three aircraft at fairly low altitude, and when he dived down saw three Hurricanes who were attacking a damaged Me 110. He saw it catch fire on its starboard side and the pilot bail out into the sea.[222] While Mayer claimed the one Hurricane wingman as having dived vertically into the sea, his number two *Uffz* Rűhl shot down the other wingman, and the British section leader

Adlertag

then fought back, damaging Mayer's Me 109 before the *Staffelkapitän* shot down this Hurricane, too.[223] These three claims against a section of Hurricanes, at 12h20–12h25,[224] have been related to the three missing pilots of 145 Squadron (F/Lt Pankratz, P/O Harrison and Sgt Kwiecinski);[225] however, Pankratz was in Blue Section of B Flight, the other two being members of F/O Rowley's Yellow Section of A Flight, 145 Squadron.[226]

Rowley in his combat report above does detail a brief engagement with three Me 109s which also involved his two wingmen, and then as the brief fight broke up he found he had an oil problem and returned home. Mayer observed his second victim turning back for the coast, smoking increasingly heavily and diving at a shallow angle towards the sea, before hitting the water.[227] If F/O Rowley's Hurricane had almost no oil left, then his engine would indeed smoke, and he did turn back for the coast, as observed by Hpt Mayer; but he did not crash into the sea, but such errors of observation were relatively common on both sides with low level combats above the water. In this regard it may be significant that Mayer's second claim, presumably against Rowley, was only accredited as a probable.[228] Some damage at least must have been suffered by Rowley's aircraft's engine, if it lost most of its oil in combat.

Uffz Koppenschläger was part of the high cover *Schwarm* of 1/JG 53, and saw a lone Spitfire behind the rest of his *Staffel* and pounced on it, shooting it down from a height of only forty metres above the sea after a short combat; despite him having no witness to his claim, it was confirmed by his *Geschwader*, based on the support of his *Gruppenführer* and *Kommodore*,[229] an exceptional practice within the strict *Luftwaffe* victory accreditation system.[230] In the German victory list, it is, however, shown as a Hurricane and only as a probable;[231] perhaps this may have been one of the two lost Hurricanes from 145 Squadron's Yellow Section, given its final *coup de grace* just above the waves?

Gruppenkommandeur Hpt Harder of III/JG 53 reported two victories near the Isle of Wight over the R/T (radio), also at 12h20 and 12h25, the same times as Mayer's above, but Harder's were rejected by the *Luftwaffe* claims system as lacking witnesses; he was last seen at 12h35 at a height of 6,000–7,000 m and was posted missing from this operation.[232] Overall in this engagement off Portsmouth and further south, 145 Squadron claimed one Ju 88 confirmed and another two unconfirmed, 1 Me 110 unconfirmed and one Dornier 17 probably destroyed.[233]

At 12h15, seven Hurricanes of A Flight, 43 Squadron, led by P/O Carey, lifted off from Tangmere and were vectored to Selsey Bill at 15,000 ft; Carey noticed a large Me 110 circle at 20,000 ft in action with another squadron (609 Squadron versus ZG 2-JG 2 circle?), and led his four Hurricanes of Red Section to attack a lone Ju 88 below, one among

Second Major Raid, Portsmouth, Radar Stations

several isolated enemy machines seen leaving Portsmouth.[234] Carey made four astern attacks using up to 20° of deflection, silencing the ventral rear gunner and causing both engines to give off a lot of black smoke as the Ju 88 lost height quite fast. Then he lost sight of it while watching out for any escorts, but Red 4 observed it flying at sea level, making a beeline for France with both engines smoking heavily.[235] Red 2 and 3 had got lost and took no part in the engagement.[236]

Frank Carey, an experienced and very successful NCO pilot, had only recently been commissioned but was already an accomplished leader, keeping an eye out for escorts and directing Yellow Section (3 Hurricanes) to attack the enemy they had sighted. Yellow 1, P/O Woods-Scawen, had also seen the Me 110 circle but led his men against a trio of bombers which, though identified as Heinkels, were almost certainly Ju 88s of *KG 51*. His combat report[237] provides a fascinating account of innovative German bomber tactics of mutual protection, and he, like many other RAF pilots chasing the Ju 88s that day, noted their high speed with this barely being compensated for by using his Hurricane's boost cut-out switch.

> I was Yellow 1 and on sighting 3 Heinkels leaving Portsmouth at 15000' I ordered my section to give chase. We were at the same height. E/A flew SSE in vic formation 2 spans apart. They maintained their formation very well indeed. I gave 3 deflection bursts and 3 from astern. On my deflection attacks I approached so that 1 e/a would shield me from the fire of the other two, but the other two e/a would promptly alter heights, one, I think the middle, going up and the other dropping so that their concentration of fire was unaffected. My other 3 bursts were from astern, one being slightly below. Fire of e/a was accurate and section attacked simultaneously but in no fixed order because section had become rather strung out in the chase, our overtaking speed with plug pulled being small. I fired twice at No 2 (beam attacks) but concentrated on their leader. On my last attack on him I encountered no return fire but No 3 fired at me throughout. One bullet passed through my engine and another through my oil tank. This caused me to break off the engagement and return. My a/c was hit 6 times in all and will be u/s for some time. (plug pulled = Merlin engine at emergency power; u/s = unserviceable)

P/O Carey claimed a Ju 88 probable and Yellow Section, three damaged He 111s, in reality damaged Ju 88s, in engagements out over the Channel, south to south-east of Selsey Bill.[238] All three machines of Yellow Section were damaged, two only superficially, but Woods-Scawen's aircraft more seriously.[239]

Adlertag

Twelve Hurricanes of 213 Squadron led by F/Lt Sing of A Flight had taken off from Exeter at 12h00, and with a flying time of about twenty five minutes to reach the Isle of Wight were the last unit to arrive over the scene of action; P/O Cottam of B Flight was a bit late getting off, and S/L McGregor only managed to get away about ten minutes behind his squadron.[240] By this time the Ju 88s of *KG 51* had all gone and a large (estimated at 70 aircraft) circle of Me 110s at about 17,000 ft south-south-east of the Isle of Wight was starting to break up and return over the Channel as well. 213 Squadron thus largely made astern to quarter-astern attacks on retreating small groups of Me 110s or single aircraft, and there were no real attempts at tackling the initial large circle and several smaller ones as the retreat across the Channel proceeded.[241] S/L McGregor did not catch up with his squadron but wisely made for mid-Channel south-east of the Isle of Wight where he found a hoped-for straggling Me 110, probably already damaged, and put it into the sea for an unconfirmed destroyed claim.[242] A few Me 109s were still around and engaged some of the Hurricanes.[243] The scattered smaller engagements typifying 213 Squadron's action are exemplified by the combat report[244] of the unit's leader, F/Lt Sing, who also experienced some rather innovative defensive tactics by a group of seven Me 110s he was tackling far out over the Channel.

> Having sighted Enemy Aircraft which were flying in a large circle, I led my section in trying to find a suitable target. I was attacked by what must have been a M.E. 109, and in the "Blacked out" turn I lost my section. When the E.A. were about 20 miles out to sea and at approx. 2,000 ft. 12 of them then broke away and started away for home. I attacked the rear machine and it crashed into the sea. As I climbed away from this attack, I sighted seven M.E. 110's flying south at 200-300 ft. As I attacked the rear machine, the two (other) rear machines turned outwards and round the next two did climbing turns outwards. Two others stayed where they were but seemed to throttle back and the leader turned round sharply to an almost head on position. This manoeuvre left me nearly in the centre of them and I received cross fire from a number of cannons. However as I broke the leader crossed my sights and I managed to get in two short bursts, whereupon he caught fire and dived into the sea. I had then used 180 rounds of ammunition per gun, but as I was low in petrol (eventually landed with 10 gallons) I broke off and returned to base.

Sing claimed two Me 110s destroyed, unconfirmed. F/O Strickland, leading Yellow Section behind Sing's Red Section, was unsure of how

Second Major Raid, Portsmouth, Radar Stations

to tackle a small Me 110 circle but did dispatch an Me 109, claimed as destroyed, unconfirmed (i.e., lacking a witness), as related in his combat report.[245]

> I was leading Yellow Section in formation with the Squadron. I got behind owing to engine trouble and on picking up enemy aircraft found myself to be the only section. There were about 70 aircraft, some went for France and about 15 stayed and went into a circle. I could not get my section in on a reasonable attack so stayed above into sun and waited for my opportunity. I saw a ME109 at sea level, so dived to the attack. I chased him to within 15-20 miles of the French Coast and got in a good burst from 200 yds dead astern. There was a large cloud of smoke and I couldn't see the aircraft; I pulled away to the side and aircraft pulled up to about 800 ft and I gave it a short 2 sec. burst. Pilot bailed out and aircraft went straight in. Pilot appeared to be alright but think he must have drowned as there were no boats in vicinity. As aircraft turned before plunging into the sea I noticed two large guns or cannon (one in each wing) sticking out.

Did Strickland despatch the *Gruppenkommandeur* of *III/JG 53*, *Hpt* Harder? He was lost at about 12h35 off the Isle of Wight.[246] A second loss of a Me 109 from *III/JG 53* did occur, where the pilot was rescued but this aircraft ditched from engine trouble later in the day, and the new *Gruppenkommandeur Hpt* Wilcke was miraculously rescued during the night.[247]

Sgt Bushell of Strickland's section got caught up in a dogfight with some of the Me 110s and set the port engine of one well ablaze before following a second diving down to escape southwards, leaving it just above the waves in a similar condition, about forty miles out from the English coast; he claimed two destroyed, unconfirmed.[248] His own aircraft was damaged in the initial dogfighting but he safely returned to base.[249] P/O Atkinson leading B Flight was involved in attacking the initial large circle before it broke up, managing to knock two Me 110s out of it, one hitting the sea on fire, the other diving out of control and burning also, both claimed as conclusive victories.[250] F/Sgt Grayson, Green 1 in B Flight knocked an Me 110 out of the initial dogfight about ten miles south-south-east of the Isle of Wight, again claiming a conclusive victory,[251] but as for Atkinson, unwitnessed. P/O Cottam of B Flight arrived behind the others and performed quarter astern attacks on three Me 110s before hitting a fourth which he left shedding pieces, smoking and beginning to spin; another conclusive but unconfirmed victory claim. He had to break away as he was himself attacked and his Hurricane slightly damaged.[252]

213 Squadron claimed one confirmed and nine probable (unconfirmed) Me 110s according to the Fighter Command Aircraft Combats records for 12 August 1940;[253] tallying the claims from the individual combat reports discussed above gives nine Me 110s and one Me 109, the vast majority being unwitnessed. In addition to Sgt Bushell's damaged Hurricane, the squadron lost two pilots, Sgts Stuckey and Wilkes of B Flight, one from each section, Blue and Green; both appear to have gone down in the initial dogfight south-south-east of the Isle.[254] It is thought that 213 Squadron's engagements were against the Me 110-Me 109 circle of *ZG 2* and *JG 2*, which had originally been located east of the Isle of Wight and as the German raid exited the Portsmouth area would have retreated south-east of the Isle towards their bases, situated in the Le Havre area and further east, mainly around Paris.[255]

Assessing overall RAF claims for this massive raid and its many engagements is difficult, bearing in mind some squadrons discriminated between confirmed and unconfirmed enemies destroyed, probables and damaged, while others merely had claims reflecting shot down enemies, those probably destroyed and those damaged. There were claims against Ju 88s comprising five confirmed, four unconfirmed, six probables and sixteen damaged. Some pilots describe actions and claims against either Do 17s or Me 110s that may have, in fact, also been against Ju 88s. Obviously, this aspect also impacts claims against Me 110s, discussed below. However, the British claims against the Ju 88s of *KG 51* are not that far off the losses suffered: ten Ju 88s were lost and three damaged;[256] the claims for bombers destroyed, confirmed or unconfirmed thus appear at first glance as reasonable. However, cognisance must be taken that at least two Ju 88s likely were shot down by anti-aircraft fire over Portsmouth, and several others were likely to have been damaged by that fire before being tackled by fighters. Of course, there would inevitably have been cases of multiple fighter attacks on the same aircraft and some of those Ju 88s claimed as damaged may have been finished off by other pilots, who then claimed a destroyed bomber.

Major claimants against the *KG 51* Ju 88s were 152, 266 and 145 Squadrons. It is basically impossible to assign specific Ju 88 losses to particular claims; 152 Squadron were likely responsible for the two bombers lost from the Ventnor attack (from *Stab* and 6/*KG 51*), but anti-aircraft fire from the radar station may also have played a role. Of far greater import to the Germans was the scale of their bomber losses: ten out of sixty-three dispatched represents an almost 16% loss rate, which was horrifically high; crew losses amounted to thirty-three dead and missing, seven POWs and two wounded, and the fatalities included the

Geschwader Kommodore, Oberst Dr Fisser.[257] The effect on unit morale of forty empty chairs around the mess tables must have been significant.

British claims against the Me 110s were excessive, at six confirmed and eleven unconfirmed destroyed, plus five probables and six damaged; there were also one unconfirmed and one probable claim against Do 17s which were likely to have been against Me 110s, but may have been misidentified Ju 88s. German losses to be equated with these claims amounted to: five Me 110s destroyed and five damaged; nine out of ten crewmen in the five shot down were lost (including the *Gruppenkommandeur* of I/ZG 2 and the *Staffelkapitän* of 8/ZG 76) with only one rescued by the Germans, and two were wounded in the damaged machines.[258] No doubt there had been multiple claims on the same Messerschmitts.

The ZG 76 circle close to Portsmouth had been attacked by B Flight of 609 Squadron, some of 257 Squadron, and by B Flight of 145 Squadron, while the ZG 2 circle off Bembridge was attacked by A Flight of 609 Squadron, Yellow Section of A Flight of 145 Squadron, and by 213 Squadron. ZG 2 had seen much more combat and suffered proportionately, four Me 110s lost and four damaged, with ZG 76 only losing one machine and having another damaged. The losses to ZG 2, coming after the very heavy losses of the previous day, must have been a grievous blow to that *Geschwader*. Three Me 109s were claimed destroyed by 609 Squadron, one from the ZG2–JG 2 circle and a brace from the ZG 76–JG 27 circle; only JG 2 reported any loss, one Me 109 being damaged in combat and its pilot wounded, who wrote off his aircraft in a crash-landing back in France. The only other Me 109 claim was a relatively late one from 213 Squadron, which, as already suggested, may fit the other Me 109 loss, that of *Hpt* Harder, *Gruppenkommandeur* of III/JG 53 who disappeared off the Isle of Wight at about 12h35, quite late in the proceedings.

RAF losses in all these engagements around Portsmouth and the Isle of Wight were six Hurricanes and five Spitfires destroyed, five Hurricanes damaged as well as three Spitfires; nine pilots were killed or missing and one wounded. Assigning German claims to specific RAF losses is no more viable than the reverse, but some inferences can be drawn. Some of the RAF fighter losses can be ascribed to return fire from the Ju 88s of *KG 51*: two damaged Hurricanes, one each from 43 and 257 Squadrons, the pilot of the latter being wounded, one Spitfire damaged (wings strained in dive) and another burnt-out after action with Ju 88s. As two pilots from 152 Squadron engaged a formation of Me 109s which were not part of a Me 110–Me 109 circle, they were likely part of the large *JG 53* fighter sweep, and the two losses of Spitfires and pilots to 152 Squadron can possibly be laid at the door of *9/JG 53*, who made two early claims against Spitfires. There is also a reasonable case to be made for *1/JG 53* having engaged with Yellow Section of 145 Squadron somewhat later, killing two of its pilots and damaging the third Hurricane.

Two other early German claims, by *JG 27* and against a Spitfire and some ten minutes later against a Hurricane, could perhaps fit the Spitfire and pilot lost from 266 Squadron and the Hurricane and pilot missing from 257 Squadron, both lost in the same general area as the *ZG 76–JG 27* circle and about ten minutes apart. B Flight of 145 Squadron had one Hurricane severely damaged (by a Spitifre according to its pilot, F/Lt Boyd) and another missing with its pilot; the latter may align with a confirmed claim by *5/ZG 76*, as the flight appears to have engaged the *ZG 76–JG 27* circle. 609 Squadron had two Spitfires damaged, one in each of the actions against the two circles, and *9/JG 2* claimed a Spitfire at an appropriate place and time for this suggestion; there were also many unconfirmed claims by Me 110 units in both circles. Finally, 213 Squadron lost two pilots missing and a third Hurricane damaged, most likely engaging the *ZG 2* circle as it broke up and returned southwards; *Hpt* Harder of *Stab III/JG 53*, who may have been killed in action with 213, also claimed two Spitfires over the radio shortly before his own demise. His two claims were unwitnessed and rejected.

The above interpretations of links between RAF fighter losses and German confirmed claims[259] have an added layer of uncertainty when the unconfirmed claims are also considered. *Luftflotte 3* recorded the claims of the various German units before they were evaluated and confirmed, or not, by the German system.[260] It is specifically bomber and Me 110 claims that were not approved for inclusion in the confirmed victory list: three claims for Hurricanes by *KG 51*; one Spitfire by *II/ZG 76*, ten more by *III/ZG 76* and one more Spitfire by *V/LG 1*; *I/ZG 2* claimed ten Spitfires and *II/ZG 2* another three. Although rejected for inclusion amongst the confirmed victory claims by the *Luftwaffe* adjudication system, this does not mean that all of these claims were necessarily invalid; no administrative system, no matter how complex and how strictly administered, can provide unchallengeable veracity.

The German tactics in approaching their target with two major formations east and west was successful as Fighter Command could not determine the targets until the *KG 51* bombers were close enough to Portsmouth and Ventnor to launch their attacks undisturbed, except by anti-aircraft fire, which was especially heavy over Portsmouth naval base. Once the targets became obvious as being located in the Portsmouth-Isle of Wight area, the 11 and 10 Group controllers lost no time in redirecting their already airborne squadrons, getting a squadron (152) to Ventnor fast enough for them to disrupt the final dive-bombing aircraft and to inflict casualties of 13% (helped also by anti-aircraft fire no doubt). While the sky above Portsmouth was a so-called gun area, RAF squadrons were directed into the area of the Nab in time to meet the outgoing Ju 88s of *KG 51*, which were dive-bombing targets at Portsmouth in small numbers of about three bombers at a time, thus providing an almost continuous stream of outgoing Ju 88s. They were met by a series of British fighter squadrons as they arrived one after the other over the fifteen- to twenty-minute time period the bomber stream was departing: 266 Squadron, then 257 and 609 Squadrons, closely followed by 145 and 43 Squadrons; the final squadron, 213 was too late for the bombers but attacked the departing escorts effectively. The two German fighter circles, one just south of Portsmouth and the other off Bembridge, while attracting a fair number of the incoming British fighters approximating to three squadrons or so, made little effort to come down to the aid of their *KG 51* comrades, who were fairly on the way to being slaughtered, suffering an almost 16% loss rate.

The Fighter Command dogma of feeding in separate and multiple small formations, mostly of squadron strength and with some of only flight strength, did not persuade too many German fighter leaders from either Me 110 or Me 109 *Gruppen* making up the two circles to come down and fight. If they had done so, then the protected airspace offered by the circles for retreating bombers would have been lost, and with strained fuel reserves due to the Channel width off the Isle of Wight, they would not have been able to do more than conduct a short dogfight and then retreat across the Channel rather than returning to the circles.

RAF squadron and flight leaders generally made the correct tactical responses to the situation facing them on arrival in the battle area: the rather disorderly retreat of the bombers in small formations negated any application of specific techniques that may have been applied to large and organised bomber formations, and most RAF unit leaders split their men into sections to tackle the disparate bomber gaggles. Under the circumstances, these were entirely the correct tactics to adopt, especially also as the German fighter circles generally retained their height and refrained from mixing in. However, some RAF formation leaders went for the Me 110 circles very aggressively, generally having to climb up to their higher level to engage them, and this particularly applied to the two flights of 609 Squadron led by P/O Overton and F/Lt McArthur. S/L Harkness of 257 Squadron was wise enough to climb for the Me 110s initially while heading away from the circle until at their level, but F/Lt Boyd who led B Flight of 145 Squadron straight up at the circling Me 110s, was himself harshly dealt with and had a colleague killed.

Adlertag

P/O Overton, leading A Flight, 609 Squadron, was lucky enough to meet the lower Me 110 circle at about the same level and charged enthusiastically right into them. While a wide range of different tactics against the circling and thus mutually protecting Me 110s was applied, particularly by 609 Squadron, the beam attack from outside the circles proved itself once again as the most efficient and suitable for average pilots, as opposed to the very difficult and highly dangerous head-on attacks against the rotation of the circling Messerschmitts. The final unit to engage the Me 110s was 213 Squadron led by F/Lt Sing, which, while displaying some uncertainty as to how to tackle the circles, then saw them breaking up as the Me 110s retreated back across the Channel, making things easier for them. The Me 109s which provided the upper part of the German fighter circles tended to display as little support for their heavier and clumsier *Zerstörer* colleagues as they did for the hapless Ju 88 bombers, with only the free chase by *JG 53* being somewhat more aggressive and thus more effective in disrupting British fighter attacks on the twin-engined machines.

While clever German approach tactics in bringing in their raids led to none of the Portsmouth bombers and only a few of those attacking Ventnor being intercepted before bombing, this is no reflection on the tactical abilities of RAF unit leaders, but they were a salient lesson for the Fighter Command and 10 and 11 Group controllers. Portsmouth suffered damage and high casualties at civilian targets but with little damage to the naval base or naval vessels; only the railway terminus serving the harbour was badly hit, though rail traffic to the harbour was not significantly affected.[261]

In contrast, Ventnor RDF station was largely wrecked, mainly by fire as the site lacked water;[262] it was out of action altogether for three days, with makeshift radar reporting being restored on 15 August through use of a mobile electricity generating plant and an operations van following repairs to both transmitting and receiving aerials.[263] But the RAF was very clever, ensuring that the real situation was masked from the Germans who followed up signals from the radar stations attacked, to judge their success against these targets; radar impulses were broadcast from another transmitter, obviously without echoes being received, but the enemy did not know that.[264] In a remarkably short span of time, a new RDF station was constructed nearby at Bembridge on the Isle of Wight by 23 August 1940, close to the transmitting and receiving masts of the original station, thereby plugging the gap in the radar chain.[265]

The German achievements in this large and complex operation were thus limited and not of long duration, and not much to set against the decimation of *KG 51*, which played little further role in the daylight assaults of the Battle, while further demoralising the Me 110 units, particularly *ZG 2*, which had already suffered grievously the previous day.

Fast raid on Manston, c. 12h45–13h00

Despite the earlier attacks on RAF radar stations at Rye, Dover and Dunkirk, enough radar coverage remained available to the Fighter Command controller for eastern Kent and the Pas de Calais, to observe the next raid developing and then coming towards the English coastline.[266] As the Fighter Command and 10 and 11 Group controllers saw through the radar network, battered though it was, by *c.* 12h20 most of the Portsmouth raiders were on their way home back across the Channel, and at precisely this same time they also noted several radar detections over the French coast opposite the Dover Straits.[267] German coordination and timing between aerial activity in the western and eastern Channel areas was thus near-perfect. The new enemy build-up comprised a formation of 20+ off Cap Gris Nez with another of about twice the size behind it, detected at 12h20, and by 12h23 another three smaller formations were detected, one at twelve miles south of Dungeness, a second some distance to the south-west, and the third off the eastern entrance to the Dover Straits.[268]

These various radar detections can be linked to specific *Luftwaffe* units: the 20+ off Cap Gris Nez were *EGr 210* with fourteen Me 110s and a close escort of seven of their own Me 109s;[269] the 40+ behind *EGr 210* were *I/KG 2*'s Dorniers at *Gruppe* strength[270] with an escort of *I/JG 52*;[271] the small formation south-west of Dungeness was from *II/JG 52*. They lost a pilot near Lewes, west of Dungeness, on this operation.[272] The small force south of Dungeness was most likely from *III/JG 3*;[273] the small force off the eastern Dover Straits, was *I/JG 54* which had taken off from Campagne-les-Guines at 12h17,[274] tasked with covering the bombers' exit.[275]

Following their detection, the situation developed rapidly. 11 Group controllers ordered 501 Squadron (nine Hurricanes) up from Hawkinge at 12h23[276] with orders to patrol Dover.[277] 615 Squadron of twelve Hurricanes led by S/L Kayll had been scrambled from Kenley at 12h20 and ordered to proceed to Portsmouth Water, but while on the way were vectored eastwards back up the coast towards a raid coming in over the Beachy Head area,[278] which comprised elements of *II/JG 52*.[279] The formation thought to be from *III/JG 3* and perhaps also including some elements of *II/JG 52* crossed the coast between Rye and Hastings to the east of Beachy Head, did a brief sweep over the coastline and then went back over the Channel without being intercepted.[280] While the unit history of *III/JG 3* also states there was no action on this mission[281] there is a claim in the official *Luftwaffe* list for a probable Hurricane at 12h50;[282] perhaps the pilot had got mixed up in the 615 Squadron–*II/JG 52* engagement.

At 11h35, the three German formations (*EGr 210, I/KG 2* and *I/JG 52, I/JG 54*) identified in the eastern Dover Straits converged with each other and began to fly over the Channel.[283] As a consequence the 11 Group controller at 12h45 ordered 65 Squadron to scramble from Manston, ordered 56 Squadron up on patrol over their forward base of Rochford, and 610 Squadron was scrambled from Biggin Hill to patrol a line from Canterbury to Hawkinge.[284] These moves were all too late, 65 Squadron being caught on the ground at take-off, and the other two units not making contact;[285] the incoming Manston raid and escorts was obviously approaching much faster than expected.

EGr 210 had lifted off from their forward base at Calais Marck soon after midday, joining up with the *KG 2* Dorniers at 11,000 ft on their way to Manston; the fighter bombers flew in front and attacked the airfield first, from an altitude of about 3,000 ft, followed soon after by *I/KG 2* who bombed from a higher level.[286] *EGr 210*'s first bombs detonated at Manston while 65 Squadron was lined up ready to scramble, yet with a single exception the Spitfires all managed to get airborne.[287] Apart from claiming that four of their SC 500 bombs exploded right amongst the Spitfires taking off, *EGr 210* also thought that they had made direct hits on hangars and billets on the airfield with another twelve SC 500 bombs and four 500 lb incendiary bombs; they claimed four Hurricanes and five other aircraft destroyed on the airfield.[288] The Manston Operational Record Book (ORB) recorded about 150 bomb strikes which caused a hundred craters on the airfield, damaged two hangars, heavily damaged one 600 Squadron Blenheim and lightly damaged another, and killed a civilian RAF clerk.[289]

The 600 Squadron ORB recorded ground crew observing two lines of incoming raiders at about 3,000–4,000 ft which then dropped their bombs.[290] This ORB also recorded the ground crews seeing twelve Spitfires (there were actually only eleven, see below) of 65 Squadron in a single large vic, ready to scramble, and the last Spitfire of the port formation having its engine stopped by blast from one of the bombs, the pilot scrambling hastily out and decamping to a safer location.[291] In fact, the relevant pilot's experience was even more dramatic, P/O Hart already being at about 30 ft off the ground when a small bomb exploded beneath his Spitfire, the resultant displacement of air stopping his engine and forcing him to touch down again immediately, miraculously unscathed.[292]

65 Squadron, when operating from grass airfields such as Manston, and very often being led by F/Lt Saunders, B Flight leader who fancied a squadron take-off in formation, would often all start rolling at the same time; they were thus lined up with Saunders' Blue Section (vic of two instead of the normal three) in front, Green Section to his left and slightly behind, Red Section of A Flight (led by F/Lt Olive) similarly disposed to his right, and the final section, Yellow also of A Flight, to the right and slightly behind Red again.[293] With a light breeze blowing across Manston from the west, the squadron had taxied across from the western side of the field to the eastern side and turned into the wind, Saunders checking radio contact with control and informing the squadron that they would scramble in one minute.[294] Before they began to move, the bombs began to fall and explode, F/Lt Olive like most of them observed to their rear the resultant fountains of earth and parts of buildings flying up into the air as Saunders told them to get going, the Spitfires already at full throttle, their pilots desperately trying to get and stay ahead of the destruction behind them.[295]

Olive looked up momentarily, observing German aircraft right above him, bombs descending, but the Spitfires were gaining speed fast and managed to outpace the advance of the bomb explosions behind them; glancing then to his left, Olive saw a line of bomb explosions behind B Flight who were ahead of his flight in their take-off run, and actually catch up and burst among them with the smoke obscuring his view of the Spitfires, before they emerged safely by some miracle, except for one which trailed back out of his view.[296] Looking the other way to see what was happening to his second section, Yellow led by F/O Quill, he saw them just ahead of an advancing wall of dark smoke and dust, before he was finally airborne.[297]

The two lines of attacking aircraft observed by the ground crew of 600 Squadron were also seen by Olive, and fortunately the left-hand line of explosions, which was more advanced, lay behind the more advanced B Flight Spitfires, while those of A Flight, a bit behind their colleagues, were chased by the less advanced right hand-line; by the Grace of God, both flights of Spitfires managed to stay just ahead of the exploding ordinance, except for P/O Hart (Green 2), who got away unharmed.[298] F/Lt Saunders' Blue Section in the lead actually comprised only two Spitfires on this scramble and not a vic of three, as Blue 2 (Sgt Kilner) did not take off due to an oxygen bottle yet being replaced.[299]

Just before he left the ground, F/O Quill saw a Me 110 pull up from its dive through the smoke and dust, and then as he got airborne a Me 109 roared past going very fast while Quill held low to the ground, weaving as he cleared Manston's boundary.[300] F/Lt Olive also saw a couple of

Adlertag

Me 109s go past at high speed, and this plus the smoke and dust partly obscuring the Spitfires saved them from being massacred by the *EGr 210* Me 109s.[301] As 65 Squadron got airborne, the sections went into line astern, F/Lt Saunders in the lead with his flight now only numbering four Spitfires, with Olive moving his section in below and behind B Flight, and Quill taking Yellow Section below his tail in turn.[302] F/Lt Gordon Olive observed the bombers, now far ahead, wheel around and turn back to the east.[303] F/O Quill and P/O Finucane (Green 3) together opened fire on a Me 109 which popped out of the cloud in front of them, but it was too far away; pulling his emergency boost which caused black smoke to pour out of his exhausts, Quill, still accompanied by Finucane, kept after the 109 but it got into cloud and disappeared.[304] P/O Gregory (Blue 3) chased a Me 109 far out to sea and claimed it damaged while P/O Finucane briefly shot at another in the clouds and thought he had hit and damaged it also.[305] P/O Smart (Green 1) also engaged a Me 109 in cloud, claiming it damaged.[306]

While these scattered actions had been taking place at about 6,000 ft and lower, F/Lt Saunders led some of the Spitfires up to 10,000 ft over Manston where he sighted about a *Gruppe* of bombers at *c.* 12,000 ft (presumably *I/KG 2*); while climbing up to them he noticed fighters some three thousand feet higher up and diverted to attack those.[307] This was a tactic 65 Squadron tended to follow often, seeing it as their duty as a Spitfire squadron to take on fighter escorts, which they did successfully on several occasions in August 1940. In the event, the 'enemy fighters' turned out to be Hurricanes,[308] and must have been those of 501 Squadron. 65 Squadron claimed two Me 109s probably destroyed and another damaged, for no losses, P/O Hart's stalled and force-landed Spitfire being none the worse for wear.[309] They had bravely faced a potentially catastrophic situation, all simultaneously making the immediate decision to take off at full revolutions, and they had survived. The 11 Group controller and his Fighter Command compatriot had scrambled 65 Squadron too late.

501 Squadron of eleven Hurricanes had been sent aloft from Hawkinge at 12h23 already and put on patrol over Dover at 7,000 ft; once the German raiders were on their way, 501 was sent northwards towards Ramsgate but were also too late to stop the bombing.[310] Once again, the controllers appear to have been tardy; perhaps the partially disrupted radar network had upset their normal efficiency. Arriving off Ramsgate, F/Lt Stoney as Red 1 leading the squadron, they were too far away to stop the bombing, and could only watch as about fifteen Me 110s flew west at 6,000 ft to bomb Manston.[311] Stoney led his men round to the north-west and made a perfect interception of the Me 110s

Second Major Raid, Portsmouth, Radar Stations

after bombing as they pulled up from bombing and climbed towards the clouds at 4,000–5,000 ft, while heading south-east back for France.[312] F/O Witorzenc, who like Stoney claimed a damaged Me 110, describes the engagement in his combat report.[313]

> I was No 2. In Red Section when the Squadron was ordered to Patrol Dover at 7000 feet and was vectored North over land to Manston. I sighted E/A when South East of Manston at 4000 feet flying West towards Manston. The Me 110 turned and dropped bombs on the aerodrome and turned South East for Home. I attacked one of them on the South East side of the aerodrome opening fire at 150 yards closing at 100 yards with 2 short bursts from the port side. The E/A emitted white smoke from the Port engine and dived into cloud. I then turned and attacked another to the left from slightly below and gave it two short bursts from 200 yards. This climbed into clouds to join other German machines, I followed them for 15 miles over the Channel before returning to base.

Sgt Lacey, the third member of Red Section, attacked a Me 110 over Ramsgate at about 5,000 ft, giving it all fifteen seconds of his ammunition in one long burst (2,400 rounds) while closing in to within 100 yards; he observed the pilot jump from the Me 110 with his chute and then lost sight of it as he evaded into cloud no longer having any ammunition.[314] He claimed an unconfirmed Me 110; what he saw is uncertain as no Me 110 from *EGr 210* or any other unit went into the Channel on this raid; perhaps the pilot jettisoned the long hood above his position. F/O K. Lukaszewicz flying as Yellow 2 behind Red Section of 501 Squadron went missing in this engagement, which continued well out over the Channel at low altitude.[315] For the squadron's claims of one Me 110 unconfirmed and two damaged, there is one Messerschmitt *Zerstörer* of *EGr 210* which had its starboard engine fail as it landed at forward base at Calais-Marck, where it was written off, the crew being safe.[316] Lt Marx of *3/EGr 210*, the Me 109 *Staffel* of the unit, claimed a Hurricane shot down into the Channel[317] and was probably responsible for Lukaszewicz's demise. *I/JG 52*, escorting the *I/KG 2* Dorniers, did not engage on this mission[318] nor, apparently did *I/JG 54*, who were meant to cover the exit of the raid.[319]

Having been redirected on their way to Portsmouth, 615 Squadron were vectored towards a position off Beachy Head where they ran into small numbers of Me 109s.[320] F/Lt Gaunce led Red Section in a sharp turn to starboard against five Me 109s flying in line astern, while the rest of the squadron turned to port; Gaunce hit the leader who appeared to be afire while in a steep dive beyond the vertical, but then he blacked out before recovering and climbing up once more and blowing a second Me 109 to pieces over the sea.[321] P/O Hugo, Red 3 hit a Me 109 which gave off smoke and vapour and dived steeply for the sea, Hugo claiming it went into the water about fifteen miles south of Hastings, the pilot waving from the water; he landed at Hawkinge where he requested a boat to be sent to collect the pilot.[322] Red 2, Acting P/O McClintock in his very first combat also made a claim, for a damaged Me 109, between Brighton and Beachy Head.[323]

With 615 Squadron claiming two confirmed (Gaunce), one unconfirmed (Hugo) and one damaged (McClintock) Me 109 (for no own losses),[324] and there being only one such aircraft lost by *II/JG 52*, a fairly common conundrum exists, as for many engagements in the Battle, and indeed, the entire war on all fronts. Perhaps all three pilots of Red Section had hit the same aircraft; it is also possible that Hugo's Me 109 actually escaped at very low level over the sea, and the pilot he saw waving from the water might have been from the earlier engagement, sometime after 08h00, between 610 Squadron and *II/JG 52*.

There were ground observers to the loss of the one Me 109 that did indeed get shot down: *Fw* Zaunbrecher who reported being shot down at 19,000 ft (the same approximate height of engagement given by both Gaunce and Hugo), and coming to earth near Lewes, where he was taken prisoner, quite badly wounded.[325] The *Gruppe* reported four victory claims on this day, but all were excluded from the official claims list[326] and thus neither times nor locations are given,[327] so it is not known whether they relate to this mid-day engagement, or to the first and/or last raids of the day in which the *Gruppe* also participated. Zaunbrecher, a member of *5/JG 52*, had his controls shot away and his petrol tank holed by a Spitfire (again the Spitfire 'snobbery') and force-landed at Mays Farm, Selmeston, east of Lewes at about 13h00.[328] The timing of the engagement between 615 Squadron and *II/JG 52*, at 12h45,[329] coincided exactly with the onset of the bombing of Manston, and this obvious decoy mission to attract RAF fighters away was thus perfectly coordinated.

An off-duty policeman observed Zaunbrecher's Me 109 flying north from Beachy Head, its engine off and belly-landing in a freshly cut cornfield relatively intact still; Constable William Laker gave initial first aid for a bullet in the shoulder, and the pilot had also suffered contusions at the back of his head from the rough landing.[330] P/O McClintock, having attacked and damaged his Me 109 much lower down at *c*. 6,000 ft[331] possibly hit an aircraft already crippled at higher altitude by one or both of his comrades.

Second Major Raid, Portsmouth, Radar Stations

While this raid severely damaged Manston, which remained unserviceable till the next day,[332] the aerial combat provided little room for innovative tactics by the RAF unit leaders due to the unexpected speed of the enemy formations. However, F/Lt Stoney brought 501 Squadron through a turn after the retreating Manston Me 110 fighter-bombers, placing them in a perfect position to attack from astern. The German escort fighters and diversion fighters did little to offset the RAF response. Victims were very few in number, Fighter Command losing only F/O Lukaszewicz of 501 Squadron, and the Germans a single Me 109 of *II/JG 52*, pilot a POW, and one Me 110 from *EGr 210* written off in France. With a relatively small incoming main formation adjudged at some sixty aircraft, plus some small diversions, only three RAF squadrons were assigned to counter the incursion. No doubt after the massive Portsmouth-Ventnor raid, the controllers were being cautious in committing too many forces. Even against the very numerous Portsmouth raiders, they had held back one squadron apiece at key bases at Exeter, Middle Wallop and Tangmere.

This was the essence of the Dowding system, based on a scientific network, advance (RDF) warning system, and getting the outnumbered RAF squadrons to the critical intercept locations as soon and as accurately as possible, when the buck passed to the unit leaders of the relevant flights and squadrons. Manston, Fighter Command's most forward and thus exposed base, was very hard to protect against fast raiders like *EGr 210*, and would in time be used as a forward base only on exceptional occasions.

Evening raids on Lympne, Hawkinge and Bekesbourne airfields, *c.* 17h15–18h15

Radar was still working well enough in the late afternoon to pick up four German formations between 16h45 and 17h22, estimated as two formations of approximately fifty aircraft each, another of about thirty and one of twenty-odd.[333] Once the first enemy force was detected, the 11 Group controller began his counter moves, sending up 64 Squadron (nine Spitfires) from Hawkinge, twelve Hurricanes of 32 Squadron from the same forward airfield, and four Hurricanes from 501 Squadron from Gravesend between 16h50 and 17h10; each was to patrol its airfield.[334] Eleven Spitfires of 54 Squadron from Hornchurch and a dozen Hurricanes of 56 Squadron from their forward base of Rochford were soon added, ordered to reinforce the Dover area, while 501 Squadron scrambled twelve Hurricanes from Hawkinge at 17h25.[335] With the exception of

Adlertag

the four 501 Squadron Hurricanes launched from Gravesend, the rest all intercepted the incoming German raids. Operations room track charts for this set of raids indicate that at about 17h33 three *Luftwaffe* formations crossed the coast: two estimated at fifty-plus each crossing in, one near Dover and the other at the North Foreland; a formation estimated to have been smaller crossed the coast further to the west, at New Romney just north of Dungeness.[336]

The raid coming in over North Foreland appeared at first to be making for Manston, already hard-hit in the earlier lunchtime raid, but it actually targeted Bekesbourne aerodrome, a field not used during the Battle and which was obstructed to hinder German gliders or Ju 52 transport machines from landing on it during an invasion attempt.[337] The Germans referred to this target as Canterbury airfield[338] as it lay some five miles south-east of the town.[339] The other larger formation was aimed at Hawkinge about six miles west of Dover, while the third, smaller formation coming in over New Romney went on to attack Lympne airfield, lying some six miles to the north-east. The fact that the Germans bothered to attack Bekesbourne airfield indicates their poor intelligence; even a cursory reconnaissance flight over Bekesbourne would have revealed no aircraft based there and it's being obstructed as well, rendering a full-sized raid unnecessary.

The three raids were carried out by the three *Gruppen* of Dornier 17s of *KG 2*, the most experienced German bombing unit in attacking Great Britain, having spent July 1940 already forming the core of the early *Luftwaffe* missions by *Luftflotte 2*. On this evening, twenty- four Do 17s from *II/KG 2* were led in over North Foreland by an additional trio of Dorniers from the *Geschwader*'s *Stabskette* (Staff flight vic of three aircraft) led by the *Geschwaderkommodore*, *Oberst* Fink,[340] who had enjoyed the title of *Kanalkampfführer* (translates, poorly, as Channel combat leader) during July. Fourteen Do 17s from *III/KG 2* made up the Hawkinge force, with twenty-one from *I/KG 2* aiming at Lympne.[341]

KG 2 was based in the general area Cambrai (*III Gruppe*)–St Léger (*Stab* and *II Gruppe*)–Epinoy (*I Gruppe*),[342] lying some eighty-five miles south-east of Calais; *I/KG 2* would thus have made north-west towards Dungeness, while II and III *Gruppen* would also have flown approximately north-west, passing over the Calais region (where they picked up their Me 109 escorts) thereafter turning more northward to fly off the eastern coast of Kent. To the south-east of Dover *III/KG 2* turned north-west heading for the famous White Cliffs of Dover easily visible from the air, and on towards Hawkinge. They were sighted by 32 Squadron coming in from the south-east while the Hurricanes were near Dover at about 12,000 ft.[343] *II/KG 2* and the *Stabskette* of the *Geschwader* flew further to the north before turning in over the North Foreland towards Manston airfield and their ultimate target at Bekesbourne,[344] lying to the southwest and about eleven miles inland.

The remaining *KG 2 Gruppe, I/KG 2*, having crossed the coast north of Dungeness at New Romney continued on north-eastward to Lympne.[345] The experienced and very professional *Oberst* Fink managed to get all three of his disparate formations across the coast at about the same time. The Bekesbourne raiders exited over the Thames Estuary, crossing the north Kent coast at Herne Bay and passing north of Margate on their way out, while those that had bombed Lympne and Hawkinge turned away towards the coast from their targets, both exiting approximately over the Sandgate area just west of Folkestone. It was precisely in this area that a Me 109 sweep by the highly efficient *III/JG 26* of *Major* Adolf Galland was carried out, claiming several successes for no known losses.[346]

As is hopefully already becoming clear in this narrative, what at first appeared to be a relatively simple set of raids, hitherto given little attention in many accounts, were in fact a much more complex operation with multiple elements, all dependent on good timing and spatial coordination, never mind some very interesting tactical innovations by both German bombers and RAF fighters. One more piece of the jigsaw puzzle was made up by *EGr 210* on yet another operation on this day; by this stage they must have been very tired after two strenuous missions already carried out. The unit history is rather vague on this third mission, merely stating that the *Gruppe* bombed Hawkinge, and that the inferred attack by Ju 88s, as reported in several accounts,[347] was actually by *EGr 210*.[348]

Hawkinge thus suffered two raids in relatively short succession, the first described by one ground witness as high level carpet bombing (obviously by the Dorniers of *III/KG 2*), and the second attack, comprising strafing and bombing by Ju 88s (again mistakenly identified!) from a lower level of about 5,000 ft.[349] In the same account, it is noted that five Hurricanes of 32 Squadron, short on fuel and thus with little choice, managed to land there in between the two raids, by some miracle not running into any craters from the first nor being hit by any of the projectiles from the second!

There were also two raids on Lympne in rapid succession; the first wave of bombers at about 17h35, supposedly Ju 88s (yet again), but actually the Do 17s of *I/KG 2* blasting this airfield from one end to the other, with a second wave of 'Dorniers' dropping smaller bombs.[350] It would thus appear that some *EGr 210* Me 110s also attacked Lympne, being responsible for the second attack there; the Lympne raid apparently had some of its attackers also drop bombs on Hawkinge.[351] This possibly indicated the Lympne Me 110s joining up with their Hawkinge colleagues near that airfield before returning across the Channel. In a history of Hawkinge airfield, a bomber formation is described as having come across the Channel at about 5,000 ft towards Dungeness, and then near Dymchurch split into two separate formations, with the first continuing inland to Lympne and the second flying parallel along the coast further towards the north-east until it reached a point off Sandgate where it proceeded inland to bomb Hawkinge.[352] This resembled the approaches made in the earlier *EGr 210* raid on the radar stations, and the two formations described in the Hawkinge account are inferred here to have been from it. The unit history does not give any aircraft numbers for this third mission of the day, but the number of bombs dropped on Hawkinge by the *Gruppe*[353] suggests twelve aircraft in that formation, thus leaving enough over for an approximately equal small formation to bomb Lympne.

Interestingly, Sandgate was about where *III* and *I/KG 2*'s Dorniers flew over the coast on their way back, and this added complexity in the German plan whereby an outgoing first bombing wave at higher altitude departed the coast about when the second wave at lower altitude (*EGr 210*) was arriving and crossing the coast in the opposite direction was tactically innovative. Such subtlety and potentially confusing routing for Dowding's reporting system carry the hallmarks of *Oberst* Fink, the ex-*Kanalkampfführer*, aided and abetted by *Generalmajor* Theo Osterkamp who had effectively been the *Luftwaffe* fighter coordinator in July 1940.[354] Osterkamp was now the fighter boss (*Jagdfliegerführer*) of *Luftflotte 2*.

Such intricate plans might also have confused the German aircrew involved, never mind some inherent dangers of different formations of bombers and their escorts becoming entangled or even colliding. Ironically, in view of several accounts of Ju 88s having attacked both Hawkinge and Lympne as discussed above, there was indeed a mission flown by the Ju 88s of *II/KG 76*, but on a different target, apparently aimed at the Rye RDF station in a follow-up to the morning raid, where twenty-eight 250 kg high explosive bombs were dropped in the evening.[355] *I/JG 3* flew the direct escort for these Ju 88s, but the unit history records that the bombers turned back due to solid cloud cover; *III/JG 3* appears to have flown either a sweep or the high cover, while *II/JG 3* were assigned to meet the out-coming bomber formation.[356] Despite *JG 3* reporting no action and apparently no bombs being dropped, about twenty high explosive bombs were recorded as having been dropped near Iden, a small village about three miles west of the RDF station.[357]

Second Major Raid, Portsmouth, Radar Stations

Presumably, the weather prevented accurate bombing and probably only seven Ju 88s actually dropped their bombload. The Ju 88s and their various *JG 3* escorts were not intercepted by RAF fighters.

The three Dornier *Gruppen* of *KG 2* each flew in a different formation; possibly *Kommodore* Fink was experimenting to see which formation performed best under combat conditions. Fink himself led *II/KG 2* at 15,000 ft to their target at Bekesbourne airfield, their twenty-seven Dorniers being arranged in three lines each comprising three vics of three bombers (thus nine to a line), the three lines arranged in line astern, with the vics stepped down from the front backwards.[358] No bomber formation could fly with other aircraft immediately behind those in front due to the slipstream of the leading aircraft, and the simplest way to avoid that was to have successive sub-units stacked at different altitudes, albeit not too far apart in order to maintain a close defensive formation. With a stepped-down formation of bomber vics, any attackers coming in from astern and above (a very common approach for fighters) would be met by the massed return fire of the dorsal rear gunners in the bombers. The best tactic for RAF fighters to apply in attacking such a formation from astern or astern-quarter, was to approach from astern and slightly below, thereby only being exposed to the ventral rear gunners of the rearmost vic of bombers. 56 Squadron would do exactly this in their attack on *II/KG 2*, as detailed below.

III/KG 2's fourteen Do 17s who bombed Hawkinge from 12,000 ft, flew in vics of three line astern, but with the vics stepped up from front to rear of the formation.[359] For such a formation to be approached by RAF fighters from astern and below would not be a good idea as they would be exposed to the massed fire of the ventral (bottom of bomber fuselage) rear gunners. An alternative fighter attack on such a formation from astern (or quarter astern) and above was an option, although many dorsal rear gunners in the bomber formation would still be able to target them; a fighter attack from directly astern at the same level as the rear vic of bombers in a stepped-up vic line astern formation would avoid a lot of return fire, but slipstream effects as the fighters got close enough to do real damage would be a problem.

For any stepped vic line astern bomber formation, whether stepped up or down, a head-on attack or one from quarter-ahead would obviate any significant return fire as most German bombers had a single effective machine gun firing forwards from the nose. Extra guns added due to casualties as the Battle proceeded helped the bombers a little, but these *ad hoc* additions never had very solid mountings in the largely glazed noses of the bombers and had to be fired by crew members already preoccupied with existing tasks (piloting, bomb-aiming/

navigating etc.). Frontal attacks were difficult to perform due to the necessity of getting ahead of the bombers at the right distance to turn in and make the head-on attack, and also due to the very high closing speeds (500 mph and more; but which also reduced the chance of being hit by bomber front gunners).

32 Squadron would make a frontal quarter attack on *III/KG 2*'s formation and one pilot made a lone head-on attack on this *Gruppe*, as will be seen below. Head-on attacks had the added advantage of being extremely demoralising for the target bombers and quite often led to break-up or partial break-up of the German formation; this was obviously a highly desirable result as it produced stragglers and damaged aircraft for other fighters to finish off. In head-on attacks on stepped up or down formations, the frontal attack concentrated on the lead bomber vics and this led *Luftwaffe* bomber leaders to fly towards the rear of the formations, their leadership thereby being less effective from a morale-boosting perspective.

With frontal attacks, another difficulty for the RAF fighters was the break-away, mostly downwards; with a stepped-down German formation this was not really possible, so a break-away over the top or to the side was needed. In the same way, breaking away from a frontal attack on a stepped-up formation basically excluded doing this over the top of the bombers. Breaking away to the side just ahead of the leading bombers was another option but demanded perfect timing, otherwise collision dangers multiplied. Sometimes in head-on attacks, RAF fighters did indeed collide with their prey; very good at breaking German bomber crew morale, but the inevitable loss of the fighter pilot was too high a price to pay. Very occasionally, some brave RAF soul would fly right through a German bomber formation, damning the risks of collision and doing excessive damage to bomber crewman morale. One such attack was performed by P/O Hamilton Grice of 32 Squadron against *III/KG 2* on the Hawkinge raid, as detailed below.

The final *KG 2 Gruppe*, *I/KG 2*, which attacked Lympne from 15,000 ft, flew a more complex formation. The twenty-one Dorniers had a leading large vic made up of three sections of three bombers flying in smaller vics followed by two further groups of bombers each comprising two sections (made up of vics of three machines) flying adjacent to each other.[360] None of the participants in this combat recorded whether the vics line astern were stepped up or down. A few pilots of 64 Squadron attempted astern attacks on these bombers but were driven off by very effective return fire from the rear gunners, and one pilot thereafter put in a brief beam attack, as will be described below. The beam attack also demanded good fighter leadership to place the RAF machines correctly

Second Major Raid, Portsmouth, Radar Stations

in time and space to close in to effective range of the bombers as these sped past at about right angles to the path of the fighters.

During this set of late afternoon raids, three German bomber formations were thus intercepted. The RAF controllers did a good job, and all three bomber formations were attacked by the British fighters using different attack methodologies. The damaged radar system retained enough capacity to ensure interceptions of each of the formations close to the coast.[361] However, only three Dorniers were damaged and none shot down. The majority of 11 Group was less experienced in meeting *Gruppen*-sized bomber formations than their 10 Group and Tangmere sector-based colleagues. But they learned fast and on the next day, 13 August, *KG 2* would suffer a stinging set of losses by fighter attack over northern Kent and the Thames Estuary. As the Battle progressed during August and into the middle of September, the RAF squadrons and their leaders would develop an ever-improving expertise in carrying out beam and head-on attacks on the German bomber formations in particular, culminating in a distinct defeat of the bombers on 15 September 1940. That this was achieved by the RAF squadron leadership despite experienced yet exhausted units being transferred out of 11 Group and replaced by relative neophytes, is a remarkable tribute to their tactical abilities and courage. It also reflects very well on 11 Group and Fighter Command leadership, who ensured that the cumulative and growing tactical abilities of the RAF fighters were passed on as new units came in to take the place of the experienced and depleted squadrons.

Each of the three German bomber formations was escorted by a *Gruppe* of Me 109s[362] and there would almost certainly also have been high cover in addition and no doubt some sweeps also. *III/JG 54* flew the escort to *II/KG 2*[363] attacking Bekesbourne airfield, and this *Geschwader*'s *I Gruppe* also flew an operation at the same time,[364] presumably as a high cover.[365] Both *I* and *II/JG 54* made single victory claims so both must have been involved in more remote escort capacities; *III/JG 54* made extensive claims and saw intense action.[366] *I/JG 52* provided the direct escort for *I/KG 2*'s raid on Lympne but made no claims nor suffered any losses;[367] the *II/JG 52* unit history does not say whether this *Gruppe* was also along or not,[368] but they may (fairly logically) have provided the high cover.

II/JG 52 claimed four RAF fighters given as three Spitfires (one only a probable) and a Hurricane in their own records,[369] but none of these claims made it through the *Luftwaffe* claims system to be included in the official victory lists.[370] As neither times nor locations are given for any of them, it is uncertain whether they were made during the earlier (08h10–08h40) raid on Lympne, or the evening one. *III/KG 2* were

Adlertag

probably escorted by elements of *JG 26* for their raid on Hawkinge; a unit history[371] describes *III/JG 26* flying a sweep over Dover and this *Gruppe* made claims south-west of Dover and around Folkestone[372] consistent with being involved in covering (remotely) the Hawkinge raid. It is probable that the direct escort for *III/KG 2* would have been one of the other two *Gruppen* of *JG 26*; one *Geschwader* history does in fact link *I/JG 26* as escort to a raid on Manston but also appears to confuse the lunchtime Manston raid with the evening raids, when there was no attack on Manston, Bekesbourne airfield being bombed, not far away from Manston.[373] There are no further *JG 26* claims for the evening raids apart from those already mentioned for *III/JG 26*.

While Oberst Fink's three bomber Gruppen all crossed the south-east English coast at about the same time, the five RAF fighter squadrons being vectored towards them engaged at slightly different times. By examining all available combat reports and the five IPRs of these squadrons, it would appear that 32 Squadron engaged first, versus the Hawkinge raiders of *III/KG 2* over the Channel, with 64 Squadron coming into action very soon afterwards, some against the escorts of *III/KG 2* and some against *I/KG 2* making for Lympne. 501 Squadron joined in only a few minutes later and also had elements involved against both Hawkinge and Lympne raiders, while 54 Squadron had most of their Spitfires engaging elements of one or both of the same two raids, mainly inconclusive action against Me 110s and Me 109s some minutes after 501 Squadron. Another part of 54 Squadron flew towards the Bekesbourne raid of *II/KG 2* but only caught up with them as they made off eastwards north of the North Foreland. 56 Squadron also engaged the Bekesbourne raiders, but a bit earlier than 54 Squadron, having met them as the Dornier *Gruppe* crossed the northern Kent coast at about Herne Bay before turning eastwards for home, where 54 Squadron intercepted them.

32 Squadron's twelve Hurricanes were led aloft from Hawkinge at 17h00 by F/Lt Michael Crossley with orders to patrol their forward base at 10,000 ft; they flew a patrol line between Deal and Dover and when at the Dover end saw the incoming German raid of about a *Gruppe* each of Dornier 17s and Me 109s at *c.* 12,000 ft.[374] Crossley recorded the following combat report on attacking this Dornier formation at about 17h30:[375]

> While patrolling behind Dover at 10,000 feet we sighted a large formation of Do 215's with Me 109's escorting coming from the S.E. towards us. We climbed up and attacked almost head on, and were almost at once mixed up with the Me 109's. I did not see what damage I did to a 215 I was attacking as a Me 109 crossed above me and I fired up at it, from about 100 yards, a burst of about 3 seconds. Yellow 1

Second Major Raid, Portsmouth, Radar Stations

saw a large red flash from it and a stream of black smoke and saw it go down steeply with thick black smoke pouring from it, on fire.

Having sighted the bombers, Crossley as the leader made an essentially instant decision to climb up to them and attack from head on, or as close as he could get to it, making in the end an attack from the starboard frontal quarter of the Dornier formation, and all his sections followed him on this, eight of his pilots reporting they attempted this attack, some getting in brief bursts of fire, others being almost immediately distracted by Me 109s and abandoning the bomber attack.[376] Some of the pilots turned a little towards the bombers as they came in, increasing the deflection angle, and P/O Hamilton Grice led his section specifically against the rearmost vic of three Dorniers. Several of the 32 Squadron pilots clearly state that the Me 109s interfered with their attack on the bombers being pushed home, and in several instances prevented the Hurricanes from opening fire due to the necessity of taking avoiding action from fighter attack. The attack on the bombers was thus a failure and they proceeded towards their target with little hindrance.

Study of the 32 Squadron combat reports suggests that F/Lt Crossley's Red Section and Yellow Section of P/O Hamilton Grice were firing on the bombers and had to break off prematurely to tackle escorting Me 109s that were attacking them; the resulting engagements with the Me 109s appear to have been rather short.[377] The Me 109s largely prevented Blue Section from opening fire on the bombers, while Green Section at the rear of the squadron formation of sections line astern was little troubled by them.[378] The escorting Me 109s were placed above the bombers, as reported by P/O Pniak, last man of Green Section; F/Lt Crossley in the lead of Red Section at the front of the squadron, also reported an attacking Me 109 close above him.[379] This was an unusual placement of the escort but allowed them to interfere rapidly and effectively with 32 Squadron's quarter-frontal attack, which could otherwise have been dangerous for the bombers if the Me 109 escort had been placed behind and above, as was common practice.

32 Squadron claimed a confirmed Me 109 (by F/Lt Crossley) in the initial combats with the escorting Me 109s, two more unconfirmed (P/O Pniak and Sgt Higgins) and a probable (F/O Humpherson); Higgins had pursued his victim to the coast off Manston, quite far to the north-east.[380] 32 Squadron lost a Hurricane in the engagements, most likely due to the initial attack by the escorting Me 109s; P/O Barton bailed out unhurt near Dover, his Hurricane crashing a couple of miles west of Hawkinge.[381]

After these initial engagements, F/Lt Crossley chased two Me 109s out over the Channel, claiming one unconfirmed victory about ten miles south of Dover, while his number two, P/O Proctor, followed an enemy formation heading north from the Dover area, claiming one of several Me 109s as a probable victory, approximately inland from Margate.[382] P/O Gardner, after the initial engagement with the escorting Me 109s, found three more below him over Deal where he claimed one as an unconfirmed victory, adding another near Whitstable on the northern Kent coast not long after, having chased four of them northwards from a location north of Ashford.[383] Altogether in these various engagements, 32 squadron claimed one Me 109 confirmed, five unconfirmed and two probable victories.[384] The diverse locations of the various Me 109 claims made by 32 Squadron illustrate how fast engagements between high speed single-engine fighters could become highly dispersed, confusing subsequent historians.

The three pilots of Yellow Section of 32 Squadron separately engaged the bombers after initial action against the escorting Me 109s. Yellow 2, P/O Smythe, joined six Hurricanes of 501 Squadron circling north-west of Dover and after some time a *Gruppen*-sized Dornier formation passed a couple of thousand feet overhead, making for France.[385] After unsuccessfully trying to get the other Hurricanes to join in, he made a lone attack on one particular bomber which had become separated from the formation by anti-aircraft fire; he set the port engine on fire and saw it side-slipping violently towards the sea before some more Me 109s chased him away.[386] This claim was confirmed by anti-aircraft gunners at Dover who 'saw' an aircraft hit the sea a few miles out over the Channel.[387] There was no such German loss, but one of *III/KG 2*'s Do 17s got home damaged and with a wounded crewman.[388]

The number three man in the section, Sgt Bayley, having divested himself of the initial escorting Me 109 attack, observed the Dornier formation they had attacked first turning back over the coast, still with some escorts present, after their attack on Hawkinge, and some five minutes after saw another raid coming in below him heading in and made a brief beam attack on the last three aircraft, forcing one to break away.[389] This he attacked from astern and below but was driven off by Me 109s and could only claim a damaged.[390] Despite Bayley stating that he had intercepted a bomber formation, it is likely he actually attacked the *EGr 210* Me 110s which followed *III/KG 2* in to bomb Hawkinge. P/O Douglas Hamilton Grice, leader of Yellow Section, 32 Squadron had possibly the most interesting experience of all three of the pilots, as appears from his combat report.[391]

> I led my Section round to attack the rearmost vic of a cloud of approx. 40 Do. 215's before we were able to fire, several Me. 109's appeared and we had to break off the attack and deal with them. In the general

Second Major Raid, Portsmouth, Radar Stations

melee I lost my section and did not find it again. Having dealt with the fighters without the necessity of firing, I chased the bombers and made a head on attack on 18 Do. 215's who were flying in Vics line astern, stepped up. I opened fire at roughly 800 yds and almost immediately the leading Vic broke up, quickly followed by the second and third Vics. Having steamed through the whole formation I broke away downwards to starboard and on looking back, one Do.215 had broken right away from the other a/c and appeared to be gliding to the ground with a suspicion of white smoke coming from it, it was roughly 2000' below the main formation. I was then attacked by a 109 but managed to get rid of it, again without having to fire. As I was then at 3000' I started to climb up again to attack the bombers. At 12000' I found 21 Me. 110 Jaguars which I attacked head on but could not split them up. I landed at Hawkinge to refuel and rearm.

It is likely that Hamilton Grice attacked both the outgoing Do 17 formation of *III/KG 2* and that of *EGr 210*, either the Hawkinge part or the combined outgoing Lympne and Hawkinge raid Me 110 formations. He probably approached both formations on their way out from approximately dead ahead, but his subsequent decision to 'steam' right through the entire Dornier formation was a very brave action. He would also have had to climb while doing so, as it was a stepped-up formation. He possibly damaged one of the bombers and may even have been responsible for separating out the one attacked by P/O Smythe, perhaps in concert with anti-aircraft fire. The effectiveness of the head-on attack method was shown by the leading bomber sections breaking up in short order. Ideally, further RAF fighters should have been in the vicinity to take advantage of this courageous manoeuvre. 32 Squadron claimed one Dornier confirmed (by P/O Smythe) and two damaged (P/O Hamilton Grice and Sgt Bayley) in Yellow Section's engagements.[392]

The 64 Squadron records are confusing regarding this action. Their Form 541 part of the Operations Record Book shows that soon after the squadron landing from an earlier patrol, four Spitfires took off from Hawkinge (F/O Woodward, Sgt Mann, Sgt Hawke and P/O Donahue) at 16h43, the first three pilots landing again at 18h05–18h10; at 17h00 hours a further four took off (F/Lt Henstock, Sgt Whelan, F/Sgt Laws and F/Sgt Gilbert), and all landed again at 18h10.[393] No landing time is shown for P/O Donahue as he was shot down, as detailed below. These entries in the ORB can suggest that two flights were being operated, each of four Spitfires, which is compatible with what F/Lt Henstock stated in his combat report, saying that he led eight aircraft of the squadron initially.[394]

Adlertag

No mention is made of a ninth pilot, P/O O'Meara, but the ORB, Form 540 clearly states there were nine Spitfires which took off, eight of them landing later.[395] The first four Spitfires to take off included members of both Red and Yellow Sections.[396] O'Meara flew as Yellow 2 once the squadron engaged.[397] There is a simple explanation for the separate take offs of two groups of four Spitfires and thereafter of a single aircraft (O'Meara): having just landed from an earlier patrol, 64 Squadron would have been busy refuelling at Hawkinge and when the scramble order came, only four machines had completed refuelling and thus took off with pilots from two sections, Red and Yellow; once the next four had refuelled, they were led aloft by F/Lt Henstock, and finally P/O O'Meara got off once he had refuelled. Being a forward base and not a sector station, refuelling facilities (fuel bowsers) would have been more limited there.

The two four-aircraft formations of 64 Squadron did not maintain those formations, as they had plenty of time before intercepting the enemy (at least half an hour) and also in being moved from a patrol over Hawkinge at 10,000 ft to one over Deal at 15,000 ft,[398] to incorporate P/O O'Meara and to sort out the normal sections of three and get the pilots flying in their correct section positions. Sgt Mann, recorded in his combat report[399] for this mission: 'Patrolling as Yellow 3 in 2nd section of 3 sections astern...' Clearly, 64 Squadron had sorted themselves out before meeting the enemy into their preferred formation of three sections of three aircraft each, line astern. At about 17h35, while they were flying inland of Dover, close to Hawkinge[400] the enemy was sighted, as described by F/O Woodward.[401]

> As Yellow One I was patrolling with the squadron inland of Dover at 10,000' when I saw a large formation of aircraft approaching from the East at about 15,000. I tally-ho'd and not knowing whether the leader had seen the e/a or not broke away with Yellow Section and climbed hard to the south side of the e/a. I saw a formation of about 50 bombers in vics of 5 astern and, above these, numerous fighters at all heights and very open formations. I circled and went in to attack behind one of the rear formations of 109's at about 18,000'. I sat behind a 109 at about 150 yds and fired a burst of 80 (counted) rounds. I saw my bullets hit the e.a., it began to smoke, then burst into volumes of smoke, turned on its back and dived down. I broke away and as I circled saw it going down in a long trail of smoke (seen by Yellow 2 and 3). I was subsequently engaged and chased by 109's without a chance to fire and at length dived to the clouds to West. I joined, for a time, a squadron of Hurricanes circling just above the clouds, not in

action. I then saw the bomber formation returning east over Hawkinge. It was still intact and there was no sign of anti-aircraft fire about it. It still consisted of about 50 a/c in tight vics astern. I climbed round to astern of the formation and tried to get in the rear of one formation of escort fighters but was observed and chased off by two others and then returned to base. (Tally-ho = code word denoting enemy sighted and attack about to be made)

F/O Woodward did not hesitate upon sighting the enemy but called in the 'Tally-Ho' and without waiting for an answer from the formation leader, F/Lt Henstock, broke away and climbed hard to the south of the enemy coming in towards Dover from the south-east; an immediate decision taken by a section leader in the heat of the interception. By climbing and taking on the escort fighters he was carrying out standard procedure, which ideally saw Spitfires tackle the escort while Hurricanes went for the bombers (in this case, 32 Squadron). Sgt Mann in Yellow Section described how, while the squadron turned through 180 degrees (they must have been flying approximately east), Yellow 1 having given a warning, broke away at only 90 degrees into the reverse-course manoeuvre, turning to port to engage the approaching enemy.[402] The circling Hurricanes noted by F/O Woodward probably belonged to 501 Squadron, and were also reported by a member of 32 Squadron, as described above.

Yellow 2 and 3 followed F/O Woodward in his climb towards the Me 109s; a *Schwarm* (two pairs) of Me 109s dived away and were tackled by the section, and Sgt Mann (Yellow 3) was witness to his leader's diving attack on a Me 109 that turned over and dived with a smoke trail behind.[403] This was very likely an example of the classic Me 109 evasive tactic, a half roll and subsequent steep dive at full throttle with exhausts shovelling out smoke from the straining engine. Despite Woodward's confirmed claim, as well as those by his two section mates described below, there are no known *Luftwaffe* Me 109 casualties which can logically be tied to any of 64 Squadron's claims.

Jackie Mann claimed an unconfirmed Me 109 destroyed which he saw lose its hood and descend in a steep, slow and tight spiral, smoking before catching fire and crashing into the sea a few miles south-east of Dover at about 17h50.[404] Yellow 2, P/O O'Meara, was initially attacked by three Me 109s, but getting rid of their attentions he flew westwards, and north of Hawkinge met another Me 109 formation at the same level as he was, 20,000 ft, flying southwards; he damaged one of the rearmost machines at *c.* 17h50 before himself being pounced on by five Messerschmitts, which he lost by a steep dive below cloud.[405]

Adlertag

F/Lt Henstock, leading the squadron and his own Red Section of 64 Squadron meanwhile proceeded westwards from Hawkinge, as recounted in his combat report:[406]

> As Red 1 leading 8 a/c over Hawkinge. Yellow section broke away to attack e/a below which I had not seen. Then I sighted 20 Do 215 flying ENE near Dungeness in sections astern, three sections leading followed by two groups of two sections each, about 150 yds. astern all in very tight form. Found I was now unaccompanied by most of Squadron so attacked No. 3 of rear section. Intense cross fire hit one in engine and wings. Broke away to try beam attack and noticed white smoke from one target which seemed to fall slightly behind. Was attacked by Me 109 from behind and forced to break off attack. Fire from Do 215s opened at very long range. E/a camouflaged very dark all over.' (Form. = formation)

Despite being aware that Yellow Section had broken away and that he was reduced to only a small rump of his squadron, Henstock courageously attacked a tight group of Dorniers, firstly from astern and then from the beam, before being driven off by the escort. The location of his attack near Dungeness and the direction being flown by the bombers points to his having intercepted the incoming *I/KG 2* formation making for Lympne airfield. Presumably, the third (Green) section of 64 Squadron broke away at the same time as Yellow Section; there are no combat reports nor even a mention of this section in the IPR.[407] Henstock's Spitfire had been hit by return fire from the Dorniers and was also damaged by the Me 109 which deflected him from the bombers; he managed to land his machine at Hawkinge.[408]

Sgt Hawke flying in the number three position in Red Section when they were near Dungeness observed several German formations to the south, flying westwards; these may have been from the *II/KG 76* raid and *JG 3* escorts making for Rye radar station, discussed above. When F/Lt Henstock gave the Tally-Ho signal upon sighting the *I/KG 2* Dorniers and escort, Hawke broke away towards Folkestone, where he intercepted a formation of what he reported as Dorniers making for Hawkinge, at about 6,000 ft.[409] Hawke attacked a straggler from astern and below, seeing bits fly off, the port engine smoke badly and the enemy aircraft dive steeply for the sea, which he claimed as a probable victory.[410] The formation he attacked was probably the *EGr 210* Me 110s, as they were flying along the coast towards Folkestone before performing a steep turn to port over the coast at Sandgate, *en route* for Hawkinge; neither this unit nor the Dorniers of *I/KG 2* suffered any losses or even damaged aircraft on this raid.[411] P/O Donahue, an American

Second Major Raid, Portsmouth, Radar Stations

volunteer, was flying as Red 2, and upon F/Lt Henstock's Tally-Ho, he broke away and had a skirmish with some Me 109s, and shortly after another with a second bunch of Messerschmitts; he was hit and his Spitfire set on fire, but he managed to bail out having suffered burns and spent about a month in hospital recovering.[412] His aircraft crashed at Sellindge, just north of Lympne, at 17h40.[413]

In their various engagements, 64 Squadron claimed one Me 109 destroyed confirmed, another unconfirmed and one damaged, along with a probable Dornier.[414] P/O Donahue may have been shot down by *II/JG 52*, who made four claims during the day (times unknown), two destroyed and a probable Spitfire, and one Hurricane shot down;[415] however, none were included in the official *Luftwaffe* victory list.[416]

The twelve Hurricanes of 501 Squadron were scrambled from Hawkinge at 17h25 and they had barely reached 7,000 ft when their forward base was bombed.[417] While the squadron Intelligence Patrol Report (IPR) states that they did not see a low level raid on Hawkinge carried out by He 111s, this probably rather reflects the Me 110s of *EGr 210*, which made the second bombing raid on this airfield soon after *III/KG 2* had bombed from high level, as already discussed above. 501 Squadron appears to have broken up near Hawkinge initially, with Yellow Section, Red 3 and the whole of B Flight leaving S/L Hogan and his number two, P/O Gibson to their own devices; some of these break-away machines attacked Me 110s and Me 109s below them and a dogfight developed in the Hawkinge area.[418] Red 3 skirmished with a *Schwarm* of four Me 109s (described as Heinkel He 113s, incorrectly), with no observed results on either side, while Yellow 3 pursued what he described as a Chance Vought machine out over the Channel.[419] The French air force had been supplied with thirty-nine Chance Vought VF 156 aircraft, better known as the Vindicator dive-bomber in its US Navy guise, but few survived the French campaign; anyway, being a two-seater with a maximum speed of only 243 mph it should have been easy to catch.[420] Exactly what aircraft Yellow 3 chased thus remains a mystery; perhaps a bomb-carrying Me 109 of *EGr 210* whose bomb had hung up?

Meanwhile, S/L Hogan and P/O Gibson, Red 1 and 2, had seen a formation coming in from the south-west towards Lympne and had flown in that direction, not yet aware that their colleagues had broken away.[421] Getting closer the two pilots observed about twenty Do 17s (presumably *I/KG 2*) with a strong top cover of Me 109s. What happened then is best related by P/O Gibson, in an excerpt from his combat report.[422]

> Looking behind own Squadron I noticed that the rear sections and red section No.3. were not there. I afterwards learnt that they had pursued

some E/A that were below us. This left only the Squadron Leader and myself and we carried on travelling West climbing into the sun. As we were turning to the right to deliver the attack I noticed in the rear vision mirror an aircraft diving. I called to Red 1 about it and pulled away to the right, and saw two Heinkel 113's on my tail. I dived into and got out of cloud and found the two E/A behind me on the left. From this time on I did not see Red 1. I began steep turning to the right and finally managed to turn to the right inside and catch up one of the E/A. I gave him two burst (sic) and suddenly saw him turn over on his back and go down over the vertical. The other E/A had been circling above and came down as I got on the tail of the first. As I dived down following the first E/A I saw white trailer coming from behind. I immediately dived into another cloud but could not find the other E/A when I emerged again. I then returned to base. (For Heinkel 113, read Me 109)

Despite his minimal formation, S/L Hogan's tactics were good, climbing into the sun before bravely taking on this raid. Despite the escort, he managed to get in an attack on the bombers as they departed what must have been Lympne, flying then towards the south-east.[423] Although the IPR states that Hogan's attack on the bombers was made on those retreating south-east from Hawkinge, the IPR also makes clear that he was then flying near Lympne, as does the combat report of his number two.[424] Having attacked one of the Dorniers without seeing any visible effect, S/L Hogan broke away but was hit almost immediately by a cannon shell beneath his aircraft from pursuing Me 109s. He managed to put his Hurricane down at Lympne without further damage.[425] In this he was more fortunate than two of his men: P/O Gibson did return to his forward base, at Hawkinge but tipped his Hurricane up onto its nose due to the damaged state of the airfield, while Sgt Lacey had his undercarriage collapse on landing there for the same reason.[426] None of the three 501 Squadron pilots was injured and their machines were all repairable. The sole claim of the squadron was P/O Gibson's 'He 113' confirmed.[427]

56 Squadron had been sent to their forward base at Rochford and at 17h13, F/O Weaver led up A Flight (Red and Yellow Sections), followed some eight minutes later by B Flight (Blue and Green Sections) led by F/Lt 'Jumbo' Gracie. His squadron was ordered initially to intercept a raid approaching Dover but soon diverted to another coming in towards Manston.[428] One Hurricane did not get off due to a technical fault, and another broke away later for the same reason, leaving Gracie with only ten of the original twelve aircraft.[429] After taking off, 56 Squadron climbed as fast as they could towards the Thames Estuary,[430] and over the

Estuary they sighted a tight formation of Dornier 17s or 215s (actually Do 17s), in three lines each made up of three vics (each of three Dorniers), with the three lines stepped down from front to rear.[431] Effectively the Dornier vics were flying in vics line astern of each other, with left hand, right hand and centrally placed vics in each of the three lines. When first sighted, the bombers (and escort of 30 to 40 Me 109s at 20,000 ft and higher) were flying north and above the squadron[432] and as Gracie led them in a hard climb over Herne Bay, the German formation crossed the coast and turned north-north-east over the sea; Gracie put his men into echelon starboard as they approached the bombers from the port side of the formation.[433]

Before the Hurricanes could get to them, the bomber and escort formation had passed in front of them and out over the Estuary, 56 Squadron then finding themselves astern of the enemy.[434] As Gracie led them after the bombers at full throttle, diving slightly to pick up speed and then pulling up again, closing the distance and altitude gap on the bombers, they were at least coming in out of the direction of the sun;[435] though the bomber gunners being higher could still see them well enough.

As it was, 56 Squadron were just too slow due to their steep climb and basically flew straight into the fire of *Oberst* Fink's well trained rear gunners.[436] F/Lt Gracie recorded his experience of the attack in a report in the casualty file of P/O Page:[437] 'I was leading the Squadron and P/O Page was No. 2 in the leading Section. We were ordered to patrol Manston at 1500 (sic, 15,000) feet. On our way we sighted an enemy formation of 27 bombers with about 30/40 escorting fighters behind and above. I put the Squadron into echelon starboard and attacked the enemy aircraft from the rear and below. The leading Section encountered very intense fire from the rear gunners and after I had expended all my ammunition, I broke away.'

Gracey's leading section (Blue) was in echelon right as it attacked, Gracie in the lead on the left, P/O Page next and slightly back, and P/O Constable Maxwell on the right, slightly behind again.[438] As Page and Constable Maxwell bored in, Maxwell saw a Me 109 pass relatively close to his left, heading straight for Page; Constable Maxwell gave the German fighter a long deflection burst and saw it jink violently before breaking away downwards.[439] This did not save Geoffrey Page from the bombers' return fire and he was caught in a cone of bullets and his header fuel tank blew up. He instinctively kicked the joystick as his Hurricane rolled over and shot straight out of the flaming inferno, badly burnt on hands and face and with a bullet in his one leg.[440] Managing to pull his ripcord despite his terribly burnt hands he landed in the sea north of

Margate, but could not inflate his mae west lifejacket due to it being fire-damaged, but did get rid of the parachute harness; with no buoyant support he managed to keep swimming until, mercifully soon, a Trinity House vessel sent a boat to rescue him.[441]

F/Sgt Higginson, leading Green Section behind Gracie's section, initially kept his men in line astern and only as he approached the bomber formation from the left quarter did he order echelon right, opening fire on the extreme left-hand Dornier from 800 yards down to 150 yards; as he broke away he observed the bomber's port engine shovelling out black smoke and could only claim a damaged enemy aircraft.[442] His own Hurricane was struck by return fire, bullets hitting his windscreen, wings, hood and side panel, and he was lucky to escape personal injury.[443] Green 3, P/O Sutton, gave one of the Dorniers on the left rear of the formation a long burst but was then hit in the radiator, glycol fumes filling the cockpit, and when he opened the hood and pushed up his goggles, both windscreen and goggle lenses were covered with a thin glycol coating.[444] Breaking away steeply, he was able to put his crippled Hurricane down in one piece at Manston (badly damaged earlier in the day), having the good fortune to land on the only open runway, marked by yellow flags, which he was not able to see.[445] One of the Dorniers flying on the left hand rear part of the Dornier formation was seen to catch fire and turn away by P/O Joubert, who did not see it crash; it had been hit by Gracie, Page or Sutton,[446] or possibly by two or all three of them.

While F/Lt Gracie had ordered the squadron into echelon starboard (right), Green Section appears to have come in to the left of Gracie's leading section, instead of to the right, based on the account immediately above. Red Section, behind Green, in contrast was in echelon right once so ordered, and being in the correct spatial placement, to Gracie's right, went for the extreme right hand rear section of Dorniers, as is evident from Red 1, F/O Weaver's combat report.[447]

> I was leading my Flight when we took off from Rochford on patrol. When airborne B Flight joined us and led us to attack E/A reported approaching Manston. We saw them 10 miles east of us, flying north. B Flight leader ordered the sections into echelon right and led us to attack. I selected the left hand E/A of the extreme right-hand rear section of the E/A, who were flying in close formation in three lines of sections of 3 in vic line-astern. I attacked from dead astern, giving a four-second burst at 400 yds., experiencing intense return fire at that range. This burst had no apparent effect. I then closed and gave him continuous burst at 250/200 yds., using all my ammunition. E/A began to give out black smoke and I broke away. Whilst at 250 yards' range after about

Second Major Raid, Portsmouth, Radar Stations

8 seconds' firing my windscreen and leading edges began to get coated with oil. On landing P/O Joubert and P/O Westmacott confirmed that they saw the E/A which I had attacked get out of control and blow up in the air. E/A kept close formation throughout the attack and adopted no evasive action.

Once more, the importance of getting close to hit a bomber effectively is illustrated. Also interesting in Weaver's report is the fact that *II/KG 2*'s Dorniers took no evasive action, relying instead on maintaining their close formation and a disciplined and controlled return fire throughout 56 Squadron's attack. While no Dornier casualties are noted in standard sources,[448] two aircraft from *II/KG 2* were damaged and apparently crashed in France.[449] A third *KG 2* Dornier from the *III Gruppe* raid was also damaged, and among the three Do 17s, three crew members were wounded.[450] One of the *II/KG 2 Staffels* claimed two 'Spitfires' shot down, which equate well enough with 56 Squadron's losses of P/O Page's Hurricane and the damaged machine of P/O Sutton;[451] six more Hurricanes were lightly damaged from the intense Dornier cross-fire.[452] The damaged Do 17 from *III/KG 2* can most likely be laid at the door of 32 Squadron, with P/O Smythe making a claim for a confirmed bomber, two others being claimed damaged by other squadron members.[453]

Yellow Section of 56 Squadron at the rear of the squadron formation had not kept up with the front three sections in their attacks on the bomber formation; instead they turned back and fired ahead of Me 109s diving down to attack F/Lt Gracie's leading section, and the German fighters were deterred by this.[454] F/Sgt Smythe, Yellow 2, climbed up and attacked a Me 109 from about 200 yds, seeing numerous hits on the wings, and then the hood flew off and it began to smoke heavily from the port wing; seeing as Sgt Hillwood witnessed it hitting the sea, Smythe's claim was confirmed.[455] Overall, 56 Squadron claimed one Dornier confirmed destroyed, another damaged and the confirmed Me 109 by Smythe.[456] The two damaged Do 17s of *II/KG 2* logically were related to the two bomber claims. *III/JG 54* which provided the close escort for *II/KG 2*'s Dorniers, suffered several casualties in this raid:[457] *Oblt* Drehs of *Stab III/JG 54* was shot down and force-landed in open ground at Hengrove, just south-west of Margate, becoming a POW; *Gefr* Stabner of *7/JG 54* went missing over the Channel; *Oblt* Schön of *8/JG 54* crashed back at base, wounded in air combat, and his machine written off (60% damage); finally, *Lt* Eberle of *9/JG 54* was also wounded in combat over the Channel, but made it back to base, his Me 109 50% damaged.

There is no logical allocation possible of these German losses to the various claims by the RAF. 54 Squadron claimed two Me 109s unconfirmed and another probable; 56 Squadron claimed one Me 109 confirmed; 32 Squadron, although largely involved against the *III/KG 2* raid escorted by elements of *JG 26*, made on Hawkinge, also seems to have had some pilots making claims near or in the general area of the *II/KG 2–JG 54* action – they claimed a total of one Me 109 confirmed (by F/Lt Crossley, between Deal and Dover) and five unconfirmed, plus two probables, with three pilots appearing to have possibly engaged *JG 54* fighters, P/O Gardner, Sgt Higgins and P/O Pniak.[458] Both *Oblt* Drehs (17h36, confirmed) and *Oblt* Schön (17h45, probable, near Ramsgate) made claims[459] before themselves being hit, which suggests they became casualties later rather than earlier in the overall actions; this would suggest 56 and 54 Squadrons possibly being the victors, rather than 32 Squadron for those two losses. 54 Squadron's two unconfirmed and one probable claims, by F/Lt Deere (one unconfirmed) and Sgt Klosinsky were made out over the Channel, about ten miles east of North Foreland[460] as the raid went back home. F/Sgt Smythe's claim in 56 Squadron was witnessed and thus confirmed, and the hood came off the Me 109, all of which is reasonably convincing for a successful claim, possibly thus *Gefr* Stabner. That would leave *Lt* Eberle as a possible victim of 32 Squadron, perhaps.

Eleven Spitfires of 54 Squadron, flying as two sections of four aircraft, Red in the lead followed by Blue Section, and Yellow at the rear of three Spitfires only, were ordered up from Hornchurch at 17h10, with orders to patrol Dover.[461] When nearing Ashford the Hornchurch controller ordered a diversion to Manston, obviously to intercept the German raid of *II/KG 2* coming in over the North Foreland, but just before this, Blue 1 gave a Tally-Ho for German aircraft over Dover and unknown to F/Lt Alan Deere leading the squadron, took the seven aircraft of his and Yellow sections off towards the south-east of Ashford.[462] Deere (Red 1) having ordered the squadron to follow him made for Manston at about 22,000 ft, and on getting closer observed a large bomber formation at about 18,000 ft accompanied by a large Me 109 escort at the same level but behind and to port, and as he watched saw the bombers turn back from west to east over what he thought was the North Foreland.[463]

This could only have been the Dorniers of *II/KG 2* turning back towards the north-east from their target at Bekesbourne, almost in direct line of sight between Ashford and Manston and North Foreland behind it; to a pilot keyed up for the action soon to be joined and with many other factors passing through his mind as he briefly looked towards the north-east, this rapid geographical mental picture can be understood. By the time Deere and his lonely four Spitfires of Red Section got to the bombers, now flying to the east off the North Foreland, he led his men in a dive out of the sun from 22,000 ft onto the bomber formation, but before getting in range to open fire, he saw the Me 109s coming in to attack them and ordered the section to break formation, after which a dogfight began.[464]

What happened next is best explained by an excerpt from F/Lt Deere's combat report.[465]

> Messerschmitt 109's appeared from the left as I closed in on the bombers, so I gave the order for my sections to break and engage fighters. After a quick turn I saw a Me. 109 shoot down a Spitfire in flames and I got on the Me.109's tail and dived from 17,000 Feet to 11,000 Feet firing short bursts at 250 Yards when enemy burst into flames and continued in a vertical dive towards the sea. On the return journey I ran into about 12 Me.110's in Mid-Channel and was able to surprise them as I was approaching from direction of French Coast. I fired a long burst at about 150 Yards and the enemy turned towards France, I fired two more long bursts using deflection and enemy prepared to pancake on sea. I followed him down and saw the man climbing into a rubber dinghy. I had a front gun exercise at him, but, unfortunately a 109 came from out of the blue and shot hell out of me I retired with 12 Boost. (12 Boost = emergency engine power)

Deere claimed the Me 109 and the Me 110 as unconfirmed victories; Sgt Klosinsky in his section also claimed an unconfirmed victory over a Me 109 in flames, as well as another probably destroyed.[466] Possibly, they attacked the same Me 109 without being aware of each other in the heat of action. *III/ZG 26* had an Me 110 damaged in combat over the Channel,[467] presumably by Deere. As he intercepted them while returning across the Channel from having been near the French coast, these Me 110s were flying north and possibly were flying a sweep-out to meet the returning *II/KG 2–JG 54* raid.

When Blue and Yellow Sections of 54 Squadron left the squadron formation just before the Ashford area, thereby leaving F/Lt Deere and his Red Section high and dry on their own to take on the raiders towards Manston, they too became depleted as Blue 3 and Yellow 2 broke away and returned to base with, respectively, engine and oxygen problems.[468] There are no combat reports for either section as no claims were made. Both sections also appear to have lost cohesion and reported diverse engagements; Blue 4 observed a long line of 'dive bombers' escorted by a 'Me 109 squadron' and made a brief attack on one of the Me 109s but was rapidly driven off by the others.[469] This vague account does hint towards *EGr 210*'s aircraft – the small Me 109 unit escorting apparent dive bombers which may have been their Me 110s, flying in a loose formation more typical of that unit than any dive bombers. Blue 1 and 2 spotted a close formation of some eighteen Dorniers flying in vics of three, and attacked their rear out of the sun followed by a second such attack by just Blue 1 on the centre sections.[470] The only geographic clue provided by the 54 Squadron IPR is given by Yellow Section who had climbed up to 25,000 ft from where the two remaining pilots spotted five separate German formations heading north over the Channel, one of them, probably of Dorniers, crossing the coast east of Dungeness.

While Yellow 1 attacked the Dorniers out of the sun, his wingman observed Spitfires and Me 109s dogfighting and attacked one of the Me 109s.[471] The two 54 Squadron sections may have spotted the *KG 76-JG 3* formations heading north over the Channel towards Rye (west of Dungeness) and the German 'Dorniers' crossing the coast east of Dungeness, could tally with the Me 110s of *EGr 210* which bombed Hawkinge soon after. Of course, it is also possible that some of the two 54 Squadron sections did in fact tackle the *I/KG 2* Dornier formation making for Lympne, which was flying essentially north – north-east of Dungeness. Either way some of the British pilots thought that some of their rounds had hit the enemy machines but did not observe any damage nor make any claims.[472] The dog fight between 'Spitfires' and Me 109s reported by Yellow 2 may have been Hurricanes of 501 Squadron in combat with Me 109s, which took place in the Hawkinge area,[473] or less likely, some of 64 Squadron's Spitfires engaging Me 109s.

JG 54 made a total of seven claims against British fighters, three Hurricanes, four Spitfires and one probable Spitfire; *I* and *II/JG 54* claimed one Spitfire each, the rest being credited to *III Gruppe*.[474] Few localities are noted for these latter claims, but the Canterbury and Ramsgate areas are given for two of them; regarding claim timing, there is one early claim at 17h20, four between 17h30 and 17h36 (one at Canterbury) of which three were by *9/JG 54*, and then from 17h40-17h45 there are two claims and a probable one, one each for the three *Gruppen* (one at Ramsgate).[475] While the middle time grouping and mention of Canterbury suggests action against a few of the 32 Squadron Hurricanes north-east of Dover towards Deal and Manston, the later times from 17h40–17h45 might have been against 56 and 54 Squadrons as the *II/KG 2* raid and escort went out again over the Channel. However there are only a few RAF losses which can logically be ascribed to *JG 54*: 56 Squadron lost one Hurricane, P/O Page seriously burnt and another damaged, but landed safely by P/O Sutton; 54 Squadron had no losses, while the single 32 Squadron Hurricane shot down was much more likely to have fallen to *JG 26*, having crashed west of Hawkinge.[476] P/O Page may have been shot down by a Me 109 or by Dornier cross-fire, or even both, as already discussed, while Sutton appears to have been hit by the *II/KG 2* bombers. *JG 54*, especially its third *Gruppe*, was rather optimistic.

While none of the escorting and supporting fighters accompanying either *I/KG 2* (attacked Lympne) or *III/KG 2* (attacked Hawkinge) suffered any losses, *III/JG 26* who were flying a sweep in support largely of the Hawkinge raid, as already detailed above, claimed two Spitfires, another probable Spitfire and had a claim for yet another rejected, all in the area between south-west of Dover and Folkestone.[477] It is likely that the 32 Squadron Hurricane mentioned in the previous paragraph fell to them. The Spitfire of P/O Donahue of 64 Squadron which came down at Sellindge may have been a further victim of *III/JG 26*, but may also have been shot down by *II/JG 52* as already discussed, and the same two possibilities would apply to F/Lt Henstock's damaged Spitfire, also from 64 Squadron, but hit also by return fire from *I/KG 2*'s Dorniers, detailed earlier. The two Huricanes of 501 Squadron which came to grief (damaged but repairable) landing at the heavily damaged Hawkinge airfield can be ascribed logically to landing accidents, indirectly related to enemy action.

EGr 210, which attacked both Hawkinge and Lympne airfields, suffered no losses, and the only Me 110 casualty was that of *III/ZG 26*, damaged 45% in combat over the Channel, and which force-landed at Calais.[478] The only relevant claim is that of F/Lt Deere of 54 Squadron who was convinced that his Me 110 went into the sea, he having immediately thereafter seen a crewman clambering into a dinghy.[479] What Deere actually saw is unclear; it is remotely possible that he lost sight of the damaged *III/ZG 26* Me 110 at low level against the sea, and observed another German, already in the drink, climb into his dinghy. The only *Luftwaffe* airman to fall into the sea on this raid was Gefr Stabner of *7/JG 54* (possibly shot down by F/Sgt Smythe of 56 Squadron) who was posted missing.

Overall, German fighters claimed nine destroyed and two probables against the RAF fighters, which have to be balanced against total Fighter Command losses of three fighters with two pilots wounded, plus four more damaged and six slightly damaged. While two of the damaged British fighters were the result of landing accidents at the bomb-damaged Hawkinge airfield, and all those lightly damaged were hit by Dornier cross-fire, the same applied to one more damaged RAF fighter while the fourth damaged fighter was the result of being hit by both Dorniers and an Me 109. Of the three British fighters which were destroyed, one was possibly from bomber return fire or a combination with Me 109 fire.

The *Luftwaffe* fighters had not achieved very much, despite greatly outnumbering their opponents. Analogously, the RAF fighters also greatly over-estimated their successes: for total claims of four Me 109s destroyed confirmed, another eight unconfirmed, three probables and one damaged, there were only two Messerschmitts destroyed with their pilots lost, another written off in France and a fourth damaged. Regarding Do 17 claims, for three of these aircraft damaged there were two RAF claims for confirmed victories, one probable claim and three assessed as damaged. The single Me 110 claimed by Fighter Command in this raid was only damaged. Both Lympne and Hawkinge airfields were heavily damaged in the raids, but both were operational again by 09h00 next day,[480] while Bekesbourne airfield was not in use at all and was thus a waste of attack effort.

From a tactical aspect, for the British it was worrying that for three of their squadrons (out of five engaged), the leaders, S/L Hogan of 501 Squadron, F/Lt Henstock of 64 Squadron and F/Lt Deere of 54 Squadron, found themselves attacking German bomber formations with most of their pilots having already broken away to pursue Me 109s, thus leaving them exposed and much less successful in the prime job of engaging *Luftwaffe* bombers rather than fighter versus fighter combats. *KG 2* was a highly experienced bomber *Geschwader*, led by *Oberst* Fink and their highly trained and coordinated rear gunners put up a superb defence against the RAF fighters that did get at them, hindering any really effective assaults on the bombers. F/Lt Crossley of 32 Squadron led his unit in a quarter-ahead attack which was close to a head-on assault on *III/KG 2* but the inherent danger posed by this attack was largely negated by an alert fighter escort placed almost above the bombers. While this would have been of little use against British astern attacks, it was perfectly placed to interfere with Crossley's frontal attack.

56 Squadron, led by F/Lt Gracie, another brave and effective leader, found themselves below and behind *II/KG 2* as the bombers were on their way out, so had little choice but to attack from that tactically poor situation or otherwise miss an interception altogether. In the event, with *II/KG 2*'s Dornier formation being stepped down (instead of the more usual stepped-up *Gruppe* formation) it was actually the right way to make a rear attack. Any attack by 56 Squadron from a higher altitude would have faced the full might of the very effective dorsal guns of the entire *Gruppe*'s Dorniers. The set of evening raids were thus not a success for the fighters on either side. Fighter Command must have been disappointed that three separate German bomber formations had fighters vectored onto them in high enough numbers to expect some good results, but due to the British squadrons breaking up prematurely (effectively poor discipline in the air) as a result of section leaders pursuing their own agendas and due to attacks on the bomber formations not being pressed

Second Major Raid, Portsmouth, Radar Stations

home fully enough in the face of the fierce return fire from *KG 2*'s Do 17s, not a single bomber was knocked down. However, the next day would see *KG 2* experience an entirely different series of events, with violent British assaults on their formations resulting in prohibitive losses. The RAF was also able to minimise squadrons breaking apart before being ordered to do so for much of the combat that lay ahead.

12 August 1940 – effective bombing raids and those raids that must be adjudged pyrrhic victories at best

Small German attacking forces, such as the nine Do 17s launched against Lympne (08h10–08h40) where a massive escort of six Me 109 *Gruppen* kept off limited intercepting fighters (610 Squadron) as well as those (54 Squadron) vectored towards a decoy raid off North Foreland, can be seen as operations intended to clear the air before the RDF station raids at about 09h30–09h45, and also to allow the Me 109s free rein on outnumbered RAF fighter squadrons. Despite variable damage to these stations, they were back on air within hours and their radar transmission signals being picked up by the *Luftwaffe* in the afternoon largely discouraged them from further attacks on such stations in the future, an immense failure in *Luftwaffe* leadership and operational intelligence.

It needs to be remembered that *Luftwaffe* philosophy greatly overvalued the ace concept, promoted successful aces to senior leadership positions and saw a planned much higher kill rate against British fighters as the key to victory. This was espoused particularly by *Generalmajor* Theo Osterkamp, *Jagdfliegerführer* to *Luftflotte 2*, as well as by the majority of German fighter leaders of individual *Geschwadern* and *Gruppen*. A similar raid to the early Lympne one was the Stuka *Gruppe* escorted by an entire Me 109 *Geschwader* sent in to attack shipping in the Thames Estuary (11h15–11h30) – ignoring two convoys, they went for a small group of minesweeping trawlers. The Me 109s meanwhile massacred the section of Hurricanes on convoy patrol and engaged one of the two squadrons vectored in, but the other managed to get at the Stukas as they pulled out of their dives and made their way back to France, without shooting any of them down. Once again, the German fighters were afforded the opportunity to bounce outnumbered opponents distracted by dive-bombers, but the raid was also no doubt planned to draw RAF attention to the Dover Straits and Thames Estuary soon before the 12h00–12h50 large raid to come, on Portsmouth and Ventnor RDF station to the west.

The 12h45-13h00 raid on Manston by *EGr 210* closely followed by *I/KG 2* and the evening (17h15–18h15) raids by all three *Gruppen*

Adlertag

of the same Dornier-equipped *Geschwader* on Lympne, Hawkinge and Bekesbourne airfields, the first two attacks accompanied also by *EGr 210* once more, dealt with forward RAF airfields close to the coast by heavily escorted bomber formations. Once more, the Me 109 escort was advantaged, and forward bases were hammered as a preliminary to Eagle Day on 13 August. In the evening attacks, the RAF controllers vectored fighters successfully onto each raid, but three of the five squadrons' performance was ruined by squadrons breaking up to attack Me 109 escorts and sweeps before the bombers were reached. Of the other two RAF squadrons, 56 Squadron reached the outgoing *II/KG 2* Bekesbourne raiders near the Thames Estuary and attacked, but doing so from behind and below came in too slowly and were effectively repulsed by excellent coordinated rear gunner fire. 32 Squadron, vectored onto the incoming *III/KG 2* raid on Hawkinge as they approached the coast, were in an ideal position for a head-on attack, which was indeed attempted by F/Lt Crossley leading them, but did not succeed due to an Me 109 escort placed, unusually, immediately above the bombers.

All of the German attacks on forward airfields, shipping and RDF stations in Kent and Sussex were rapid raids against targets close to the coast and thus difficult to counter. With short penetration depths over land there was minimal time for RAF squadrons to make multiple attacks on bomber formations, and they were forced to accept the conditions imposed on them at the time of interception, as in the case of 56 and 32 Squadrons. One member of the latter squadron, P/O Hamilton Grice, was accorded a rare second chance of attacking the *III/KG 2* Hawkinge raiders as they exited the coast from a head-on closure and made full use of it, but the partial breakup of the tight Dornier formation he achieved was of no use as there were no other fighters to take advantage of this; the Germans were already over the narrow Dover Straits and homeward-bound.

None of the interceptions in this set of raids was successful, but for that against the Portsmouth-Ventnor raiders, where different conditions pertained. In the first instance this was a much larger raid, a full Ju 88 *Geschwader* of sixty-three Ju 88s, with two large and equally unwieldy Me 110–Me 109 circles placed south of Portsmouth and further south, to the east of the Isle of Wight, with Me 109s also sweeping ahead as all this came in. Even though most of the action was over the sea, there was significant penetration distance of well defended British airspace, allowing time for serious attacks on the retreating bombers and also for the circles to be well addressed.

The combination of larger German formations, longer penetrations depth of a well defended area provided many more opportunities for

Second Major Raid, Portsmouth, Radar Stations

RAF fighter attack, in direct contrast to what had occurred over the narrows of the Channel to the east throughout the day. Also, seven RAF squadrons intercepted the Portsmouth-Ventnor raiders. Another permanent disadvantage in the central-western Channel, which was significantly wider than that at the Dover Straits, was that this allowed little time for short- ranged Me 109 escorts to provide effective top cover. They could not accompany incoming bomber formations without using up too much fuel as they flew circles and figure eight courses keeping pace with the much slower bombers. The Me 109s of JGs 2, 27 and 53 were thus forced to make use of sweeps, both ahead of bombers or Stukas, or meeting them on the way out, or by arriving over particular parts of a targeted area at a specific time, likely to be critical within a complex attack plan.

An alternative was to make use of staggered take off times of Me 109s to maintain a more constant presence above attacking and retreating bombers, but perforce in much smaller numbers. Recourse in the central-western Channel reaches was had to using Me 110s as bomber protection, often through large circles of Me 110s, which, though they did attract British fighter attention, those fighters soon became adept at countering them with high casualties to the *Luftwaffe*.

For the *KG 51* raid on Portsmouth and Ventnor, the Ju 88s over the main target of the Portsmouth naval base resorted to dive bombing, in *Ketten* of three aircraft at a time, after which they left the target area and made off south-south-east of the port and past the Isle of Wight to its east, giving the waiting RAF fighters a continuous stream of small disorganised formations of bombers, many already damaged by flak; this went on for some fifteen to twenty minutes. Of six and a half British fighter squadrons, the equivalent of three and a half went for the bombers, the other three taking on the fighter circles. There was enough time for numerous attacks on the unfortunate Ju 88s, which were suitably massacred, losing ten bombers with three more damaged. The fighter circles showed little interest in aiding the Ju 88s, and especially the Me 110s put up another rather dismal performance. The British fighter squadrons in this area had already learnt from the previous day's large actions against Me 110s how best to tackle the circling *Zerstörer*. Raids in the general Isle of Wight–Portland areas and inland thereof by *Luftflotte 3* were thus largely doomed to fail due to inadequate German fighter protection. With the massive Stuka raids in mid-August, particularly on 16 and 18 August to come, the same basic principles applied: being much slower and more vulnerable than the twin-engined *Luftwaffe* bombers in having a single, liquid-cooled engine, they would suffer in the same way from the RAF fighters even on their generally shorter penetration depths,

Adlertag

attacking coastal airfields (naval fields near Portsmouth, Tangmere etc.), their low speed allowed significant interception time to Fighter Command.

In the 11 Group area bordering the Channel narrows to the east, earlier attacks on Channel convoys, naval assets, ports, and coastal forward RAF airfields during July 1940 and up until 12 August, suffered few effective interceptions of bomber formations, due to fast raids of short penetration depth being the norm. Excessive use of the dangerous and efficient *EGr 210* fighter-bombers was made, and this unit must have rapidly become over-tired. Their nemesis was on 15 August on a long penetration attack on Croydon airfield; their colleagues of *KG 2* met their come-uppance earlier, on 13 August, when their vaunted coordinated return fire did not spare them excessive losses on a deeper penetration raid on Eastchurch on the Isle of Sheppey, Thames Estuary. *EGr 210* had the misfortune to run into the combined talents of 32 and 111 Squadrons on 15 August, while *KG 2* were intercepted by 74, 111 and 151 Squadrons on 13 August – these were all Fighter Command units of experience, determination and ability, led by expert tacticians, as will be seen on Eagle Day.

Interestingly, the Dornier units, *KG 2, 3* and part of *KG 76* were concentrated in *Luftflotte 2* where they were due to battle it out against the RAF fighters right through the Battle until the famous 15 September 1940 defeat over London. The most modern bombers, the faster Ju 88s of *KG 54, KG 51* and *LG 1*, were in their turn concentrated in *Luftflotte 3* to the west, where they struggled, having been sent into combat before the new aircraft was fully tested and evaluated beforehand. Despite their speed, as they carried much of their bombload externally, they became not just slower but also more ungainly in action. The Dorniers with their air-cooled radial engines were the only German bombers so blessed and carried the major weight of the *Luftwaffe* day bomber offensive in the Battle of Britain. At the end of the day, longer penetration raids, no matter how large, complex and in spite of well-planned diversions, escorts and supporting sweeps that might be set in motion, would be subject to that most distinct and common martial phenomenon of things often going wrong, with concomitant casualties and pyrrhic victories, despite effective bombing having been achieved.

3

Eagle Day: 13 August 1940

Unescorted attack on Eastchurch airfield and Sheerness naval base, *c.* 06h45–07h30

KG 2 was slated to attack Eastchurch airfield on the Isle of Sheppey, as well as the nearby Sheerness naval base early in the morning of 13 August 1940; *I Gruppe* was assigned Sheerness as its target, while *II, III Gruppen* and a *Kette* of three Do 17s from *Stabstaffel/KG* 2 were to destroy the RAF Coastal Command base at Eastchurch in the plan.[1] Sheerness lay on the north-western tip of Sheppey, and accommodated some of the anti-invasion naval forces of the Nore Command;[2] Eastchurch was situated a bit to the north of centre on the island. Despite Eastchurch being an airfield assigned to Coastal Command, on this day it actually hosted two Fairy Battle-quipped light bomber squadrons, the Spitfires of 266 Squadron and those of B Flight of 19 Squadron.[3] Both Fighter Command Spitfire units had been transferred temporarily there on 12 August, 266 Squadron to provide escorts for the Battles in attacking German light naval forces across the Channel, while the 19 Squadron flight led by S/L Pinkham was supposed to strafe Channel ports and especially to attack e-boats.[4] Attacks on the e-boats in French and Dutch ports by these forces were planned by the RAF for 13 August,[5] but *KG* 2 would ensure that such attacks were delayed for several days.

Eighty-four *KG* 2 Dorniers took off from their bases in the Arras area at dawn, between 04h50 and 05h10, comprised of the three *Gruppen*, each twenty-seven machines strong, with an additional *Kette* (vic) of three Dorniers from the *Stabstaffel* (staff flight) of the *Geschwader*, which included the *Kommodore* of the unit, *Oberst* Fink, experienced, disciplined and professional.[6] This mass of Dornier bombers proceeded to Amiens, a city with a distinctive radiating road pattern situated just

Adlertag

downstream of a major confluence of the river Somme, and thus easily spotted from the air; here they assembled the large body of aircraft into three *Gruppen* formations at 12,000 ft.[7] This took time, about half an hour,[8] but they were not in any particular hurry; they were unaware that RAF radar had picked them up almost immediately, at about 05h30–05h40, at the extremely long range of 110 miles already.[9] Considering the depredations wrought by the attacks on radar stations on the previous day, this was a fine performance by the British warning network.

At about 06h10 the Dorniers finally started to move northwards, flying towards the Pas de Calais where they were to meet their escort of sixty Me 110s of *ZG 26* led by their *Kommodore*, *Obstlt* Huth.[10] However, as the weather rapidly deteriorated from the clear conditions predicted the day before and new weather reports came in from reconnaissance missions, the entire operation (and others proceeding simultaneously further to the west) was scrubbed by Göring; the low cloud rapidly growing thicker northwards would have forced bombing over the Thames Estuary at low altitudes where barrage balloons and anti-aircraft guns were relatively plentiful.[11] The recall signal went out at 06h15, but Fink's radio was out (unknown to him) and the radio operator of *II Gruppe Kommandeur Obstlt* Weitkus had flu and did not understand the message in his fuddled state; Huth did receive the order and was surprised to see the bombers continue flying up from the south, and he left his Me 110 formation to try and warn Fink by calling them on the radio, and when that elicited no response, by diving and zooming up close to the Dorniers while gesticulating wildly.[12]

Fink, not comprehending any of this, went on his way.[13] Only *I/KG 2* heard the message, and landed back at their base at Epinoy.[14] Presumably, *III/KG 2* like the *II Gruppe*, did not receive or understand the recall signal either. Despite the lack of an escort, Fink went ahead with the mission, a brave and determined man. His *Geschwader* would suffer significant losses on this mission and Fink himself would see both his wingmen disappear close to Eastchurch as Spitfires attacked but still managed to drop his bombs on the assigned target. His left hand wingman did not return (this aircraft also carrying the *Staffelkapitän* of the *Stabstaffel*), the other managed to struggle back to base with a badly damaged Dornier and two wounded crewmen.[15] Fink's *Stabskette* was right at the back of the formation, behind *II/KG 2*, with *III/KG 2* flying in front; in the leading aircraft at the head of *III Gruppe* was a *Staffelkapitän* in direct radio communication with Fink, ready to carry out any further orders from the *Kommodore*, which would also be heard by the entire formation, all on a common inter-aircraft radio frequency.[16]

Eagle Day: 13 August 1940

Turning now to the Fighter Command controller's reactions to the *Luftwaffe* activity over the Pas de Calais area: by 06h15, the same time as the cancellation order had been sent out to *KG 2* and *ZG 26*, the RAF had three squadrons on patrol, protecting potential targets.[17] 151 Squadron, up from North Weald was covering a convoy in the mouth of the Thames, 111 Squadron (Croydon) was over their forward base of Hawkinge near Dover, and 74 Squadron (Hornchurch) was patrolling Manston, their own forward base.[18] In the meantime, Fink's Dorniers proceeded out over the Channel in the two *Gruppen* formations, *II/KG 2* behind the *III Gruppe*, flying off the eastern Kent coast in a north-north-westerly direction, heading for a spot north-east of the North Foreland, where they were to turn westwards and fly up the Estuary towards the Isle of Sheppey.[19]

In further reaction, at about 06h20–06h25, Fighter Command scrambled more fighters: a section of 17 Squadron sent up from their forward base at Martlesham to patrol there, 257 Squadron launched from Northolt with instructions to patrol Canterbury, and three sections of 64 Squadron (Kenley) ordered to fly towards the Thames Estuary.[20] However, the latter two squadrons were soon redirected towards the Tangmere–Portsmouth area down the Channel to the west, where another large German raid was incoming; in an ominous development, this was the first time the *Luftwaffe* had launched simultaneous large attacks against widely separated parts of southern England.[21]

Although it is often asserted that 74 Squadron was the first to intercept Fink's Dorniers, 151 Squadron's records make it clear that this unit in fact intercepted them significantly earlier and much further away from Eastchurch than 74 Squadron's Spitfires. First up from 151 Squadron at North Weald was Red Section, at 05h21, led by S/L Gordon and originally instructed to intercept another radar plot, but only nine minutes later the other three sections were ordered off as well and all twelve Hurricanes proceeded towards Rochford, their forward base, on the northern side of the Estuary.[22] Before reaching Rochford, they were diverted to Dover and almost as rapidly then diverted once more, to intercept a raid off the eastern coast of Kent.[23] During these movements, Red Section became separated and took no further part in the engagement that ensued,[24] due to the thick clouds encountered.[25]

The remaining three sections of the squadron, Blue, Yellow and Green, were led by F/Lt Roddick Smith, the B Flight Commander, and met up with Fink's incoming Dorniers south-east of Manston, flying over the sea in a stepped-up, wedge-shaped formation at 8,000–13,000 ft, and proceeding north.[26] Although no single report by any of the three squadrons which intercepted the *KG 2* formations is definite about the nature of the formation which they maintained, many individual combat reports mention seeing or attacking *Ketten* of three Dorniers, and the crew of the Do 17 most probably shot down by 151 Squadron also reported flying in *Ketten* of three machines, when interrogated.[27] F/Lt Smith's combat report, quoted below, shows that he was not to be rushed, calmly placing his squadron in the best attacking position, and also illustrates his concern for his colleagues, most of whom were inexperienced.[28] He also refers to three formations of Dorniers, which they attacked; these likely correspond to the three *Staffeln* making up *III/KG 2*, each presumably flying in vics of three (*Ketten*) line astern, stepped up.

> I was leading the sections of 151 Squadron (Blue, Yellow, Green) – its C.O (sic) and Red s. having been separated coming through the clouds from Rochford due to the hurry to get into the patrol which was ordered for 12 miles South of Manston. The clouds were from 3000 to 5000 ft, and in continuous layers everywhere, with a small parting towards Dunkirk, so that it was difficult to keep the formation. At approximately 06.25 (guessed) I heard base tell the CO to intercept E/A which were 20 miles S.E. of Manston, so proceeded there myself, with the three sections. P/O Ramsey reported "aircraft at 4 o'clock" after 5 minutes, and I saw 3 formations of aircraft stepped up about 5 miles to starboard going North at about 8,000ft. Seeing the rear top squadron to be twin-engine fighters, I spent ten minutes or more positioning myself dead into sun, at 16000 ft and about two miles astern. I ordered the attack, telling my aircraft (which I hoped were all there, although one section was not visible in my mirror, and my no. 2 could not keep up) to dive through the enemy formation, and into the clouds (as I assumed that the rear squadron was Me 110's, and ¾ of my pilots were new). I opened fire at about 300 yds with my cannons, firing into the general mass, as the enemy were in exceptionally close formation. One immediately burst into flames and another started smoking. Then my windscreen front panel was completely shattered by enemy fire, and I broke away downwards & returned to North Weald. (Red s. = Red section; 4 o'clock = example of use of clock system to give direction relative to the reporting pilot's aircraft, 12 o'clock being directly ahead and 6 o'clock directly behind, and thus 4 o'clock is a bearing to the enemy in this case as being to the right hand side and somewhat behind the pilot)

151 Squadron intercepted well to the south-east of Manston, but Smith was mistaken in seeing Me 110s at the rear – they were most likely *II/KG 2* and *Oberst* Fink's *Stabskette* bringing up the rear, but they were not attacked by 151 Squadron. Smith was flying one of the two cannon-armed

Eagle Day: 13 August 1940

Hurricanes which 151 had on strength, and closed in to 100 yards while giving his victim a four-second burst, this Do 17 being claimed as destroyed, confirmed and witnessed by Sgt Clark.[29] Smith's 'bulletproof' windscreen was completely starred and cracked by a single enemy bullet, which also penetrated the windscreen, leaving a large hole but by some miracle missing the pilot; on landing he found a small piece of perspex had gone into his right eye (and was never removed) while the pockets of his flying suit were filled with small pieces of perspex and glass.[30]

Sgt Savill, flying Smith's wing as Blue 2, also opened fire at a Do 17 on the extreme right of the formation, closing to *c.* 150 yards with a six-second burst of machine gun fire, and claimed it destroyed (witnessed by two of his fellow sergeant pilots), having seen it appear to break up and fall through the clouds.[31] Only one of the five Dorniers lost by *KG 2* on this mission can logically be tied exclusively to 151 Squadron's attack, one from 7 *Staffel* that came down reasonably intact on Puxton Farm, near Stodmarsh, some four miles north-east of Canterbury at about 06h45; the crew were all unwounded and during interrogation stated that they were on a reconnaissance mission and carrying only parachute flares and no bombs.[32] The attack caused one engine to fail, also cutting petrol and oil leads; this aircraft was heavily armoured and had five defensive machine guns.[33] Perhaps it was intended to photograph the results of the Eastchurch raid.

Both F/Lt Smith and Sgt Savill recorded the time of their attacks on the Dorniers as 06h45, and at a location approximately fifteen miles east-north-east of Manston. It is suggested that Smith's close attack using cannons seriously damaged this Dornier, and that Savill possibly saw this hard-hit machine falling through the clouds; equally logical, the German pilot took a course to the south-west from his position over the sea north-east of Manston to ensure coming down on land with his dying aircraft. Of course, Savill may also have hit (and presumably only damaged) a separate *III/KG 2* machine. The other two *KG 2* Dorniers which came down on or very near land, the one that crashed just off the coast and the other which crashed into the Thames Estuary mudflats, all came down a good half hour later than the one at Stodmarsh.[34]

F/O Milne, an experienced member of 151 Squadron, was leading a section of three Hurricanes behind Smith.[35] He adopted a different tactic to Smith, diving his men down behind and below the enemy formation, zooming up behind the Dorniers from below, as described in an excerpt from his Combat Report (which comprises two sub-reports):[36]

> At 0530 hrs the Squadron took off for forward base but was ordered to intercept enemy Dornier formations at 8000 ft above 10/10 s cloud.

Adlertag

Only three sections managed to form up together. We were over an hour before finding the enemy and when we sighted them they were flying North. They flew in three large formations stepped up. All were Dorniers. We climbed up and positioned ourselves in the sun, taking our time. When in the perfect position we attacked the last large formation. I led my section in an astern attack from below following a dive down. I opened fire at 200 yds but was travelling too fast and only got in a two seconds burst. While firing I saw an E.A. leave the formation and go down but did not see it again.

Sgt Savill attacked the Dornier formation three more times, once from astern and then making vertical diving attacks from above onto the formation.[37] Milne was also not done with *III/KG 2*, not by a long shot. As he himself describes, in a further excerpt from his combat report, at about 07h00 or shortly before:[38] 'I zoomed to several thousand feet above them and decided on a head-on attack to beat their armour plate. I tried one attack but did not fire owing to E.A. formation commencing to turn.'

The important point to bear in mind is that during all these attacks by 151 Squadron on *III/KG 2* (by Smith, Saville and Milne), the German *Gruppe* was not standing still, but was still flying northwards. Having been about twenty miles south-east of Manston when first sighted by 151 Squadron's Hurricanes, when Smith first attacked at about 06h45 they had already reached a location east-north-east of Manston, and when Milne launched his first head-on attack at about 07h00 they would have been even further north, before starting a turn westwards up the Thames Estuary. *III/KG 2* was by about 07h00 somewhat off course, too far north of the North Foreland area when they finally turned westwards for their target of Eastchurch up the Thames Estuary. Having suffered attacks by 151 Squadron, from above and astern, from below and astern, from vertically above and finally from Milne from head on, as well as some casualties (a few likely damaged, and one shot down Dornier), the cohesion of their formation would have suffered and very likely they had to reassemble the close formation of Do 17s before proceeding towards Eastchurch. They would have had to fly back south-westwards to get close to the north Kent coastline to find Eastchurch as they went up the Estuary.

II/KG 2 behind them, with Fink at its rear, had not been attacked, their formation and navigation was undisturbed, and when they turned westward up the Estuary for Eastchurch they would have become the leading *Gruppe* of the *Geschwader*, with the disrupted and off-course *III Gruppe* behind them. *Oberst* Fink was fortunate enough to have spotted

Eagle Day: 13 August 1940

Margate below him in a short-lived opening of the thick cloud cover, and was able to turn accurately for the flight up the Thames Estuary; he ordered the formation to spread out to avoid the chances of collisions as they would have to descend through the clouds to attack Eastchurch.[39] Thus do detailed plans go awry in war.

With *II/KG 2* (and the *Stabskette* with *Oberst* Fink) now flying up the Estuary and heading for Eastchurch, *III/KG 2* having reorganised themselves followed suit behind them, reversing the formation order as it was in the plan until 151 Squadron's attack. F/O Milne who had broken off his head-on attack on *III/KG 2* due to it starting its turn westwards did not give up but followed and attacked once more, as outlined in the later part of his first combat sub-report:[40] 'I again pulled up and turned to head them off. I got several miles ahead and then attacked the outside member of formation from head on. I held a steady bead and opened fire when quite close. I was flying slowly and held fire for about 4 seconds. I pulled up after (word illegible) attack and saw starboard side of E.A. in flames. He was a long way ahead now but I followed up and after hearing over R.T. "Achtung" "Achtung" (illegible) three of the crew bailed out. The aircraft dived down for the clouds in flames, and I followed but did not see it on emerging over the sea. I searched for some time but was short of petrol.' (R.T. = radio-telephone)

Three of the crew of a Dornier from *8/KG 2* which crashed onto the mudflats at Seasalter just west of Whitstable managed to bail out but only one survived, to be taken prisoner badly wounded.[41] Three crewmen bailing out is known only from this one Dornier and not from any of the other three which came down on land or close to the seashore. The crew of a fifth Do 17 down in the sea were all killed and one washed ashore.[42] This is circumstantial evidence that Milne was involved in the destruction of this specific Do 17.

Two other pilots from two different squadrons, Sgt Skinner of 74 Squadron and F/O Ferriss from 111 Squadron, also each engaged a Dornier just east of Eastchurch and observed several crewmen bailing out.[43] Ferriss additionally located his claim as being over Seasalter. It is thus likely that the *8/KG 2* Do 17 smashed to pieces on the mudflats at Seasalter was actually attacked by three fighters from three different squadrons.

When *II/KG 2* got near to the Isle of Sheppey, flying at *c.* 5,000 ft above thick cloud at about half that altitude below them, they had no clear view of their target; the Dornier *Gruppe* thereupon flew a wide turn to the south-west towards London, but kept turning right around and while flying towards the east on the reciprocal course the crews caught site of Eastchurch airfield through a break in the clouds.[44] Once more

Adlertag

they performed a 180° turn, accurately coming out near the hole in the clouds, through which they descended towards Eastchurch now close ahead of them.[45] *Oberst* Fink, being the seasoned veteran combat leader that he was, had stayed calm and instructed the *Gruppe* to make the appropriate manoeuvre to give them another run in towards Eastchurch and this time, they got a good view; fortune favours the brave.

Things were about to change rapidly for the worse for the rearmost Do 17s. 74 Squadron's twelve Spitfires led by the redoubtable S/L 'Sailor' Malan had been accurately vectored by the Hornchurch controller from their original position over Manston, up the north Kent coast and intercepted *II/KG 2* near Whitstable, just as they emerged below the cloud through the hole they had spotted.[46] With the Spitfires coming in from the east out of the early morning sun shining through the gap in the clouds, the *Stabskette* of *KG 2* was unpleasantly surprised, suddenly hit by machine gun salvoes; *Oblt* Schlegel flying the machine on *Oberst* Fink's port side had an engine hit and the fuselage, wounding both rear gunners.[47]

The interception of the Dorniers below the clouds was very sudden and left S/L Malan with very little time for an effective squadron attack on the rear of the German formation before the rest of them had begun their bomb runs on Eastchurch.[48] Malan had already introduced sections of four (two pairs) rather than the outmoded vics of three favoured by Fighter Command;[49] his number two, F/Lt Brzezina describes how they initially saw three Dornier formations (no doubt the three *Staffeln*) and were about to attack them when a fourth formation emerged from the clouds behind and they broke away to renew their attack on this vic of three aircraft.[50] Malan's own combat report describes their attack.[51]

> Whilst leading the Squadron into attack against enemy bombers (Do.17) in the Estuary I came across three in a vic formation on my beam. I closed to within 100 yards and raked them with machine gun fire. I then swung into line astern and fired at No. 3 of the formation. I fired at 150 yards using four two second bursts. This machine burst into flame in mid air and was last seen heading for the sea. I then attacked the leader of the formation and gave him a three second burst at 150 yards and one of the engines was put out of action, and bits and pieces fell off. This machine could not possibly have reached home. I attacked the third of the section and used my last ammunition but did not see any result. No evasive action was taken by these three machines. I carried a cine camera gun film which was in operation during the combat.

Malan's tactics involved an initial beam attack on the entire vic, followed by his swing into line astern behind the bombers at the short range of

Eagle Day: 13 August 1940

150 yards; as he always did, 'Sailor' Malan was economical with his ammunition, firing only short bursts. As one of the best shots in the RAF, he could afford to be so. The German number three would have been the left-rear machine in the vic, that flown by *Oblt* Schlegel, and clearly Malan had done major damage to this aircraft. The leader of the *KG 2* vic was *Oberst* Fink himself, whose aircraft suffered no serious damage in the combat, while the number two Dornier at the right rear was flown by *Oblt* Langer who managed to get his damaged Dornier back to base, two of the crew wounded.[52] F/Lt Brzezina recorded:[53]

> I attacked No. 2 and gave him a long burst and saw him gliding down towards the sea with smoke coming from one engine. I did not see him go into the water. I then attacked No. 3 of the formation and must have got to within fifty yards when there was a sudden explosion in my cockpit and I found myself falling fast. I managed to get out of the machine at about 2,000 feet and made a successful parachute landing. I did not see what happened to this Do. 17 but I was at such close range that it must have been severely damaged.

He came down over Herne Bay (just over a mile to the east of Whitstable) at about 07h15. His machine went into the sea.[54] Malan and Brzezina each claimed a confirmed Do 17, with one more probable for Malan and another damaged for Brzezina.[55] Exactly who did what damage to which of the two Dornier casualties is debatable, but the pair of them did cripple the aircraft of Schlegel and damage that of Langer, wounding two of his crewmen.

Fink's two wingmen were observed by 74 Squadron to peel away to left (Schlegel) and right (Langer, the starboard wingman).[56] Schlegel with a dying aircraft turned away to the south-east of the target, taking the shortest homeward route across Kent to escape the carnage. He had not had a chance to drop his bombs.[57] Two more RAF fighters appear to have attacked Schlegel's dying Do 17 before it ploughed into the ground, near Barham, Kent, about eight or nine miles south-east of Canterbury at approximately 07h30.[58] Once more, the validity of the generalisation that the larger German aircraft required multiple attacks to bring them down is supported. The rest of *II/KG 2* as well as *Oberst* Fink bombed Eastchurch airfield very soon after 74 Squadron had attacked the *Stabskette* at the rear of their formation. The time of the initial bombing was a few minutes after 07h00: while the 12 and 142 Squadron records give a time of 07h00,[59] 266 Spitfire Squadron, also caught on the ground like the two Battle bomber squadrons mentioned, recorded a time of 07h05 for the onset of the bombing and a duration of the attack until

07h20.⁶⁰ A third time of 07h02 was apparently given by a controller for the start of the bombing.⁶¹

There was no further interception of *II/KG 2* and Fink's remaining lone machine of the *Stabskette KG 2* after the *Kommodore's* two wingmen had been detached by 74 Squadron. The mass of the *II Gruppe* turned to starboard after bombing, flying out over the Thames Estuary eastwards, some shooting up the barrage balloons as they went.⁶² They would have flown down the Estuary just below the clouds so as to be able to pull up into them if endangered.

While this had been going on at Eastchurch airfield itself, 111 Squadron, having been vectored from a position near Dover, also arrived in the general area east of the Isle of Sheppey not long after 07h00, and there was fierce action between *III/KG 2* (coming up the Estuary behind *II/KG 2* after having reorganised themselves after the attack by 151 Squadron) and 74 squadron plus the new arrivals, 111 Squadron, from approximately 07h10–07h30.⁶³ S/L Thompson's combat report provides a good overview of how his squadron began the battle and of his tactic of applying head-on attacks wherever possible.⁶⁴

> At 0550 hours No. 111 Squadron took off on a vector of 125° height 12,000'. After 12 minutes we were told to orbit. Shortly after we were ordered to patrol forward base (HAWKINGE) below clouds and look for enemy aircraft approaching from N.E. We were then told to proceed on a vector of 340° below clouds and look for enemy aircraft returning from the direction of the ISLE of SHEPPEY. No enemy aircraft were seen on this course. On arrival over EASTCHURCH I was unable to contact the ground station by R/T and, owing to poor visibility went above the clouds. At approximately 0710 hours a formation was observed approaching from the East about 1,000' below us. It was a formation in section of 3 astern of about 10 aircraft, but owing to the distance they could not be identified. I instructed 'A' Flight leader to remain where he was whilst I took my flight past these aircraft on the port beam to identify them. When I identified them as Dorniers I instructed 'A' Flight leader to carry out a head on attack whilst I took my flight round to the rear. At that moment I observed another formation astern of the first one, so I carried on and executed a head on attack on this from below. Little return fire was observed until the break away. These head on attacks had the effect of breaking up the enemy formation. I then attacked the formation from the rear closing to within 200 yards of the right hand aeroplane. I broke away from this attack and observed another enemy aircraft (Dornier 215) alone over SITTINGBOURNE flying East. I carried out a full

deflection attack on this aircraft closing to astern at about 50 yards range. Both engines of this enemy aircraft emitted clouds of white vapour but the pilot pulled up into the clouds which were about 50' above. This enemy aircraft could not possibly have flown much more than a few miles. On the return to base over W. MALLING a Dornier 215 appeared out of the clouds ahead of me and I gave him a 2 second burst from about 400 yards dead astern but he immediately went back into the clouds again. Then owing to shortage of fuel I returned to base and landed. (A Flight leader = F/O Ferriss)

Both flights of 111 Squadron thus carried out head-on attacks on two formations of *III/KG 2*, Thompson himself leading his attack from below as the second Dornier formation would perforce have been higher than the leading one, due to slipstream effects. Thompson originally planned for his flight to attack the leading formation from astern after they had been broken up by Ferriss's attack from ahead; these were sound tactics. During all this action, of course, the Dorniers were continuing as best they could to fly towards their target at Eastchurch, and the lone Do 17 Thompson met over Sittingbourne (about five miles south-west of Eastchurch) was flying east, not westwards like *III/KG 2* coming in to their bomb runs. This bomber was very likely the aircraft of *Oblt* Schlegel from *Stab/KG 2*, bearing in mind he was badly hit by 74 Squadron just east of Eastchurch, and is known to have broken away without dropping bombs, towards the south-south-east,[65] the most direct route home in his badly damaged state.

The bulk of *II/KG 2* had turned out over the Estuary after bombing, heading eastwards for the Channel again. Schlegel, turning away to port after being hit, would have turned through well over ninety degrees to get on a south-easterly course and this logically would have placed him initially around the Sittingbourne area before proceeding south-eastwards across Kent. Thompson's full deflection attack, using small calibre machine guns, would have been unlikely to have crippled both engines, and the white smoke given off by both suggests already existing serious damage. It is thus postulated that Thompson added to *Oblt* Schlegel's problems as he despairingly headed towards home across a still considerable distance over cloud-covered and hostile Kent. Thompson claimed a Do 17 destroyed (Schlegel, most likely) and a second as damaged. There were more problems to come for the Schlegel crew, which would see their attempted escape come to naught.

An already familiar opponent of *KG 2*, F/O Milne of 151 Squadron, who had already contributed to the *8/KG 2* Dornier down at Seasalter (described above), now continued his relentless pursuit of the remnants of this *Geschwader*. From his description of the crash of this machine (below) it can only fit that down near Barham, some eight or nine miles south-east of Canterbury; the aircraft's tail and rear fuselage broke off in the crash and it ended up upside down on the local railway line, exposing its blue underside. The only other Dornier which could have raised a lot of dust as Milne related (the other three came down in coastal to seaward situations) was that at Stodmarsh (detailed above), but that aircraft was essentially intact after a good belly-landing and lay right way up.[66]

The determination of many Fighter Command pilots to pursue their enemies and to get them down is well illustrated by F/O Milne's actions, as described in his second combat sub-report of this raid (below).[67] 151 Squadron was an outfit of considerably high morale and a squadron with an unusually strong animus against Germans; Dickie Milne displayed these characteristics, despite his calm demeanour, as recounted by a newly arrived pilot, P/O John Ellacombe.[68]

> Whilst returning from air action earlier on, I encountered a lone Dornier 215 flying towards me and below. I was just about over Eastchurch. I half rolled onto him and continued my dive below, pulling up slightly and opening fire at 200 yds after a short run up. After about four seconds fire his right rudder crumpled and he commenced diving slightly. I held fire and saw everything I fired simply pouring into the fuselage. His dive became steep now and I broke off the attack at 50 yds, passing to starboard then pulling up and out. I only encountered slight fire from bottom rear gunner which ceased earlier on. The Dornier was now well below me and dived through the clouds at about 60 degrees. I followed closely after and saw on emerging a huge cloud of dust and debris over a field with the remains of a blue fuselage bottom and planes, hardly recognisable as an aeroplane. I circled and saw a Spitfire approach and look at the crash. I now returned to forward base with only a couple of gallons left. (Dornier 215 = Dornier-17)

Milne claimed this aircraft as an unconfirmed (i.e. unwitnessed) victory but appears to have been the fourth RAF pilot to attack it. Once more, multiple fighter attacks were necessary to bring down a bomber when using .303 ammunition.

74 and 111 Squadrons attacked the Dorniers of *III/KG 2* east of Eastchurch in a number of confused actions in and out of the clouds, which seem to have accounted for two more bombers, both from *7/KG 2*; one came down in the sea in the Thames Estuary (crew killed, one washed ashore near Whitstable), and the other just off Birchington (about five miles west of North Foreland) at about 07h30.[69] Sgt Dymond

led Yellow Section of 111 Squadron, part of A Flight, who performed a head-on attack on *III/KG 2* flying westwards east of Eastchurch, on the instructions of their squadron leader who was at the head of the other flight, as already related. Dymond was an experienced pilot and claimed one Dornier destroyed and another damaged at *c.* 07h20.[70]

> Enemy aircraft were sighted approaching from East approximately 15,000' below. Red and Yellow sections were ordered by Blue 1 to deliver head-on attack. Red and Yellow sections formed line astern. The enemy aircraft flew into cloud and Yellow section followed Red section below cloud. During the dive Yellow section overtook the first wave and were positioned about 500 yards to the right of enemy aircraft and slightly below. This position was favourable for an attack so Yellow section turned right around to meet the second wave with a head-on attack, opening fire at 500 yds and holding fire until 100 yds. Only Yellow 1 and Yellow 3 delivered this attack as Yellow 2 became detached from his section. Yellow 1 and 3 broke down and to the left and then climbed to deliver an astern attack. One 215 broke to the left of his formation and was attacked by Yellow 1 and 3 in succession. I saw pieces of cowling fall from enemy aircraft and smoke issued from starboard engine during a 3 sec burst. I broke away and positioned myself for an attack after Yellow 3 had delivered his attack. I attacked enemy aircraft again from dead astern with a 3 sec burst. The aircraft was losing height gradually. I broke away and engaged another 215 that was heading East and delivered several attacks from beam and head-on. Aircraft was seen to be damaged but as ammunition was expended I returned to base. My aircraft was hit in 8 places. (215 = Do 17).

Despite an immediately unfavourable position for a head-on attack after following the bombers flying into and through the cloud, Dymond turned his section through 180° to apply that most effective method. He describes attacking the second wave of Dorniers, and thus most likely attacked the same Do 17s as S/L Thompson. The attack by Sgt Dymond did indeed detach a single bomber, which he and his number three then attacked further as the hapless Dornier tried to get away to the east. Yellow 3, Sgt Craig describes his part in assisting in this action, which he located over Herne Bay (about six miles west of Birchington).[71]

> I stayed with Yellow 1 and delivered a short head-on attack on the second wave, breaking away underneath and coming up for an astern attack. One Dornier broke away from his section and I attacked it after

Yellow 1. I saw pieces of cowling break away from aircraft and after two attacks in succession from Yellow 1 and myself (burst of 5 sec each attack), Yellow 1 broke away to follow another 215. I decided to stay with the first Aircraft and after another 5 sec burst from astern the rear gunner bailed out just off Herne Bay. I broke away to allow the rest of the crew to leave the aircraft which by this time was losing height rapidly with the port engine idling. As the crew did not appear to wish to abandon aircraft, I went in again and delivered an astern attack firing the remainder of my ammunition (except 8 rounds each gun), from approximately 150 yards. It was during this final attack that my aircraft was damaged. As I was getting very short of petrol and enemy aircraft appeared to be completely disabled, I broke away and return (sic) to base.

Craig's pause in his attack to allow further crewmen to bail out is noticeable; the gunner was observed to bail out over Herne Bay, about one and a half minutes' flying time west of Birchington, which is very likely where this machine plunged into the waters just offshore of that town. The crew of the machine down off Birchington were all killed and their bodies all recovered,[72] being close to shore. Sgt Dymond's second and separate attack on a second lone Do 17 which he claimed damaged while it was retreating eastwards, was also from ahead (and the beam). The determination to apply head-on attacks by 111 Squadron pilots was a distinct facet of their tactics in the Battle of Britain.

P/O Freeborn of 74 Squadron described chasing three Do 17s eastwards, attacking one from astern with a long burst, and then seeing it dive straight into the sea off Birchington.[73] Presumably he also contributed to the demise of the Birchington Dornier; as so often was the case, multiple attackers, especially when from different squadrons, failed to assign any significance to the attacks of other RAF machines – nothing dishonest in this, just human nature at work.

The fifth and last Do 17 lost by *KG 2*, another 7 *Staffel* machine, came down in the Thames estuary; no location is known and all the crew were lost, with one member's body being washed up at Whitstable.[74] Presumably, it went into the sea in that general area, to the east-south-east of the Isle of Sheppey. F/O Ferriss, commanding A Flight of 111 Squadron, reported attacking a Dornier in this general area at 07h10 together with his one wingman, which was flying in from the east and thus presumably from *III/KG 2*:[75]

> At approximately 0710 hours a formation of bombers was sighted and Hydro leader ordered me to prepare to carry out a head on attack

> while he approached the enemy aircraft to identify them. I saw Hydro leader taking his flight into attack and I positioned mine in sections line astern, each aircraft also being in line astern. As we were approaching the enemy aircraft they dived through the clouds and I was forced to abandon this attack and I turned over them and dived through the clouds parallel to them. I located them and their direction by the pattern bombing, and turned into the leading wave and delivered a head-on attack, while Yellow 1 made exactly the same attack on the second wave. All Red aircraft fired from 5-10 seconds at these twelve aircraft, which were flying in sections of three line astern stepped up. They pulled up as they saw us approach and wavered rather. No result was able to be observed as Red section broke away in the clouds. I was hit once in the breakaway. Red section was still in formation when we saw a single D.O.215. I carried out a Beam to Quarter attack, and was followed up by Red 2. The aircraft was seen to pull up immediately and then fall away. (Hydro leader = S/L Thompson of 111 Squadron; Yellow 1 = Sgt Dymond; D.O.215 = Dornier-17)

Ferriss was actually followed up by his number three wingman, P/O McIntyre, and not his number two; McIntyre reported his side of this engagement.[76]

> I followed Red section leader in a head on attack on a Vic of 3 Dornier 215. I took the centre aeroplane of the vic. I attacked and gave long burst opening at 300 yards, and closing to about 80 yards. I broke away above the aircraft, I attacked and noticed enemy formation had broken up. I rejoined Red 1 in line astern and intercepted a single Dornier flying E. I followed section leader's beam attack with one from slightly ahead closing in to point blank range. I raked the front fuselage of enemy aircraft and saw my bullets entering front cockpit, the nose of enemy aircraft went up and appeared to stall, and as I turned to attack aircraft once more, I saw its port wing had dropped and was losing altitude while still in stalled position. It was obviously so disabled that I refrained from further attack. (Dornier 215 = Dornier-17)

F/O Szczesny of 74 Squadron attacked a Do 17 in the same general area which had been separated from its formation:[77] 'One of the machines was out of formation and I attacked it from astern. At this point the Do. dropped several bombs in the sea. I got a good burst in from very close range and the Do. started to dive towards the sea. He tried to land there but as he flattened out he burst into flames and toppled straight into the water. This must have been somewhere in the Estuary East of the Isle of Sheppey. I did not know where I was and managed to force land at Maidstone with my undercarriage up, as I could not get it down.'

Szczesny may have observed the final demise of this aircraft, and it is thus suggested that this particular bomber was brought down by the two 111 Squadron pilots, Ferriss and McIntyre and the 74 Squadron pilot. The latter actually landed at West Malling (not Maidstone) on one wheel and crashed, damaging his Spitfire, at about 07h40, but he was unhurt.[78] Of course, any deductions relating claims and losses to each other will never be certain, but what is probably more realistic is that with five Dorniers lost and total claims for destroyed bombers amounting to fifteen assessed as destroyed (confirmed and unconfirmed),[79] there were most likely multiple attacks (and thus claims) on the same aircraft, for all five lost. Additionally, three more Do 17s were claimed as probably destroyed and nine damaged.[80] These additional claims must be balanced against seven Do 17s damaged, in which seven of their crew members were wounded.[81]

Information on localities and times of engagements resulting in damaged machines is of course much rarer than for aircraft shot down, especially those falling on land. For the latter there are witnesses in the air and often on the ground too, but not always. An example is a combat report by P/O Walker of 111 Squadron who claimed a Dornier destroyed over Herne Bay, given below,[82] which does not give any details of observed damage; possibly this pilot contributed to the demise of one of the Do 17s shot down, but very likely his last target may only have been damaged.

> I was flying Blue 2, and broke away to intercept a Dornier which was diving under the clouds, I lost that one and returned above cloud and saw enemy aircraft trying to reform, and made a half and half ¼ attack and he disappeared into cloud. I broke to port and saw a Dornier in front of me. I made a head on attack, closing to point blank range and he pulled up sharply and fell away to port, I followed him down but lost him in the haze at about 1500'. I noticed rear gunner fire cannon at me as I passed over the top.

RAF losses in the engagements with *Oberst* Fink's *KG 2* Dorniers were one Spitfire of 74 Squadron shot down (F/Lt Brzezina bailed out, unhurt) and two more damaged; 111 Squadron had three Hurricanes damaged.[83] So the disciplined and steady return fire from *KG 2*'s well drilled crews flying in tight formations hit six British fighters but only one was a total loss, and there were no personnel casualties inflicted. The *Luftwaffe* claims lists contain no mentions of any *KG 2* claims.[84]

Eagle Day: 13 August 1940

The major achievement of Fink's men was against their ground target, Eastchurch airfield, but this was not a Fighter Command station, and although elements of two fighter squadrons happened to be present, their losses were small, at least in machines and pilots, as detailed below.

Various standard sources on the Battle of Britain record the loss of five Blenheims (from 53 Squadron, Coastal Command) at Eastchurch airfield as well as one or even all twelve of 266 Squadron's Spitfires on the ground.[85] 53 Squadron did indeed lose five Blenheims to German bombing, but at 16h00 in a raid on another Coastal Command airfield, at Detling.[86] In addition to 266 Squadron, a flight of Spitfires from 19 Squadron and two Fairy Battle bomber squadrons, 12 and 142 Squadrons, were based at Eastchurch; none of those three units suffered any casualties to either personnel or aircraft.[87] 266 Squadron's experiences and losses are detailed in their Operational Record Book for 13 August 1940.[88]

> Warm Sky overcast – visibility moderate. EASTCHURCH aerodrome bombed and machine gunned by enemy aircraft from 07.05 hours to 07.20 hours. Two waves of 15 DORNIERS in Vic formation from South and East appeared over the Aerodrome dropping over one hundred High Explosive and Incendiary bombs. Airmen's quarters suffered severe damage and sixteen service personnel were killed and several injured. Squadron casualties were one killed (No. 916446 A.C.2. SHAWLEY J.D.), one severely injured (No. 973446 A.C.2. CROSSLEY H.) and four airmen slightly injured. Pilot Officer H.H. Chalder received severe cuts on foot. These casualties were admitted to County Counel (sic) Hospital at MINSTER. Several other airmen received minor cuts and bruises but after treatment resumed duties. All hangars were hit and the hangar occupied by the Squadron was set on fire. Three SPITFIRE Aircraft and two MAGISTER Aircraft were in the hangar at the time, but were removed after One SPITFIRE had been damaged by ..... (unclear, fire?), causing damage to both main planes – tail plane, elevator and airscrew. All Squadron ammunition, spare ammunition tanks and a quantity of equipment was destroyed. One bomb fell on officers' quarters shattering windows and dislodging plaster. Water supplies were seriously affected.

The courage of the ground personnel who removed the aircraft from the burning hangar was of a high order. 266 Squadron thus suffered one Spitfire damaged at about 07h10[89] and a pilot wounded in the bombing, with one member of their ground crew killed and another seriously injured. All the hangars at Eastchurch were damaged, the operations block was badly hit, the runway extensively cratered, electricity and telephone links were cut off and a quantity of fuel destroyed.[90] Forty-eight people were wounded in the bombing.[91] The fifteen minutes during which bombing occurred saw attacks by both *Gruppen* of *KG 2*, with *II/KG 2* and the *Stabskette* first, followed by *III/KG 2*. While most of the damage was caused by *II/KG 2*, who were relatively undisturbed by fighter attack (except for 74 Squadron's leading elements which attacked the *Stabskette* just prior to the initial bombing), the follow-up by *III/KG 2* was much less effective due to RAF fighter attacks, especially by 74 and 111 Squadrons.[92]

The first formation of *II/KG 2* dropped a few bombs on Leysdown airfield, close to the coast of Sheppey and about five miles east of Eastchurch, while scattered bombs from *III/KG 2* fell in the Herne Bay and Whitstable areas[93] as Dorniers jettisoned bombs when under fighter attack. Two Do 17s even bombed a couple of small merchant ships at Sheerness.[94] Despite the severe damage to airfield facilities, Eastchurch was operational by 16h00 on 13 August; both fighter squadrons, 19 and 266, were returned to Fighter Command control the same day without having flown any missions from Eastchurch.[95] The one bright spot in all this was the almost perfect functioning of the radar chain, despite the previous day's attacks on a number of RDF stations by *EGr 210*, ably assisted by the Observer Corps who accurately plotted Fink's formations flying up the Thames Estuary despite the extensive cloud cover.[96]

There is one more vignette in the Eastchurch 13 August 1940 story, and it involves two of those aboard the *Stabstaffel/KG 2* Dornier which came down at Barham. Apart from a sophisticated interrogation programme run by RAF Intelligence,[97] the British War Office also ran a secret programme which recorded the conversations between recently captured German POWs amongst themselves, using hidden microphones, where they tended to put Germans of similar rank but different units together; this was before they were transferred to normal POW camps.[98] Unfortunately, the actual names of the POWs are not given in the preserved transcripts of these conversations and the participants are all identified by a code number; the reports are, however dated.[99] In a few cases amongst many hundreds of such reports, it is possible to identify specific POWs from these documents, including two from the *Stabstaffel/KG 2* Do 17 who were shot down on 13 August: *Oblt* Schlegel (code number A346), the pilot and *Oblt* Oswald (A345), the *Staffelführer* (acting *Staffelkapitän*); the third POW in some of these conversations was another *Oberleutnant*, who had been the observer on a *KG 51* Ju 88 (code number A349).[100] During the Battle of Britain period, the vast majority of incoming German prisoners were from the *Luftwaffe*, hence the prefix 'A' for each POW's code number, representing 'Air'.

Eagle Day: 13 August 1940

National Socialism enjoyed wide acceptance in Germany amongst the general public during the Second World War.[101] This is well illustrated by a very expressive term, 'participatory dictatorship'.[102] The influence of Nazism in the German armed forces was less pervasive and this remains a complex subject,[103] but it should be remembered that the *Luftwaffe* was in many ways a Nazi creation, having been formed in the 1930s once Hitler was in power. Be that as it may, the three *Luftwaffe* pilots A345, A346 and A349 appear to have been rather convinced Nazi supporters, as can be gleaned from the transcripts of some of their conversations. At the end of one report on a conversation between *Oblt* Schlegel of *KG 2* and his unidentified comrade from *KG 51* (A349), the British intelligence officer recorded his own summary: 'Morale of both P/W high. Supreme contempt for everything English, absolute confidence in German victory.'[104] In another recording involving the same two, Schlegel tells A349 that 'A345 was exceedingly unpopular and is a coward.'[105] A345 is his own *Staffelführer*, Oswald! Despite flying with Schlegel as his observer on this mission on 13 August 1940, he was not a regular member of that crew. In a third conversation, *Oblt* Schlegel tells his *KG 51* comrade what happened to them on this operation.

> We made a forced landing in a "Do 17". We were making an attack on Eastchurch. The *Staffelkapitän* went below the clouds at 1500 metres. The *Kommandeur* forbade him to do that, but it was too late. We were due over the target at 7 o'clock. We arrived at 8, but none of our fighters was there then. There were clouds over the target. In the East there was a break in the clouds. Spitfires came out of it.... The left engine stopped. The armouring was really splendid. I shot down a Spitfire before I received the order to cease fire.[106]

The *Staffelkapitän* referred to by Schlegel is not his own (Oswald) but a II/KG 2 *Staffelkapitän* flying at the head of this *Gruppe* and in direct contact with *Kommodore* Fink in the *Stabskette* at the back of the II/KG 2 formation. The final partial transcript, cited below, is of a conversation between Schlegel, Oswald and A349, and shows that these men were Nazi supporters.[107]

> A346: The opposition of the Catholic priests to National Socialism is appalling. A345: These people (the Catholics) [parenthesis by British intelligence officer] consider themselves better than we, they consider themselves intellectually superior to the armed forces, I think it will slowly get better – with the people who have been through the "Hitler-Jugend". A346: If it doesn't get better, then it will get worse for them

Adlertag

(the Catholics)... A priest once tried to influence my parents against National Socialism. In consequence my father did not want to go to church any more; not a single one of the peasants went any more; the church was empty!

This illuminates the state of mind of at least three young and junior *Luftwaffe* officers at the time. For RAF Intelligence it certainly gave them good insight into exactly why they were fighting the Germans and why they really had to win the Battle of Britain. It is unknown but also rather doubtful whether such transcripts or pertinent comments therefrom were ever made known, obviously with heavy obfuscation of the means by which they were obtained, to any of the RAF fighter pilots. However, the latter knew what they were fighting for, and how vital it was that they stand fast until relieved; and that is exactly what they did. The determination of the RAF fighter pilots to get at their enemies was obvious in this early morning raid on Eastchurch, in the multiple attacks by 111 Squadron and by Sgt Savill and F/O Milne of 151 Squadron.

Unsuccessful large raid, RAF Farnborough and Odiham air bases, *c.* 06h40–07h15

Approximately at the same time as the Eastchurch raid carried out by *KG 2* under the auspices of *Luftflotte 2*, *Luftflotte 3* planned a large raid on the RAF station at Farnborough and on RAF Odiham a few miles to the west. Assigned to this mission were twenty Ju 88s of *I/KG 54*, slated to attack Farnborough and armed lightly with an average of just over 500 lbs of bombs per aircraft, predominantly small 110 lb bombs, and with only four 550 lb high explosive bombs and two similar-sized incendiaries.[108] Eighteen Ju 88s of *II/KG 54*, whose target was Odiham, were much more heavily armed, carrying an average of about 1,700 lbs of bombs, this time mostly the larger 550 pounders but still with only four incendiary bombs of the same size, as well as some 110 lb projectiles.[109] Quite why the supposedly more important target at Farnborough, which housed the RAF's Royal Aircraft Establishment research unit, was only to be attacked with a limited number of small bombs remains unclear. In addition to *KG 54*, eighty-eight Ju 87 Stukas of *StG 77* were launched against Portland naval base, but due to cloud cover over their target they turned away before reaching it and jettisoned their bombs in mid-Channel.[110] This large array of bombing power was protected by 173 Me 109s from all three available *Luftflotte 3 Geschwadern*, *JG's 2*, *27* and *53*, and sixty Me 110s from *I/ZG 2* (twenty-eight in number) and *V/LG 1*.[111]

Eagle Day: 13 August 1940

The RAF radar network picked up the first German formations at about 06h10, comprising about 100 machines near Dieppe, with a second force estimated at forty-plus to the north of Cherbourg.[112] The Dieppe detection most likely reflected the two *Gruppen* of Ju 88s from *KG 54*, which were based in the Evreux area some 60 miles south of Dieppe, and possibly also *I/ZG 2* (based near Amiens, *c.* 37 miles east of Evreux). *I/JG 2* (based about 15 miles west of Evreux), assigned to a sweep ahead of *KG 54* over the Brighton area, probably also formed part of this detected large force.[113] However, *I/ZG 2* broke away from this mass of German aircraft as they traversed the Channel and probably joined up with *II/JG 2* and flew as top cover or even as a sweep for the *KG 54* raid towards the west of Tangmere and inland, where the Me 110s spread out.

The more direct escort to *KG 54* was made up of *V/LG 1*,[114] which took off from their base just south of Caen[115] and then flew directly northwards to join up with their charges. *I* and *II/JG 53* (based at Rennes and Dinan, respectively)[116] were tasked with a sweep of the Isle of Wight area, which they found largely cloud covered; *I Gruppe* had no contact with British fighters, while their *II Gruppe* compatriots had some minor combats but suffered no losses and made only one claim,[117] which must have been rejected as it does not appear in the *Luftwaffe* claims list.[118] *I/JG 53* used a forward base in the Cherbourg area, while *II Gruppe* used Guernsey, RAF radar picking up a force estimated at twelve-plus off Guernsey at 06h24.[119] The force of forty-plus previously detected north of Cherbourg was most likely *StG 77*'s Stukas; their escort would have been elements of *JG 27*, which belonged to the same VIII Air Corps as the *Luftflotte 3* dive bomber units.[120]

In response to the radar detections, at 06h15 Fighter Command put up a section each from 43 Squadron and 238 Squadron over their respective base airfields, at Tangmere and Warmwell.[121] As the radar network indicated that the German formations were making their way out over the Channel, by 06h25 these two sections were reinforced by the balance of their squadrons, to leave twelve Hurricanes of 238 Squadron over Warmwell and a dozen from 43 Squadron flying a north-south patrol line just east of Tangmere.[122] At 06h17 Fighter Command ordered nine Hurricanes of 257 Squadron into the air from Northolt, with instructions to patrol Canterbury in Kent; upon arrival there at 06h25, however, they were vectored towards the south coast of Sussex and ordered to patrol south of Tangmere.[123] Applying the standard cruising speed of the Hurricane, they would have arrived at their new patrol area by about 06h40.[124] Such changes are an example of the balancing act forced upon the Fighter Command controller by two simultaneous raids on southern England; as the indications grew that the raids approaching the general area Tangmere-Isle of Wight–Portland appeared to be more extensive, so were dispositions altered. Similarly, nine Spitfires of 64 Squadron from Kenley, originally vectored towards the Thames Estuary after their take-off at 06h40, were also soon sent towards Sussex, meeting the enemy on the way, over Horsham at about 07h00.[125]

Finally, Fighter Command scrambled a dozen Hurricanes from 601 Squadron from Tangmere at 06h30 with orders to patrol their base, followed some five to ten minutes later by another dozen from 213 Squadron as well as six more from 87 Squadron, both from Exeter and placed to protect Portland naval base.[126] In the meantime, 238 Squadron had been dispatched from their patrol over Warmwell and sent eastwards to a position south of the Isle of Wight and arrived there by *c.* 06h40.[127]

While these RAF Fighter Command moves were afoot, the German formations were approaching the southern coast: one formation (easternmost) approached Littlehampton on the Sussex coast, while a second was making for the Spithead area (between the Isle of Wight's north-western coast and Portsmouth) a little way to the west; the third German formation was still in mid-Channel.[128] The easternmost formation was the *KG 54* raid, with *I/JG 2* sweep ahead and escort of Me 110s from *V/LG1* as top cover; that making for Spithead was almost certainly *I/ZG 2*'s Me 110s and the Me 109s of *II/JG 2*, while the mid-Channel force was most probably the two *Gruppen* of *JG 53* making for the Isle of Wight. At about 06h35, the *KG 54* raid group crossed the coast near Littlehampton with some elements like *I/JG 2* being further eastwards near Worthing; the Spithead force crossed near Portsmouth at about 06h40, with the third formation located some 20 miles south-west of St Catherine's Point, Isle of Wight.[129]

The force approaching Spithead would have steered clear of the formidable anti-aircraft defences of Portsmouth (already experienced by the *Luftwaffe* on the previous day), and would have passed to the east of the harbour. At the same time, *c.* 06h40, both 43 and 601 Squadrons were airborne out of Tangmere and heading eastwards towards Littlehampton, with 43 Squadron having been first off and thus placed a bit further east and at a higher altitude than 601's Hurricanes.[130] 257 Squadron which had been vectored post-haste from an original assignment in the Canterbury area had just arrived south of Tangmere[131] and must have passed below the incoming *KG 54* raid getting there; they were lucky not to be spotted, or worse, attacked by the German fighter escort.

S/L Badger led 43 Squadron eastwards from Tangmere, vectored towards where the controllers thought the enemy raid would cross the coast. The location of the engagement is noted as over Littlehampton and northwards.[132]

> I was leading No. 43 Squadron as Green 1 when we were ordered to patrol base 10,000' and contact Red Section who were already in the air. After rendez-vous we were ordered to 18,000' and warned of large formation of bandits approaching from South. At 13,000' approx. Red 1 gave Tally Ho. and Bandits were seen approaching our starboard beam. They were in two large formations of approx. 25 each. I climbed squadron up sun of nearer formation and turned S to meet them. When 1000' above I turned in to attack with sections in line astern. I went in behind one Ju 88 and gave him two steady bursts of five secs. I could see I was hitting but the target did not seem distressed except for the emission of black smoke which I believe was due to full throttle and turning I then noticed tracer passing me from the port quarter so broke away and gave alarm that me 110's were attacking us. I returned to attack a straggler in the other formation and gave him two bursts to finish all my ammunition but E/A did not go down. Return fire was fairly intense and appeared to be controlled as it was withheld until I was about 400 yds astern. The me 110's did one dive and then climbed out of reach showing no willingness to fight. I saw one E/A crash just west of Arundel and one parachute descending N. of Littlehampton. For the third time in succession that my squadron has been ordered to intercept E/A I have heard German being clearly spoken on our wavelength. (Red 1 = F/Lt Carey)

P/O Upton, flying number three in Blue Section behind Badger's Green Section, clarified the tactics adopted by his squadron leader in his combat report:[133] 'I was Blue 3 when Squadron Leader (Green Sec) sighted enemy crossing coast at 15000 in the vicinity of Worthing. Leader wheeled into sun to gain advantage of surprise – then South and through 180° to North where astern attack was delivered on 25 Heinkels 111.' The two *KG 54* bomber formations were flying about a mile apart and approximately parallel, each comprising vics of three Ju 88s (not He 111s as identified by Upton) line astern of each other and stepped down from front to back of the formations, to avoid the slipstreams of aircraft in front affecting those behind; the nearer formation was estimated at 23 aircraft and the further one as possibly 30 machines.[134]

While 43 Squadron documentation does not indicate which of the two parallel bomber formations S/L Badger and his men attacked initially, it can be surmised to have been the one flying on the left or western side of the two *Gruppen*, thus *II/KG 54*, carrying the heavier bomb loads intended for RAF Odiham. This is based on the fact that several 43 Squadron combat reports record that several Ju 88s were detached from the formation attacked,[135] and 257 Squadron, at approximately the same time (*c.* 06h40) located south of Tangmere close by and over the sea, encountered several straggling machines heading southwards, Ju 88s as well as a few Me 110s and Me 109s.[136] By the time 601 Squadron engaged the same two *KG 54* formations some minutes later and further to the north, they observed the nearer (western formation) group to be only nine strong.[137] So 43 Squadron appears to have detached nine of the eighteen Ju 88s originally making up the *II/KG 54* formation.[138]

While S/L Badger led most of his 43 Squadron pilots up into the sun and then down towards the approaching *II/KG 54*, flying past them and turning in to attack from astern and above as the Ju 88s headed northwards from the coast, three of his very experienced pilots did something different. Sgt Hallowes flying as number two to S/L Badger had seen extensive combat over the UK, Dunkirk where he was wounded, and in the early Battle of Britain, with seven victories to his name.[139] Instead of flying past the incoming Ju 88s, Hallowes turned in towards the bombers and made a deflecton shot at their leading aircraft. Seeing no results, he closed up behind them and made three attacks, two from astern and one from the port rear quarter; his first target was observed diving away, smoking from its port side, over Arundel, just north of Littlehampton.[140] He was then attacked ineffectually by an Me 110 from astern, broke away from the bomber formation and had a brief squirt at a Me 110 from head on before running out of ammunition.[141]

Hallowes also observed Green 3, Sgt Noble's Hurricane, going down streaming glycol[142] and indeed Noble's aircraft had been hit in the glycol tank and radiator, but he managed to put the damaged machine down at Tangmere with no further damage.[143] F/Lt Dalton-Morgan, while following with his section behind S/L Badger and before they had passed the incoming Ju 88s, saw that he was ideally placed to deliver a head-on attack on the bombers and, receiving permission from Badger to do so,[144] carried it out:[145]

> I was Blue Leader and took off with Green Section and Yellow section to join Red Section over base. We soon sighted e/a heading inland from the sea in 2 separate close formations 200 yards apart. I engaged an e/a in the rearmost formation delivering a head on level attack. He burst into flames and P/O Woods Scawen saw it dive steeply enveloped in flames. I carried on through formation and tried to engage a second but he swerved away and I engaged a Ju88 straggling behind the forward formation.' (Woods Scawen should be hyphenated)

He had succeeded in partially breaking up the formation he attacked. His reference to two separate Ju 88 formations and then to 'rearmost'

Eagle Day: 13 August 1940

and 'forward' formations should not be confused with referring to the two separate *KG 54 Gruppen* formations, but rather to two parts of the western, *II/KG 54* formation, which comprised a forward element of nine machines and a rearward element of nine. It was this rear bunch of nine Ju 88s that 43 Squadron's combined attack detached, a few of which were soon to be engaged by 257 Squadron over the sea to the south as they fled homewards. Dalton-Morgan observed some of the bombers split up as he attacked them from the rear after his head-on pass and also saw two Ju 88s diving away giving off flames and smoke.[146]

F/Lt Carey, already an RAF legend with eleven single and eight shared victories, promotion from Sergeant to acting Flight Lieutenant since the beginning of the war, a DFM and two DFCs awarded, and who had been wounded in France,[147] led Red Section of 43 Squadron as they closed on *KG 54*'s bombers.[148]

> I was leading Red Section and took off at 0615 with orders to patrol Brighton at 15000', afterwards changed to contact remainder of Squadron and patrol Tangmere at 18,000'. After joining up with them I sighted large bunch of E/A approaching Worthing at same height and gave Tally-ho. Leader turned Squadron to left to use sun as background, but E/A were too close and we attacked in waves, each section in line astern, from the E/A's Starboard bow. I followed in and attacked the Ju88 formation, "jinking" about in between each burst to watch E/A fighter escort and to foil E/A rear gunners. After first wave of attack it became mainly individual combat. After firing at the 3 Ju88s, on starboard of formation, they each showed signs of distress with smoking engines and falling back from main formation. Leading aircraft and left hand aircraft continued though losing height slowly but right hand aircraft dived steeply into layer of cloud with black and white smoke coming from engines and fuselage. I was attacked then by 3 Me. 110s so had to break off attack on Ju88s. ME. 110's pulled up and refused to mix it although I appeared to be isolated at the moment. When I had a moment to spare to attempt to look for E/A formation they had disappeared. I patrolled above and below cloud waiting for E/A to return and later saw one M.E. 10 (sic, 110) flying just above cloud heading S. at coast between Bognor and Littlehampton, but ammunition gave out after short burst and E/A was lost in cloud. I returned to base and landed at 0700. While waiting for return of E/A, I noticed large palls of smoke at following places:-
> 2 mls N. of Arundel
> 1 mile N. of Bognor,
> About 10 mls N.W of aerodrome in hills. ('Aerodrome' presumably Tangmere)

Adlertag

Carey's lone attack from starboard quarter ahead on the Ju 88s (his section, like Dalton-Morgan's did not follow him, but stayed with S/L Badger) detached a full vic of three bombers. The actions he describes took place while the bombers flew from Littlehampton at the coast to somewhere south of Petworth, and thereafter Carey returned to the coast to await retreating German aircraft. It is important when discussing actions such as this (and in fact almost all air actions in the Battle) to bear in mind that while an interception may have begun in a particular location (in this case, Littlehampton), the German bomber formations and their escorts to a lesser extent, generally forge on, aiming for their inland targets. The entire action therefore took place on the move, so to speak, bombers cruising at about 180-200 mph often, and the action would move at something like 3 or 4 miles a minute, with different individual actions hiving off as formations split up. This led to the common experience on both sides of an individual pilot suddenly finding himself, after some violent manoeuvre, flying apparently totally alone in the sky.

Section leaders in RAF Fighter Command played an important and indeed essential role in action, as is very obvious from the 43 Squadron accounts. A squadron leader (or senior flight lieutenant leading a squadron) would make the decision to put in an attack on an enemy formation, having assessed time and space available, the proximity and type of escort present and whether to divert any of his men to distract the escort while the bombers were attacked. The squadron leader would adopt a specific attack method (astern, beam, head-on attack etc.), but once it came down to the attack itself, very often sections followed each other in in line astern and circumstances changed while the sections attacked sequentially. Each section leader thus made tactical decisions for his own three-man formation, and with section leaders being experienced men by definition, they often made their own tactical moves.

In the present scenario, with both Blue (F/Lt Dalton-Morgan) and Red (F/Lt Carey) Section leaders having broken away suddenly to attack II/KG 54's Ju 88s from ahead, this left their two wingmen in each case rather at a loss. Both Sgt Deller (Blue 2) and P/O Upton (Blue 3) followed behind S/L Badger and attacked the Ju 88 formation from astern; the former fired three bursts at the bombers but saw no result, while the latter was unable to draw a proper bead on the bombers and did not get to fire in this first attack.[149]

F/Lt Carey's two wingmen were similarly left hanging. While Red 2, Sgt Crisp, did get in an astern attack on the Ju 88s, he did not get into effective range before being attacked by Me 110s; he fired at one closing in from head on but saw no result, then got onto the tail of the rearmost Me 110 now following the bombers, gave it a long burst and saw both

Eagle Day: 13 August 1940

engines smoking, claiming it damaged.[150] So often, smoking Daimler Benz engines signified over-throttling on the part of their pilots rather than significant damage, and as *V/LG 1* suffered no damaged or destroyed aircraft in this mission[151] this would appear to have been the case here. Carey's other wingman (Red 3, Sgt Mills), while approaching the Ju 88 formation from behind, observed an Me 109:[152] 'I was Red 3 and after taking off with Red Section at 0615 sighted a me (sic) 109 behind and rather lower than bombers just approaching coast. I dived on his tail and he headed out to sea. He took evasive action by steep turns and half rolls but I managed to keep on his tail and fired as opportunity offered. After my third burst smoke emerged and bits of a/c dropped away and he started a steady dive, still out to sea. Still in this dive of about 30° he hit the sea and submerged immediately. Nothing was seen to float and just a little oil covered the water. I returned to base direct and landed at 0700.'

This dogfight took place out to sea as the Me 109 retreated across the Channel. Presumably this Me 109 was from *I/JG 2*, which had done a free chase or sweep ahead of the *KG 54* raid. *I/JG 2* lost one Me 109 shot down that belly-landed in a field just south of Shoreham airfield in this raid, *Oblt* Paul Temme, adjutant of the *Gruppe* being taken prisoner.[153] The *Gruppe* suffered one other loss, a 2 *Staffel* Me 109, thought to have been flown by *Uffz* Schwentick, which was 80% damaged and written off when it belly-landed at Theville in the Cherbourg peninsula; the seriously wounded pilot never returned to his unit.[154] This casualty better fits the claim made by Sgt Mills; it was not that uncommon for pilots to 'see' a damaged opponent hit the sea, who had actually dived close to the water surface and managed to get away; the surface of the sea was continuously displaying breaking waves of different sizes and a brief glance at such a phenomenon as an opponent dived close to the water could easily lead to an impression of the enemy having gone into the drink.

Yellow Section of 43 Squadron were flying at the rear of the squadron and as befits that position, which often equated to flying the rearguard for the rest (although there is nothing in squadron documents to confirm this on this occasion), climbed up astern of the *II/KG 54* bomber formation and Yellow 1, P/O Woods-Scawen, attacked an enemy from above and astern, without visible result.[155] He failed to specify what type of German machine he had attacked over Littlehampton and inland thereof, but his wingman P/O Lane's combat report is more specific:[156] 'I was Yellow 2 in sections vic astern when e/a were sighted 3000 ft above crossing coast travelling N. I climbed with my section and attacked 2 Me 110s who crossed my sights. They were behind the bombers. No results were observed and I spun out of the combat.' Yellow 3, P/O Gray's combat report is not available, but as he claimed a Do 17 damaged[157] he would appear also to have engaged the Me 110s, presumably of *V/LG 1*, but without very concrete results. While the escorting Me 110s of *V/LG 1* did thus obstruct the astern attack by 43 Squadron, they did so without inflicting any serious damage, and as noted in the squadron Intelligence Patrol Report:[158] 'They were too far astern to render immediate assistance and when they did dive to attack our fighters, they seemed to have done so in a rather half-hearted manner.'

After 43 Squadron's four sections had attacked the *II/KG 54* formation near the coast, with most attacking either bombers or escorts from astern while Sgt Hallowes, F/Lt's Dalton-Morgan and Carey had attacked the bombers from beam and ahead, two members of Blue section continued to pursue the German bombers northwards, inland from the coast. Dalton-Morgan (Blue 1) after his daring head-on attack, flew after the remnants of the *II/KG 54* formation, now reduced to its forward *c.* nine Ju 88s and attacked a straggler. In a report included in his casualty file (he was wounded) he describes what happened.[159]

> I have the honour to report that during the morning of the 13th of August, 1940, I was with the Squadron during an engagement with about one hundred enemy aircraft. Whilst carrying out an astern attack on a straggling Ju.88 two other Ju.88's throttled back from the main formation and proceeded to direct controlled fire against me as I was breaking away. My aircraft was hit in the reserve petrol tank and somewhere in the glycol system. It caught fire, so I decided to endeavour to make a forced landing. I switched off the petrol and opened the throttle. I switched off the engine when the petrol had run out of the system. I then proceeded to glide the aircraft from 15,000 feet. When I reached 6,000 feet the flames were getting a grip on the cockpit, and glycol flames were beginning to suffocate me. I decided to abandon the aircraft and loosened my harness, oxygen tube and R/T lead, in readiness to jump. I opened the hood and tried to open the emergency panel, but it failed to release. I closed the hood again as to open it made the flames worse. After reducing the speed of the aircraft to 100 m.p.h. I again opened the hood and heaved myself out of the cockpit, and over the starboard side. After a few seconds I found the rip-cord of the parachute, and pulled it. I made a successful parachute descent on Cocking Downs, and only sustained a sprained ankle and twisted tendons as a result. I saw my aircraft crash in flames about 300 yards from where I finally descended.

While Blue 1 had followed the rump *II/KG 54* formation north from the coast, his one wingman, Blue 3 P/O Upton, also flew north following his

Eagle Day: 13 August 1940

initial attack and then attacked a formation of about twenty-five aircraft that he thought were Dornier bombers. His combat report[160] suggests that following his unsuccessful initial attack on *II/KG 54* he pursued the other Ju 88 formation of *I/KG 54* which was still intact, and at least seriously damaged one of their Ju 88s.

> I then broke away and headed North where I could see some 25 D.O. 17's. I got astern of one and opened fire at 300 yds with a short burst of 2-3 Secs – his port engine immediately issued streams of black smoke – I then closed to 150 yds where emptied all my ammunition into him – (his starboard engine then caught fire) and by this time his Port engine was burning – the machine went down into a zoom then slipped into a steep dive – burning furiously. I followed him to a thin cloud layer at approx. 4-5000 ft. and then turned in a wide arc to look for other members of the Squadron. I could see no one so returned to base and landed 0700. I cannot pinpoint position of enemy going down – but it was I should say 10–15 miles North of Tangmere beyond the Downs. I observed 5 parachutes in all – 3 North of Downs – 2 South.

The two German bomber formations went north away from the coast where they had crossed near Littlehampton, proceeding west of Arundel (and east of Tangmere) towards Midhurst-Petworth and on over Haslemere, some elements of 43 Squadron still following. 601 Squadron airborne from Tangmere a few minutes behind 43 Squadron also became involved, having had first to climb up to the bomber's level and above, flying parallel to the Ju 88s on their port (western) side, before engaging them in the Haslemere area.[161] Their actions will be detailed below, once brief descriptions of those of 43 Squadron who had continued to engage have been completed.

Arriving over Haslemere with *I/KG 54* still essentially intact on the starboard (eastern side) and the rump of nine Ju 88s of *II/KG 54* on the port (western) side, each *Gruppe* changed rapidly from a northern course onto western headings. *I/KG 54* spotted a hole in the solid cloud cover to the west of Haslemere, and dived down into it having made a sharp turn to port, and *II/KG 54* (smaller formation) also turned westwards, parallel with them but rather than diving down formed a circle.[162] *I/KG 54* released their bombs willy nilly through the gap in the cloud cover over an approximately five-mile zone stretching from Bordon in the north to Longmoor Liss in the south, lying about five miles west of Haslemere; their targets of Farnborough and Odiham lay some eight to ten miles further north and were not attacked at all.[163] Three pilots of 43 Squadron engaged the two bomber groups as these manoeuvres proceeded.

Adlertag

Sgt Deller, Blue 2 of 43 Squadron, described attacking the diving bombers of *I/KG 54*, in an excerpt from his combat report:[164] He 'saw several machines diving for the clouds and picked out a straggler – Ju 88 - & got 3 bursts in from astern concentrating on starboard engine. Bits fell off and it smoked badly. As I had something on my tail I broke away and before I could attack e/a again another Hurricane attacked it firing the other engine. Two of crew baled out. Not knowing this sector well I can't say where it was, being above 10/10 cloud, but can't have been very far from coast. I returned to base, having finished my ammunition at 0700, having taken off at 0635.' The second attacking Hurricane would have been from 601 Squadron. P/O Tony Woods-Scawen, the leader of Yellow Section of 43 Squadron engaged the *II/KG 54* Ju 88s and made repeated attacks on their circling formation. He was shot down, narrowly escaping a burning aircraft.[165]

> I broke away and attacked the other formation as they turned round from flying North and veered South again. A long burst into one e/a which I thought was a He 111 but might have been a Ju 88 made his port engine stream with black smoke and his starboard propeller stop. He continued South away from the formation which was circling back to the North again losing height when I saw him attacked by another Hurricane which I think had a grey nose and I presumed to be 601 squadron. So I followed the main formation round and attacked a Heinkel 111 (or maybe Ju 88) which gave forth jet black smoke and vivid red flames from port engine. E/a dived steeply through clouds. I was above 10/10 cloud but must have been somewhere N of Midhurst. I attacked a section of 3 bombers straggling behind the rest and fired at the starboard machine of the vic but my engine was hit repeatedly and I had to force land at Millard 12 miles N of Midhurst. Machine caught fire immediately I had got out. ('Millard' was Milland, north-west of Midhurst.)

Just like Sgt Deller, his one opponent was also attacked by a 601 Squadron machine. P/O Lane, flying behind Woods-Scawen as his number two, after spinning out of his initial engagement with some Me 110s over the coast, climbed for height before making his attack on the circling machines of *II/KG 54*:[166]

> When I regained control I had lost sight of the combat & was over Worthing. I saw a squadron of Hurricanes circling. I then saw many e/a by the black smoke that was coming from exhausts and their loose formation. I climbed up to 20,000' into the sun & dived down between

10 Mes 110 and about 20 e/a that I think were Heinkels 111. They went into a circle with (illegible) very loose vics & I singled out one following him round with a continuous burst closing right up and breaking away underneath. I didn't notice the rear gunners fire at all but there was plenty of cross fire from other e/a & I was not hit at all & circled about 4000 ft below formations as no one came to attack me. I climbed to attack the formation. Two Me 110's came down then to meet me, the first opening fire head on at 1000 yds and to which I replied at 400 expending my ammunition & passed underneath & returned to base, noticing a solitary Hurricane circling well below me. This was the only friendly a/c seen during my second attack. Returned to base at 0700.

Thus ended 43 Squadron's depredations against *KG 54* and their escorts. The Hurricane squadron which P/O Lane had observed circling was most likely 601 Squadron just before they engaged. Just like their other attacks on 43 Squadron over the coast, the Me 110s of the *V/LG 1* escort appear to have been ineffective, as related above by P/O Lane. 601 Squadron's attacks overlapped with the later engagements of some of 43 Squadron as just described, and 601 Squadron's Intelligence Patrol Report provides a succinct and very clear explanation of what they saw and how they engaged their enemies.[167]

Twelve Hurricanes of No. 601 Squadron took off at 0630 hours with orders to patrol base at 10,000 feet, and fifteen minutes later sighted 20-30 Ju.88s escorted by large numbers of Me.110s and 109s, at 12,000 feet flying North over Arundel. E/a were in two large formations of bombers, one of nine, the other about eighteen Ju.88s flying abreast and about a mile apart in sections of three stepped down slightly in line astern, in fairly close formation, while the fighters were stepped up in tiers into the sun. No. 601 Squadron were just to the West of the bomber formations, climbed and kept abreast of the enemy, at 180 m.p.h. When about to attack, the larger formation dived for a small hole in cloud, which was 10/10 at 5,000 feet, loosed off their bombs, and made off South. Squadron delivered beam attack on the whole of the other formation (nine) as they flew across the bows of No. 601 Squadron. They formed a defensive circle and a dog fight then developed... The other formation of Ju.88s was also attacked as they came out of their dive.

This report also gives the cruising speed of the Ju 88 formation, equating to *c.* three miles per minute, placing 601 Squadron's first attack (over

Haslemere) some twelve miles north of 43 Squadron's initial engagement over the coast, within a short space of time. Fascinatingly, there is an account from a most unusual ground witness, Wolfgang Edelstein, a Jewish schoolboy from Germany, to their passing over Haslemere on his birthday. A German-born child was watching his countrymen being engaged by the RAF, the enemies of his country, and upon whose success his life depended in the longer term. (His account is given later.)

601 Squadron was led by F/Lt Sir Archibald Hope (Red 1), their senior flight commander, who would soon succeed to command of the unit. An excerpt from his combat report makes it clear that he first attacked the smaller Ju 88 formation (*II/KG 54*; in the vicinity of Haslemere) and then the larger one (*I/KG 54*) as they pulled up from jettisoning their bombs, hitting two of the latter, each in company with another Hurricane, presumably from his own squadron.[168]

> Just as I was preparing to order the squadron to attack, the furthest formation (the larger one to the east) turned west and dived and at the same time the nearer nine turned west also but were not seen to attack. There was nearly 10/10 cloud at 5000 ft inland from the coast and the E/A just dived at a small hole and loosed off their bombs and then made off south. I first delivered a beam attack right across the whole of the nine formation as they flew across our bows, with no visible result. I then turned right through 180° and attacked the Ju 88's as they came out of their dive. I attacked one in company with another Hurricane and after breaking away it had vanished. I think we got it. I then attacked another Ju 88 and finished my bullets on it. As I broke away another Hurricane attacked it and almost immediately the starboard engine appeared to give out white smoke and the a/c was last seen losing ht and going very slowly. I landed at 0700 and by 0715 all our a/c had returned safely.

Red 2, F/O H. J. Riddle, who had a brother flying as number three in Green Section this day (and who made no claim in this engagement), became detached from his section as Hope went in, but managed to attack a straggling Ju 88 which had just been attacked by another Hurricane, and after a couple of bursts had his windscreen covered in oil from the struggling bomber, which appeared to be badly damaged.[169] He probably attacked one of the stragglers from the *I/KG 54* formation, and logically the other Hurricane was that of F/Lt Hope. The third man in Red Section, P/O Mayers, had to break off his attack on the bombers of *II/KG 54* as their escort intervened, and later tackled stragglers from *I/KG 54*:[170]

Eagle Day: 13 August 1940

I started to attack the bombers but as all the escort came down in a dive I made a climbing right turn into the 110s. I saw part of the roof and fuselage of one 110 break away as I fired one burst of about 3 seconds from almost head on. The E/A continued in a dive but I did not see what happened to it. Turning I saw a JU88 1000 ft below me. I dived and fired a long burst of 5 seconds giving full deflection. I saw the E/A explode just behind the pilot and go down in flames. Three of the crew jumped using parachutes. This combat is confirmed by F/O Dalton (sic: Doulton) of 'B' Flight 601 Squadron. While searching for my section I ran into 5 JU88's making for France. I climbed and made one beam attack sweeping the formation from front to rear. One E/A dropped behind and went into a cloud. I followed above the cloud and found it 800 ft under me when the clouds ended over the coast. I dived and fired all my remaining rounds into it at about 300 yds. One engine started to burn giving off black smoke and the E/A lost height. I followed it about 10 to 15 miles out to sea and last saw it losing height in a cloud of smoke. I landed at 0715.

Mayers was nothing if not persistent; having taken on a Me 110 from almost head on and where he was hazarding the very heavy nose armament of that machine, he attacked a lone Ju 88 separated from its formation and after observing three of its crew bale out, relentlessly pursued further retreating stragglers far out to sea. Three crew members successfully bailed out of a Ju 88 belonging to Stab *I/KG 54* which crashed and exploded at Treyford (south of Midhurst), killing the unfortunate pilot, *Oblt* Ostermann.[171] This particular crew had a rather unusual mission assignment, as became apparent during interrogation of the surviving three prisoners: after a very early morning lone take off from Gütersloh in Germany and carrying extra fuel tanks, they met the incoming *I/KG 54* at the coast and flew ahead as a reconnaissance machine and were then shot down by anti-aircraft fire.[172]

Ascribing a loss to anti-aircraft fire rather than a skilled aerial opponent was by no means an uncommon assertion of captured *Luftwaffe* aircrew. F/O Doulton described its loss in an excerpt from his combat report:[173] 'When my ammunition was finished I watched a Ju88 hit and set on fire by a Hurricane, three of crew jumped and their parachutes opened above cloud, I believe, 5 miles north of Goodwood the Ju88 ½ rolled and dived almost vertically in flames.' It is quite possible that the Ju 88 was already damaged by someone else from the squadron before Mayers settled its hash for good. The location given by Doulton is near Midhurst.

Red and Yellow Sections of 601 Squadron were observed by F/O Clyde, the leader of Blue Section, to dive after the formation of nine Ju 88s,[174] thus of *II/KG 54*; Yellow Section followed in behind F/Lt Hope's three machines of Red Section, in the Haselmere area. Their leader, F/O Davis also had his engagement with this *Gruppe* interrupted by Me 110s of the escort, but before that managed to make a head-on attack on the rear section of the nine Ju 88s:[175]

> I picked the leader of the last section and did a head-on attack, starting fire at 400 yds and breaking off at about 50. By then I was firing a full deflection shot. I saw bullets hitting but did not see what happened to him. The bullets were hitting fuselage and I think it likely that pilot was killed. Request confirmation of JU88 within 5 miles of target they were bombing. After attack on 88 I met ME 110s coming down and after one got on my tail I broke away. On my way home I heard P/O Fiske calling for help and found him near base with no amm^n and a damaged JU88. I fired remainder of my amm^n into JU88 at 250 yds. Killed gunner but no other effect. 88 went out to sea over Portsmouth with 1 engine disabled. AA guns did not fire at it, which surprised me. I landed at 0704 hrs.

Once again, the Me 110 escort's performance was distinctly lacklustre; Davis expended his remaining ammunition on a straggler from *I/KG 54* initially engaged by Billy Fiske whose experiences are detailed later. Yellow 2, P/O McGrath, tackled two stragglers from the nine aircraft of *II/KG 54*, and set on one of them, very likely already damaged by another member of 601 Squadron, and chased it southwards, out over the sea. He dispatched this machine.[176]

> I did three beam attacks on it and after the Second he went into a shallow turn with smoke pouring from the fuselage. I placed myself in front and beneath him and again did a beam attack from his right. After this his starboard engine caught fire and he spiralled through cloud into the sea. On hitting the sea there was an explosion and bits of wreckage could be seen floating. I climbed again and found another straggler who was travelling very fast and I could not manoeuvre into position. I fired 3 or 4 bursts from astern at 200 yds closing to 100 yds. Both engines were smoking badly and I saw an explosion in centre of fuselage after which smoke poured out and E/A went into a shallow dive. All guns pointing to rear had ceased firing. I watched him go down to the clouds but due to no ammunition I had to return to base as there was danger of meeting the escort fighters. I landed to refuel and rearm at 0700.

The second straggler he tackled likely also belonged to the same *Gruppe* of bombers; having seen no conclusive result to his second victim,

Eagle Day: 13 August 1940

McGrath could only claim a probable success. Yellow 3, F/Sgt Pond made no claim.[177] F/O Clyde led Blue Section in a beam attack on the larger *I/KG 54* formation, all three pilots using the same tactic in their initial attacks. Clyde's persistent attacks on this formation, which replied with intense fire, led to him being hit, his machine badly damaged and himself lightly injured; he made it back to base but had a lucky escape.[178]

> I led my section in a beam attack on the formation of 21 Ju88 in Vic formation – I attacked 1 Ju88 and saw it break away from the formation. Blue 2 later attacked this a/c with no definite result although he jettisoned his bombs and one engine was smoking. I then turned and attacked on the outside of the formation another Ju88 from quarter and finished into line astern. This a/c slowed right down and dived straight thru cloud with both engines smoking. I think this was a good "Probable". I was unable to follow it down as my a/c had been hit in both mainplanes and in the oil sump and I had been hit by splinters on the leg – later it was found that bullet had come thru the front armour plating and pierced the air pipes making guns u/s also broke flying wire and one elevator control. Bombers kept very good formation with the exception of the outside men who seemed inexperienced. Very heavy cross fire encountered. Landed 0710.

P/O Grier was flying in the Blue 2 position and after giving the Ju 88 detached by his section leader three bursts, singled out another straggler, this time from the smaller *II/KG 54* formation which had formed a defensive circle; he gave it three bursts also, and left it in a shallow dive, both engines apparently burning and issuing lots of black smoke.[179] Blue 3, P/O Fiske hit a Ju 8 from *I/KG 54* in his initial beam attack, which left the formation and was immediately pursued by another Hurricane, so Fiske went for another diving Ju 88 at the right rear of the bomber formation:[180]

> I put in a burst and starboard propeller stopped. E/A broke away and dived straight from about 8000 ft. through cloud to 2800 ft. I followed him all the way firing in an attempt to put port engine out. Unsuccessful, but E/A could not gain enough height to get back into cloud. He had no more ammunition, at least all firing ceased. I called for other Wepon a/c over South Downs and all way to Thorny. Wepon yellow 1 came up but I thought he also was out of ammunition. E/A last seen in gentle glide over Solent about 2500 ft. proceeding towards Bembridge with A.A. bursts all around him. (Wepon = 601 Squadron radio call sign; Wepon Yellow 1 = F/O Davis; Bembridge lies on the east coast of the Isle of Wight)

Adlertag

F/O Doulton led in the last section (Green) of 601 Squadron, and he observed F/Lt Hope making for the smaller *II/KG 54* formation before clearly seeing the larger *I/KG 54* formation peeling off into a dive, with dive breaks on, right in front of him. He attacked this from astern:[181] 'I turned left and followed one JU88 in a steep dive but had no difficulty in overtaking it. My first burst from dead astern made the Ju88 pull out of this dive and my windscreen was covered with black oil. The Ju 88 then levelled out and slowed to 150 mph enabling me to close in and get two long and steady bursts from dead astern. Answering fire from the rear gunner ceased during my last burst and the Ju88 dived gently into the clouds and I lost it.' F/Lt Hope appears to have attacked this same Ju 88 after his initial attack on the smaller *II/KG 54* formation. Green 2, Sgt Hawkings, made repeated attacks on two separate Ju 88s from the *I/KG 54* formation, seeing the first jettison its bombs and an engine catch fire, before leaving it to further attack by another Hurricane, presumed to have been Blue 2, P/O Grier; the second dived into the clouds, the crew bailing out as it went.[182] His second claim appears to overlap with the *I/KG 54* bomber downed at Treyford and which had been engaged by P/O Mayers (Red 3), as reported earlier.

Ground witness to *KG 54* flying over Haslemere: Wolf Edelstein's twelfth birthday, 13 August 1940

Wolfgang Edelstein (who later changed his name to Elston, and nicknamed 'Wolf', an alias also favoured by Hitler, ironically) celebrated his twelfth birthday on this day. While his first-hand account of living as a non-Aryan within Nazi Berlin in the late 1930s is both fascinating and unsettling, what is remarkable is that his parents and his private Jewish school still placed great emphasis on German patriotism and culture despite all the restrictions, humiliation and physical danger imposed on them. His later move to England under the life-saving auspices of the Quaker *Kindertransport* movement was to place this young lad of only ten in muddy emotional waters during the Battle of Britain. Wolf attended the *Goldschmidt-Schule* in Berlin, a Jewish private school, after non-Aryans were expelled from the public schools. Prior to that he attended *Volksschule 15* where he was brutally bullied by classmates and the many party member teachers, though his *Klassenlehrer* (form teacher) tried to protect him, the only non-Aryan boy in the school.[183]

His memories of schooldays in Berlin during 1938-1939 that follow he kindly provided to the author.[184] Amongst Wolf's classmates in

Volksschule 15 before these public schools were closed to non-Aryans was Norman, the son of Hans Frank, notorious legal advisor to Hitler and the Nazi Party and later the murderous ruler of the rump of the Polish state, the General Government. Wolf was ten years old when he started at this school and only attended it for six months. Strangely, while brutally bullied by his classmates, Norman Frank protected him. When Wolf was targeted by his fellows for his dark hair, Norman told them to leave him alone as his father and the *Führer* had dark hair! The six months he spent there encompassed also the Sudetenland crisis, the Munich agreement, and *Kristallnacht*, 9-10 November 1938; his parents then realised there was no future for the family in Germany.

At the *Goldschmidt-Schule*, the approach was conservative and pro-German. Ancient German ancestors such as Arminius were the ideal, a German who had become a Roman citizen and received military training, and who later defeated three Roman legions in the Teutoberg forest in 9 BC. Wolf's parents were in full agreement with such sentiments and regarded themselves as proper German patriots as opposed to the false prophets of Nazism. His father had volunteered immediately the First World War broke out and served for four years, rising to *Unteroffizier*; as a front-line veteran he was allowed to practise as a lawyer after the 1935 anti-semitic Nuremburg laws imposed restrictions on most freedoms and activities of Jewish people. His mother, who began her studies towards a medical degree in 1914 and who interrupted these to serve as a nursing sister throughout the war in military hospitals, was denied such rights as she was not recognised as a front-line campaigner, and so was forbidden to practise as a doctor after 1935.

While the *Goldschmidt-Schule* was a Jewish private school, Wolf did not attend the Jewish religious studies there, as his father's family had converted to Christianity three generations earlier; he thus attended a special evangelical Christian class as part of a small group of what he termed 'Goyim'. The lives of the Jewish children shrank steadily, things like movie theatres and public swimming baths being out of bounds, and gangs of Hitler Youths on the streets became an ever-present and considerable danger. During the 1938 Sudeten crisis, all males had to register for military service of some kind, and despite being a non-Aryan his father had to as well, being placed in *Ersatzreserve 2*, the lowest reserve category. Wolf was witness also to squadrons of Ju 52s passing overhead; he realised that the same few squadrons were being used repetitively in a mock show of force. For him, the Munich peace agreement was highly significant as it saved his life; had war broken out in 1938 before he could get out of Germany, he would have been swallowed up in the Holocaust.

Adlertag

In early November 1938, Wolfgang noticed that there were several empty seats in his classes. This was due to Jewish families who possessed Polish passports and thus felt themselves safe in Nazi Germany. This was a big mistake as the Polish authorities suddenly decreed that all such Jews must return to Poland within forty-eight hours or lose their citizenship. It was this cruelty, visited also on his parents, that led the seventeen-year-old Herschel Grynszpan in Paris to assassinate a Nazi diplomat at the German embassy, which in turn led to the pogrom of *Kristallnacht*, 9 November. On the following day the synagogue behind Wolf's apartment block was burnt down, and the *Goldschmidt-Schule* was closed down for several days. Wolf had been sent to spend this dreadful night with friends where the husband was already in a concentration camp, and whose house was thus deemed safe. Meanwhile, *Gestapo* coming to arrest his father at their apartment just missed him as he slipped out a back door, but assaulted his mother seriously and threatened her and her elder son of fourteen with execution.

When the school re-opened, the Jewish students had to walk to school in groups as protection against marauding bands of Hitler Youth, and classes shrank as children were got away to the USA, UK, Palestine and Holland (the latter tragically in vain). The *Goldschmidt-Schule* had been sold to an English teacher, thus providing British protection against further Nazi moves. By now Jewish children were leaving in numbers, many under the auspices of the Quakers in the US and UK; over ten thousand were to be rescued before it was too late.

During 1939 New Year celebrations, Wolf's mother quietly provided family members with fatal doses of Veronal, a sleeping drug. In 1942, his paternal grandmother used hers the night before she was to be transported to the East. His maternal aunt and uncle (a decorated World War 1 veteran) did not use theirs and perished in Majdenek extermination camp. And still, both in the *Goldschmidt-Schule* and at home, German patriotism and culture were emphasised to Wolf in 1939.

While adults now struggled to be able to leave Germany, children could be got out, and were allowed into the UK, with Wolf's paternal cousin assisting with the trip for him and his elder brother. The two brothers sailed for England from Hamburg on 11 February 1939, and would not see their parents again until 1945; the parents were very lucky to get out also, in 1941 and via unoccupied France, Spain and Portugal, to the US. In 1939, the family's pastor was placed under house arrest by the *Gestapo*, accused of baptising Jews, but he had only handled the confirmation for Wolf's brother; in the neighbouring parish of Dahlem, the famous anti-Nazi Pastor Martin Niemöller was put into a concentration camp, an ordeal that was to last for seven years.

Eagle Day: 13 August 1940

Wolf thus found himself in England in early 1939; he had got out in time and now faced a new and uncertain existence in a country where he was regarded in some quarters as an enemy alien. Thanks to support from his father's cousin once more, the Edelstein brothers found themselves at the Stoatley Rough School, just outside Haslemere in Surrey, where Wolf was to remain until 1945. His depiction of life in the Haslemere district including witnessing the Battle of Britain going on above his head is from a memoir he wrote in 1990,[185] unless otherwise indicated.

The school was founded by Dr Hilde Lion in 1934, using a large country house given to the Quakers by Mrs Marjorie Vernon;[186] they took in about 100 mainly Jewish refugee children fleeing from Nazi Germany under the *Kindertransport* scheme, organised by the Quaker Germany Emergency Committee under the leadership of Bertha Bracey.[187] The teachers at the school, which wisely and unusually allowed siblings of both sexes to remain together, included both German exiles who had voluntarily left including some senior members who had belonged to the women's movement of the Weimar Republic, and British educators. Instruction was in both German and English.

On 3 September 1939, Wolf and some of his friends saw the RAF squadrons fly overhead, heading for France when the war broke out. The children at the school suffered anxiety with the string of German victories ending in the Dunkirk evacuation and the fall of France. The latter was accompanied by the issuing of Alien Registration Cards to those fourteen years and older, which made an ironic accompaniment to the children's German passports, stamped with a large and bright scarlet letter J to signify that they were non-Aryans in their homeland. The local people however, ignored all such strictures and accepted them. Despite the vast majority of the children being of Jewish ancestry, the establishment was essentially secular, with limited religious instruction of any kind.

On 13 August 1940, Wolf's twelfth birthday, he was awoken by the sound of many aircraft throbbing overhead at about 06h00, and dashing outside spotted neat formations of silver dots high in the sky as Göring's *Adlertag* got off to a somewhat shaky start due to the weather. Then, a major thrill as two Hurricanes swept past above them and climbed up into the sky, and they could also hear distant thuds and machine gun fire. Only then did the Haslemere and school air raid alarms go off and the children took shelter in the coal cellar. Here the singing and congratulations for Wolf's birthday enabled him also to express his thanks to Hermann Göring for providing the fireworks to mark the occasion.

Over the next few months, the children saw twisted contrails high in the sky and on occasion spent cartridge cases fell out of the heavens onto

Adlertag

corrugated iron rooves. Almost every night there were air raid alerts over the next nine months with, in the earlier ones, several alerts during the day also; this largely came to an end with June 1941 and the German invasion of Russia. Ironically, during the winter of 1940-1941, while Wolf was being kept awake in Haslemere by the *Luftwaffe* overhead, his parents were being robbed of their sleep in Berlin by RAF bombers. Wolf's former German neighbours were hellbent on their destruction, while those who risked their lives to keep them safe (RAF day and night fighter pilots) considered them enemy aliens. This strange somewhat schizophrenic reality would have pervaded the scholars' thoughts during the Battle of Britain.

Additional engagements in the Farnborough–Odiham raid

While 43 Squadron was engaging *II/KG 54* and some of their escorts near Littlehampton at about 06h40, nine Hurricanes of 257 Squadron led by S/L Harkness were waiting just south of Tangmere over the sea, where they intercepted a few straggling Ju 88s and Me 109s; these were almost certainly from 43 Squadron's engagement, which split off about half of the bombers from their formation.[188] Harkness first spotted a few enemy machines above them while they were at 12,000 ft and he led his Blue Section up to about 18,000 ft, where he found a few enemy strays making off southwards; after seeing a lone Me 109 dive away from a higher altitude, he sighted a single Ju 88 which he attacked from abeam and astern before it dived into the clouds.[189] His one wingman P/O Cochrane attacked another single Ju 88 but was interrupted by a couple of Me 110s whom he avoided easily, making a deflection shot at one before they, too, vanished in the clouds below.[190]

While Red Section lost contact when Harkness dived after his Ju 88, F/O Mitchell led his Green Section up after Harkness's original climb to *c.* 18,000 ft, and while trying to place his section into the glare of the sun, noticed four Me 109s above doing exactly the same thing; the Germans then came down and attacked them ineffectually as Mitchell led his men into a steep turn. Green 3 Sgt Hulbert was hit yet managed to get his badly damaged Hurricane to Tangmere for an emergency landing, unscathed himself.[191] As Mitchell came round onto the tails of the rapidly diving Me 109s, the enemy leader broke away and took energetic avoiding manoeuvres, but Mitchell thought he had hit him from about 400 yards range, before this machine also vanished into the clouds.[192] Lance Mitchell followed and as he came out below the cloud saw a Ju 88 in front of him being fired on by a Hurricane that broke off as both the

Eagle Day: 13 August 1940

enemy's engines gave off smoke trails. Following several more attacks from astern by Mitchell, the bomber dived to sea level wreathed in smoke and disappeared into the haze.[193] Mitchell claimed the Ju 88 as a probable, with his Squadron Leader apparently having damaged it first.[194]

At approximately the same time, just a few minutes behind the *KG 54* raid, the sweep by *I/ZG 2* and *II/JG 2* arrived south of the Isle of Wight, then skirted this island and crossed the coast east of Portsmouth, and elements of *II/JG 53* swept in towards the south of the Isle, as described above.[195] 238 Squadron, operating from Warmwell, became briefly involved with these elements of the overall *Luftwaffe* raid. The squadron had sent up Green Section initially, which was vectored eastwards to the north of the Isle of Wight and once north-east of it was turned towards the south, flying at about 30,000 ft.[196] From their great height they observed a Me 110 formation which rapidly turned away and disappeared and thereafter had no further enemy contact.[197] F/O Hughes led the other nine Hurricanes of the Squadron up from Warmwell, and while they did not link up with Green Section, were vectored to the south of the Isle of Wight, flying at about 25,000 ft.[198]

Both sections of the ORB describe how they were surprised from above by enemy aircraft, which Blue Section leader P/O Urwin-Mann saw only just in time to shout a warning; Sgt Batt flying as Yellow 2 was separated from his squadron by this attack,[199] while Sgt Seabourne (Blue 3) was shot down, and their colleagues took frantic avoiding action and got away. Sgt Batt clearly saw that their attackers were Me 109s,[200] and logically these would have been from *II/JG 53* who engaged the RAF south of the Isle of Wight; they claimed one Hurricane without loss,[201] but their claim was not confirmed in the *Luftwaffe* victory list.[202]

They almost certainly did shoot one down, that of Sgt Seabourne, who was seen from a destroyer at sea and from ground observers on the shore to take on three Me 109s, apparently dispatch two and then succumb to the third.[203] Seabourne force-landed in the sea, badly burnt, where he was very lucky to be picked up by the destroyer HMS *Bulldog* that had witnessed his combat.[204] He had displayed great presence of mind in his ordeal; with his engine seized after a cannon shell hit the radiator and with the Hurricane burning and the hood jammed, he turned it on its back and literally fell out with the hood, and after delaying his drop for 16,000 ft to escape the combat zone, managed to open his chute and inflate his Mae West before landing in the water about seven miles south of the Isle of Wight.[205] He was to spend seven months in hospital and undergo numerous plastic surgery operations.[206]

Meanwhile, Sgt Leslie Batt, finding himself alone, spotted some Me 110s below and while starting a turn and dive to tackle them felt the Hurricane take an enormous impact, the machine diving almost vertically out of control, streaming glycol coolant and with a large dollop of oil inside his windscreen, his hood wide open as the cold air howled in.[207] As his senses returned he found his eyelids gummed shut with oil, prised them open and got the aircraft level again, and turned north towards land and closed the hood.[208] At this, the large amount of oil inside his windscreen which the slipstream blast had been sending out of the cockpit in the dive landed in his lap; gliding north and steadily losing altitude he broke cloud at about 2,000 ft over Selsey Bill, much to his relief, and landed unhurt, wheels-up in a field near Tangmere, at Eartham.[209]

The Me 110s he had seen would have been from *I/ZG 2* and their top cover of *II/JG 2* (who made one confirmed claim for a Hurricane)[210] were probably responsible for downing Sgt Batt; these Me 110s and Me 109s were carrying out a sweep to the east of Portsmouth and passed up the eastern side of the Isle of Wight on their way to the coast. 238 Squadron did not make any formal victory claims.[211]

Eight 64 Squadron Spitfires from Kenley were initially sent towards the Thames Estuary,[212] presumably to counter the Eastchurch raid. However, they were later redirected towards the south-west along a vector of about 240° and when flying over Horsham about ten miles north of Worthing on the south coast at about 07h00 saw six to eight 'Do 215s' in a loose vic formation about three miles to their starboard, heading northwards.[213] Upon sighting the Spitfires, the German aircraft lost no time in reversing course and making off to the south-west at speed; 64 Squadron only caught up with them near Chichester after a chase of about fifteen miles, where they observed two other enemy formations converging upon the first from both east and west, all three then making off southwards.[214] The speed of these supposed Dornier bombers indicates that they were in fact Me 110s, obviously those of *I/ZG 2* which had spread out over the region where the raid was supposed to take place.

F/O Woodward, leading the squadron on this occasion, ordered an attack by sections from quarter astern, and a slew of skirmishes ensued between the eight Spitfires and various small formations of Me 110s fleeing southwards, some forming small defensive circles.[215] He himself attacked one Me 110 from the beam and astern, assisted by two more Spitfires, leaving the Me 110 with one wing and engine on fire, P/O Simpson seeing it spiralling down steeply, burning.[216]

Simpson attacked another Me 110 repeatedly, leaving it with a silent rear gunner and its undercarriage down, before running out of ammunition and breaking away.[217] Woodward claimed a confirmed victory, Simpson one severely damaged, and three more squadron members reckoned they had damaged their opponents, but with little

Eagle Day: 13 August 1940

direct observation of any meaningful damage. This is illustrated by the combat report of one of them, F/Sgt Gilbert:[218] 'Ordered to patrol at 15000ft and given vector of 240°. I was leading Blue Section and enemy a/c were observed on starboard about three miles distance. Enemy appeared to be on Northerly course but immediately on sighting us made South at high speed. I carried out No.2 attack on Port aircraft. Observed rear fire which appeared to be inaccurate. After 2nd attack e/a stopped firing, but no further damage was noticed.' (No. 2 attack means by sections, from quarter astern.) Against these claims there were two damaged Me 110s from *I/ZG 2* which managed to get back to base, three of the four crewmen being wounded.[219] Presumably, one of these was damaged by F/O Woodward and two of his squadron mates, and the second hit by P/O Simpson (and possibly others also). Simpson's own aircraft was damaged in return, but he was unhurt and got his Spitfire safely back to base.[220]

What then was the upshot of the German raid on Farnborough and Odiham? Based on the detailed accounts presented above, a reconstruction is possible. 43 Squadron intercepted the *KG 54* bombers and escorts as they approached the coast neat Littlehampton, attacking the formation of eighteen Ju 88s of *II/KG 54* as they rapidly approached the twelve Hurricanes from their beam. S/L Badger had seconds to react and took the only possible sensible action, which was to immediately turn to port, flying just ahead of the bombers and gaining height before turning through 180° and diving through another 180° and attacking from close astern of the rear nine bombers before the escort came down.

A few members of the squadron broke away to attack from beam, head on and from quarter ahead before the bulk went in from astern. 43 Squadron got in a set of rapid attacks on the Ju 88s and detached nine of them, before disruption from some of the Me 110s from the escort who made ineffective dives on them before breaking upwards again. A few members of the squadron followed the Ju 88s as they flew north attacking the rump of *II/KG 54* and some of *I/KG 54*. In the Haslemere area, with 601 Squadron closing in on the two bomber formations, the larger and still relatively intact *I/KG 54* dived into an opening in the solid cloud cover, jettisoning its bombs while the remnant of *II/KG 54* lost height and formed a circle. Both Ju 88 formations had turned abruptly from northern to western courses just as 43 Squadron's final attacks were made and those from 601 Squadron began, the latter hitting both bomber formations effectively. F/Lt Hope leading 601 ensured that both German bomber formations were attacked from beam to astern as they altered course rather unexpectedly. That expert air fighter, F/O Carl Davis, even managed a brief head-on attack on the *I/KG 54* formation.

Adlertag

Claims by the two squadrons encompassed one Ju 88 confirmed, three unconfirmed, two probables and five damaged by 43 Squadron, while 601 Squadron claimed one Ju 88 confirmed, another unconfirmed, eight and a half probables and three and a half damaged. As generally occurred in the Battle, multiple attacks on the bombers were common, and 601 Squadron's pilots noted six shared claims amongst bombers assessed as probably destroyed or damaged. Some pilots described He 111s rather than the Ju 88s involved.

I/KG 54 lost one aircraft which crashed at Treyford (near Midhurst; one killed, three POWs) which was attacked by P/O Mayers and Sgt Hawkings of 601 Squadron (if not others also), and another aircraft and crew in the Channel, with six more damaged carrying three wounded crewmen home.[221] *II/KG 54* suffered equally badly, with one Ju 88 lost and crew killed near Arundel (close to Littlehampton, probably by 43 Squadron with F/Lt Dalton-Morgan at least involved) and another and second crew in the Channel (attacked by P/O McGrath, 601 Squadron, probably others too); five were damaged from which one crewman died of his wounds and four more were wounded.[222]

With the multiple attacks and likely sharing of lost and damaged enemies between the members of the two squadrons, it is not possible to assign detailed *KG 54* casualties to specific attacking Hurricanes. Suffice to say that four Ju 88s were lost and eleven damaged out of a total of thirty-eight, a very high casualty rate, and all for a totally failed raid, not a bomb being dropped anywhere near either target, nor even any serious attempt to reach either RAF Farnborough or Odiham. The response of the *V/LG 1* Me 110 escorts was pallid, they suffered no losses against four claimed damaged, three by 43 and one by 601 Squadrons. 43 Squadron claimed an unconfirmed Me 109 destroyed, probably the written-off machine of *Uffz* Schwentick, 2/JG 2 who was badly wounded,[223] probably by Sgt Mills.

The other lost Me 109 of *Stab I/JG 2*, flown by *Oblt* Paul Temme who became a POW after bellying-in near Shoreham, may possibly have been engaged by F/O Mitchell, who also claimed a Ju 88 probable previously shot up by his boss S/L Harkness of 257 Squadron south of Tangmere. They had a Hurricane damaged by the Me 109s. 238 Squadron were bounced by *II/JG 53* south of the Isle of Wight, and probably also by elements of the *II/JG 2* top cover to the Me 110s of *I/ZG 2*, losing two Hurricanes (probably one to each Me 109 *Gruppe*) and one pilot seriously wounded, for no claims. Two of the *I/ZG 2* Me 110s were damaged in running skirmishes with 64 Squadron in return for a damaged Spitfire, over Chichester and out to sea. 43 Squadron had two aircraft shot down by Ju 88 return fire (one pilot slightly injured) and one damaged, possibly

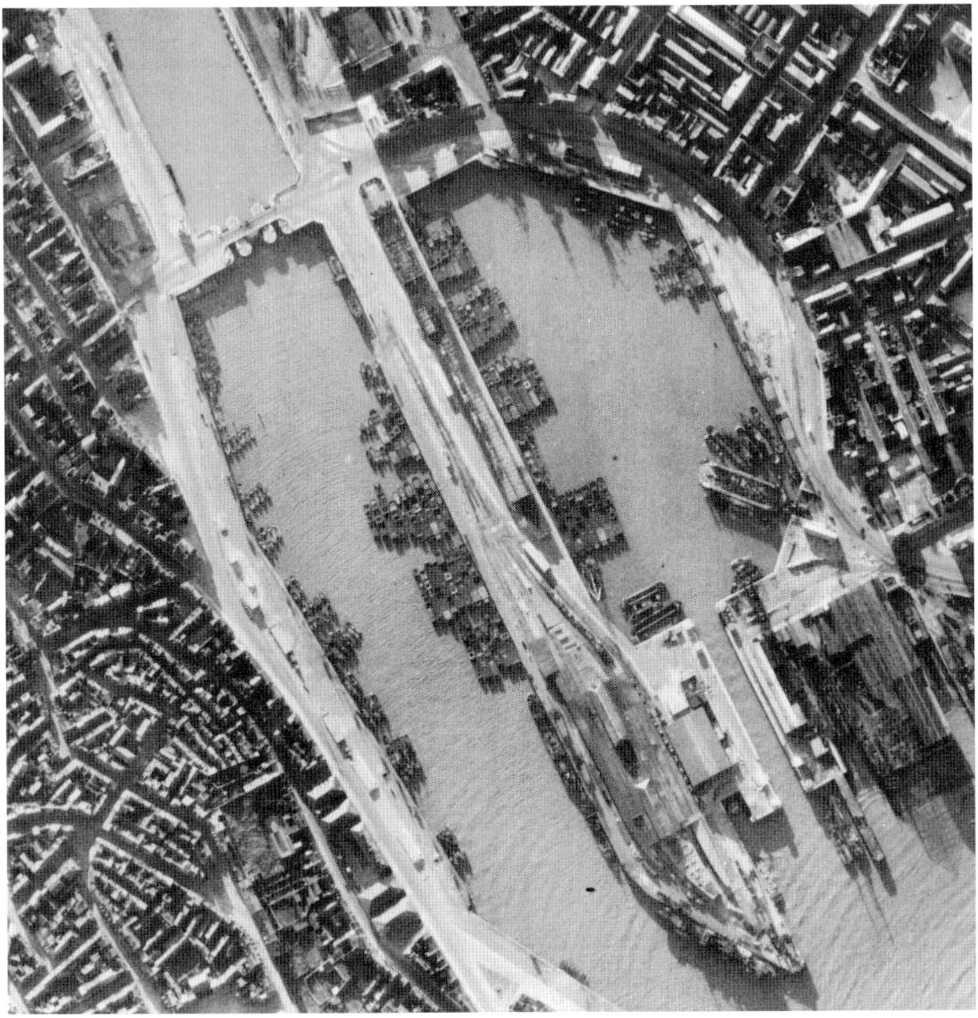

Above: The Battle of Britain was fought to maintain adequate RAF air superiority to ensure the German invasion fleet never set sail; invasion barges in Boulogne harbour for Operation *Sealion*.

Right: Generalfeldmarschall Albert Kesselring, commander of *Luftflotte 2*, stationed in north-eastern France, Belgium and Holland.

Above left: Generalfeldmarschall Hugo Sperrle commanded *Luftflotte 3* in Normandy and Brittany; Hitler half-jokingly called him his most intimidating field marshal.

Above: Major Theo Osterkamp, highly decorated First World War ace, in a pre-war Nazi military parade, mid-1930s. As a *Generalmajor* and *Jagdfliegerführer* of *Luftflotte 2*, he enjoyed the confidence of Kesselring and was an influential figure in *Luftwaffe* fighter strategy and tactics.

Left: Hanns Trübenbach led *I/LG 2*'s Me 109s as a *Hauptmann* during 11–13 August 1940, before taking over as *Kommodore* of *JG 52* later that month.

Right: Faith Winter's statue of Air Chief Marshal Lord Dowding outside the RAF church, St Clement Danes, in the Strand, London; no man deserves the recognition more. (Courtesy Elliott Brown under Creative Commons 2.0)

Below: King George VI and Queen Elizabeth visit Dowding at Fighter Command headquarters, Bentley Priory, September 1940.

Wing Commander Alan Deere, right, and Squadron Leader Dennis Crowley-Milling later in the war. During the Battle 'Al' Deere flew as the senior flight commander in 54 Squadron, and P/O Crowley-Milling in Douglas Bader's 242 Squadron.

The beautiful and immortal Spitfire shows off its lines; rebuilt wartime Mark IX model based in New Zealand, of later vintage than the Battle but in Al Deere's markings in his honour.

Above left: The famous South African S/L A. G. Malan in his Spitfire at Biggin Hill, probably 1941. 'Sailor' Malan, a pre-war merchant marine officer, led 74 Squadron in August 1940; an outstanding aerial tactician and innovator.

Above right: Cuthbert Orde's portrait of F/O John Dundas, leading light in 609 Squadron, who flew in action on all three days, 11–13 August 1940. (Air Ministry, public domain)

A typical squadron scene: pilots of 19 Squadron discuss a recent mission with a beer in hand at Fowlmere, satellite aerodrome to Duxford sector station, September 1940. Far right is S/L Brian Lane, their C/O, in the middle at the back towering above everyone is F/O H. S. L. Dundas of 616 Squadron, and second from left with his dog Flash, F/Sgt George Unwin.

A *Schwarm* (two pairs) of Me 109s flying in echelon starboard low over the Channel waters close to white chalk cliffs. Possibly a propaganda photograph from the French Channel coast rather than the English one, due to the very vulnerable tactical situation of the fighters.

Two crews in front of a Ju 88 being briefed for an operation; note bombs carried on external pylons inboard of the engines.

A Do 17 P-2 reconnaissance aircraft, often mis-identified as a Do 215. These Dorniers were earlier models than the prolific Do 17 Z, with the P-2 being equipped with a bomb rack, as opposed to the P-1.

A Do 17 Z of *KG 2* having an engine changed on a frontline airfield; the ground crews were the unsung heroes of the Battle on both sides. The white stripe across the nose indicates *I Gruppe* of *KG 2*.

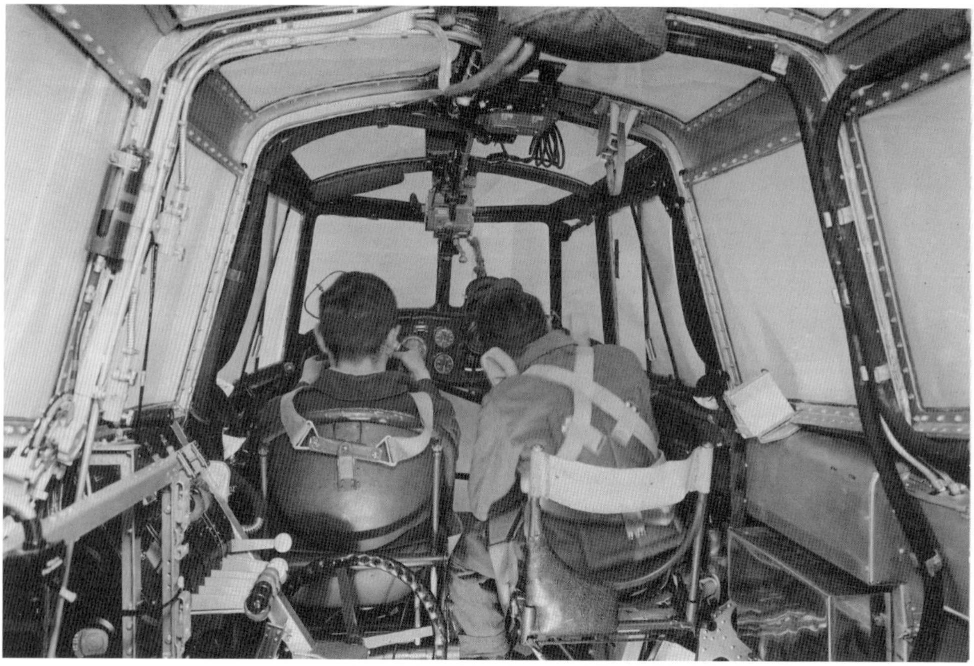

Above: View forward from the dorsal rear gunner's position in a Do 17, pilot on the left, probably observer to his right; horribly exposed to the fire from eight-gun British fighters.

Left: The flag for a *Luftflottenkommandeur*; fitting as Field Marshals Kesselring and Sperrle, leaders of *LFl 2* and *LFl 3*, were the greatest influences on Luftwaffe strategy and tactics in the Battle. The flag border is red, and eagle and swastika gold. (Courtesy Fornax under creative commons)

Above: The slow and clumsy Stukas excelled as accurate dive-bombers; only retention of RAF air superiority could keep them away.

Right: A rather fanciful artist's impression of combat, with two gallant Spitfires overflying a ditched He 111, the crew clambering into their life raft. The realities of aerial combat were much less sanguine, being fast, often chaotic and always brutal; ditched aircraft rarely floated for more than tens of seconds, and experienced fighter pilots seldom came low to observe their victim's demise.

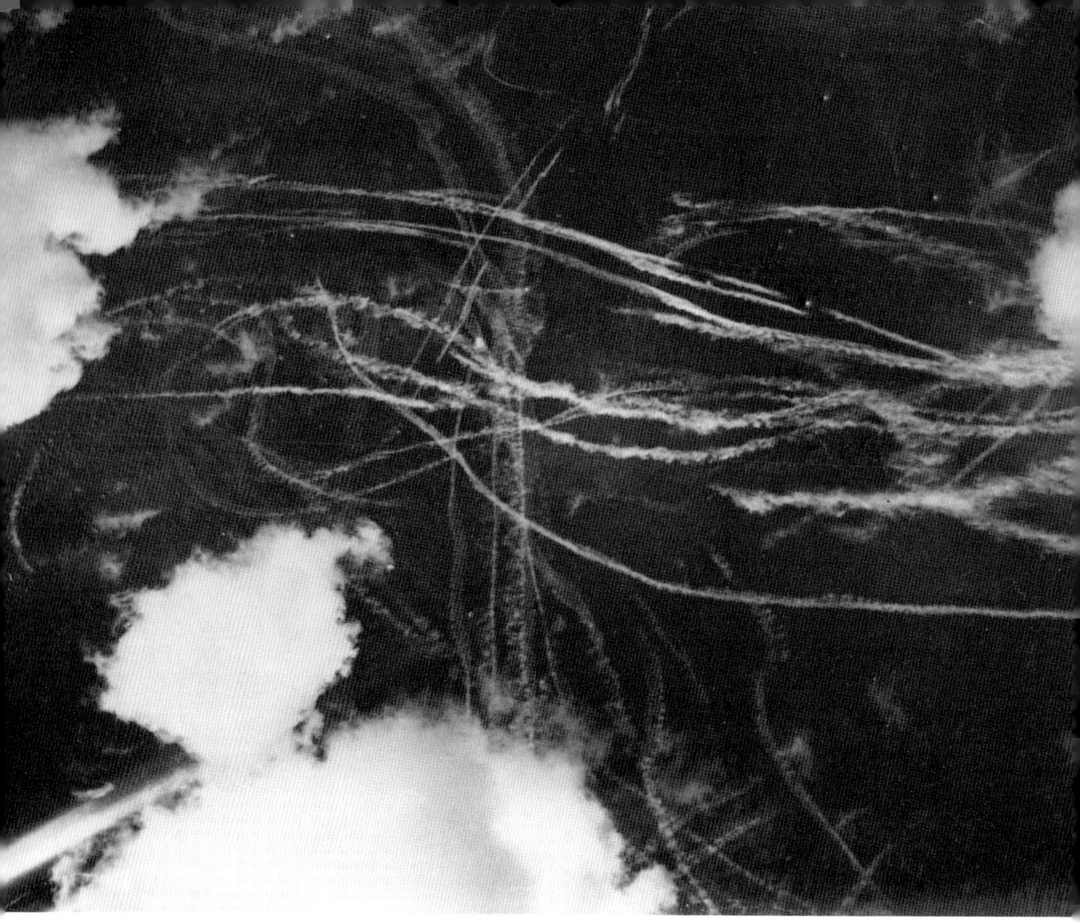

Opposite, top: Vapour trails photographed high in a Battle of Britain sky. Their complex patterns reveal small formations still intact, lone machines and several plunging downwards, either in a steep dive or mortally hit. Rapid dispersal of chaotic dogfights sometimes led to clear skies within minutes, an oft-reported phenomenon of the Battle.

Opposite, bottom: Rear-gunner's position on the improved Ju 88 A-4 model, which succeeded the Ju 88 A-1 predominantly used in the Battle of Britain. Better MG 81 machine guns were installed, with two in place of the single MG 15 weapon of the A-1, and the gunner's position significantly better protected. This resulted from the experiences of Ju 88 crews in the Battle.

Right: Ju 87 Stuka dive-bomber releases its ordnance over a target; Detling Coastal Command airfield was devastated by such an attack on *Adlertag*, 13 August 1940.

Below: Remarkable German photograph of Ventnor radar station on the Isle of Wight being bombed by fifteen Ju 88s of *Stab* and *II/KG 51* soon after noon on 12 August 1940. Top of photograph towards approximate north-west.

The terrible destructive power of cannons, illustrated here by the tail of an American B-17 Flying Fortress later in the war, where the rear gunner's position has been obliterated and extensive damage caused to both rudder and elevators. Remarkably, the machine got home to Eastchurch. In the Battle of Britain, the German fighters had them, but the RAF lacked them, apart from a single squadron. Fighter Command won the battle of attrition despite this handicap.

The tangled, almost unrecognisable wreckage of Me 110 D, W. Nr. 3374 of *Stab/ EGr 210* downed on 15 August 1940; shot down onto Redhill aerodrome by two Hurricanes, pilot *Oblt* Horst Fiedler dying of his wounds some days later while gunner *Uffz* Johann Werner miraculously survived as a prisoner. *EGr 210* saw action each day on 11–13 August 1940.

British Red Cross form accompanying a photograph of the grave of *Lt zur See* K-W. Brinkbaumer at Tangmere Churchyard, for his next of kin. The naval *Leutnant* was the observer on board a Ju 88 of *8/LG 1*, killed with his comrades when shot down at Siddlesham at *c.* 16h35 on 13 August 1940 by no fewer than seven Hurricanes.

Proudly surrounded by the Home Guard is a Ju 87 Stuka of *II/StG 77* which force-landed almost intact on a golf course near Littlehampton on 18 August 1940 after both crewmen were seriously wounded by a Spitfire pilot; only one survived. Clearly, the game of golf still took precedence over barricading a potential landing site with airborne invasion obstacles.

Restored Bristol Blenheim fighter in the colours of 23 Squadron, with which this machine actually flew night-fighter sorties during the Battle. Blenheims of Fighter, Bomber and Coastal Commands suffered losses on all three days, 11–13 August 1940. (Courtesy Airwolfhound under Creative Commons 2.0)

Remains of one of the two 9.2 inch coastal defence gun emplacements at Culver Downs just south-west of Bembridge, Isle of Wight, covering the Solent approaches to Portsmouth naval base, which was heavily raided on 12 August 1940. (Courtesy Geni under Creative Commons 4.0)

S/L Peter Townsend C/O of 85 Squadron climbs down from his Hurricane P3166 in July 1940 at Castle Camps. In August the squadron was in the maelstrom of action in 11 Group of Fighter Command. Townsend was shot down in this aircraft on 31 August 1940, losing a big toe to a German fighter.

Above: RAF Odiham, which the Germans unsuccessfully targeted early on *Adlertag*, 13 August 1940, eventually became the training camp for the RAF Regiment, a unit founded in 1942 and dedicated to airfield defence.

Right: The cost of war and the price of victory in the Battle of Britain: just one of many memorials, this one for 601 County of London Squadron, Royal Auxiliary Air Force, at the RAF Museum, Hendon, features the squadron's emblem, a flying sword. The sculpture was designed by Sam Bofey. The squadron lost four pilots missing in a single combat on 11 August 1940. (Courtesy AndyWebby under Creative Commons 3.0)

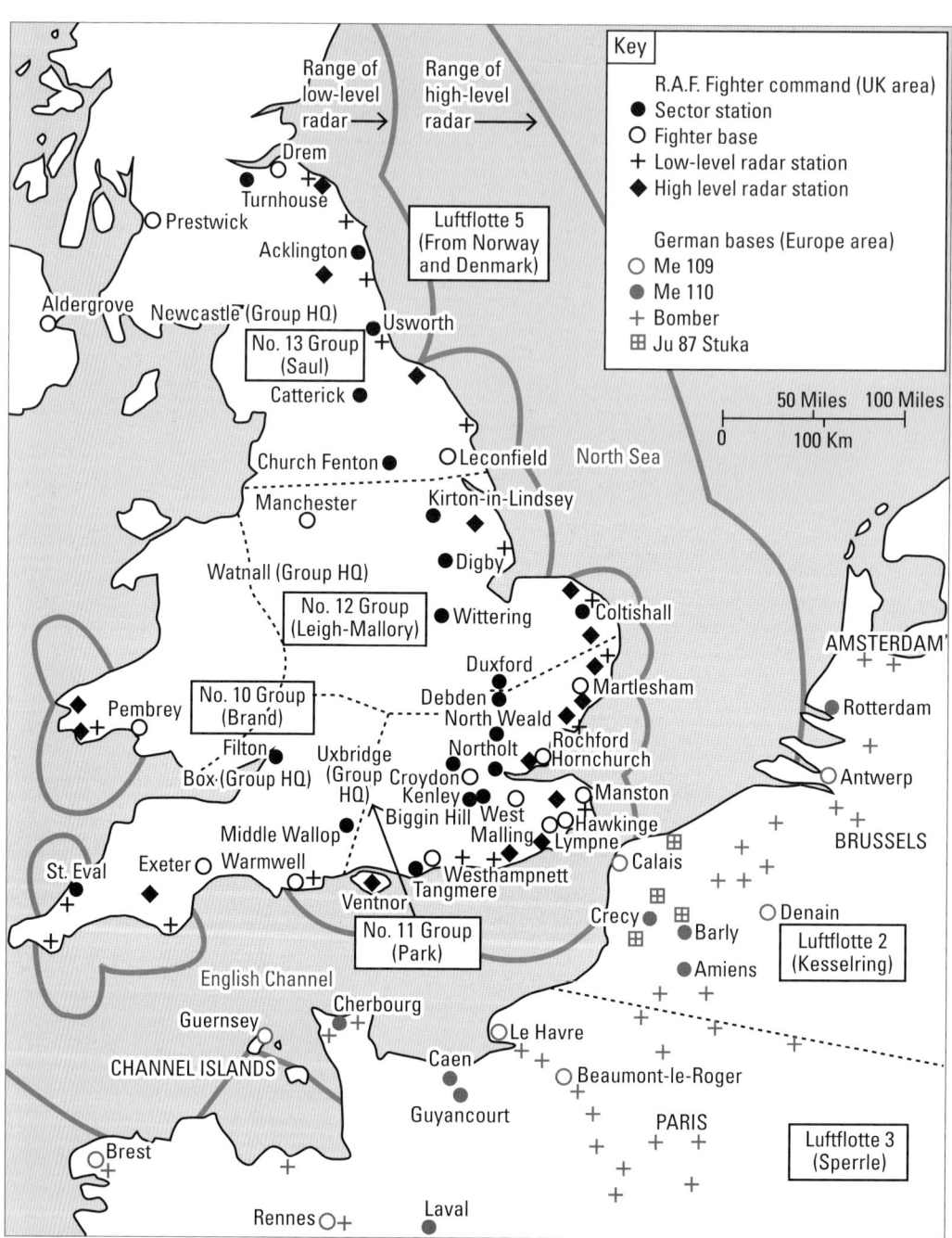

Map showing Fighter Command, RAF and *Luftwaffe* dispositions for the Battle of Britain. For 11–13 August 1940, most German incursions originated in the Pas de Calais region (fighters and Ju 87s) or its hinterland (bomber bases) for the Straits of Dover and surrounds; for the Central-Western Channel, German raids were launched from the Cherbourg peninsula (especially the shorter-ranged Me 109s and Ju 87s who used this as a forward base), from the Guernsey-Caen-Le Havre transect (Me 110s and Me 109s) and from inland bomber bases.

Eagle Day: 13 August 1940

by a *I/JG* 2 Me 109; 601 Squadron had one Hurricane damaged, its pilot lightly wounded, again to bomber return fire.[224]

The two *Gruppen* of *KG 54* each claimed seven RAF fighters, many assessed as Spitfires,[225] thereby doing nothing to counteract over-claiming or 'Spitfire snobbery'. None of those claims made it onto the *Luftwaffe* official claim lists, which logged a confirmed Spitfire and Hurricane near Brighton at c. 06h50–06h55, a probable fighter to *Oblt* Temme, all from *I/JG* 2, one confirmed victory to *II/JG* 2, and one confirmed Spitfire south of Guildford (presumably near Haslemere) by *V/LG 1* at about 06h45.[226] There is no clear RAF casualty to relate to the latter claim. There was one further casualty on this raid: *Gefr* Niessl, the flight engineer on a 6/*KG 54* Ju 88 which suffered engine trouble flying north past the Isle of Wight, the captain then promptly ordering abandonment of the machine, which order Niessl immediately followed.[227] Unfortunately, on his very first operation he was found wandering around in the countryside just east of Tangmere, while his comrades succeeded in getting their ailing machine home without him.[228] It is a moot point whether he or RAF Intelligence was the more baffled by a crewman found on the ground but no aircraft wreck.

About half an hour after the raiders had flown back across the Channel, S/L Dewar led three Hurricanes from 87 Squadron up from Exeter and while flying east over the Nab (east of the Isle of Wight), sighted what they thought was a Ju 88 on their port side, making south.[229] They wheeled round in pursuit as the German dodged in and out of cloud and caught it about 20–25 miles south of Selsey Bill, where they dispatched the hapless bomber, seeing it hit the sea about two minutes after a crewman bailed out, and sink slowly.[230] As they returned northwards to base, F/O Glyde's machine was seen losing white vapour and when next Dewar looked he had vanished and a search revealed nothing.[231] This once again illustrates the reality that it often took two to three RAF fighters to shoot down a bomber with machine gun fire, and that such prey were always dangerous in terms of return fire, especially in operations over the sea. This was probably a He 111 of *III/KG 27*, possibly on reconnaissance after the raid or looking for *Luftwaffe* crewmen down in the sea, indicated as falling to fighters north of Cherbourg, three crew dying but the pilot being rescued by the *Seenotdienst*.[232] Presumably he was the one to bail out.

Fighter sweep, Portland–Weymouth Bay–Bournemouth, c. 12h00–13h00

After the early morning raids on Farnborough-Odiham and Eastchurch, there was an approximately four-hour lull in bomber operations before an enemy formation assessed as twenty-plus aircraft was detected by the RDF stations (excluding Ventnor knocked out the previous day) in the greater Isle of Wight–Portland region, at about 11h40.[233] This enemy force was located on the eastern edge of the Cherbourg peninsula, following a north-westerly course, and it was next detected at 11h54 about forty five miles south-west of St Catherine's Point. At this time a second formation assessed at twelve-plus was located a short distance to the west, on a parallel course aimed at Portland.[234] Despite Ventnor RDF station being out of action, the radar net still worked well enough to allow plotting of these enemy forces in the central Channel,[235] encouraging for Fighter Command and no doubt somewhat baffling to their enemies who were intercepted. The larger force detected by the RAF comprised twenty-three Me 110s of *V/LG 1* that had taken off from their base at Rocquancourt (near Caen) at 11h10, led by *Gruppenkommandeur Hpt* Liensberger.[236]

According to *Luftflotte 3* documents, they were to perform a free chase of the Portland area.[237] However, the unit history states that the Me 110s were to escort bombers with a target area of Bournemouth–Portland–Isle of Wight, where airfields and radar stations were the allotted targets.[238] The bombers were apparently to have come from *KG 54*, who were briefed for a second raid on this day.[239] This is one more example of an excess of German higher command confidence, that a bomber *Geschwader* which had flown an early morning raid some four hours prior to this envisaged mission could undertake another after such a short interval. In reality, *KG 54* returned from their first raid in rather poor shape: out of thirty-eight Ju 88s dispatched on that raid, four were lost and eleven damaged with four crews lost, and another crewman died of his wounds and seven more were injured. This is almost certainly why *KG 54* were not sent out for the second raid. The assertion is often made[240] that while the bombers were not launched following an order from Göring at 10h00 to delay the second set of attacks of 13 August 1940 until about 14h00 in the early afternoon, that this message was not sent to the bomber escorts of *V/LG 1*.[241]

That the Germans could make a second such mistake after the *KG 2* raid on Eastchurch had been sent off while its Me 110 escort was recalled in that early morning raid, is unlikely. To support this assertion, *Hpt* Liensberger was briefed before *V/LG 1* took off and instructed to make a landfall near Portland, following which he was left to his own devices.[242] This suggests that the despatch of the twenty-three Me 110s towards Portland was deliberate and done with the full knowledge of the *Luftflotte 3* staff. Were they sent off without any bombers with the express purpose of determining if the destruction of the Ventnor RDF station on the previous day had left a vulnerable gap in Fighter Command's defences?

Eagle Day: 13 August 1940

From the radar plots it is clear that *V/LG 1* flew a direct course from their base at Rocquancourt near Caen, past the north-east tip of the Cherbourg peninsula and on to Portland; that there was no attempt to disguise their destination does provide some support for this being a mission designed to test the results of the previous day's attacks on radar stations. The accounts of the aerial combat which resulted, from both German and RAF sides, show that the Me 110 mission became spread across the Portland–Bournemouth area and also penetrated inland, *V/LG 1*'s claims being located over Salisbury and Blandford Forum.[243] Interestingly, there are no RAF records recording claims anywhere near that far inland, only over the sea and adjacent coastline along the Portland–Bournemouth axis and to the south of it; why give claim locations much further inland (seven to fifteen miles from the coast) unless this had been part of their briefed area to fly over?

While the *JG 53* unit history[244] gives no information on any operations at this time and date, there is a claim for a confirmed Hurricane at 11h50 by *III/JG 53* in the official German victory claims list.[245] Additionally, one crew of *V/LG 1* recorded being saved from RAF fighter attack by a couple of Me 109s, probably from *JG 53*[246] and several RAF pilots mention sighting Me 109s of approximately *Gruppe* strength. There was no plan for a combined Me 110–Me 109 fighter circle on this operation, unlike the preceding major central Channel raids on 11 and 12 August, when huge fighter circles were placed short of the bombing target to provide a distraction to incoming British fighters and a secure airspace below through which retreating bombers could head homewards. While these huge circles did attract many RAF fighters as the Germans had planned on these two preceding days, the Me 110s themselves suffered devastating casualties, and in both cases the bomber formations were intercepted and hit hard by other British fighters.

On 13 August 1940, a different approach is apparent in the first two raids from *Luftflotte 3*. As recounted above, the early morning *KG 54* raid planned against Farnborough and Odiham had included a Me 110 sweep of *I/ZG 2*, which clearly split into three parts over southern England, one of which was intercepted by the RAF some ten miles inland from the coastline. The *V/LG 1* Me 110 sweep at about midday on 13 August also penetrated inland from the sea, and the unit may have planned to fly some fifteen miles inland from the coast and spread out across a relatively wide area from Portland to Bournemouth. So the large, fixed fighter circles over a strategic location were abandoned on 13 August, to be replaced by wide-ranging small Me 110 sweeps in the general area of the bombing raids: a new *Luftwaffe* tactic. While it worked well on the early morning raid where only a couple of Me 110s were damaged, on the midday sweep, *V/LG 1* was to be very roughly handled. Thus, another Me 110 tactic was easily negated by Fighter Command.

Despite Ventnor RDF being out of action, the Fighter Command and 10 and 11 Group controllers were able to direct three Hurricane squadrons towards the incoming German incursion: eleven aircraft from 238 Squadron from the nearby Warmwell forward base took off at 11h50, with orders to patrol Portland at 25,000 ft, 601 Squadron (twelve machines, Tangmere, up 11h55, to patrol Swanage at 20,000 ft), and finally 213 Squadron of thirteen aircraft from Exeter, took off 11h58, with orders to patrol Portland, probably at 10,000 ft.[247] The German fighter formations had reached the Portland area just after midday where they remained for some ten minutes before the first two RAF squadrons intercepted between about 12h10 and 12h20; both were well placed at relatively high altitude and 238 Squadron arrived first, as 601 Squadron pilots observed an ongoing dogfight between Hurricanes and circling Me 110s at a somewhat lower altitude when they arrived.[248]

Me 110 circles were always characterised by the Messerschmitts flying essentially vertically banked over and thus perforce descending as the combat ensued; aerial combat generally in the Battle of Britain (and indeed, World War 2) tended to lose altitude as it proceeded. One of the Me 110 crews, pilot *Uffz* Schümichen and gunner/radio operator *Ogefr* Giglhuber of *15/LG 1*, provided a detailed account of the *V/LG 1* formation over Portland just as the first RAF fighters pounced: the whole *Gruppe* formed defensive circles as the enemy were sighted, with *15 Staffel* at 7,200 m, *14 Staffel* c. 1,000 ft lower and finally, *13 Staffel* another 1,000 ft lower again, one below the other.[249] These defensive circles formed in reaction to sighting the British fighters as a defensive measure in contrast to the much larger fighter circles employed by the *Luftwaffe* on the preceding two days, which were meant to attract RAF fighters and which were thus offensive in nature and intended to dominate, at altitude, a chosen piece of enemy airspace close to a bombing target.

238 Squadron's eleven Hurricanes were led by F/O Hughes (Red 1) and were vectored towards Portland with instructions to patrol there at 20,000 ft.[250] Upon reaching the Portland area, the squadron was still climbing and at *c*. 16,000 ft they saw about twenty Me 110s flying north 2000–3000 ft above, and higher still at about 25,000 ft were about the same number of Me 109s.[251] Hughes ordered the five Hurricanes of B Flight to keep on climbing and tackle the top cover while he led his A Flight up against the Me 110s.[252] Red 1 and 2, Hughes and P/O Davis,

Eagle Day: 13 August 1940

got up to 22,000 ft, up sun of the *Zerstörern* and dived down on them from there, while PO Simmonds as Red 3, despite having his throttle through the gate at emergency power, could not keep up and turned in on about ten Me 110s at about 18,000 ft.[253] As F/O Hughes opened fire, the Me 110s began to form a circle, and when P/O Simmonds turned into the ten at *c.* 18,000 ft they were also just starting to form their defensive circle.[254] P/O Davis, Red 2, attacking from above against the top Me 110s, saw them begin to form their circle and joined by some twenty more.[255] P/O Charles Davis of 238 Squadron should not be confused with F/O Carl Davis of 601 Squadron – both pilots were in action against V/LG 1 in this engagement.

Red 1 and 2 of 238 Squadron attacked the uppermost Me 110s after having climbed above the enemy, and as the individual *Staffeln* began forming their defensive circles they also joined up together.[256] It is entirely logical, with three separate small Me 110 circles forming above each other at vertical spacings of *c.* 1,000 ft, that the three German *Staffeln* would also get closer together for mutual support; the easiest way to do that would be for the two upper *Staffeln* to descend closer to the lowermost one, ending up at about 18,000 ft. 601 Squadron which attacked soon after 238 Squadron, reported seeing a dogfight between Hurricanes and Me 110s in progress and noted that the circling Me 110s formed a combined mass of rotating aircraft with a depth of 2,000-3,000 ft.[257] V/LG 1's *Gruppenkommandeur*, *Hpt* Liensberger was not aware of the presence of enemy fighters until one of his rearmost Me 110s gave an alarm, upon which he immediately ordered his aircraft into a circle.[258] F/O Hughes and P/O Davis thus most likely attacked *15/LG1*, the topmost *Staffel*, while their wingman, P/O Simmonds flying the Red 3 position and having a slower Hurricane that fell behind in the climb, most likely attacked the lowermost *Staffel 13/LG 1* twice, as related in his combat report.[259]

> I was Red 3 and was at 16,000 ft. when I sighted 4 flights of ME 110's approximately 2,000 ft. above. Red 1 ordered line astern, gave chase gaining height. I pulled the boost out but my machine was not quite so fast as Red 1 & 2 and I dropped behind. A section of approximately 10 ME 110's on my port beam were starting to form a circle. I noticed tracer and cannon about 50 yds. to port. I pulled up sharply to the left, turning in underneath the end machine and fired a four second burst into the cockpit but hit the fuselage and tail unit. The machine dropped down out of control. I followed for 7,000 feet approx. I broke away and on pulling up to gain height saw more 110's immediately above. I gave a 4 sec. burst into the bottom of fuselage before breaking away.

Adlertag

F/O Hughes' leadership was clever as he chased after the northward-flying Me 110s, climbing at full boost to achieve surprise when he dived down on them from a superior altitude.[260]

> I ordered A Flight into line astern and dived to attack out of the sun. I opened fire on a DO 17 at 250 yds. (1 sec. burst). As soon as fire was opened the E/A commenced to circle, but the DO 17 which I had attacked dived down. I followed him down and fired at ranges varying from 250 yds. to 100 yds. The E/A's evasive tactics were S turns and circling. I observed that the rear gunner was out of action and closed to 20 yds. and gave a deflection shot of 2 secs. The starboard engine was smoking and as I passed over and across him, within a few feet, I observed the pilot climbing out of his cockpit. The E/A crashed in the sea. I saw the pilot descending by parachute but did not observe where he fell. Landed 12.40. Rounds fired 1040. (For DO 17, read Me 110)

Hughes got really close to this Me 110 having put the rear gunner out of action, his final burst from only twenty yards most likely proving lethal. From the German side, *Hpt* Liensberger described how one of his Me 110s banked off to starboard away from the formation apparently unscathed, while a second dived away hotly pursued by a RAF fighter, and that two of his fighters were lost before the circle closed.[261] Although claiming his victim mistakenly as a Do 17, Hughes' account above describes how his chosen victim dived down with him in close pursuit. The second straggler which left the formation before the circle closed may have been engaged by Red 2, P/O Charles Davis, whose combat report follows.[262]

> I was Red 2 and the squadron was ordered to intercept raid over Portland. I saw 20 110's pass overhead going N. about 3,000 feet above. Red 1 gave line astern and we climbed into sun above reaching about 22,000 feet. The E/A formed a defensive circle being joined by about 20 more. The section became split up and I took a straggler and fired a long burst downward deflection at 400 yds. closing to 250 yds. (3 secs.). Unable to observe result, but bullets entered E/A. I climbed again and picked another straggler well away from the main body and dived on his tail and fired long burst closing rapidly from astern (about 4 secs.). Port engine caught fire and E/A went down apparently out of control. Unable to confirm due to cloud, but most likely to have crashed. Landed at Warmwell, 12h50. Number of rounds fired. 1250.

Yellow Section of 238 Squadron climbed up into the sun, following the lead of Red 1, but got higher up to 25,000 ft before they also dived

Eagle Day: 13 August 1940

onto the disorganised incipient circles; Yellow 1, Sgt Marsh, attacked a straggling Me 110, and like Hughes was able to observe its pilot bailing out and the machine was seen to crash on land.[263]

> I was Yellow 1 and the squadron was ordered to patrol Portland at 20,000 feet. At 15,000, I sighted ME 110's above and I climbed into sun with section. At 25,000 feet I delivered attack against a slightly separated ME 110. I fired 1 burst of about 4 secs. at 100 yds. from quarter, to astern deflection. Port engine started smoking. E/A climbed to left, headed West. I followed and saw pilot bale out and A/C dived straight through cloud, and crashed on and just West of St. Albans Head (on cliff). There are two crashed E/A there, and mine was the eastern most (nearest the head). Two enemy pilots landed just West of St. Albans Head and were picked up. Landed at Warmwell because windscreen was oiled over. Landed 1245. Number of rounds fired 1150.

While there was only one Me 110 which came down some three miles west of St Alban's Head, its two crew members did bail out into the sea off that section of coast: clearly this was the machine from *15/LG 1* crewed by pilot *Uffz* Schümichen and gunner *Ogefr* Giglhuber who both survived their ordeal unscathed and were rescued to become POWs, the abandoned aircraft coming down at Kimmeridge.[264] While both Hughes and Marsh claimed solo victories over their Me 110s other 238 Squadron Hurricanes may also have hit them. P/O Wigglesworth, leading the two rear-guard 238 Squadron Hurricanes of Green Section, climbed up even higher than Yellow Section, to 32,000 ft and then calmly circled descending slowly to 25,000 ft before selecting a lone Me 110 and diving onto it, damaging it significantly.[265] Overall, 238 Squadron claimed four Me 110s confirmed and a fifth unconfirmed, the latter Wigglesworth's claim.[266]

601 Squadron having taken off from their more distant base at Tangmere, arrived after 238 Squadron were already engaging the Me 110s as they performed their standard left hand defensive circle manoeuvres, at about 19,000 ft, the spiral being c. 2,000-3,000 ft in depth.[267] S/L Ward flying as Red 1 had returned to base soon after take-off with oxygen trouble, and F/Lt Sir Archibald Hope, their senior flight commander, had taken over the lead.[268] Hope was an excellent leader as demonstrated in his combat report; he was much occupied by the fate of the aircrew down in the waters of Weymouth Bay.[269]

> I was leading 601 Squadron when ordered to proceed to Swanage and then to Weymouth to engage enemy fighters @ 20000. There was a layer

of cloud at 9000' and another about 4500. As we approached Portland I saw about 20-30 aircraft going round in circles. We were at 20 gs and their highest a/c was just below us. There may have been Hurricanes about 5000' below. The squadron went into line astern and 5 turned left towards the E/A who were still circling left-handed in a sort of spiral about 2–3000 feet deep. I went for the top me (sic) 110 and fired a deflection 60° burst at it. It continued to turn and I followed on its tail firing until it appeared to go down and I thought I had gone down far enough. It had continued to turn left and I was by now circling with the E/A so I turned to go against their circle. I fired a short burst at one E/A head on and as I passed it took another the same way. He tightened his turn and pulled straight up across me so that I could see all his pale blue underneath and I finished my bullets into his bottom in a full deflection shot. I then spiralled steeply down and watched the sea. I saw one parachute go in and circled it for a minute or two until I saw a boat going straight for it. This was about 10 miles E of Portland. I flew west for about 4 miles and found another British pilot in the water and what looked like a dead German. I marked the place by the oil where an a/c had gone in and went SW. to where I found two more pilots in the water one British and one doubtful. By this time I had been joined by Blue 1 and 2 and I left them to circle the last two while I went back to the others. In the end all were picked up though we had considerable difficulty in showing the boat where the German was. The boat that had picked up the first pilot went straight back to shore and I couldn't make it come towards the others. I took one look around Weymouth Bay without seeing any more and returned home as I was getting short of petrol. I am convinced that unless we had circled these pilots in the water at least three of them would not have been picked up. They were easy to see from the air as long as their parachutes were floating ie. for half-an-hour at most, which seems to show the importance of getting to the scene by air early. Once found it was comparatively easy to keep the pilots in the water in sight though it would have helped if we could have dropped some sort of marker. I landed at 1336.

Hope's Red Section had been reduced to two aircraft by the return to base of his commanding officer. One of the beneficiaries of F/Lt Hope's efforts to guide boats to airmen in the water was his wingman, P/O Mayers, who was shot down and wounded by the Me 110s, as recounted in his combat report below.[270] Watching one of your victim's descent towards the sea during a dogfight rapidly sets you up to become a target.

I was flying Red 3, 'A' Flight 601 Squadron when ordered to intercept enemy fighters at 20,000 ft off Weymouth. I first saw E/A at about

Eagle Day: 13 August 1940

20000' South of Portland at 12.50 hours. They were being attacked by Hurricanes and had formed a defensive circle. I went into line astern as the leader gave the order to attack and delivered my first attack, quarter deflection head on, with a burst of about 6 secs. This attack appeared to be ineffective. I turned to the left coming round for the second attack, this time going the same way as the defensive circle of the E/A. I picked out one ME110 and fired a long burst from dead astern, opening at about 300 yds and closing when it appeared that I was just about to ram. I saw one rudder and part of the elevator or fin break away as the machine dived away in a left spiral apparently out of control. I turned a little to the right and up in order to watch the E/A go down. It had just gone through the clouds at 7000' when my Hurricane was hit by what felt like a tornado. I felt a pain in my right buttock and leg, felt the engine stop, heard hissing noises and smelt fumes. My first reaction was to pull back the stick but there was no response. The next thing I remember was falling through air at high speed and feeling my helmet, flying boots and socks torn off. Lack of oxygen must have dulled my senses as the combat ended at 19000' and my parachute opened just about (above?) the clouds at 7000'. At about 5000' between two layers of clouds a ME110 fired at me while being chased closely by a Hurricane. I landed in the water about 3 miles from Portland. Just before landing I saw an MTB about a mile away but the C.O. told me later that they did not see me coming down although they saw a German parachutist not 200 yds from me. After about 20 minutes I saw a Hurricane searching the bay which I soon recognised as belonging to my Flight Commander F/LT Hope. He waved to me and spent some considerable time trying to inform the MTB of my where abouts by flying backward and forwards between the boat and myself. Even when the MTB came in my direction it very nearly went too far to the South, missing me. I am quite sure that if it had not been for F/LT Hope that the MTB would not have found me. The C.O. of the MTB told me that it was extremely difficult to see anything, very far away, in such small craft. It appears that the Radio in the MTB cannot be tuned to pick up our R.T. so that any communication between aircraft and boat is impossible. I was taken to Portland Naval Hospital where my schrapnel wounds were X rayed and dressed. The wounds were only superficial and I was allowed to proceed to Warmwell where I obtained transport in a Battle, arriving back at Tangmere at 21.30 hrs. I would suggest that Pilots carry marker flares and that organised air searches be made after each battle over the sea. (MTB = motor torpedo boat)

Hope and Mayers each claimed a Me 110 probable, with Hope claiming damage to a second machine.[271] The German *Luftwaffe* had a highly organised and well-manned air-sea rescue service, based firstly on rescue floatplanes (He 59s) or flying boats (Do 18s), but also with moored rescue floats in the Channel containing emergency supplies, shelter and communications equipment, and they also commonly followed up raids by airborne reconnaissance machines and/or the floatplanes, quite often with fighter escort.[272] Their aircrews had bright green dye containers to help their location in the water. The RAF fighter pilots had to rely in the first place on the Royal National Lifeboat Institution (RNLI), a service of great tradition, high efficiency and brave crews, but generally reliant on reports received from sea-borne or land-borne observers and without aerial support. That provided by F/Lt Hope and colleagues, as described above, could make all the difference, but these squadron-level initiatives were *ad hoc* and a more organised service of aerial observation following large actions over the sea would have helped a lot. There were a limited number of RAF fast rescue launches and local fishermen and small naval patrol auxiliary craft, plus larger vessels, both naval and merchant marine, involved much less often.[273]

An examination of the activities of the Weymouth RNLI Life-boat Station related to this raid reveals their hard work and frustrations. At 12h15 the station received a report of an aircraft down in the sea off 'Whitenose' (actually, more correctly, White Nothe, a chalk headland at the eastern end of Ringstead Bay, East of Weymouth), and within minutes launched the *Queen Victoria* motor life-boat, temporarily attached to Weymouth station; this vessel was recalled thirty minutes later, reaching home by 13h42.[274] This report can only have referred to F/O Mayers who came down off that headland at 12h15.[275] At 12h30 the Weymouth life-boat was launched but could only find some wreckage of a *Luftwaffe* machine.[276] At 14h00 a report came in to Weymouth RNLI station of an airman swimming about two miles off Osmington in Weymouth Bay, and the *Queen Victoria* went out once more, searched, found nothing and was once more recalled, the airman having been rescued by another boat.[277] The life-boat crews had to be tireless in their efforts, reacting to each incoming report, but without aerial support to guide them could never see far over the choppy waters of the Channel from their low freeboard boats.

In the air, the engagement between 601 Squadron and *V/LG 1* continued. F/O Carl Davis led Yellow Section in behind F/Lt Hope and his wingman in the reduced Red Section. Davis's combat report (below)[278] underlines the skill and aggression of this pilot and section leader, soon to become a flight commander in the Squadron. He managed to carry out three head-on attacks against the rotation of the Me 110 circle.

Squadron took off at 1150. I was Yellow 1. We climbed west to 20000 ft over Portland. We had been told to go for fighters and saw them to south dogfighting. We joined in. I attacked defensive circle against rotation thereby being in position to do head on attacks. After one or two bursts saw ME I fired at break away. Followed and put in burst from 200 yds astern. He stalled turned and dived into sea. I was then at 15000 ft so climbed to south and attacked from south with sun at my back, again doing head-on attacks against defensive circle. My second burst set a machine on fire between starboard engine and fuselage. He disappeared into cloud band in flames. I then saw an E/A by itself. As I turned towards him he did the same and I gave him a burst head-on we both then stalled turned and I attacked head on again. He went into a gentle right hand turn and dived. As I was out of ammunition I followed him down to sea. My camera gun was switched on in this combat and I took a picture of the splash. An RAF launch nearby over which I flew should confirm this last machine. I landed at 1255 hrs.

Yellow 3, F/Sgt Pond, also attacked the Me 110 circle against its rotation, but without any visible success, so climbed back up into the sun and attacked a Me 110 from below and astern, stopping its right hand engine.[279] Both he and the Me 110 were in steep right hand turns at the time, and the Messerschmitt steepened its turn so much that Pond spun out.[280] While Pond could only claim a damaged Me 110, Carl Davis clamed three destroyed, one confirmed and the other two unconfirmed. The third member of Yellow Section, F/O H. J. Riddle, did not make any claim. He had a brother in the Squadron, F/O C. Riddle who was flying as Green 2 in this engagement.[281]

F/O Clyde led B Flight of 601 Squadron and when Hope led A Flight down into the Me 110 circles, Clyde kept his men at about 21,000 ft as there was a large number of Me 109s at about 30,000 ft; they did not come down and, as with 238 Squadron, avoided combat despite a height advantage.[282] Clyde was leading Blue Section, with Green behind, and once he realised the Me 109s were not going to become involved, he led his men down into the circling Me 110s below. Clyde had two inconclusive combats with Me 110s, damaging one and sending another down in a vertical dive with an engine smoking, claiming an unconfirmed victory.[283] Blue 2, P/O Grier, went into the circles against their rotation and fired at three Me 110s from head on before a fourth frontal attack ended in a near collision, leading to this Messerschmitt diving down immediately; he followed it down firing, seeing it go into the sea for an unconfirmed (unwitnessed) victory claim, leaving just a patch of green dye and oil.[284] Both Grier and Clyde responded to F/Lt Hope's call for assistance in spotting downed flyers in the sea off Portland and Weymouth, helping to guide boats to struggling airmen in the water.[285]

Adlertag

The third member of Blue Section, P/O Fiske, made four attacks on the Me 110 circles, from the beam, quarter astern, astern and head on, claiming two probables and two damaged, before himself being hit by a cannon shell which jammed his one aileron, forcing him to leave the engagement, but he landed safely back at Tangmere.[286] Only Green leader, F/O Doulton, made a claim for that section in this engagement, for a damaged Me 110. His combat report[287] reveals how the Hurricane could effortlessly turn inside the Messerschmitts in their circles, but accurate sighting was significantly reduced by the steep turns. He also records how the Me 109s above the engagement did not become involved and left the Me 110s to their fate.

> As Green (1) I led the astern section of the Squadron. At 12.05 a large mass of A/c seen 5 miles to the S.W. of us. Ordered section line astern climbed into sun and engaged Me110's at 22,000' which had formed defensive L.H. circles. On getting inside circle I had no difficulty in turning inside this Me110 and keeping position but turn was so tight that sighting was very difficult. Me110's dived on me but more often climbed up beneath. After nearly 10 minutes managed to get on 1 Me110's tail. This aircraft immediately rolled onto back and as he fell out of this roll I gave him a quick deflection burst at 100yds range, smoke and slight flame seen in cockpit of this Me110. On turning away to re-engage I lost sight of the remainder of E/A. Landed Tangmere. 13.05. Me 109. Seen at 25,000 – before engaging Me 110 but these apparently kept up and out of the engagement.

The same sighting difficulties must also have affected RAF pilots attacking the Me 110s head-on, against the rotation of the circles. As always with fighter pilots, victories tended to be scored by those with superior gunnery skills; such pilots were rare – not everybody could aspire to the daring and skill of someone like Carl Davis. Doulton's Hurricane was damaged during the combat.

V/LG 1 suffered high losses in this engagement with 238 and 601 Squadrons.[288] Five Me 110s were total losses, with three crews and their machines plunging into the waters off Portland and into Weymouth Bay, only one body being recovered after washing ashore at Portland. These three Me 110s comprised one machine from each of the three *Staffeln*, 13, 14 and 15/LG 1. A fourth Me 110 flown by *Fw* Datz with gunner *Uffz* Lammel of *13 Staffel* was hit in the engagement, caught fire and Lammel was wounded in the leg and was not able to bail out on his own. Datz cleverly half-rolled the big fighter, throwing the gunner out of the aircraft, but he did not survive and washed ashore at Portland.

Eagle Day: 13 August 1940

Datz himself got out and landed safely in Weymouth Bay with a burned face and was finally rescued after several hours in the water.

The fifth total loss was a machine of *15/LG 1*, piloted by *Uffz* Schümichen with gunner *Ogefr* Giglhuber and appears to have been an early victim. They were hit when in a defensive circle at *c.* 23,000 ft having already flown about six full circuits, an attack by three fighters coming out of the sun. The port engine immediately lost revolutions, the instrument panel was damaged by bullets and a fuel tank was likely also hit, as the pilot managed to pull sharply to port and get out of the stream of bullets and dived the machine away smoking. Then there was a loud bang behind the pilot and fire and smoke forced Giglhuber to try and bail out, which, due to their speed, was at first impossible; a second bang saw him thrown out and he hit the tail a glancing blow, always a hazard in any bail-out. The gunner retained consciousness, opened his chute and some ten minutes later landed in the drink, a few miles out to sea as the wind had carried him.

Schümichen meanwhile, with gunner, his machine gun and the rear canopy all gone, felt the Messerschmitt pitch steeply down, rapidly speeding up and he became jammed against his cockpit hood. After a struggle he managed to get his legs into the slipstream of the diving, flaming wreck, was flipped over and fell clear, losing a boot and sock as he did so to the strong slipstream. After a few seconds he pulled his ripcord, and the shock of the parachute opening rendered him unconscious for a few seconds. He was brought round by the noise of a British fighter circling him and its pilot waving. He was also blown out to sea and before landing in the water observed his gunner splash down a couple of miles away.

They had been hit over Lulworth at about 12h35 and descended to the west along the coast, passing over Swalland Farm shedding pieces,[289] with the crew being observed to bail out from the ground before the Me 110 crashed at Kimmeridge.[290] According to the Messerschmitt's crew when interrogated, they had been shot down by four RAF fighters.[291] While there is little clarity on which RAF pilot attacked any specific Me 110, Sgt Marsh flying Yellow 1 in 238 Squadron was involved in the downing of the Schümichen-Giglhuber Messerschmitt of *15/LG 1*, having seen his victim hit the ground just west of St Albans Head, a couple of miles east of Kimmeridge.[292]

In addition to the five aircraft which failed to return, *V/LG 1* also suffered five damaged machines.[293] One of these from *13 Staffel* was 50% damaged but made it back to France with a wounded crew, while two others from the *Gruppe* (*Staffeln* unknown) were written off after making it back: one crash-landed at Cherbourg airfield with 80% damage, and the other belly-landed at their base of Rocquancourt. Remarkably, three of the four crewmen in these two machines were unharmed, but Fw Jecke, a pilot from *14 Staffel*, was wounded in the legs, thus indicating one of the two aircraft was from that *Staffel*.

Another *V/LG 1* Me 110 suffered only light damage of 10% in the engagement off Portland, and can be linked to a crew from *14 Staffel*, being flown by *Staffelkapitän Oblt* Junge: this was aircraft L1+FK which was damaged on 13 August in the hands of this pilot in a combat some twelve miles west of Bournemouth, in which rear gunner *Gefr* Haas was wounded, losing his leg as a result.[294] As this aircraft was shot down and Oblt Junge and his new gunner killed in it on 4 September 1940[295] it must logically have been the aircraft amongst the five damaged from the *Gruppe* on 13 August that suffered only minor damage, repairable at unit level.

The fifth 'damaged' Me 110 from *V/LG 1* in fact suffered no damage at all, except perhaps to the dignity of its rear gunner. *Lt* Altendorf of *15 Staffel* while flying in the defensive circles, saw the Me 110 in front of him being attacked by an RAF fighter, and after firing at it himself, saw it roll and dive away, and he followed optimistically. Unbeknownst to him, gunner *Uffz* Arndt had failed to secure the ammunition drum for the cannons properly and as they dived it flew up and hit the back of his head, knocking him out cold. Through some quirk of *Luftwaffe* bureaucracy Arndt was classified as wounded in combat.[296] Quite apart from the comic opera aspects of this story, they were lucky to have survived, as while Arndt was unconscious and at low level over the sea a British fighter came up behind them, but they were saved by two Me 109s which shot down the enemy.[297]

Presumably their rescuers were from JG 53,[298] who otherwise appear to have avoided any involvement in the tribulations of *V/LG 1*. No British fighter can be identified to fit this German account of a victory. However, a confirmed victory for *7/JG 53* over a Hurricane at about 11h50 is recorded in the *Luftwaffe* claims list, which also gives five probable claims for members of *V/LG 1*.[299] Against these claims there are only two damaged 601 Squadron Hurricanes and F/O Mayers of 601 Squadron who was shot down and lightly wounded, as already recounted. 238 Squadron had no casualties. *V/LG 1* lost five Me 110s missing, two written off and another two damaged, with seven crew killed, three POWs and four wounded; from twenty-three aircraft, a very high loss rate of 30%. The German losses are balanced against total claims by 238 Squadron of four confirmed and one unconfirmed destroyed, with another five destroyed (four of which were unconfirmed), five probably so and six damaged by 601 Squadron (total for this squadron taken from combat reports). Elements of 213 Squadron who intercepted outgoing stragglers (Me 110, Me 109, Ju 88) claimed a Ju 88 and an Me 109 destroyed.[300]

Only Blue Section and one member of Red Section engaged outgoing German stragglers for 213 Squadron, the other nine Hurricanes not making contact.[301] F/Lt Strickland, Blue 1, spotted a single Me 110 east of Portland at about 12h35, dived after it only to see it shot down into the sea by another Hurricane with a red and white spinner and nose,[302] probably from 601 Squadron. Strickland had fleeting ineffective engagements with two more Me 110s and made no claims. Sgt Llewellyn (Red 3) made two attacks on what he identified as a Ju 88, and followed it down; he then saw a white patch in the water with boats moving towards it and claimed the Ju 88 as a victory.[303] However, his claim is not included in the squadron total in the Intelligence Patrol Report (nor is there a combat report for him this day in the records), which only lists two made by P/O Laricheliere (Blue 2). He followed Strickland down when that pilot went for the Me 110 he spotted, while Laricheliere sighted a Ju 88 through a gap in the clouds; this he attacked from astern and followed it south-east through the clouds for about a quarter of an hour.[304] He fired again in a clear patch setting its port engine on fire and the enemy dived into the sea, where he saw a small boat heading for the wreckage.[305]

While observing all this, Laricheliere was attacked by an Me 109 which he evaded in the clouds and then found it again over the wreckage in the water, and claimed it shot down into the sea in flames.[306] The Ju 88 claims of Llewellyn and Laricheliere have some common elements, and with Strickland having seen an Me 110 shot down into the sea (probably by another squadron) this may have been what both claiming pilots saw in the water. No Me 109 was lost on this raid.[307] Approximately an hour after the Portland engagements had ended, RAF radar plotted a 9+ formation flying into the Portland area; it was not intercepted nor did it make any aggressive moves and was most likely searching the sea for missing airmen[308] from *V/LG 1*. This was common German practice and if the spotters sighted any airmen in the water, either floatplanes or boats would follow.

Raids on Andover, Middle Wallop airfields, RAF Thorney Island and Southampton, *c.* 16h00–17h10

After the fiasco of the early morning raids, where partial cancellation orders and the cloudy weather had led to confusion, missed targets and relatively heavy losses, followed by the midday Me 110 sweep over Portland (also heavily engaged), the planned afternoon raids were intended to really launch the thus-far abortive Eagle Day assaults. The weather was still uncooperative, again leading to losses, missed targets and plenty of confusion. The importance of the weather as a controlling factor on air operations, particularly on the *Luftwaffe*'s ability to launch large, multi-formational escorted raids, has been stressed by one of the Battle's veterans, Peter Brown, who served with 611 and 41 Squadrons.[309] As he clearly demonstrates in his book, the weather 'made the decisions' in the first place, providing an unavoidable framework for practical use of large German formations and for more successful RAF fighter interceptions thereof, with losses significantly increased for both sides when the weather was fine. Concomitantly, bad weather reduced the efficiency of both sides, generally and also reduced losses.[310] This is a factor much neglected in many Battle of Britain histories and was certainly of great importance on 13 August 1940.

Interestingly, losses were still quite high, for the *Luftwaffe* at least, on this day. There were complex cloudy conditions, which allowed interceptions and combats to take place in clear patches and between vertically separated cloud formations. Notably, 13 August also saw an enhanced amount of the over-claiming endemic to aerial combat. This was at least partially related to widespread, rather thick individual cloud layers, separated by thousands of feet of altitude, into which aircraft from both sides would often dive at high angles with smoking engines. Often during the Battle, and in air combat generally through World War 2, this indicated engines throttled up to maximum power to escape attack rather than damage, as inferred by those eternal optimists, fighter pilots.

The *Luftwaffe* plans for the afternoon attacks on *Adlertag* were a two-pronged affair in the central-western Channel region, encompassing two Stuka raids against two RAF airfields to the north of Portland, and three Ju 88 raids against inland RAF bases at Boscombe Down, Andover and Worthy Down.[311] In the event, thanks to the weather, neither Yeovil nor Warmwell in the hinterland of Portland, nor Boscombe Down and Worthy Down north of the Southampton area, were bombed at all. Instead, at least in the latter set of raids north of the Solent, a string of localities endured minor bombing attacks, these spread from far (*c.* 40–45 miles) inland near Swindon and Reading to the coast at RAF Thorney Island, along an approximately north-west/south-east trajectory. However, Southampton was hit by an entire Ju 88 *Gruppe*, Middle Wallop sector station by six Junkers, and Andover by a round dozen; RAF Benson, Perham Down, Bishops Waltham, Stockbridge and Wroughton suffered a few projectiles.[312] As so often owing to the poor

Eagle Day: 13 August 1940

quality of *Luftwaffe* intelligence, Fighter Command facilities were in the minority amongst the planned targets.

Fifty-two Ju 87 dive bombers from *StG 3* were to attack two RAF bases: twenty-five from *I/StG 1* had Warmwell as their target, and twenty seven from *II/StG 2* were assigned to bomb Yeovil.[313] *StG 3* had three subordinate Stuka *Gruppen*, *I/StG 3* and the two *Gruppen* just mentioned;[314] several Battle of Britain sources erroneously suggest a second assault in addition to *I/StG 1* and *II/StG 2*, by another fifty-two Stukas from *StG 3*, due to this illogical unit make-up. Further to the east, *LG 1* put up three Ju 88 formations, comprising nineteen aircraft from *I/LG 1* (intended target: Boscombe Down), sixteen from *II/LG 1* (target: Worthy Down) and twenty-three Ju 88s from *III/LG 1* (target: Andover).[315] Escorts and more remote fighter support were to be provided by all three of *Luftflotte 3*'s Me 109 *Geschwadern*, *JG*'s 2, 27 and 53, plus Me 110s from both ZG 2 and ZG 76.[316]

While the details for the operations of *JG 2* and *JG 27* on these raids are unclear, *I/JG 53* was given the mission of flying a fighter sweep ahead of the raids north of Portland, *II/JG 53* was to act as direct escort for the Warmwell raiders of *I/StG 1*, with *III/JG 53* not involved in these afternoon missions.[317] The earliest German fighter claims were made by *I/JG 53*, and *II/ZG 76* made claims at the same time[318] and was thus presumably associated with this Me 109 fighter sweep. The first RAF fighter squadron in action was 152 Squadron, which engaged both Me 110s and Me 109s.[319] The sweep ahead of the Ju 87s was intended to draw off defending fighters to the west, away from the intended targets.[320] The first Stuka raid, by *I/StG 1*, which failed to locate its target in the prevailing weather conditions, took place under the cover provided by *II/JG 53*, and the dive bombers turned back without bombing and were not engaged by RAF fighters; *II/JG 53* stayed on in the general Portland area on an impromptu free chase.[321] *JG 27* provided escort for Stukas,[322] specifically for the second Stuka raid, by *II/StG 2* (target Yeovil).[323]

Defending RAF fighters from 213 and 238 Squadrons also reported engaging Me 110s while fighting against the incoming *II/StG 2* raid and its Me 109 escorts,[324] and 609 Squadron who engaged these Stukas also reported Me 110 escorts behind the dive bombers and too far back to assist them.[325] These Me 110s could only have been *III/ZG 76*; Me 110s from this *Gruppe* are known to have escorted Stukas on the afternoon raids[326] and the *Gruppe* also suffered losses while flying sorties over the sea off Portland[327] at this time.

Operations to the east, commencing in the general Isle of Wight area, were equally complex, and also staggered in time, analogous to the two Stuka raids in the Portland region which were about 20 to 25 minutes

Adlertag

apart.³²⁸ *II/LG 1*'s Ju 88s took off first at 15h20 from their base at Orleans-Bricy³²⁹ with fighter support from elements of *JG 2*, these units approaching the Isle of Wight and overflying it just east of its centre, basically above Ventnor's destroyed RDF site, bombed the previous day.³³⁰ Details of *JG 2*'s actions are not available, and bearing in mind the much wider Channel in this area, Me 109s would have had limited penetration depth; possibly there was also a sweep ahead. *II/JG 2* claimed a Hurricane shot down but this was not accepted and is shown in the *Luftwaffe* victory list as having been rejected.³³¹ *II/LG 1* proceeded north towards Worthy Down airfield but could not find it with the cloudy weather, and while flying south-eastwards towards Selsey³³² to cross over the coast once more, probably dropped many of the scattered bombs reported above, at localities between Worthy Down and Thorney Island airfields.³³³

A gunner's diary from the *Gruppenkommandeur's* aircraft of *Stab II/LG 1*, which was shot down on 17 September 1940 and fell into RAF Intelligence's hands recorded a large-scale attack (no doubt that was the intention) and the destruction of two bombers at take-off.³³⁴ One Ju 88 of the *Gruppe* crashed on take-off killing all aboard while a second was 50% damaged after a tyre burst on lifting off at Orleans-Bricy.³³⁵

Twenty minutes after the *II/LG 1* lifted off, *I* and *III Gruppen* took off, the former also from Orleans-Bricy and the latter from Chateaudun.³³⁶ These two units were supported by fighters from, respectively, *JG 27* and *ZG 2*.³³⁷ *I/LG 1*, supposed to attack the RAF base at Boscombe Down,³³⁸ approached the southern English coast a few miles west of St Alban's Head and then flew along the coast towards the Solent, where it was detected by radar, and went on to bomb Southampton without any real interference from the defences.³³⁹ Bombing was accurate and hit a number of warehouses and a cold storage facility heavily. Anti-aircraft guns at Southampton claimed a bomber shot down,³⁴⁰ but *I/LG 1* suffered no losses.

Hpt Kern who was leading *I/LG 1* on this mission made the decision to attack an alternative target,³⁴¹ a decision that must have been made as the Ju 88 *Gruppe* approached the English coast and saw the extensive and thick cloud cover extending far inland. *JG 27* thus appears to have provided fighter cover to both *I/LG 1* and to the second Stuka raid, that by *II/StG 2* further to the west; flying generally from the Cherbourg peninsula, this would have been quite within their range. A pilot from *4/JG 27* claimed a Hurricane, which was disallowed in the victory list;³⁴² it was not recorded whether this was related to the *I/LG 1* raid or that by *II/StG 2*.

III/LG 1's route took it over the western Isle of Wight, Middle Wallop and then to its intended target of Andover airfield, the Ju 88s flying out over the Channel for home again via Westhampnett.³⁴³ Of *III/LG 1*'s twenty-three attacking Ju 88s, a dozen claimed to have bombed Andover and half that number to have dropped their ordnance on Middle Wallop, claiming several direct hits on hangars and eight to twelve aircraft destroyed on the ground at the former airfield.³⁴⁴ Of a total of thirty-six 250 kg bombs, twelve equally heavy incendiary bombs and sixty 50 kg projectiles dropped by this *Gruppe*, only twelve bombs landed within the Andover airfield boundary, but they destroyed the station headquarters building and officer's quarters, damaged one aircraft and killed two personnel, S/L L. De. L. Leder and P/O A. D. Mountstephen, with F/Lt (Ret) A. E. Dark wounded.³⁴⁵ While six Ju 88s claimed to have bombed Middle Wallop sector station, only one bomber appears to have actually found Middle Wallop at all, and dropped its load on the village, well clear of the RAF base.³⁴⁶

Establishing a timeline for all the different parts of this complex *Luftflotte 3* operation is challenging. The times provided in many records and published sources vary quite a bit. One way round the dilemma is to estimate flight times from German bases in France to either target areas or areas over which they were engaged by RAF fighters. Using *III/LG 1* (base Chateaudun) as an example and applying a loaded cruising speed of approximately 217 mph,³⁴⁷ the *Gruppe* would have reached its target of Andover at *c.* 17h00. This airfield was hit by twelve bombs as noted above, at 17h00.³⁴⁸ This correlation suggests the method has some viability.

8/LG 1 lost a Ju 88 shot down on the way in at about 16h35 just inland from the coastline, at Selsey.³⁴⁹ Both *I* and *II/ZG 2* provided fighter cover for *III/LG 1* and were engaged by RAF fighters north of Southampton.³⁵⁰ Applying similar logic to the *I/LG 1* (base: Orleans-Bricy) raid suggests Southampton being bombed at about 16h48 and *II/LG 1* (same base as *I Gruppe*) reaching the general Worthy Down area (which target was not located and thus not bombed under existing weather conditions) at *c.* 16h38. If *I/LG 1* had actually attacked its intended target at Boscombe Down, that would have occurred about four minutes later than the time of the alternative bombing of Southampton. The three Ju 88 *Gruppen* of LG 1 each approached the coast in the general area of the Isle of Wight but at different locations, and thus seem to have operated independently of each other.

Further towards the west, in the general area of Portland and north thereof, the sweep by *I/JG 53* and the associated sortie by *II/ZG 76* were the first *Luftwaffe* incursions. The Me 109s crossed the coast west of the Isle of Wight soon before 16h00.³⁵¹ Having crossed in over Poole, *I/JG 53* swept westwards, flying close past Warmwell and crossing back

Adlertag

out over the coast at Lyme Regis.[352] The Me 110s of *II/ZG 76* are not reported as having crossed the coast and probably flew an approximately parallel arc over Portland, passing over the port from north-north-east to the south; when intercepted by 152 Squadron they were flying south, over Portland.[353]

Elements of *I/JG53* and *II/ZG 76* engaged with British fighters over the Portland area around 16h00. At about the same time as this sweep took place, the first Stuka raid (*I/StG 1*, took off from forward base Dinard, just west of St Malo) which had picked up their escort from *II/JG 53* over Guernsey, reached the coast north of Portland but due to the clouds could not find its target at Warmwell, and dropping bombs randomly along the coast, the Ju 87 *Gruppe* in reasonable formation crossed back to France.[354] *Major* Hozzel, *Gruppenkommandeur* of the Ju 87s had taken the trouble to fly to Guernsey the previous day to discuss their escort with the *Kommandeur* of *II/JG 53*, *Hpt* von Maltzahn, who, while agreeing not to abandon them, insisted on his *Gruppe* not being a persistent close escort.[355]

In the event, when the Stukas turned round at the coast it was the Me 109s of *II/JG 53* that were abandoned, and they then carried out an unplanned fighter sweep over Portland.[356] In this they became involved with the second Stuka raid (*II/StG 2*, up from their base at Lannion in Brittany) and provided some protection to that raid's Ju 87s and also to their direct escort of Me 110s from *III/ZG 76*. The engagements of Stukas, Me 110s and Me 109s occurred to the north, north-west and north-east of Portland at *c*. 16h10–16h15, with some *II/JG 53* dogfights extending to about 16h40.[357] Despite the Stukas suffering heavy losses from the RAF, without the fortuitous appearance of these Me 109s from *II/JG 53* they would have been even harder hit. *II/StG 2*'s own escort from *JG 27* appears to have been of little if any help, while their Me 110 cover was too far back to help, and also under attack itself.

The German plan for these raids thus encompassed one raid followed up by a second soon after in both west (Portland area) and east (north of Isle of Wight), the earlier ones presumably aimed to draw RAF fighters into combat and exhaust their fuel and ammunition prior to the second incursion. The concept was enhanced with a fighter sweep ahead, known from the Portland raids and possibly also applicable in the east around the Isle of Wight (elements of *JG 2*?). What is much harder to understand is the German strategic decision not to attack major Fighter Command sector stations at Tangmere (north-east of the Isle of Wight) and Middle Wallop (north-west of Southampton) before planning attacks on RAF targets further inland such as those intended in this set of raids: Yeovil, Boscombe Down, Andover and Worthy Down. In contrast, what

Eagle Day: 13 August 1940

did make sense was the plan for the earlier raid in the west to target Warmwell, a forward fighter base close to the coast near Portland.

152 Squadron had been the first RAF squadron to take off, at 15h00, and was on patrol at about 15,000 ft in the Portland area where its ten Spitfires engaged the *I/JG 53–II/ZG 76* sweep.[358] When they first sighted the Me 110s, these were flying southwards over Portland and were above the Spitfires who climbed about 1,000 ft above them before attacking,[359] as described by the 152 Squadron formation leader, F/Lt Boitel-Gill in his combat report.[360]

> I was Maida Leader, with instructions to patrol Portland at 15,000 feet. I sighted a formation of 30 ME 110s and gave the order to attack in line astern. The A/C were proceeding in a southerly direction and it took me quite a long time to catch up with them. I delivered a stern attack from slightly above opening fire at about 1000 yards maintaining fire until about 100 yards. I did not see the effect of the fire, but consider several machines were damaged as the formation was tightly packed and I sprayed six A/C during the attack. Rounds fired 390. Stoppage Starboard 1. (Maida = call sign of squadron)

The engagement mainly took place some six miles south of Portland, and the Me 110s rapidly formed a large circle for defence once attacked.[361] Some Me 109s were observed by the Spitfire pilots and two of them reported being attacked by these machines towards the end of their engagements.[362] *Hpt* Mayer, the *Staffelkapitän* of *1/JG 53*, led his *Staffel* in a break-away from the rest of the *Gruppe* during their sweep across the southern coastline between Poole and Lyme Regis, and would have required only a few minutes to reach their Me 110 comrades in need; they claimed four victories, of which two were confirmed, one by Mayer himself, and the other two are classified as probables in the *Luftwaffe* claims list.[363] *5/ZG 76* claimed two Spitfires, all six claims being at c. 16h00;[364] while *1/JG 53* claimed only Hurricanes, at least *II/ZG 76* got the aircraft type right. The Spitfires of 152 Squadron suffered no losses apart from F/O Inness, whose Spitfire had a single bullet come through his seat's armour plate, graze his elbow and wound him slightly and end up smashing into his instrument panel.[365] He was able to return to base in his damaged machine and having received medical attention was back on duty the next day.[366]

152 Squadron were only slightly less expansive in their claimed victories than *1/JG 53* and *II/ZG 76*, asserting one Me 110 destroyed (by Inness) and two more damaged.[367] Neither German unit reported any losses.[368] With both sides observing their opponents diving steeply away

into cloud below the fighting, with engines smoking as throttles were shoved through the gate by German and British pilots, this may have encouraged many of the claims. For 152 Squadron several pilots reported seeing one Me 110 engine that they were firing at belch smoke and the machine descend steeply. It is quite likely that the second engine of these aircraft, which they did not observe closely while concentrating their fire on the other wing and its engine, gave off just as much black smoke as it was suddenly throttled up to the maximum. The combat report of P/O Williams of 152 Squadron is instructive regarding the excessively optimistic claims made by both sides.[369]

> I was Black 2, and at about 15,000 feet saw about 30 ME 110s above us, climbed behind them, and attacked from astern. I picked out an ME 110, he turned to the right; I followed firing full deflection shot for about 7 seconds. The incendiaries hit the ME 110, but another ME 110 fired at me from head on. I turned over left and another ME 110 fired at me. I turned on my back and dived down, I saw a plane in my mirror, which looked like a ME 109, so went on through the clouds and returned to base. Owing to the quickness with which things happened, I could not tell whether the ME 110 was damaged or not.

He reports his incendiaries hitting his one Me 110 opponent – these were more likely to have been some of the De Wilde rounds which resulted in small explosions against the enemy aircraft upon making contact. In aerial combat, many aircraft would be only lightly affected by a few machine gun rounds impacting in non-vulnerable places, and such light damage which was repairable by unit mechanics at their base was often not formally reported to higher authorities.

Following the sweep discussed above (which engagement occurred within a few minutes pre- or post-16h00, approximately), three RAF fighter squadrons intercepted German raiders in short succession of one another in the general Portland area and north thereof: 213, 238 and 609 Squadrons, in that order. While 213 Squadron met *Gruppen*-sized formations of Me 110s and Me 109s some fifteen miles south of Portland Bill (engagement *c.* 16h10-16h20), 238 Squadron flying above Portland itself, reported a large armada of bombers (two pilots reported these as Ju 88s or Ju 87s, respectively[370]), Me 110s and Me 109s numbering up to *c.* 300-400 machines (engagement *c.* 16h15-16h30), spread widely laterally and stepped up backwards for several miles.[371]

The last to intercept, 609 Squadron met the enemy over the coast at Lyme Bay (*c.* 16h25 onwards) and reported engaging Ju 87s and some Me 109s, with a *Gruppe*-sized formation of Me 110s seen in the distance

Eagle Day: 13 August 1940

and engaging Hurricanes, but too far back to help their charges.[372] The approximate times estimated for these three successive engagements were not really discrete, as overlap occurred, the late part of an engagement of one squadron overlapping with the early part of the action of the next unit. Possibly the three successive engagements were separated by only minutes.[373] That the three squadrons saw rather different enemy incursions in rapid succession to each other over a distance of about twenty miles is rather confusing.

However, there is a logical explanation. The twenty-seven Stukas of *II/StG 2* lifted off from Lannion in Brittany as already noted; this base lay almost due south of Torquay in Devon and was west of the Cherbourg peninsula. They thus likely flew a north-north-east course towards Lyme Bay, north-west of Portland. Their close escorts of *III/ZG 76* were based in Laval (south-south-east of the Cherbourg peninsula), while the more remote Me 109 cover from *JG 27* was forward-based in the Cherbourg area in general. Due to the very slow speed of the Ju 87s compared to both fighter types, and bearing in mind the width of the Channel here restricting Me 109 range considerably, it would have been essential to have the escorts fly at their most fuel-economic speed (faster than the Ju 87s at *their* economic speed with bombload), and thus a rendezvous closer to Lyme Bay, about over the Portland area (an easily identifiable landmark from the air) would have been logical.

213 Squadron, initially below the clouds, caught sight of the *III/ZG 76* Me 110s and some of the *JG 27* Me 109s. 238 Squadron was much higher at about 22,000 ft and patrolling above Portland were most likely witness to a much larger German formation once rendezvous between Stukas and escorts had been effected; they possibly also saw further *JG 27* Me 109s flying northwards to the east and even some of the *I/LG 1* Ju 88s approaching towards the west of the Isle of Wight. Over-estimating the size of an enemy formation was a common feature in the Battle for both sides. By the time 609 Squadron engaged not long after, *JG 27*, being short of fuel after their engagements with 213 and 238 Squadrons, had turned back while *III/ZG 26*'s Me 110s were in combat with 238 Squadron a couple of miles behind the Ju 87s. The Me 109s engaged by 609 Squadron were from *II/JG 53*, which after early departure of their dive-bomber charges due to the cloud-covered coastline and adjacent interior, were performing a fighter sweep in the area and had contact with these Spitfires. *II/JG 53* possibly also engaged some of the other two squadron's Hurricanes further south, as the Messerschmitts turned south and made off across the Channel again at the end of the overall complex aerial action.

213 Squadron's Hurricanes were on patrol south of the Portland area, flying below the clouds, as ordered by the 10 Group controller.[374]

215

Adlertag

The cloud on this day was a major factor, with a thick layer of 10/10 cloud from about 2,000–5,000 ft and a second at 6,000–9,000 ft.[375] While squadron documentation makes clear they were patrolling south of Portland Bill below cloud, it is not clear which cloud layer was pertinent. However, the leader of 213 Squadron on this mission, F/Lt Sing, sighted the enemy at 12,000 ft, suggesting they were flying beneath the second, higher cloud layer, as is apparent from his combat report.[376]

> I sighted approx. 30 M.E. 110's and 20 M.E. 109's, 15 miles south of Portland Bill at 12,000 ft. I lost Red 3 climbing through cloud but Red 2 remained with me. We approached the enemy from above but as we were attacked by M.E. 109's we lost one another in the coming "dog-fight". I got in two 4 sec. bursts at two M.E. 110's when diving down at them but did not have time to see what effect they had on them. An M.E. 109 attacked me without success and before it could get away up to the cloud I got in two bursts of 4 secs. each and it burst into flames and crashed into the sea. I returned to base to rearm. In the two M.E. 110's there were four guns firing aft from rear turret.

F/Lt Sing's regular number two in his section was Sgt Norris; Norris took off from Exeter ten minutes after the rest of his squadron, but caught up with them while they were patrolling below the cloud south of Portland Bill.[377] It appears that Sing managed to attack a couple of the Me 110s before the Me 109s came down and disrupted these attacks and also separated F/Lt Sing from his wingman, Norris. The second section (Yellow) which climbed up behind Sing's Red Section was led by P/O Osmand, who reported:[378]

> I was on patrol below cloud above Portland when a "Tally-ho" was given from above a cloud. Our section climbed up and contacted a circle of M.E 110's with attendant M.E 109's… One passed slightly in front of me at close range and I fired two bursts which resulted in black smoke pouring from his engine. I followed it through cloud and found signs of three aircraft being shot down into the sea. Two with signs of having fallen recently. This was about fifteen miles to the South of Portland.

JG 27 suffered no losses in this mission, and Osmand's description of a Me 109 descending into cloud, its engine pouring black smoke, is another example of the classic Me 109 evasive manoeuvre when attacked: dive and push the throttle through the gate, thereby sending black smoke pouring from the exhausts.

Eagle Day: 13 August 1940

With the lack of any *JG 27* casualties, F/Lt Sing might also have been a victim of this misleading German evasive manoeuvre. Red 3, Sgt Bushell, claimed a Me 109 damaged while P/O Atkinson, leader of Green Section, claimed another in the sea.[379] With 213 Squadron's engagement mainly being at about 15,000 ft and with cloud below them, observing a machine hit the sea would not have been easy. P/O Laricheliere (Blue 2) climbed up like the rest of the squadron and on passing through cloud, at 10,000 ft suddenly saw a Me 110 sitting right in front of him, and at which he fired a one second burst, claiming that it exploded.[380] In his combat report,[381] he noted: 'DEWILDE AMMUNITION was used for the first time in No. 4 Port gun.' An older pilot, twenty-seven at the time, and a graduate of Montreal University in his native Canada, he joined the RAF in 1939 and had one of the shortest and most intense fighting careers in the Battle:[382] three victory claims on 13 August 1940, three more two days later, and missing the next day off Portland.

His claim for an exploding Me 110 in this particular engagement after a very short burst of fire of only one second does ask a lot of small calibre .303 inch bullets. The first experience of the De Wilde incendiary rounds, which ignited when they hit their target, causing small flashes to be observed, if close enough[383] may also have played a role in his observations. However, he may also have made a lucky hit on something very vulnerable like an empty or partially empty vapour-filled fuel tank; one will never know. 213 Squadron claimed a total of three Me 109s destroyed, another damaged and Laricheliere's exploded Me 110.[384] In turn, they lost Sgt Norris, F/Lt Sing's wingman who went missing about ten miles south of Portland, where he was last seen by some of his fellow pilots who were in action at the time, 16h15.[385] His body was washed ashore near Le Touquet, far to the east in the Pas de Calais, many weeks later.[386] Channel currents[387] reaching the Le Touquet area of the French coast suggest he landed/crashed into the sea quite far south of Portland.

III/ZG 76 lost two Me 110s missing off Portland with one crew surviving to be picked up by the German air-sea rescue service, one lost machine each to *8th* and *9th Staffeln*.[388] With competing claims from 238 Squadron, whose engagement will be detailed below, there is no way to assign specific German losses to particular RAF claims against these Me 110s.

213 Squadron from its documentation does not appear to have had a major engagement with the Me 110s of *III/ZG 76* – one was claimed and only two pilots reported engaging them at all. The majority of this Me 110 *Gruppe* can thus be assumed to have continued their flight northwards as part of the initially remote escort for *II/StG 2*'s Ju 87s, and once rendezvous between these two groups of aircraft plus the

Adlertag

Me 109s of *JG 27* had been effected, they were sighted by 238 Squadron's Hurricanes, who were to have a much more intense engagement with the Me 110s. The eleven Hurricanes of 238 Squadron, all they could muster after intense combat with significant losses since 8 August 1940, were led on this mission by twenty-two-year-old F/O David Hughes, who, despite only joining them nine days earlier, was already acting flight commander and acting squadron commander.[389] His C/O, S/L Harold Fenton had been wounded on 8 August and could not fly, though he was fulfilling the other duties of a commanding officer.[390] In his combat report, Hughes describes what happened when they sighted the enemy.[391]

> I was Red 1. At 1530 hours the squadron was ordered to patrol Portland at 20,000 feet. Over Portland a formation of ME 110's were seen travelling North. I ordered line astern and attacked out of the sun. At 250 yds. I gave a short burst (1 sec.). The enemy commenced a steep turn to the left. I broke away and climbed. The 110's commenced circling and before they had closed the circle I dived on the last 110 and fired a deflection burst (2 secs.) at 200 yds. closing to 50 yds. The enemy went into a long spiral and burst into flames. I again dived on a 110 from astern and gave a burst of 1 second, continuing the dive. I pulled up underneath the ME 110 and fired a very short burst at point blank range before breaking away. The E/A dropped its nose and commenced a slow downward spiral with smoke and flames pouring out of the port engine. I fired several bursts (1 sec.) at other machines whenever the opportunity presented itself. With the sun directly astern of the E/A, I saw a ME 109 cruising straight and level. I turned into attack but before I was in range I observed in my mirror two other ME 109's on my tail, and I broke off the attack. This manoeuvre of the enemy occurred again and I made a feint attack on the leading ME 109, and then did a tight "side loop" and found myself on the tail of the rearmost ME 109. I gave the E/A a burst of 2 secs. and pieces flew off the machine and I think his empennage was badly damaged. I then broke off the attack as the other two ME 109's were working round onto my tail. Landed 17.00 hrs.

Hughes had ordered Red, Yellow and Green Sections to perform a number 1 attack (line astern, from behind and slightly below) from their height of about 5,000 ft above the Me 110s, and they struck the outside machines on the port side, while leaving the three Hurricanes of Blue Section aloft as a rear-guard against Me 109 attacks.[392] With his relative lack of fighter combat experience, the past few days had taught David Hughes a lot, and his dive out of the sun caught the Me 110s by surprise, with the top cover Blue Section Hurricanes giving them a window of opportunity to make multiple attacks on the Me 110s as the latter formed a defensive circle. The tactical innovation and rapid learning curve followed by the youthful leadership in Fighter Command's squadrons are amply demonstrated in this engagement. Red Section detached the three port outside Me 110s of the *III/ZG 76* formation, which then turned around and fled southwards; F/O Hughes claimed two of the Messerschmitts with Red 2, P/O Davis following one of them and dispatching it into the sea after a *c.* ten mile chase across the Channel, as related in his combat report.[393]

> I was Red 2. Squadron ordered to patrol Portland 20,000 ft. sighted about 400 E/A at 16,000 ft. heading North. Red 1 gave line astern and dived down towards E/A. Red 1 and I picked the two extreme left hand A/C and both fired from about 250 yds. I fired 3 sec. burst whereupon the E/A dived into the cloud and turned for home. I caught up about 10 miles S. of Portland and fired a very long burst from 250 yds. closing to 50 yds. The E/A then righted itself and dived into the sea leaving long trail of oil on the surface. I noticed a cannon firing out of the tail of the ME 110.

It is possible that Davis in fact followed and attacked a Me 110 already damaged by F/O Hughes; what is certain from Davis's report is that, as was the norm, destruction of the Me 110 necessitated multiple attacks and very close-range machine-gun fire. P/O Simmonds, the other member of Red Section, claimed four damaged Me 110s.[394] None of the other sections of 238 Squadron claimed any Me 110s, illustrating the success of the defensive circle adopted by *III/ZG 76*; their losses to Red Section occurred before this manoeuvre could be completed. Relatively late in the action, Me 109s did interfere, as related by Hughes. Blue Section leader, P/O Urwin-Mann, once having ensured that the Me 109s did not immediately disturb his comrades' attacks on the Me 110s, bounced a section of Me 109s behind the Me 110 formation.[395] He claimed one shot down but *JG 27*, providing the Me 109 cover to this Stuka raid on its way in, did not report any casualties. As was so often the case in the Battle, minor damage suffered by either side and repairable at their bases was often not reported up the line.

238 Squadron, having claimed a total of three Me 110s, another four damaged, one Me 109 dispatched and another damaged, suffered the loss of two Hurricanes, one pilot missing and five machines unserviceable on return to Middle Wallop.[396] *III/ZG 76* lost two Me 110s off Portland, one each from *8* and *9 Staffeln*, one crew being saved by their air-sea

rescue service;[397] these were likely victims of 238 Squadron's pilots, but 213 Squadron may also have scored a victory, as already discussed.

In their turn, ZG 76 claimed the enormous total of eleven Hurricanes and Spitfires in the actions involving *II Gruppe* in the earlier sweep action and *III Gruppe* over Portland[398] against 213 and 238 Squadrons. Yellow 1, Sgt Marsh, was missing after the engagement over Portland. His No. 3 in the section, Sgt Bann, in a letter to his parents, described how he had fainted momentarily from exhaustion and lost sight of his section leader;[399] once alone a pilot became much more vulnerable to the marauding Me 109s. Sgt Little, the third man in Blue Section, probably also became separated and vulnerable; he was badly shot up but managed to glide over the coast near Burton Bradstock where he skilfully carried out a crash-landing at Bredy Farm, one mile north-north-west of Swyre and not far from Dorchester, slightly wounded.[400] The relevant casualty file for Sgt Little[401] details the damage to his Hurricane, which was a write-off: a one foot diameter hole in the fuselage behind the cockpit; splinter holes in starboard wing; damage to glycol coolant and electrical systems; broken tail wheel; engine damaged and had failed.

Sgt Little's aircraft had come down some twelve miles north-west of Portland where the main Me 110 battle occurred, and both he and Sgt Marsh are recorded as having been shot down at about 16h30,[402] late in 238 Squadron's engagement. With Little's machine coming down in an area where 609 Squadron (who attacked next in the sequence, after 238 Squadron) had their main engagement with the Stukas of *II/StG 2* and the Me 109s of *II/JG 53* (discussed below), the two 238 Squadron aircraft may well have been the victims of the latter unit's Me 109s. As already noted, once the Stukas of *I/StG 1* had seen the clouds over the coast and inland and had turned back, their escort of *II/JG 53* had remained behind, carrying out an impromptu fighter sweep that met 609 Squadron. As they in their turn withdrew due to dwindling fuel reserves back south across the Channel, they would likely have met any RAF stragglers over Lyme Bay and further south. *5/JG 53* claimed three Spitfires at about 16h10–16h15, two north of Portland (one confirmed, one probable) and another confirmed south of it, with *4/JG 53* claiming a further Spitfire (probable) and a confirmed Hurricane north of Portland some 20 minutes later.[403]

With 609 Squadron suffering only a single Spitfire damaged to Stuka return fire, the three confirmed claims by *II/JG 53* may fit the two lost Hurricanes of 238 Squadron, and that of Sgt Norris missing from 213 Squadron. The times of the German claims may be a little early for the relevant RAF actions, but not by more than a matter of minutes. While *JG 27* made only a single claim, this was rejected by the *Luftwaffe* system.[404]

Eagle Day: 13 August 1940

Effectively, 609 Squadron attacked as the last of three successive intercepting Fighter Command units (after 213 and then 238 Squadrons) attacking the *II/StG 2* raid and its escorts, doing so from a position approximately west of Portland and then north towards Lyme Bay. The two flights of 609 Squadron had become separated in the cloudy weather while patrolling over the Portland area.[405] While the Intelligence Patrol Report (IPR) states that A Flight preceded B Flight into action by some seven to eight minutes, this is an error in the IPR, which can be explained as it was only written up three days after the event.[406] The combat reports, being almost always filled out immediately after the engagement in question, often provide a more accurate picture, and from S/L Darley's combat report[407] it would appear that the six Spitfires of Blue and Green Sections which he led were the flight to intercept first, namely B Flight.

> The Squadron was ordered to patrol base at 20,000 ft. Owing to 10/10 cloud from 2/5000 ft and again from 6/9,000 ft. I lost contact with A flight. After patrolling for about 35 min. I saw a mixed force of about 40 JU 87's and in 4 Vic formations of about 10 each and about 40 Me 109's and 110's stepped up and above the 87's all heading North. I was at 20,000 ft. and attacked a formation of 87's passing in front of the enemy fighters. The attack was badly judged and I had to go into an extremely steep dive to keep my sights on. I gave a burst of 2 secs. duration from 400–100 yds. and broke away to the right. No results observed. On my way down I experienced crossed fire from the formation of 87's about 400 yds. to my port. On recovering from my dive I saw the 87's turning left and back to the South. I gave a full deflection burst of 2 secs. at the last formation as it turned and then met fire from the ME's 109 & 110 and (should probably read 'who') then went into a series of left hand turns covering the retreat of the 87's. Having experienced the trap before I left the E/A and flew below cloud to Portland where I heard other A/C ordered to patrol. After orbiting for 10 mins. I picked up Blue 2 again and I was then ordered to pancake. (Pancake = land)

When S/L Darley saw the Ju 87 formation and stepped up Me 109 and Me 110 escorts behind it, all heading north, B Flight of 609 Squadron dived down on the Ju 87s just before 238 Squadron attacked the rearmost German fighters, namely the Me 110s of *III/ZG 76*. A few minutes later and further north towards the coast at Lyme Bay, when A Flight of 609 Squadron attacked the Ju 87s they observed how the Me 110s were being engaged by a Hurricane squadron and were too far behind to intervene.[408] 238 Squadron's attack on the Me 110s thus coincided

Adlertag

with Blue Section (B Flight) of 609 Squadron diving down onto *II/StG 2*'s Ju 87s. While the follow-up attack by A Flight of 609 Squadron took place some minutes later, overall thus 609's attack can be seen as just after 238 Squadron's attack, with an overlap in time as both 238 Squadron's and B Flight's dives into combat coincided.

If this sort of detail is confusing to the reader (it certainly was to the author), it is worth remembering how Dowding's excellent system led typically to a number of discrete attacks by separate squadrons in short succession, from differing directions; this must have played merry hell with German attempts to keep their large and unwieldy formations together and to apply the often complicated chronological coordination so often built into their overall raid plans. Dowding's defensive foundation and indeed his genius were thus complicated (and complemented) by the tactical *nous* of the RAF leaders in the air.

As already described in S/L Darley's combat report, his attack on the Ju 87s was ill-judged and made at too steep a dive angle and thus too fast; as a consequence he made no claim for damage to any Stuka, and the same applied also to Blue 2, F/O Ostaszewski.[409] Blue 3, P/O Appleby, managed only a short burst at a Ju 87 as he dived rapidly past them, only pulling up far below in cloud and then climbing back up into the fray overhead, to find just two lone Me 109s which he proceeded to stalk and fire upon, claiming one damaged Stuka and two damaged Me 109s.[410] S/L Darley similarly lost considerable altitude in his wild dive, recovered and saw most of the Ju 87s turn back south again to go home; he made a rapid deflection attack on the last section of them before being dissuaded from further attack by some accompanying Me 110 and Me 109 stragglers.[411]

While Blue Section had thus attempted to attack *II/StG 2*'s Stukas with little success, Green Section, the other half of B Flight, had been at a higher altitude (above 20,000 ft and in the sun), to provide a rear guard.[412] S/L Darley placed his flight above and in the sun, well situated to surprise both Ju 87s and some Me 109s which had suddenly appeared. P/O Crook flying the number three slot in Green Section had spotted five Me 109s passing just below his section and reacted promptly by diving on the hindmost and hitting him hard with a long burst from close range; the Messerschmitt appeared to catch fire and plummeted down, spinning and giving off black smoke for many thousands of feet before vanishing into the clouds.[413] The British pilot followed through and on breaking cloud some five miles north of Weymouth observed smoke rising from burning wreckage in a field below, which he quite understandably assumed was his Me 109 victim.[414] In fact, the wreckage was from one of

Eagle Day: 13 August 1940

II/StG 2's Ju 87s which had crashed near the Grimstone Viaduct between Rodden and Portisham, killing both crewmen.[415]

Crook is credited in many Battle of Britain sources with having dispatched a Me 109 which fell into Poole Harbour, some twelve miles to the east. The few Me 109s which Green Section of 609 Squadron had found suddenly flying close beneath them were from *II/JG 53*, the erstwhile escorts of the slightly earlier abortive Stuka raid by *I/StG 1*, targeting Warmwell; it may be recalled that they remained behind to perform an impromptu sweep around Portland after the early departure of their charges. By chance, a few had landed up just below Green Section, who were in a very advantageous position to attack from up-sun.

When P/O Crook broke away from his section to take on the rearmost hapless Me 109, his two section mates must have seen this and followed suit immediately. The Me 109s split all over the sky, Crook's victim flying north from Weymouth, another two over Weymouth Bay and a fourth towards Poole Harbour to the east of Weymouth, as described in the combat reports of Green 1 F/Lt McArthur and Green 2 F/O Nowierski.[416] P/O Crook emerged from the clouds approximately above Dorchester, a few miles north of Weymouth. The Ju 87 crash he observed lay a few miles to the south-west, and one of *4/JG 53*'s Me 109s was hit over Dorchester, *Oblt* Schulze managing to get his damaged machine home despite being badly wounded.[417] This is the most logical Me 109 to have been in combat with P/O Crook.

5/JG 53 lost three Me 109s, two into the sea in Weymouth Bay and one into Poole Harbour; *Ofw* Trutwin was killed over Weymouth Bay, *Lt* Pfannschmidt bailed out and survived to become a POW, and Uffz Hohenseldt bailed out badly wounded over Poole but survived, also as a prisoner.[418] When the five-odd Me 109s of *II/JG 53* had been surprised by the attack from the sun by Green Section of 609 Squadron and split in all directions, pursued by the Spitfire pilots, surprise must have been complete for three of them to be lost and another damaged.

F/Lt McArthur, Green 1, gave his Me 109 an approximately five-second deflection shot and then avoided four more of his fellows who were after him by going into the clouds.[419] After emerging from the clouds at about 3,000 ft, McArthur observed two bombers, which he thought were Ju 88s making for Swanage, and he pursued them to the French coast without being able to get close enough to attack them properly.[420] Swanage lies about five miles due south of Poole Harbour and thus places McArthur's engagement close to where the wounded Uffz Hohenseldt bailed out of his stricken Me 109; he would appear to have a stronger claim against this machine than P/O Crook. F/O Nowierski's combat

Adlertag

report, given next, places his combat over Weymouth Bay[421] where two *5/JG 53* Me 109s were lost.

> I was Green 2 and we sighted a large number of enemy aircraft coming from the South. We circled above them, and Green 1 dived to attack. At that moment I saw one Me. 109 above me and ahead. I climbed up behind him and fired three bursts at fairly close range and from astern. White smoke appeared from his fuselage and he turned over and started to dive. Some large object probably the cockpit door or roof flew away and the pilot got out and opened his parachute. I then saw 2 Me's 109 behind me and I dived and pulled out in a violent left hand turn and 'blacked out'. Ten minutes later I saw another Me. 109 ahead and approached him from behind and gave him a good burst at very close range. White smoke appeared from the fuselage and he dived steeply into a cloud and disappeared. I dived through the cloud and a minute or so later saw another aircraft dive into the sea. This occurred too late for it to have been my victim. Before attacking my first 109 I saw a Spitfire attack and shoot down a Me. 109.

This was probably P/O/ Crook. Having seen the enemy pilot take to his parachute over Weymouth Bay, Nowierski can be credited logically with having shot down Lt Pfannschmidt's Me 109. Nowierski had seen the German formation approaching from the south initially, like S/L Darley, and like F/Lt McArthur was also harassed by further Me 109s, presumably of *II/JG 53*. He probably saw P/O Crook sending *Oblt* Schulze's aircraft down spinning and smoking to its assumed demise, just as Crook himself had inferred; Schulze made it home across the Channel despite being badly wounded. *Ofw* Trutwein who crashed into Weymouth Bay and was killed was either the victim of F/O Nowierski, who claimed a second Me 109 damaged from close range in his combat report above, or of P/O Appleby, Blue 3, who pursued two Me 109s after his brief and abortive attack on the Stukas.[422]

After S/L Darley led B Flight (Blue and Green Sections) in his abortive attack against the *II/StG 2* Stukas near Portland and some minutes later towards the coast of Lyme Bay north-west of Portland, A Flight came into action against the Stukas, still in good formation but lacking any effective escort, the Me 110s of *III/ZG 76* being too far astern and in action themselves (with 238 Squadron), and no Me 109s close by to assist them. A Flight's attack coincided approximately with Green Section's engagement with the Me 109s of *II/JG 53* and this distracted and drew off the only possible Me 109s that may have helped the Stukas. Their own escort from *JG 27* had already withdrawn back across the Channel,

Eagle Day: 13 August 1940

no doubt short of fuel. How A Flight's attack unfolded is well illustrated by the combat report[423] of F/O John Dundas, ace pilot in 609 Squadron and with the finest eyesight as well.

> I was spare pilot and joined squadron as Red 4. Above cloud at 10,000 ft. sighted fighters in sun above my head and informed Red 1, who told me to take lead. I climbed into sun at 18,000 ft. with Flight in line astern behind me, when I turned in towards three Vic formations of Ju's 87 (18 in each formation) silhouetted against clouds below us, heading North. Red 1 then took lead and I fell into line astern as Red 4. First three aircraft of Red section dived on rear section of 3 87's out of the sun. E/A took no avoiding action. After three attacks carried out singly from line astern by Red 1, 2 and 3, the three Ju's 87 were all destroyed. I attacked starboard Ju' 87 of next section to port, opening fire at 250 yds. Though well throttled back I had rather too much overtaking speed and had closed to point blank range within 4 secs. I saw E/A burst into flames and dive into cloud. I broke away and then attacked a second Ju. 87 which was already being attacked by a Spitfire as I closed in. For this reason I had to hold my fire till I was so close and could only get in a two second burst, all but colliding with E/A as I broke away. During this attack I ran into some rear-gun fire and a bullet punctured my oil system. I came down through cloud with no oil pressure and forced landed on Warmwell aerodrome with a dead prop. Ju's 87 took no avoiding action. Our attack developed straight down sun and must have surprised them. I think escort fighters Me's 110, whom we saw about 3 miles astern as we went into attack, were already engaged. They were too far away from Ju's to protect them adequately and appeared only to be flying at same height as Ju's. No Me's 109 seen.

The 'spare pilot' referred to in Dundas' report was an additional thirteenth fighter which took off with a full squadron of twelve machines, there in order to replace any aircraft that had to abort the mission due to any technical failure and thereby maintain the unit at full strength once action was joined. Not all fighter squadrons adopted this practice, which obviously also depended on enough aircraft being available to the unit, something that became much less common as the Battle unfolded and casualties rose. Very keen pilots flying number thirteen such as John Dundas would stay with the formation to enter combat rather than turning back before the engagement began. One of the German Ju 87 pilots witnessed the entire *Kette* (vic) of three Stukas being shot down in short order in the first attack by Red 1, 2 and 3.[424] F/Lt Frank Howell,

Adlertag

Red 1 and the leader of A Flight also demonstrated excellent leadership in letting Dundas take over the lead until the enemy had been sighted, after which Howell led them down from up-sun in a perfect attack.[425] Yellow section followed the four Spitfires of Red Section into an equally devastating attack on the hapless Stukas.[426] The Stukas never got near their inland target of Yeovil.

Six of the *II/StG 2* dive-bombers were shot down by 609 Squadron with the loss of five crews, only one of whom became a POW, the sixth crew survived a ditching in the Channel and being rescued by a German e-boat.[427] Four of the dive-bombers ended up in the sea, one off Portland, another in Weymouth Bay and one almost made it home only to crash into the water near Guernsey; two crashed on land, one near the coast of Lyme Bay, the other near Dorchester.[428]

Inevitably, 609 Squadron over-claimed: a total of eight Ju 87s destroyed, another probably so and three damaged; this was in addition to the two Me 109s and four more damaged claimed by B Flight with Sgt Feary of A Flight claiming a straggling Me 110 damaged.[429] 609 Squadron suffered no casualties apart from F/O Dundas's damaged Spitfire detailed in his combat report.

As already outlined, the three *LG 1* bomber formations appear to have operated independently of each other, despite all three crossing the coast within the general area of the Isle of Wight. Applying take-off times for each Ju 88 formation and cruising speed for the loaded bombers, suggests all three crossed the coast within about fifteen to twenty minutes of each other. While elements of *JG 2* and *JG 27* provided Me 109 cover for the Ju 88s, they had very little contact with the RAF defenders. It was only the Me 110 escorts of *I* and *II/ZG 2* that had anything more than fleeting combat with Fighter Command aircraft. Parts of four fighter squadrons were directed against these bomber incursions and escorts by the controllers, but in the generally prevailing cloudy weather successful interceptions were greatly reduced, mostly being skirmishes against single or a few aircraft. The only exception was an engagement between 601 Squadron and *ZG 2*'s Me 110s in the Winchester-Botley area (north-north-east of Southampton) at *c*. 16h25; the Me 110s were intercepted while flying on a southerly course and thus appear to have carried out a sweep inland ahead of the bombers, being caught on their way out before the Ju 88s flew inland.[430]

The dozen Hurricanes of 601 Squadron took off from Tangmere at 15h35 and were initially vectored to Bembridge, Isle of Wight below the clouds.[431] The squadron were flying an unusual formation consisting of three sections, Red Section being four strong, Yellow the more normal three Hurricanes, and Blue had five machines.[432] Why they were is unclear; possibly Red Section was flying a diamond formation, a vic with one in the box behind and either slightly above or below; Blue Section likely comprised a vic in front and a pair behind, the latter possibly placed higher as a rear-guard for the squadron. F/Lt Hope was leading 601 Squadron on this mission[433] despite the presence of their short-lived and inexperienced new squadron commander, S/L The Hon. E. F. Ward, who served in that capacity only between 10 and 19 August before being moved to the Tangmere operations room.[434] He seems to have been flying in the Red 2 position, but without any combat report, his actions are unknown.

The squadron was soon ordered to Selsey at 5,000 ft before being informed that the enemy machines were west of them.[435] Proceeding in that direction and climbing to 12,500 ft, they met sixteen Me 110s over Winchester who were below them at about 11,000 ft[436] and flying south; the Me 110s also used an unusual formation, six led, followed by a *Schwarm* of four and at the rear two vics of three *Zertstörern*.[437] The squadron attacked them and a dogfight ensued during which the engagement moved further southwards, towards Botley, just east of Southampton; here F/O Davis reported meeting what was most likely a second Me 110 formation comprising ten Jaguars, fighter-bomber Me 110s carrying four light bombs inboard of each engine nacelle.[438]

Three pilots (F/O Clyde, F/Sgt Pond and Sgt Guy, one from each section) had engagements with straggling Ju 88s over the Selsey area and out over the Channel, while P/O McGrath had a skirmish with Me 109s, presumably from *JG 2*, far out to sea.[439] It is likely that *II/ZG 2* were carrying the bombs (with *I Gruppe* being involved in the main engagement), and perhaps the idea had been for the former Me 110s to drop their light bombs as part of the overall mission as some sort of distraction; in the event, the weather probably prevented this and when F/O Davis spotted and attacked them on their way out, those he saw from close-up still carried their projectiles.

F/Lt Sir Archibald Hope led his squadron in to the attack, hitting the Me 110s now strung out in two line astern formations from head on, before they could form their normal defensive circle, and watching his target turn, expose its belly and disappear downwards vertically.[440] Red 3, Sgt Guy, followed Hope in, giving two Me 110s short bursts before hitting another from below and astern, seeing flame and smoke pour from it as it dived steeply away.[441] By the time F/O Cleaver flying as Red 4 came in, the circle was forming and he flew against the rotation of the Me 110s, firing a full deflection burst from head on and slightly on the quarter, well ahead of his target, which then obligingly flew straight through the bullets, as Cleaver observed its glasshouse cockpit cover shatter, and as he spun out trying to stay with his turning victim, he last saw the Messerschmitt turn half over and go down.[442]

Yellow Section came in next and after relatively brief attacks on the circle, mostly from head on and less from astern, each pilot followed one or more Me 110s that broke from the circling German formation. Yellow leader, F/O Davis, saw two Me 110s heading south and stopped the starboard engine of one prior to it disappearing in the clouds.[443] P/O McGrath, Yellow 2, similarly followed a Messerschmitt he had separated from the circle southwards over the Channel, its engines smoking heavily; he chased it right into the sea as a final long burst finished it off, the pilot jumping but his parachute not opening in time, about thirty miles south of Selsey Bill.[444]

As McGrath climbed above the lower cloud layer to make his way home, he met six Me 109s who tried to prevent his return, but the British pilot managed to evade them and even claimed one damaged, the Me 109 being seen smoking.[445] Seeing as *JG* 2 reported no casualties at all, this was possibly normal Me 109 escape behaviour – smoke issuing from an over-throttled engine. Yellow Section's third man, F/Sgt Pond, after making several attacks against the circle from head on and below the Me 110s, attacked another from astern which broke away and dived for the clouds; he pursued what was likely the same machine in and out of the clouds until he caught sight of the French coast.[446] He then turned north again and only saw the ground once more when north-west of Southampton, whereupon he turned east towards base.[447]

All five Hurricanes of Blue Section attacked the circle of Me 110s from outside; Blue 1, F/O Clyde, gave one a long burst and it turned over, bits fell off and it dived down, and he then attacked a second just above and in front of him and observed it descend well on fire.[448] Climbing back up, Clyde came across a Ju 88 which he followed out over the Channel in and out of cloud for some twenty-five miles, but lost it after a forlorn burst from 500 yards.[449] Blue 2, P/O Grier, while turning inside the Me 110 circle, stood his Hurricane on its tail and fired at a Messerschmitt from below, seeing it fall away seemingly in trouble; pursuing it, he gave a long burst into its tail, both engines caught fire and it fell into cloud burning all the way.[450] Sgt MacDonald, number four in the section, gave two short deflection bursts at a Me 110 not quite within the circle yet, and as it dived away for the clouds he gave two more long bursts and saw the port engine afire as it disappeared into the cloud above the sea, two miles off Selsey.[451] Blue 5 F/O 'Jack' Riddle entered the Me 110 circle against its rotation, firing head on, then from the middle of the circle fired at a Me 110 from above and behind while turning steeply, and watched pieces fly off and its perspex roof shatter before it turned onto its back and went down vertically.[452]

After leaving the circle fight to pursue two Me 110s fleeing south, F/O Davis called Tangmere control and was directed to Botley where he found ten Me 110 'Jaguar' fighter-bombers, each carrying what appeared to be four light bombs inboard of each of their engine nacelles. Attacking the rearmost of them, he killed the rear gunner and stopped the starboard engine, followed by two more attacks from quarter ahead, after which he last saw it descending steadily off the Isle of Wight.[453] His number three man from Yellow Section, F/Sgt Pond, was flying east towards Tangmere having returned from a fruitless pursuit to within sight of the French coast, when two anti-aircraft bursts in front of him marked a Ju 88 just ahead of them; following as the Junkers flew north over Portsmouth and towards its balloon barrage, Pond had enough wisdom to break away as the bomber entered cloud in that dangerous area.[454] Turning away, he spotted yet another Ju 88 flying west below the clouds, and as the bomber went up into the vapour, Pond followed and as he emerged from the clouds, saw it proceeding south across his beam at only 200 yards. He gave it a long deflection burst and saw it dive away back into the cloud shovelling out black smoke.[455] Whether this was real damage or merely a German pilot giving emergency power is unknown.

Sgt Guy, who had headed for Tangmere after engaging the Messerschmitt circle, saw two Hurricanes circling a 'Me 110' which appeared to him to be evading their attentions; he climbed in, gave a burst at the port engine and saw the starboard one already glowing, and the enemy machine crashed into a field at Selsey, bursting into flames.[456] This can only have been the Ju 88 of *8/LG 1* which came down at Siddlesham and exploded at *c.* 16h35; this particular bomber had been attacked by 257 Squadron en route to bomb Andover, and the crew including pilot *Major* Scheuplein all perished.[457] Scheuplein was *Staffelkapitän* of the 8 *Staffel*; his posthumous promotion to *Major* was backdated to 1 August 1940.[458] Ironically, of the three 601 Squadron pilots who engaged Ju 88s, only Sgt Guy played a role in the destruction of one of them, and he claimed it to be a Me 110. Aircraft recognition always suffered during aerial combat. These Ju 88 stragglers engaged by 601 and 257 Squadrons probably broke away from the main formation of twenty-three Ju 88s flying in to attack Andover. With twelve bombing that target and six more attacking Middle Wallop,[459] this suggests that five may have come adrift when faced with the solid cloud cover over that part of southern England as they approached the coast, and they probably turned back, some of them being confronted singly by the two RAF squadrons.

Adlertag

601 Squadron claimed a total of one confirmed Me 110, four and a half unconfirmed destroyed, five probables and two damaged (plus one damaged Ju 88 and a damaged Me 109). German Me 110 casualties in this engagement listed only a single machine lost, from *1/ZG 2*; the pilot Lt Münschmeyer survived a harrowing ordeal: his machine was hit from below while diving on some Hurricanes over Winchester, damaging the elevator controls and he was himself hit twice in one foot, and as a result could no longer control the Me 110 and both crewmen bailed out.[460] The gunner fell dead close to the wreck, which crashed at North Baddesley; the wounded pilot had the further misfortune to hit the elevator as he left the stricken machine, breaking both legs and landed in a tree.[461] Lt Münschmeyer had been flying in the tail-end Charlie position[462] in *I/ZG 2*, which meant he was the last to gain some protection within the defensive circle.

A second Me 110 from *I/ZG 2* was damaged in the engagement but managed to reach forward base at Le Havre where it force-landed, the crew unscathed.[463] With so many claims by 601 Squadron there is no practical way of relating any of them to the two casualties suffered. The many Me 110s breaking off from the defensive circle to dive into cloud below, over-throttled engines smoking as they did so, no doubt was responsible for some of the RAF over-claiming, as was the very intensity of the combat between 601 Squadron and *ZG 2*.

While Green Section of 257 Squadron had been scrambled from Tangmere at 15h09 to investigate an x-raid (unknown aircraft detected by radar or Observer Corps) which turned out to be friendly, Blue and Red Sections of the squadron were sent up at 15h31 to patrol the Isle of Wight below cloud.[464] The six Hurricanes were led by S/L Harkness, who reported:[465]

> I was 257 Squadron leader acting as Blue I. When flying at 5,000 ft. south of Tangmere I saw black puffs of A.A. fire at about 3,500 ft. which appeared through a gap in the clouds. Seeing a Ju 88 above the A.A. puffs I dived and did a quarter attack from above. The e/a flew into cloud and I followed it pouring into it most of my ammunition and broke off at 80 yds. The bomber did a right hand turn and flew out to sea. I saw another Hurricane come in from behind and take up the attack.

The second Hurricane was that of P/O Capon.[466]

> I was Blue 2 257 Squadron. After I had been flying for nearly one hour in Blue section with the Squadron circling in line astern Blue leader

Eagle Day: 13 August 1940

> dived steeply from a height of about 7,000 ft. I fell back slightly coming third in the line astern. At this moment I lost my section and seeing a Ju 88 in thin cloud about 1,000 ft. below me I dived to the attack. Just as I was about to open fire another Hurricane attacked from slightly above me. Losing sight of it, I followed the e/a up and down through cloud. I was fired at from TWO top rear guns in the turret. The fire was almost continuous for about 7 seconds. I was hit in my Glycol. tank, port petrol tank and oil cooler. After I had flown to the port side of the e/a I made a 50 degree beam shot. I then turned inside, firing at it all the time as it made an almost vertical left hand turn. I noticed that its port engine was on fire and that flames were coming out of the wing root starboard. Return fire had ceased when the e/a straightened out and I saw about 5 Hurricanes do beam attacks on it. I watched it glide down into field west of Selsey Bill when it appeared to explode.

This combat account emphasises some home truths about bomber engagements in the Battle: bomber return fire, even from a single aircraft, was dangerous, and it generally took attacks by multiple British fighters to bring down these larger machines. P/O Capon got his damaged aircraft safely back to Tangmere. In fact, all six Hurricanes from Blue and Red Sections of 257 Squadron attacked the hapless Ju 88,[467] as did Sgt Guy of 601 Squadron. Green Section of 257 Squadron, while ordered to join the other two sections of Hurricanes, did not find them in the murky conditions but were briefly attacked from out of the sun by four Me 110s (presumably from *ZG 2*); fortunately for them, Green 2 P/O Bonseigneur saw them coming just in time for the section to turn out of the way before the Me 110s vanished into the clouds, Green 2 sending an encouraging burst after them.[468] Apart from the Ju 88 destroyed by 257 Squadron and Sgt Guy of 601, one more bomber from the Andover raid of *III/LG 1* was missing and another damaged enough (70%) to be written off after force-landing at Cherbourg.[469] These further German bomber casualties can be ascribed to attacks on straggling Ju 88s made by 92, 43 and 145 Squadrons.

One section of 92 Squadron had been scrambled from Filton, led by F/Lt Robert R. S. Tuck, whose combat report[470] provides a detailed account of their subsequent actions against three separate Ju 88s in the Selsey Bill area and out to sea.

> Blue Section vectored by Filton down to Portland Bill. On arriving Portland Bill at 1500 feet saw many Spitfires and Hurricanes so decided to fly out to sea. When about 20 miles due South of Portland and having seen no enemy aircraft decided to fly toward Southampton.

When approximately over Isle of Wight climbed up through cloud heading N.E. and when clear of cloud at 3000 feet immediately sighted one Ju. 88, heading S.W. I put Section into line astern and gave chase. Enemy aircraft saw us immediately we broke cloud surface and dived straight into cloud. Enemy aircraft lost sight of. After having chased down through cloud to try and contact E/A again, found myself due South of Selsey Bill. Heading inland and through large break in cloud saw a burst of A.A. fire directly above Selsey Bill at approximately 6000 feet. Immediately climbed towards it and sighted another Ju. 88 heading out to sea S.E. Immediately gave chase. Enemy aircraft tried to climb to cloud layer at 8000 feet, but we were on him before he could make it. Enemy aircraft did steep dive 430 miles p.h. I got in one burst of 5 seconds from dead astern at about 200 yards as he commenced his dive saw a large splash from port engine and streams of white smoke. I now withheld my fire till he was on the surface of water. As he was crabbing along surface owing to his Port engine being out of action myself No's. 2 and 3 executed beam quarter and astern attacks on enemy aircraft until he crashed into the sea at a point approximately 40 miles S.E. of Selsey Bill. As soon as enemy aircraft hit water it disappeared from sight and on flying very low over debris and oil patch saw two of crew floating and waving their arms. Immediately set course back to Selsey Bill at 1500 feet in order to try and signal a rescue boat to pick the crew up. When in sight of and about 10 miles from Selsey Bill observed one Ju. 88 heading S.E. straight at me and on same level. Immediately gave Tally-Ho and half rolled on to the enemy aircraft. He dived straight for water and carried out violent evasive actions by means of steep turns on the water. Carried out one attack on him then my ammunition finished. My other two aircraft appeared to have more ammunition left and were doing attacks on him so I carried out dummy attacks in order to harass him. When we had all three finished our ammunition the enemy aircraft appeared to be flying satisfactorily and heading towards French coast. I reformed my Section and returned to Warmwell and re-fuelled. Rounds fired: 2800. No stoppage.

Tuck's leadership encompassed a relentless search for enemy machines and an equally relentless pursuit of them when sighted. Once more it had taken multiple attacks to dispatch the Ju 88 that crashed into the sea. This can only have been the missing Junkers from *III/LG 1*. 92 Squadron aircraft also carried an extra 400 rounds of ammunition. 'Bob' Tuck was one of the RAF's major aces in the Dunkirk/ Battle of Britain period, and thereafter. Bearing in mind that this set of engagements by 92 Squadron was some thirty minutes after 257 Squadron had intercepted a straggling

Ju 88 as *III/LG 1*'s formation came in over the coast, clearly Tuck's section had engaged some of the *III/LG 1* Andover raiders on their way out after bombing their target.

In contrast, 43 Squadron whose nine Hurricanes had taken off from Tangmere at 16h00, appear to have engaged Ju 88 stragglers earlier, over the coast and out to sea,[471] at about the same time that 257 Squadron and one pilot from 601 Squadron intercepted a few Ju 88s that turned back from the incoming *III/LG 1* raid heading for Andover. 43 Squadron landed at 16h49, about a quarter of an hour before 92 Squadron had their action, indicating 43's combat was against the earlier stragglers.[472] Nine Hurricanes of 43 Squadron had first been ordered to patrol over Beachy Head, and after doing just that were vectored back to the west and informed of a dogfight over Southampton, thereafter proceeding to the Isle of Wight to cut off the Germans' retreat over the Channel.[473]

While two other members of the squadron fired ineffectively at stragglers at long range as they lost them in the cloudy conditions, Green 2 Sgt Hallowes met a lone Ju 88 over the Isle of Wight from head on, giving it a burst and seeing it immediately crash into a wood at Thorness Bay[474] on the north coast of the island. No German aircraft was lost there or even close by on this mission, and possibly Hallowes had engaged a retreating Ju 88 still carrying bombs, which had turned back early and, when attacked, jettisoned them; their explosion at Thorness Bay may have looked as though the machine itself had crashed there, as it dived away Channel-wards unseen by the 43 Squadron pilot.

Climbing back up to 9,000 ft over the Isle of Wight, Hallowes espied a Do 17 over Yarmouth through a gap in the clouds; as Green 2 manoeuvred onto its tail, the German flew a half circle south and west from Yarmouth.[475] Having closed to 300 yards astern of the enemy aircraft, and gaining on him only a short distance and firing on him when possible as the German dived and turned alternatively left and right, Hallowes saw the aircraft catch fire, emitting large amounts of dense smoke and he broke away.[476] As he passed over Ventnor, he last saw the enemy machine head north again in the direction of Ryde[477] on the northeast coast of the Isle of Wight. From the speed of this aircraft and its being described as a Do 17, it may have been one of the ZG 2 Me 110s. Whether it was on fire or just over-throttling will never be known. There is no obvious German casualty to fit this reported engagement.

In a final encounter, anti-aircraft fire over Portsmouth drew Hallowes' attention to a Ju 88 about twenty miles south of that location; he easily caught up with it as it was doing only about 160 mph and was probably already damaged.[478] His single burst of fire knocked pieces off the

Junkers before it dived into clouds about 35 miles south-south-east of Selsey Bill.[479]

The final RAF squadron in action was 145 Squadron (nine Hurricanes), up from Westhampnett, the satellite field to Tangmere sector station at 16h15–16h20, with orders to intercept enemy aircraft; only one pilot, F/Lt Dutton contacted an enemy[480] but there is neither a combat report for him, nor an Intelligence Patrol Report in the relevant files. This probably reflects the fact that 145 Squadron transferred out to Drem that same evening, having been relieved from their frontline station; record-keeping likely took a back seat during such a move. A brief note in the squadron Operational Record Book[481] describes F/Lt Dutton joining a combat between some Spitfires and a Ju 87, which Dutton claimed to have sent into the sea. The take-off time and distance to fly to where the Ju 87s operated over Portland and to the north-north-east, as described earlier (*II/StG 2* versus 609 Squadron), provide no logical time window for Dutton to attack one of those machines. It is more plausible that he joined the fight with the 92 Squadron Spitfire trio, who did indeed dispatch a Ju 88 into the sea.

Heavy raid on Detling and failed attacks on Rochester and Rochford, *c.* 16h00–16h30

The Detling raid is one of particular interest as it indicates a new Me 109 escort tactic for Ju 87 dive-bomber formations, one also applied in the approximately coeval set of raids (just described) against mainly airfield targets north of the Portland and Isle of Wight areas, further to the west. In the latter raids, a sweep ahead by Me 109s of *I/JG 53* flew in over the coast near Poole, carried on westwards and exited the coast over Lyme Bay, just a few minutes ahead of the incoming Ju 87s of *I/StG 1*, due to bomb Warmwell not far away. In the event, the Stukas turned back due to cloud cover, and their escort of II/JG 53 lingered behind, becoming involved with the subsequent incoming Stuka raid by *II/StG 2* by chance. However, the intersection of outgoing *I/JG 53* sweep and incoming *I/StG 1* Stuka raid was intentional.

To the east over Kent at this same time, a sweep ahead by elements of *JG 51* crossed the east Kentish coast, flew overland towards the west and then south-west, exiting approximately over the Dover area. As it did so it provided the first element of fighter protection for the incoming Stukas of *II/StG 1* and *IV/LG 1* west of Dover. With the slow speed of the dive-bombers, Me 109s could not practically or in terms of efficient fuel usage accompany them directly, instead preferring to fly in behind the Ju 87s and rendezvous with them as they neared the target. Such an outgoing sweep ahead thus provided an initial element of protection as the Stukas crossed the coast – seen both over Kent and further west in the Lymne Bay area. In addition to this apparent new *Luftwaffe* tactic, the direct escort tasked with looking after the Kent dive-bombers, *I/LG 2* applied a new tactic of their own, deliberately strafing Detling airbase just ahead of the Stukas' bombing – another new tactic, but one reliant on the initiative of the escort commander and apparently not part of the overall *Luftflotte 2* plan.

As was normally the case, the first indications of incoming German attacks were provided by the radar warning system. The first enemy force (termed here force #1), estimated at thirty or more machines was plotted at 15h39, located some fifteen miles north of Cap Gris Nez.[482] This location would have been a few miles due east of Dover, with the force heading northwards. *EGr 210* had taken off at 15h15 from their forward base at Calais-Marck, with the assigned target of Rochford airfield near Southend on the northern shore of the Thames Estuary; escort was provided by *ZG 26* (elements of *I* and *III Gruppen* are known to have participated) who were based at St Omer and Crecy.[483] What can only have been this combined Me 110 force was next detected at about fifty miles due east of Sheerness by British radar, a location some twenty-five miles off the North Foreland (and directly north of Gravelines on the French coast and south of St Omer, one of the *ZG 26* bases)[484] before altering course to fly westwards up the Estuary.[485] Force #1 thus flew due north from the Pas de Calais, parallel to the eastern Kent coast, past the North Foreland still quite far out to sea before turning west up the Estuary towards their target of Rochford, reaching the Southend area, obscured below cloud, at 16h00.[486]

Being much faster than the Stukas tasked with attacking Detling (and Rochester, not bombed) on the southern side of the Estuary, they reached their more distant target area only about five minutes before the Detling raiders got to their closer one at 16h05.[487] This was good fulfilment of the obviously planned coeval attacks on the two separate targets. 56 Squadron had been sent up from their forward base at Rochford at 15h50 and vectored to Manston,[488] obviously to counter the Me 110 raid detected coming up the east Kentish coast. As the latter then turned again from their course up the Estuary, north-westwards towards Southend-Rochford which they approached from the east, 56 Squadron was hastily diverted to defend Rochford; however, the Me 110s and their similarly equipped escorts had immediately turned away southwards upon observing the solid cloud cover of their target area, and 56 Squadron intercepted them further south.[489]

Adlertag

Only one minute after the detection of force #1 due east of Dover, at 15h40 a second German force (here called force #2) was picked up some five miles north and west of #1;[490] this would have placed it near Deal on the east Kent coast. This second force (a fighter sweep by elements of *JG 51*[491]) crossed the coast between Deal and Sandwich at 15h45, making for Canterbury.[492] At this stage, A Flight of 65 Squadron from Manston was already patrolling over Dover and B Flight lifted off from that same base at 15h30 and soon joined their compatriots above Dover.[493] A section of Hurricanes (17 Squadron) was over a convoy near Clacton and another pair (1 Squadron) above another convoy, off Harwich;[494] they were well placed in case the raid detected going northwards off the east Kent coast made for that shipping.

In addition, a flight of five Spitfires (19 Squadron) was ordered off at 15h55 from their temporary base at Eastchurch to protect Martlesham airfield, just north of Harwich; ten minutes earlier, seven more Spitfires (64 Squadron) scrambled from Kenley were vectored towards the Straits of Dover.[495] However, neither Spitfire unit intercepted any enemy aircraft. The Fighter Command controllers had done their best, but their inherent difficulties in countering multiple and complex *Luftwaffe* incursions in very cloudy weather will soon become clear.

Finally, among the earlier radar detections was a third German force (force #3) located about seven miles south of Dover, some time during the 15h45–15h55 period.[496] This force would have been the Stukas assigned to hit Detling and Rochester; while sources agree on it comprising the two *Luftflotte 2* Stuka *Gruppen*, *II/StG 1* and *IV/LG 1*, many of those sources also suggest that a reinforcement *Gruppe* from *Fliegerkorps 8* of *Luftflotte 3* was also present, some naming it as *I/StG 1*.[497] However, *I/StG 1* was in fact operating in the Portland region on a coeval raid under the auspices of *Luftflotte 3*, as already discussed. A few references are clear on the raids only being mounted by *II/StG 1* (intended target Rochester) and *IV/LG 1* (targeting Detling).[498] A clincher in favour of the latter raid composition is a German source dealing with the history of *JG 77* about who provided the escort for the two Stuka *Gruppen*, namely *I/LG 2*.[499] This source makes it clear that *I/LG 2* escorted both Stuka *Gruppen*, and that after the Rochester *Gruppe* (*II/StG 1*) found it socked in under cloud, both dive-bomber *Gruppen* hit Detling. Rochester, a civilian airfield on which the Short aircraft works was situated (where the initial Short Stirling bombers were being constructed),[500] lay only some four miles north-west of Detling. The Stukas would appear to have crossed the Kent coast west of Dover,[501] not far north-north-west of where radar had first picked them up seven miles south of Dover as force #3.

Eagle Day: 13 August 1940

Close to the time that the Ju 87 dive-bombers crossed in west of Dover, the outgoing early sweep of *JG 51*, including elements of at least *II* and *III Gruppen* went out over the Dover area in the opposite direction; they were intercepted by 65 Squadron just to the south over the Channel, who pursued them to the Calais-Cap Gris Nez area of the French coast.[502] The outgoing sweep having thus provided an initial, if brief, fighter protection for the incoming Stukas, the latter continued on towards the Detling area, just north-east of Maidstone, lying about ten minutes flying time from the coast west of Dover. During this time their direct escort of *I/LG 2*[503] would have easily caught them up having flown in behind them at their much higher cruising speed. Ground observers at Langley, a couple of miles south-east of Maidstone, saw the Stukas approaching their target at Detling from the south-east, flying below the cloud base.[504]

By taking a risk in flying at low level beneath the clouds, the Detling raiders of *IV/LG 1* were able to find their target, unlike their compatriots aiming for theirs at Rochester (*II/StG 1*) and Rochford (*EGr 210*). Presumably, the Rochester raiders, unable to locate their bombing target had been flying above the clouds, and then turned back south-east and past Detling (just a few miles distant) by then under attack by *IV/LG 1*, where they joined in. Detling was visible due to breaks in the cloud cover,[505] and this Coastal Command airfield was easy to locate, being near the Thames Estuary but on higher ground, its three main hangars visible from miles away.[506]

While Detling was devastated by the Stuka bombing attack, this was preceded just before the bombing began by a low level strafing attack by Me 109s.[507] There is an eyewitness account of this from two members of the ground crew at Detling, who observed what they estimated as some fifty Me 109s breaking their formation and coming in for a low-level strafing attack, followed very soon after by the Ju 87s diving to their attack.[508] *I/LG 2* was commanded by *Hpt* Hanns Trübenbach, a highly experienced airman whose flying had begun in the later 1920s and who had a penchant for low-level airfield attacks. The author had the privilege of corresponding with Hanns Trübenbach for many years, who ended his war service as an *Oberst* and senior fighter controller in the Battle of Germany. During the Battle of Britain, he succeeded to command of *JG 52* on 19 August 1940, to which *I/LG 2* was subordinated for some months despite being essentially tied to *JG 77*.

As the C/O of this temporarily expanded *JG 52*, Trübenbach on his own initiative led several low-level attacks on RAF airfields, before being forbidden to continue these by higher authority.[509] It is thus plausible that Hanns Trübenbach was responsible with his *I/LG 2* for the initial strafing attack by Me 109s observed from the ground. The records of

53 Blenheim Squadron of Coastal Command at Detling recounted a heavy bombing and machine gun attack, and ascribed the loss of five of their bombed-up and fuelled Blenheims (standing ready for night attacks on invasion barges in the ports across the Channel)[510] to incendiary machine gun fire.[511] While the first volume of the history of *JG 77*, dealing with 1940, does not record any victory claims for *I/LG 2* on 13 August 1940, the claims lists for the *Geschwader* for the entire war do contain two: a Hurricane and a Blenheim, supposedly shot down.[512] There is no known aerial combat for this *Gruppe* on this day, nor are these two claims included in the official *Luftwaffe* claims list,[513] so do they rather refer to two ground victories at Detling?

Detling airbase was very hard hit by the Stukas' bombing and the strafing by *I/LG 2*: unfortunately, station personnel had just lined up for tea to be served when the attack occurred and all three mess halls were hit, the operations block destroyed by a direct hit, taxiways, runways and aircraft hardstands cratered. Sixty-seven people were killed and many wounded, and twenty-two Coastal Command aircraft were destroyed and many damaged.[514] While Detling had clearly been caught by surprise,[515] the Dowding system did not fail, as the Observer Corps in Maidstone repeatedly tried to phone through a warning of the approaching raid, but could not get through as all lines were busy.[516]

Detling was a particularly vulnerable target, with few and antique defences, the airmen's mess and sleeping quarters being built of wood and many personnel under canvas; as tragic ill luck would have it, two shelters suffered direct hits as well as the airmen's mess, and the station commander Group Captain E. P. M. Davis was killed instantly at the entrance to the Station HQ, as well as several of his staff including S/L J. H. Lowe and six other ranks, with three more officers and twenty-one other ranks (including one WAAF) injured.[517] 53 Squadron, the resident Coastal Command Blenheim unit lost S/L D. C. Oliver, another officer and seven ground crew killed, one presumed killed whose body was never identified, as well as two air gunner sergeants and nine ground crew wounded.[518]

Only the previous night, S/L Oliver and his Blenheim crew had carried out a lone raid over Ijmuiden at 21h15-23h38.[519] The resident Coastal Command Anson-equipped 500 Squadron suffered three killed, including two sergeant air gunners, one missing and eight injured personnel.[520] Total RAF casualties thus numbered twenty-two dead and forty-three wounded; some of the wounded may have succumbed later to their injuries. Three of those killed in the raid were civilians, and the majority of the fatalities belonged to army troops stationed at or very near the airbase, including sappers from the Royal

Eagle Day: 13 August 1940

Engineers, and anti-tank gunners from the Royal Artillery attached to the infantry of the East Surrey Regiment.[521] The station adjutant, F/O Anthill survived being blown off his feet twice by bursting bombs, as the Stukas and Me 109s bombed and strafed for several minutes.[522] The attack on Detling was made beteen 16h00–16h05[523] and lasted for several minutes.[524] Despite the terrible damage and casualties, RAF Detling was able to send up its first Blenheim of 53 Squadron on patrol at 07h15 the next morning.[525]

Quite a few Battle sources ascribe the successful Stuka attack on Detling to a timely sweep by *JG 26*.[526] The *Geschwader* history authored by a previous *Kommodore*[527] refers to a sweep east of Maidstone by *I* and *II Gruppen*, while *III/JG 26* had the frustrating job of escorting air sea rescue floatplanes and boats. One prominent Battle historian finds that the *JG 26* sweep was timed to overlap the withdrawal of two of the three Stuka *Gruppen* postulated to have come in over Kent, while the third *Gruppe (IV/LG 1)* was on the way in.[528] The early radar detections of German formations[529] do not include the *JG 26* sweep, only that made earlier by elements of *JG 51* (plus *EGr 210* and the two incoming Stuka *Gruppen* targeting Detling and Rochester). It would make more sense that the *JG 26* sweep did in fact roughly coincide with the conclusion of the Detling raid and the retreat rather than the advance of the Stuka raiders.

Some of these *JG 26* Me 109s became involved in aerial combat with the 56 Squadron pilots who were pursuing the *ZG 26* escorts to *EGr 210* southwards from the Thames Estuary towards the Hawkinge area, with combat reports and losses for the RAF squadron being timed at 16h15-16h30. *JG 26* itself suffered only one combat loss, in an engagement over Folkestone at 16h15.[530] The other RAF fighter squadron in action, 65 Squadron, fought against Me 109s south of Dover and towards the French coast near Calais at *c.* 16h00.[531] It was actually the sweep by *JG 51*, unlucky enough to be intercepted by 65 Squadron off Dover as it flew back to France short of fuel, that probably eased the passage of the Stukas towards Detling. If 65 Squadron had not been drawn off by the retreating *JG 51*, they may have been vectored onto the incoming Stukas not far to the west of Dover, or have found them by mere chance.

However, the sweep by *JG 26* and the earlier one by *JG 51* were by no means the only German fighter efforts put up by *Luftflotte* 2 over Kent; a very large proportion of the available German fighter *Gruppen* in the air related to the raids assigned to *II/StG 1, IV/LG 1* and *EGr 210*. *I/JG 52* (take-off at 16h02, landing at 16h40) was sent up to meet returning *Luftwaffe* units in mid-Channel,[532] while *I/JG 54* (15h25–16h05) were dispatched earlier.[533]

Adlertag

JG 3 sent up two of its *Gruppen*, *I/JG 3* (15h13–16h45) and *II/JG 3* (took off at 15h20), the first on a sweep and the second to engage British fighter forces.[534] *Luftflotte 2* thus used the majority of its Me 109 fighters to support this set of Stuka and *EGr 210* raids on the three chosen targets, and Kentish airspace would have been saturated by them. Quite obviously, the Germans intended to cause high casualties to responding British fighters. However, the cloudy conditions appear to have worked against them, though the combination of large numbers of enemy fighters and cloudy weather created dangerous conditions which might well have caught a number of Fighter Command units by surprise, potentially. That the two RAF squadrons which did in fact intercept the *Luftwaffe* formations, 65 and 56 Squadrons, were not decimated must be seen as rather good fortune in the circumstances.

65 Squadron, having taken off from their forward base at Manston, had been sent to patrol over the Dover area before the German formations came in.[535] Despite all the dangers inherent in the many marauding *Luftwaffe* Me 109 formations, they had the good fortune to run into elements of the early *JG 51* sweep as they left the coast in the vicinity of Dover on their way back to France, at about 16h00. In the succeeding engagement which took place over the Channel off Dover and towards Calais in France, they initially met about a *Gruppe* of Messerschmitts a couple of thousand feet below them and making for France post-haste.[536] Being by this time almost certainly short of fuel, the German fighters were understandably reluctant to engage and most tried to escape into the clouds somewhere between 5,000 and 12,000 ft as they dived for the French coast. The combat report of Sgt Kilner illustrates what transpired over the Channel in this engagement.[537]

> At 15.30 hours on the 13th August 1940, "B" Flight of 65 Squadron was told to join "A" Flight over Dover to intercept raiders. The squadron flying at 21,000 feet towards Calais met enemy fighters which were 2,000 feet below and attacked. As Blue 2, I followed Blue 1 in line astern and selected a Me.109 on his starboard, as the e/a did a gentle climbing turn to the left. I gave one burst at 1½ rings deflection, and saw ammunition enter round the pilot's cockpit. Apparently out of control, probably due to injuries sustained by the pilot, the Me.109 dived vertically with a slight aileron turn and was not seen to recover before entering clouds 15,000 feet below.

F/Lt Gordon Olive, leading A Flight of 65 Squadron, had a really intense set of engagements against several different formations of Me 109s, as detailed in his combat report.[538]

Eagle Day: 13 August 1940

At about 14.50 hours on the 13th August 1940, "A" Flight took off to intercept 3 e/a flying from Chatham but no interception was made. On returning to land we were instructed to join up with "B" Flight which we did about 15.40. We intercepted about 15 to 20 Me.109's flying at about our own height (19,000ft.) engaged about five with my section in a dog fight and noticed four above to the east at about 23,000ft. I climbed and after a dog fight shot down the rearmost which blew up and descended in flames. The remainder dived for France. I was then returning when I noticed four Me.109's at about 26,000ft. I climbed and approached down sun and shot another down in flames. I saw it explode on the way down. I then started to descend when about 30 Me.109's tried to attack me, but as they were the same level I outclimbed them into the sun and attacked the nearest one of my pursuers. They gave up the chase and I was diving to cloud level when I saw a single Me.109 going back to France. I attacked at about 430 A.S.I. and I fired about a four second burst and noticed him rock violently and pieces flew off the machine. I fired the remaining ammunition into him before he reached the cloud, when I lost sight of him. I then returned to Manston and landed. (A.S.1. = presumably, air speed indicator)

He appears to have intercepted four different formations of Messerschmitts, an initial *Gruppe* diving for Calais, then two small formations at higher altitude, and finally another *Gruppe*-sized formation at about his then altitude. 65 Squadron claimed a total of four Me 109s destroyed, three more probably so, and another damaged,[539] as against three Messerschmitts which were 80% damaged on reaching France and all written off (one pilot wounded), plus one more with lesser damage.[540] The three write-offs were all from *9/JG 51* and were all badly damaged in action close to the French coast in the Calais-Cap Gris Nez-Coquelles area.[541] Logically these all fit the claims made in that area by 65 Squadron.

The one less damaged German machine was from *II/JG 51* and may thus have belonged to one of the apparently different formations tackled by F/Lt Olive. This RAF pilot may even have engaged a lone Me 109 of *JG 26*, once over Kent again on his way home, as described in his combat report above, related to 56 Squadron's engagement with this *Geschwader*. Five pilots of 65 Squadron fired their guns, one even expending 2,650 rounds (clearly 65 Squadron carried extra ammunition above the 'official' quota of 2,400), while making no claims; there are thus no combat reports to describe their engagements. In return, the *Gruppenkommandeur* of *I/JG 51* claimed a Spitfire confirmed[542] but

Adlertag

65 Squadron suffered no damaged machines.[543] All three *Gruppen* of *JG 51* thus took part in this early sweep, again underlining the large numbers of *Luftflotte 2* Me 109s dispatched over Kent in this set of raids.

Unlike 65 Squadron, which met the outgoing Me 109s of *JG 51* in an advantageous tactical situation, of which they took full advantage, 56 Squadron's Hurricanes were less fortunate. Scrambled at 15h50 and sent to patrol over Manston, they were rapidly diverted to Rochford, then being threatened by *EGr 210* and its *ZG 26* escorts, as already described in a preceding paragraph. Emerging through low cloud at about 5,000 ft two miles east of Rochford, the ascending Hurricanes spotted what they thought were a dozen Heinkel 111 bombers about 10,000 ft higher, with about a *Gruppe* of Me 110s above and behind them.[544] With the bombers already too far away and retreating rapidly southwards, F/Lt Gracie led 56 Squadron up against the escorting Me 110s.[545] The engagement with the Me 110s of *I* and *III/ZG 26* began about 16h15 and endured for about fifteen minutes[546] and is well described by F/O Percy Weaver, leading A Flight of the squadron behind Gracie's flight.[547]

> I was leading 'A' Flight, which was in the rear of 'B' Flight. On emerging above 10/10 cloud at 4000' I saw a number of HE 111's followed by probably 30 ME 110's, about 8000 ft above us. Owing to a lack of height it was not possible to catch the bombers so I climbed as fast as possible towards the ME 110's. These started breaking formation, some of them forming a defensive circle. My No. 3 broke away towards a 110 which was above him and to the left. I then realized that a 110 was getting on to his tail, so I pulled up very steeply, & tried to fire at the second 110 vertically from underneath. As I commenced to fire, I saw No 3 (P/O Joubert) dive away with a glycol leak, & observed no damage to my 110. I then stalled. I attacked another 110 from dead astern & about 200 yds, and fired at him for about 5 seconds. He turned sharply away and dived with glycol pouring out of one of his engines (I believe the port one). I did not continue the attack as there was a 110 on my tail. I broke sharply away, and got on the tail of another 110. At about 150-200 yds I fired off the remainder of my ammunition (about 6 secs) dead astern, and after a few seconds violent twisting and turning, he turned over on his back and went vertically downward into the clouds with both engines on fire. I broke away and joined up with Yellow 3 (P/O Wicks) who confirmed that this E/A was destroyed.

Weaver was hit by one bullet in his port aileron. In the engagement the squadron lost three Hurricanes from which the pilots bailed out, over the general area of the Isle of Sheppey on the southern side of the Thames Estuary; a fourth Hurricane was written off in a crash-landing at Hawkinge by F/O Brooker towards the end of the fight.[548] 56 Squadron chased the retreating Me 110s southwards from the Rochford area and over Sheppey, with the engagement petering out towards Hawkinge. P/O Joubert, the wingman whom F/O Weaver had seen diving away streaming glycol coolant, had a rather dramatic exit from his Hurricane, as described in an excerpt from his combat report.[549]

> I did a quarter attack against one of the machines in the circle, silencing his rear gunner. Shifted aim to port engine & this commenced to give out black smoke. By this time I was drawn into the circle and attacked from behind. A cannon shot hit my radiator and the glycol came into the cockpit. I then came down to 2000' with the idea of making a forced landing. The radiator suddenly exploded & I shot out of the side of the Hurricane and landed by parachute at Faversham Kent. I have a little cannon splinter in my left leg, and I landed in an apple tree which caused me no injury.

While Joubert came down near Faversham, lightly wounded, F/O Davies bailed out severely burnt and landed close to the shore at nearby Seasalter; Sgt Hillwood had to abandon his machine after a head-on attack by a Me 110 off Sheerness, and battled the waves for a distance of about two miles, almost succumbing to exhaustion before being spotted by two gunners from a coastal anti-aircraft battery who swam out to save him.[550] Retribution exacted by 56 Squadron encompassed claims for two Me 110s confirmed, another unconfirmed destroyed and five damaged.[551] Their assessed victory claims were not far off the mark, their opponents losing three Me 110s (two of which were written off in crash-landings), three more damaged and one other hit on the ground and damaged at a forward base by one of their own crash-landing Me 110s (which was one of the two write-offs).

ZG 26 were hard hit by 56 Squadron, losing one *I Gruppe* Me 110 over Sheppey, which broke up while still in the air, scattering wreckage over a wide area and killing the crew; this is ascribed to F/O Weaver's attack.[552] The *Gruppe* had two more machines damaged that made it home to France while a third had the misfortune to crash at St Omer and hit another of the unit's aircraft (30% damaged), being written off, the crew lucky to have escaped injury.[553] The bad weather resulted in a few Me 110s of *III/ZG 26* getting lost on the way home, one with some damage force-landing at Amsterdam with an injured crew member, while a second was written off crash-landing at Vlissingen.[554] While *ZG 26*'s sacrifices protected the fleeing fighter-bombers of *EGr 210* from any harm, these dropped their bombs blindly, many in the Crundale area south-west of Canterbury as they made their way home over Kent.[555]

While the three 56 Squadron Hurricanes of Joubert, Davies and Hillwood were apparently the victims of ZG 26's Me 110s, the one written off by F/O Brooker in his crash-landing at Hawkinge is not ascribed to a specific German foe.[556] The *JG 26* sweep may have been responsible. On the southern side of the Thames Estuary, P/O Constable-Maxwell observed the retreating bombers (*EGr 210*'s Me 110s) which he mistakenly identified as Ju 88s, saw them jettisoning bombs near Canterbury, and then noted Me 109s high above the 56 Squadron Hurricanes; they came diving rapidly down and zoomed back up to altitude again, not causing any visible damage, but Constable-Maxwell saw a lone Hurricane above in a swarm of Me 109s.[557]

The *II/JG 26* had led the *Geschwader*'s sweep, coming in near Dover and then encountering solid cloud at about 6,000 ft, with *Gruppenkommandeur* Ebbighausen navigating by compass and time flown.[558] *Lt* Borris of *5/JG 26* dived down on a Hurricane formation sighted below, setting one on fire before pulling up and hitting another already being attacked by another Messerschmitt, and this Hurricane also went down on fire.[559] Borris's aircraft was attacked by a Hurricane and, unbeknownst to him, hit by a single bullet in the starboard wing, rendering the flaps on that side inoperative, making for an interesting, high-speed landing.[560] Boris's claims were both confirmed, and were made over the Maidstone–Detling area and two minutes later over Maidstone-Ashford,[561] showing a north-west to south-east course for the *5/JG 26* pilot. The first area was close enough to Sheppey where 56 Squadron's engagement with the Me 110s of ZG 26 had begun, while Ashford was en route to the Hawkinge area, where F/O Brooker's Hurricane was written off in its crash landing.

5/JG 26 also suffered a loss of their own in this engagement: *Uffz* Wemhoner was shot down in a combat near Folkestone, his machine crashing at Denton. He parachuted down over Elham at *c.* 16h15, being taken prisoner burnt and with a broken leg.[562] While 56 Squadron may have shot him down, it could also have been a Spitfire of 65 Squadron returning from their combat over the Channel off Calais. Wemhoner's Me 109 was hit by a lucky shot in the engine from some 500 yards away,[563] and his victor may thus not have realised his own success at that excessive range.

While there seems little doubt that *JG 26*'s sweep coincided with the end of the Detling raid and the retreat of the relevant Stukas, 56 Squadron's interception of the outgoing ZG 26 Me 110s escorting the

Eagle Day: 13 August 1940

fleeing *EGr 210* would have been at about the same time, which may well have overlapped with the later activities of 65 Squadron Spitfire pilots as they returned towards and past the Folkestone–Dover area. F/Lt Olive did attack a lone Me 109 with the last of his ammunition, seeing it hit and descending into cloud beneath him before returning to Manston[564] and may have been responsible for the lost Me 109.

Some of the 56 Squadron Hurricane pilots reported the fleeing bombers south of Rochford as having been He 111s, and their leader, F/Lt Gracie, had a fleeting shot at what he clearly identified as a Heinkel, as reported in an excerpt from his combat report:[565] 'I then fired a short burst at one of the bomber aircraft which passed across my sights. I did not see the effect of this burst, but no other member of the squadron engaged.' A lone He 111 reconnaissance aircraft of *3(F)/122* was in fact damaged through enemy action over the east coast of England, managing to return to its base at Amsterdam-Schipol with a wounded crew member.[566] This aircraft may have become caught up in the engagement over Kent and been hit by F/Lt Gracie.

Some conclusions concerning the Eagle Day raids

Just as on 11–12 August 1940, the *Luftwaffe* only used part of its bombing forces available on 13 August: for *Luftflotte 3*, only the Ju 88 bombers as well as some of the relatively large Stuka force, whereas *Luftflotte 2* utilised only a portion of *Fliegerkorps II*: KG 2's Dornier-17s, its two Stuka *Gruppen*, and *EGr 210*. Both Sperrle commanding *Luftflotte 3* and Kesselring's *Luftflotte 2* did, however, use the vast majority of their Me 109s and many of the Me 110s to protect the bombing forces. Only from 15 August 1940 onwards did the *Luftwaffe* finally launch full-scale bombing assaults on the United Kingdom, using most of their available bombing forces. Arguably, 15 August should be seen as the real *Adlertag*.

This raises the question of what the real purpose was of the 13 August raids, still regarded in most sources from both sides as marking the onset of Göring's highly optimistic four-day estimate of the time needed to defeat Fighter Command. The only thing that set *Adlertag* aside from the rest of the 11–13 August time period was that the *Luftwaffe*'s raids were for the first time on RAF airfield targets which lay some distance inland from the coastal bases, ports and naval and merchant marine shipping attacked up to that point. There was no increase in the rather limited bombing forces used on 13 August, but the risk to them from going further inland for their targets was thereby enhanced. This also went hand-in-hand with some new escort tactics, applied both by Me 110 and Me 109 units, which makes sense.

The real winner on 13 August was the weather. Widespread cloud cover ruined the early morning attacks on Odiham and Farnborough for Sperrle's men, while similar conditions over Kent and the Thames Estuary resulted in command confusion and unescorted Do 17s of the intrepid *Oberst* Fink's *KG 2* pushing through to Eastchurch, but at significant cost in casualties to the RAF bombers. The *Luftflotte 3* Ju 88s were also roughly handled in the west, despite the cloud cover. In the afternoon a repeat performance of somewhat more complex raids on targets inland from Portland and the Isle of Wight were once again largely scotched by weather, but Detling in Kent was hammered by Kesselring's two Stuka *Gruppen*. Some of Sperrle's Stukas were caught over the coast at Lyme Bay and one *Staffel* rather massacred by Spitfires. However, both Eastchurch and Detling belonged to Coastal Command and not Fighter Command, thus rather undermining the Germans' two main successes of the day. RAF interception efficiency also suffered with the widespread cloud cover, as tracing of enemy raids once across the coast with its radar chain and heading inland rested in the hands of the Observer Corps, who were seriously handicapped by such weather.

One could perhaps argue that the two heavy raids on the Coastal Command stations badly hit represented a successful *Luftwaffe* tactic to attack airfield targets when the Dowding system was on the back foot due to the cloud cover. Though it is doubtful whether the rather clueless *Luftwaffe* intelligence outfit were overly aware of the subtle distinctions between the capabilities and duties of the two main detection arms, radar and Observer Corps. However, the Germans could also not afford the luxury of launching numbers of inland attacks on the RAF organisation and having only two achieve meaningful success while another nine raids failed, and one of the successful attacks, that on Eastchurch, was achieved at the price of significant *KG 2* casualties. The RAF fighters were almost always going to get lucky in bad weather every now and then.

In addition, several German formations which turned back for home having observed the cloud cover were also hit hard by the British fighters: the Stukas of *5/StG 2* and the Ju 88s of *KG 54*. The British fighter pilots were also capable of coming up with some good tactics of their own in response to several of the German raids on 13 August. Both 43 and 601 Squadrons in the early morning raids successfully followed bomber formations inland, having picked them up at the coast first. Other British fighters remained by the coast after German raiders had headed inland, in the knowledge that bombers that went inland in cloud had to come

Eagle Day: 13 August 1940

back out again over the coastline, where they would be happily received by the RAF.

The Thames Estuary in this regard represented a rather special case in that British radar stations along the coastal areas to the north and south of the estuary faced each other across fairly narrow waters. There was thus radar coverage provided to the opposite shore for some distance inland from the estuary's coastal areas, if the Observer Corps struggled with inclement weather conditions. For much of the Battle the Germans seemed to view the Estuary as a preferential route to targets north and south of it, as well as for London later in the conflict, possibly thinking that by flying over water as they headed up it, the risks of interception were perhaps lower. This especially applied to the Dorniers of *KG 2* and *3* from Kesselring's *Luftflotte 2*, whose base locations in north-eastern France and Belgium made the Estuary a logical choice of route.

13 August 1940 witnessed a very distinct change in Me 110 tactics. The large *Luftflotte 3* raids on 11 August (Portland) and 12 August (Portsmouth and Ventnor RDF station) were characterised by large Me 110 circles at altitude with Me 109 top cover, which were each retained in a specific location during the raid itself. On 11 August, two such circles formed, one near the Isle of Wight, the other south-east of Portland and later these joined up. On 12 August again, there were two circles, one just south of Portsmouth and the other circle was placed east of the Isle of Wight. The purpose of these large circles was to provide a distraction, even a trap for British fighters just ahead of a raid's bombers coming in, and also, by remaining in their locations, to give protection to retreating bombers, most likely by then in somewhat ragged formations. On 11 August, it worked very well in drawing RAF fighters away from the incoming bombers, but despite this and relatively high British casualties, a superb beam attack by 213 Squadron severely disrupted the Portland bombing raid of *KG 54*; and the Me 110 and Me 109 casualties were high from the circle itself.

Next day, on the Portsmouth raid, the Me 110-Me 109 circle placed east of the Isle of Wight, was too far from Portsmouth. The German fighters in the other circle, ideally sited just south of Portsmouth, were reluctant to leave their altitude and relative security and descend to the aid of the bombers. As the *KG 51* raiders exited that naval harbour in small three-aircraft groups (determined by successive three-machine *Ketten* or vic dive-bombing formations over Portsmouth, which needed to be small to enable accurate bombing), they were slaughtered by the British fighters between Portsmouth and the further 'protective' circle off the isle of Wight. The latter, too, was assaulted by other RAF machines and also suffered heavy casualties.

Adlertag

On 13 August, these tactics were not repeated. The fiasco of partial cancellations on the early Eastchurch raid saw the Me 110 escort to those bombers withheld. On the Farnborough–Odiham coeval early morning raid, *V/LG 1* was placed as a direct escort above the incoming *KG 54* bombers. To the west, *I/ZG 2* flew a sweep that split into three *Staffel*-sized formations which spread out over the coastal hinterland and penetrated inland covering a wide arc over the general area of the planned raids. Me 109 top cover of short duration was provided for both Me 110 formations, but essentially the longer range Me 110s were being used in the same way as Me 109s normally were, as bomber escorts and associated sweeps. With the much wider Channel in the general Portland–Isle of Wight area, Me 109s could not adequately perform such duties due to range limitations.

In the event, the three *Staffel*-sized sweeps of *I/ZG 2* were lucky – only one was intercepted (by 64 Squadron Spitfires), turned tail and fled to the coast where it had a fortunately minor skirmish with the RAF fighters and joined up with its two sister *Staffeln* to flee across the Channel. In their turn, the *V/LG 1* Me 110 escorts to *KG 54*'s Ju 88s used a new tactic in defending their charges – flying above and behind, when RAF fighters closed in (especially those of 43 Squadron, the first to engage) the Me 110s did a steep dive, leading to a brief attack before zooming back to altitude. The Me 110 was quite fast in level flight, but with poor manoeuvrability, though it did have a good dive and zoom performance which exposed it to little risk while maintaining a threat at altitude.

There were thus two new Me 110 tactics on 13 August, denoting a marked departure from the previous large *Luftflotte 3* raids of the 11th and 12th. In the event, the dive–zoom–climb tactic of the Me 110s would be used more extensively from late August 1940 onwards, before being negated by the RAF fighters, by then used to it. In any case, by that stage of the Battle Me 110s and crews were in ever shorter supply and played no meaningful role in protecting the large London attacks commencing on 7 September 1940. Occasionally, from 15 August onwards, Me 110 circles over a specific location were still used, but they were no longer the dominant tactic applied by these twin-engined heavy fighters. In this context, it is important to note that Me 110s when intercepted or surprised by British fighters often tended to form *ad hoc* defensive circles to try and minimise their losses. These defensive circles are not to be confused with the much bigger, Me 109-topped circles carefully planned in advance and located over a specific area, to attract RAF fighters and provide a fighter umbrella for outgoing German bombers, as typical of 11–12 August.

Eagle Day: 13 August 1940

Other new German fighter tactics related to the Me 109 escorts of Ju 87 dive-bomber raids. In both the afternoon Stuka raids, that in the west aimed at Yeovil and Warmwell, and that in the east which targeted Rochester and Detling, a sweep ahead by Me 109s exited the English southern coast in the two areas about where the Ju 87 dive-bombers were about to cross it on their way into their targets. Obviously, this made for some confusion, particularly for Fighter Command's plotting and understanding of German aerial manoeuvres, which paralleled the confusion on the German side engendered by multiple single squadron RAF fighter attacks on incoming raids and escorts. Quite apart from the inherent advantage to the *Luftwaffe* in causing some confusion to the British fighter interception system, it also provided an immediate fighter cover to the slow and vulnerable bombed-up Stukas as they overflew the coastline en route to their chosen targets.

It was practically impossible for Me 109s (cruising speed of five miles per minute) to effectively escort loaded Ju 87s (cruising speed of 2.7 miles per minute). The solution was to have the much faster fighters catch up with their Stuka charges as they flew into British airspace, thereby giving them some temporary cover while they cruised around above the slow-moving Junkers machines. But wastage of fuel and flying slowly themselves made the Me 109s doubly vulnerable in their own right. Hence, having an initial 'escort' present over the coast as the Ju 87s came in not only gave them cover for some minutes but also had the Me 109s flying at normal cruising speeds. Once they had departed, a second 'catch-up' fighter escort could rendezvous with the Stukas closer to their targets, which were normally not too far inland (targets further inland were reserved for the *Luftwaffe*'s heavier medium bombers, Do 17s, He 111s and Ju 88s).

The first application of these new Me 110 and Me 109 protection tactics on 13 August might explain why a somewhat limited use was made of the *Luftwaffe*'s bomber fleet by both Kesselring and Sperrle. To test the suitability of the new tactics, it was obviously better to try them out with fewer bombers, thus exposing their attack force to less risk if they did not pan out. In the event, they appear to have worked reasonably well, Me 110 losses being smaller than on 11–12 August, and Me 109 casualties also reduced. The enhanced protection of Stukas was moot on *Adlertag* as shown by a successful and casualty-free raid on Detling, but balanced by a failed attack on Yeovil with heavy Stuka losses to *5/StG 2*. In Kesselring's Stuka and Me 110 fighter-bomber raids aimed at Rochester, Detling and Rochford in the afternoon, the wily Field Marshal swamped the skies over Kent with Me 109s, making use of the majority of his available single-engined *Gruppen*.

Adlertag

The radar operators would have been able very often to pick up which were fighter formations and which bombers, due to the speed with which they neared the coastal areas. The large prevalence of fighters over bombers in the Kent raids by *Luftflotte 2* may explain the limited response by Fighter Command, with only 65 and 56 Squadrons intercepting German aircraft and indeed both making contact with fighter escorts, respectively Me 109s and Me 110s. Kesselring would continue to use his fighters to the maximum, with highly complex Me 109 sweeps, direct and remote escorts scattered across much of the 11 Group area on many future missions during the rest of August and early September 1940. This approach also owed much to Kesselring's fighter boss, *Luftflotte 2 Jafü Generalmajor* Theo Osterkamp, who held to the view that fighter versus fighter combat and a high kill ratio for the Me 109s was the way to win the Battle.

4

Conclusions

This chapter is based on those preceding it, without repeating use of supporting sources unless new ones are included. The three days of 11–13 August 1940 were marked by both *Luftflotten* 2 and 3 moving from the limited raids of the preceding July and early few days of August to larger operations against a wide variety of targets. With the weather causing the launch of Eagle Day to be moved forward several times, the gloves were off and both Field Marshals Kesselring of *Luftflotte* 2 and Sperrle of *Luftflotte* 3 were able to launch a series of much more intense raids, including several really large missions. These reinvigorated operations allowed both *Luftflotte* leaders to implement their own unique strategies, which set the scene for much of the rest of the Battle of Britain. In a way, the chosen short time in this volume was the nursery period for launching Kesselring's and Sperrle's brands of aerial warfare. In addition, 11–13 August saw a very rapid evolution in the use of the Me 110 twin-engined fighters as escort aircraft, while also ushering in an innovative way of using outgoing Me 109 sweeps as a way of short-term support for incoming Stuka raids.

After an initial experiment by *Luftflotte* 2 using large Me 110 circles (topped by similarly rotating Me 109s) on 10 July, emplaced at relatively high altitude near the targeted convoy just offshore of Folkestone, similar tactics were employed on a large scale on both 11 and 12 August by Sperrle's *Luftflotte 3* in the central Channel. The idea of having large circling fighter formations at altitude was to firstly establish an aerial presence in a specific location, close to the chosen bombing target, which would threaten any attacking British fighters struggling for altitude to get at the bombers; the circles would (and did) attract British fighters on their own. Secondly, the circles provided a safe area below which retreating bombers could leave their target as they sped back home for France. While the circles did to

Adlertag

a certain extent fulfil these envisaged functions on 11–12 August, they suffered heavy losses of Me 110s to RAF fighter attack, with British pilots rapidly applying effective tactics to counter them. #

Beam attacks mounted into the rotating flank of such Me 110 circles proved very effective and were well within the capabilities of the average RAF fighter pilot; their more skilled and more daring comrades attacked right into the teeth of the circling Me 110s from head on, which, while difficult and dangerous, was very productive. The bombers they were supposed to protect were on both days heavily attacked by other Fighter Command units, as was implicit in Dowding's approach of multiple single squadron attacks rather than single larger formations. On 12 August in particular, *KG 51*'s Ju 88s suffered very heavily from RAF attack. The Me 110 circles had been used by *Luftflotte 3* in the central Channel rather than by *Luftflotte 2* over the Straits of Dover and surrounds.

On 13 August, the Me 110 circles were abandoned and replaced with Me 110s flying sweeps ahead of bombers and forming escorts above and behind them, similar to the Me 109s. In addition, the Me 110s used a new dive and zoom tactic to deter British attackers. The Me 110 was well suited to such tactics having a good zoom climb performance, and while these attacks were not pressed home very hard on 13 August, they would be applied rather effectively at the end of August 1940 and in the first few days of September. Another German tactical innovation in the period concerned support for Ju 87 formations. The Stukas were the hardest aircraft to provide with fighter support due to their low speed, and thus Me 109 sweeps ahead of the bombers would be tasked to overfly British airspace before exiting the southern English coast close to where the incoming Stukas would cross over it on their way to their targets. The sweep provided the first fighter cover at the coastline without having to try and keep pace with the sluggish dive-bombers. This new tactic by the Me 109s was implemented first on 13 August by both Kesselring's and Sperrle's men in the afternoon attacks over Kent and the Portland region.

The table which follows is a summary of the actions which took place on the three chosen days giving major targets, bomber units which were employed, the number of *Stukagruppen* which were utilised as well as the extensive use made of *EGr 210*, the specialist fighter-bomber outfit. In addition, the number of escorting *Gruppen* of both Me 109s and Me 110s sent in are listed. Use of the term *Gruppe* here is fairly informal as sometimes smaller fighter formations from a particular *Gruppe* were engaged rather than an entire full-strength unit. The operations mounted by the two *Luftflotten* are also distinguished from each other, and for *Luftflotte 2*, an approximate ratio of Me 109 *Gruppen* to bomb-carrying *Gruppen* (whether twin-engined bombers, dive-bombers or fighter-bombers) is provided.

Conclusions

Summary of raids, 11–13 August 1940

(shading = *Luftflotte 3* area (Isle of Wight–Portland); unshaded = *Luftflotte 2* area (eastern-central Kent, Dover Straits, Thames Estuary). Ratio (R) = Me 109s/bomb carriers, *Luftflotte 2* only.

Time	Target	Bombers	Me 109 escorts	Me 110 escorts
11 August 1940				
c. 07h37-08h10	Dover harbour	*EGr 210*, small formation of *KG 2*	c. 2 *Gruppen* (R=1)	
c. 09h50-10h30	Sweep – Dover		6 *Gruppen*	
c. 10h20-11h00	Portland	2 *Gruppen KG 54*	9 *Gruppen*	2 *Gruppen*
c. 10h50-11h25	2 rescue aircraft – Dover Straits		1 *Gruppe*	
c. 11h40-12h15	Convoy off Orfordness	*EGr 210*, small formation of *KG 2*	1 *Gruppe* (R=c.0.5)	1 *Gruppe*
c. 12h45-13h00	Convoy east of Clacton	1 *Stukagruppe*	1 *Gruppe* (R=1)	
c. 13h30-14h15	Shipping off North Foreland	2 *Gruppen KG 2*, 1 *Stukgruppe*	4 *Gruppen* (R=1.3)	
12 August 1940				
c. 08h10-08h40	Lympne airfield (decoy of escorted bomber formation off North Foreland not engaged)	1 *Staffel KG 2* (decoy comprised Do 17s)	7 *Gruppen* (R=7+)	
c. 09h30-09h45	Radar (RDF) stations: Dover, Rye, Pevensey, Dunkirk	*EGr 210*		
c. 11h15-11h30	Shipping Thames Estuary (minesweeper trawlers)	1 *Stukagruppe*	3 *Gruppen* (R=3)	
c. 12h00-12h50	Portsmouth, and Ventnor radar station (I of Wight)	3 *Gruppen KG 51*	9 *Gruppen*	4 *Gruppen*

253

Adlertag

Time	Target	Bombers	Me 109 escorts	Me 110 escorts
c. 12h45-13h00	Manston airfield	EGr 210, 1 Gruppe KG 2	4 Gruppen (R=2)	
c. 17h15-18h15	Lympne, Hawkinge, Bekesbourne airfields; Rye RDF	3 Gruppen KG 2, EGr 210 (airfields); II/KG 76 (Rye radar)	10 Gruppen (R=2) (c. 7 for airfields, 3 for Rye raid)	
13 August 1940 (Eagle Day)				
c. 06h45-07h30	Eastchurch airfield (Sheerness naval base – aborted)	2 Gruppen KG 2 (Sheerness – 1 Gruppe KG 2)		
c. 06h40-07h15	Farnborough and Odiham airfields (Ju 88s) and Portland (Ju 87s) (latter raid aborted)	2 Gruppen KG 54 (airfields) and 3 Stukagruppen (Portland)	4 Gruppen (airfields), c. 2 Gruppen (Portland)	2 Gruppen (airfields)
c. 12h00-13h00	Sweep – Portland-Weymouth-Bournemouth (mainly Me 110s, Me 109s in indirect support)		c. 1 Gruppe	1 Gruppe
c. 16h00-17h10	(a) Airfields at Andover, Middle Wallop, Thorney Island, and raid on Southampton. (b) Airfields at Warmwell and Yeovil	(a) 3 Gruppen LG 1; (b) 2 Stukagruppen	(a) c. 3 Gruppen (b) c. 3 Gruppen	(a) 2 Gruppen (b) 2 Gruppen
c. 16h00-16h30	(a) Detling and Rochester airfields; (b) Rochford airfield.	(a) 2 Stukagruppen; (b) EGr 210	(a & b) 10 Gruppen (R=3.3)	(b) 2 Gruppen

Convoy attacks dominated on 11 August, along with a raid on Dover (a naval port), and a large operation against Portland (another naval base) by Sperrle's men. In distinct contrast, 12 August was exemplified

Conclusions

by airfield attacks, with concentrations on forward bases at Manston, Hawinge and Lympne; RAF radar stations were attacked three times on the day while the naval base at Portsmouth was heavily raided. On Eagle Day itself, large-scale attacks were launched (or attempted unsuccessfully) against a number of RAF airfields further inland than the Kent–Sussex coast or the 10 Group southern coastline. These included particularly severe raids on Eastchurch and Detling on 13 August; however, neither were Fighter Command airfields. The large port of Southampton was also targeted on Eagle Day.

Generalfeldmarschall Hugo Sperrle in his *Luftflotte 3* had three *Fliegerkorps*, the *VIIIth* with all his Stukas as well as some of his fighters, and the *IVth* with two bomber *Geschwadern* (*KG 27*, first three *Gruppen* of *LG 1*) as well as the *Vth* with three (*KGs 51, 54, 55*). His most modern aircraft were the Ju 88-equipped *LG 1, KG 51* and *KG 54*, the other two bomber *Geschwadern* flying the venerable He 111. From the word go almost, Sperrle used his most valuable bombing resource with both available *Gruppen* from *KG 54* operating in full strength on 11 and 13 August, and *KG 51* using all three available *Gruppen* on 12 August, with the three Ju 88 *Gruppen* of *LG 1* engaged on 13 August. Sperrle thus used his most valuable attack asset right from the start and spared none of his three Ju 88-equipped *Geschwadern*; he also used several of his *Stukagruppen*. Presumably he assumed, as did Göring and much of the *Luftwaffe*, that the RAF would be crushed in a few days.

Sperrle had only three Me 109 *Geschwadern* plus three *Gruppen* of Me 110s (and access to two more from *Luftflotte 2, II* and *III/ZG 76*). With the much greater Channel width in the Cherbourg-Isle of Wight region, his Me 109s had only limited fuel reserves for a short combat period and lesser penetration of the southern English coastal areas, compared to *Luftflotte 2* sitting across from the narrow Dover straits region. Sperrle only operated his fighters at full stretch when launching large *Geschwader*-strength raids (such as by *KG 54* on 11 August, *KG 51* next day), otherwise tending to use one or two *Gruppen* only from any specific fighter *Geschwader*.

Luftflotte 3 already suffered significant casualties to its Ju 88s on 11, 12 and 13 August, as well as substantial numbers of Me 110s especially from ZG 2 on the same days, and meaningful Me 109 losses. In effect, Sperrle's approach was to use the 'big battalions' from the beginning and as a result he decreased his fighting power within the three days. *KG 51* suffered the loss of ten Ju 88s in the raid on Portsmouth on 12 August, largely due to the idiotic tactic of having them stack up over that port and then carry out dive-bombing attacks in *Ketten* of three aircraft at a time, following which that small formation departed for home and into the arms of enthusiastic Fighter Command squadrons awaiting them south of Portsmouth and off the Isle of Wight. The RAF were very happy to receive this long stream of strung-out small Ju 88 *Ketten* (vic) formations while much of their escort fighters were sitting within two large circles at higher altitudes and thus ineffective at protecting their charges, as few felt it worthwhile coming down to aid only three bombers at a time.

In very distinct contrast was the strategy adopted by *Generalfeldmarschall* Albert Kesselring's *Luftflotte 2*. Kesselring's two subordinate commanders, his Chief of Staff, *Oberst* Paul Deichmann and his *Jagdfliegerführer* (*Jafü*) *Generalmajor* Theo Osterkamp also played a key role in influencing Kesselring in his approach to the air assault on the United Kingdom. Deichmann was a bomber man in essence, who constantly pushed for the maximum protection of these charges by the Me 109 fighters.[1] In this he also had an influence on Göring whose cries for better and closer fighter protection of his vulnerable bombers by the fighters became more strident as bomber losses rose with the missions flown in August and early September. By striving to place the fighters ever closer to the much slower bomber formations, the *Reichsmarschall* also made the protectors that much more vulnerable, as they perforce flew at minimum speed and pursued curved courses closely around the slow bombers, instead of maintaining the high altitudes and high speeds that better supported the Me 109 pilots' penchant for free hunting rather than close escort, and the bounce tactics so suited to the performance of their Messerschmitts.

The third man in the *Luftflotte 2* triumvirate, Theo Osterkamp, was a high scoring ace from the First World War (thirty-two victories, decorated with the *Pour le Mérite*), who had led *JG 51* over France in May and June 1940, and then over the Channel during July, again scoring several successes before his appointment as *Jafü 2* on 23 July 1940.[2] His replacement, the famous ace Werner Mölders, only arrived at *JG 51* on 27 July, and ignoring Osterkamp's warning about the dangers of the opposition on the Channel coast[3] was shot up the very next day and wounded.[4] Osterkamp thus had to look after *JG 51* from 23 July to 7 August, when Mölders came back from hospital and could lead his *Geschwader*, from the ground at least.

As a consequence, Osterkamp did not immediately change how Kesselring's fighters would operate, but examination of the *Luftflotte 2* fighter-to-bomber ratio in the table above shows that from 12 August 1940 onwards the new *Jafü* was in charge, as there was an immediate and sustained increase in escort fighter numbers.

It is important to understand what Theo Osterkamp's duties entailed in order to better comprehend the influence he had on the tactics adopted by *Luftflotte 2*. Osterkamp's orders on becoming *Jafü 2* clearly stated that he was responsible for the tactical operations of all the fighter forces in *Luftflotte 2*; however, discipline and logistics were placed under the authority of *Fliegerkorps II* commanded by General Loerzer.[5] Loerzer's *Fliegerkorps II* thus had direct authority over the entire *Jafü*. Poor Osterkamp received orders from *Fliegerkorps* and *Luftflotte* as well as frequent orders direct from Göring, who liked to interfere in the Battle personally, usually from a distance.[6] It was thereby left largely to the *Jafü* to pick out the order that suited him best from the variety offered! He only ever saw Loerzer once in his *Jafü* headquarters, otherwise the general remained ensconced in his castle in Ghent.[7] The orders that did come through from him were largely unimportant and Osterkamp soon began to ignore them. In his early period as *Jafü* he saw more of Kesselring, who gently chided him when he had worked his way around an order from either *Luftflotte* or *Fliegerkorps*, and when Osterkamp explained to him why he had done so, Kesselring was remarkably accepting.[8]

After Kesselring had observed Osterkamp rapidly and skilfully handling a fighter escort emergency, unaware that his boss was in his headquarters at the time, Kesselring told him that he was convinced that he could get on perfectly well without him, and thereafter he saw little of him.[9] In time, Kesselring gave both disciplinary and logistical responsibility to Osterkamp within an independent *Fliegerdivision* under the *Luftflotte*.

Kesselring had complete confidence in his *Jagdfliegerführer*, and Osterkamp had a free hand in controlling the fighter operations and the tactics employed within *Luftflotte 2*. As Sperrle's fighters were largely transferred from his *Luftflotte* to Kesselring's late in August 1940, this meant that Osterkamp then controlled the operational employment of most of the *Luftwaffe*'s fighters ranged against the UK. Osterkamp sought to foster favourable air combat conditions between his Me 109s and the Hurricanes and Spitfires of Fighter Command; he thus encouraged complexity and cunning at all levels in the employment of his single-engine fighters, with the emphasis on ambuscade and surprise from a superior tactical position. Like many in the *Luftwaffe*, he laid the emphasis on fighter versus fighter combat, relying on their dearly held belief in the superiority of German fighter aircraft and pilots.

Concomitant to this doctrine was the focus on major aces and their importance in inflicting high casualties. High-scoring German pilots received much more support and encouragement than in other air forces. As aces rapidly ascended the ranks and attained command of fighter units at different levels, they were further enabled by flying at the head of a specific formation, enjoying first rights to attack while backed up by wingmen in numbers designated to protect their leader. Osterkamp firmly believed in using all fighter assets that were available and not needed elsewhere on a specific mission; his protégés would thus most likely outnumber their opponents. Through these measures, Theo Osterkamp strove for his pilots to achieve a scoring ratio against their opponents of 5 to 1, which he considered necessary for the *Luftwaffe* fighters to win their duel against Fighter Command.[10]

Dowding, ably supported by Park and Brand, respectively the 11 and 10 Group commanders, adopted a deliberate battle of attrition approach to the Battle of Britain from the very beginning, carefully husbanding the strength of his forces while striving to meet each German raid before it reached its objective, and Kesselring and Osterkamp also took an attritional approach. However the *Luftflotte 2* battle of attrition was never intended to be more than a short-term policy against RAF Fighter Command, victory to be achieved within a week or two. The genius of Dowding was in planning his battle of attrition to last, and to be supported by adequate reserves of aircraft and pilots, highly efficient decentralised repair services, and high aircraft production. Through his self-discipline, calm courage and clear vision maintained through stressful months, he along with his two senior colleagues was able to achieve this. In contrast, the Kesselring-Osterkamp attrition approach lessened the strain on their bomber *Geschwadern*, which flew relatively fewer missions; this is clearly seen in the first instance during the three days of 11–13 August 1940, when he husbanded most of his bomber units, using mainly only *KG 2* (as well as his two *Stukagruppen* and *EGr 210*) and sparing his other five bomber *Geschwadern* for battle still to come.

The price paid for this was that the fighter units were subjected to a much higher pace and intensity of operations; according to the adopted doctrine, fewer bombers engaged did not translate into fewer escort fighters involved, quite the opposite. The Me 109 aircraft were thus worn out faster, especially their engines, the maintenance crews got little respite, and pilots were subjected inexorably to operational fatigue and stress. Most German veterans recalled the fear of having to transit the Channel to get home, often in a damaged machine. The fighter arm of *Luftflotte 2* thus wore down much faster than the bombers, and not only became significantly reduced in numbers but also in efficiency, as aircrew became exhausted as August 1940 wore on. By the time the *Luftwaffe* turned their daytime offensive onto London on 7 September, serviceable Me 109s had been reduced to only 533[11] and this reduced number limited the bombers that could effectively be escorted safely, thereby reducing the *Luftwaffe*'s overall fighting power.

Conclusions

The Kesselring-Osterkamp fighter-use policy thus carried the seeds of the loss of the entire Battle of Britain. This application of fighter operational policy was first used by *Jafü* Osterkamp (fully supported by Kesselring) during the period 11–13 August. As an aside, if Air Vice Marshal Leigh-Mallory, in charge of 12 Group of Fighter Command, had been allowed free rein for the widespread adoption of his 'big wing' tactic across all Groups, as he and his Air Ministry supporters wanted, that might have lost them the Battle within a relatively short period of time, as they would effectively have bought into the shorter-term effectiveness of the Osterkamp-Kesselring tactics.

Notes

Preface

1. Townsend, Peter, *Duel of Eagles* (London: Weidenfeld and Nicolson, 1970) (pp. 289-297).
2. Osterkamp, Theo, *Durch Höhen und Tiefen jagd ein Herz* (Heidelberg: Kurt Vowinckel Verlag, 1952) (pp. 360-363).
3. Green, William, *Aircraft of the Battle of Britain* (London: MacDonald-Pan, 1969) (pp. 47-64).
4. Osterkamp, Theo, *op. cit.*

1. The first major raid, Portland:
   11 August 1940

   1. James, T. Cecil G., *The Battle of Britain* (Abingdon: Routledge, 2012) (pp. 56-57).
   2. *ibid.*
   3. Vasco, John, *Messerschmitt Bf 110 Bombsights over England: Erprobungsgruppe 210 in the Battle of Britain* (Atglen: Schiffer, 2002) (p. 53).
   4. Nowarra, Heinz J., *Luftschlacht um England: Verlorener Sieg* (Friedberg: Podzun-Pallas-Verlag, 1978) (p. 30).
   5. James, T. Cecil G., *op. cit.* (pp. 56-57).
   6. Intelligence Patrol Report (IPR), 32 Squadron, 11 August 1940 (Air 16/955 records, National Archives).
   7. *ibid.*
   8. *ibid.*
   9. *ibid.*

Notes

10. Tidy, Douglas, *I Fear no Man; the Story of No 74 (Fighter) Squadron Royal Flying Corps and Royal Air Force* (Cape Town: Purnell, 1972) (pp. 84-85).
11. *ibid.*
12. Combat Report (CR), S/L A. G. Malan, 74 Squadron, 11 August 1940 (Air 50 records, National Archives), copy in: Tidy, Douglas, *op. cit.* (pp. 83-84) (take off time *c.* 08h00; were two later CRs for Malan this day, take off times *c.* 09h50 and *c.* 13h56).
13. Tidy, Douglas, *op. cit.* (pp. 84-85).
14. IPR, 74 Squadron, 11 August 1940 (Air 16/955 records, National Archives) (take off time *c.* 08h00; were three later 74 Squadron IPRs this day, take off times *c.* 09h50, *c.* 11h45 and *c.* 13h56).
15. James, T. Cecil G., *op. cit.* (pp. 56-57).
16. Website, Wood, Tony, *Tony Wood's Combat Claims and Casualties Lists*, website accessed via Don Caldwell's website: don-caldwell.we.bs/claims/tonywood.htm (with many relatively minor edits by fellow historians).
17. *ibid.*
18. Eriksson, Patrick G., *Alarmstart* (Stroud: Amberley, 2017) (pp. 131-132).
19. Kaplan, Philip, *Sailor Malan; Battle of Britain Legend Adolph Malan* (Barnsley: Pen and Sword Aviation, 2020) (p. 89).
20. James, T. Cecil G., *op. cit.* (p. 57).
21. *ibid.*
22. James, T. Cecil G., *op. cit.* (p. 57); IPR, 32 Squadron, 11 August 1940 (Air 16/955 records, National Archives) (take off time *c.* 10h05; was one earlier IPR this day, take off time *c.* 07h42); IPR, 64 Squadron, 11 August 1940 (Air 16/955 records, National Archives) (take off time *c.* 09h32; were two other IPRs this day, take off times *c.* 07h30 and *c.* 11h45); IPR, 74 Squadron, 11 August 1940 (Air 16/955 records, National Archives) (take off time *c.* 09h50; were three other IPRs this day, take off times *c.* 08h00, *c.* 11h45 and *c.* 13h56).
23. James, T. Cecil G., *op. cit.* (p. 57).
24. IPR, 64 Squadron, 11 August 1940 (Air 16/955 records, National Archives) (take off time *c.* 09h32); CR, S/L A. R. D. MacDonell, 64 Squadron, 11 August 1940 (Air 50 records, National Archives) (take off time *c.* 09h32; was one later CR for MacDonell this day, take off time *c.* 11h45).
25. *ibid.*
26. IPR, 64 Squadron, 11 August 1940 (Air 16/955 records, National Archives) (take off time *c.* 09h32).

27. *ibid.*
28. Ramsey, Winston G. (ed.), *The Battle of Britain: then and now* (London: Battle of Britain Prints International Ltd., 1982), (*Luftwaffe* entry for 11 August 1940).
29. Ramsey, Winston G. (ed.), *op. cit.* (RAF entry for 11 August 1940); ORB, Records of Events, 64 Squadron, 11 August 1940 (Air 27/589/22 records, National Archives).
30. Prien, Jochen and Stemmer, Gerhard, *Messerschmitt Bf 109 im Einsatz bei Stab und I./Jagdgeschwader 3* (Eutin: Struve-Druck, 1997) (p. 79); Prien, Jochen and Stemmer, Gerhard, *Messerschmitt Bf 109 im Einsatz bei der II./Jagdgeschwader 3, 1940-1945* (Eutin: Struve-Druck, 1996) (p. 18).
31. IPR, 74 Squadron, 11 August 1940 (Air 16/955 records, National Archives) (take off time *c.* 09h50); CR, S/L A. G. Malan, 74 Squadron, 11 August 1940 (Air 50 records, National Archives) (take off time *c.* 09h50), copy in Kaplan, Philip, *op. cit.* (pp. 64-65).
32. *ibid.*
33. IPR, 74 Squadron, 11 August 1940 (Air 16/955 records, National Archives) (take off time *c.* 09h50).
34. CR, P/O J. C. Freeborn, 74 Squadron, 11 August 1940 (Air 50/32/87 records, National Archives) (take off time *c.* 09h50; were two later CRs for Freeborn this day, take off times *c.* 11h45 and *c.* 13h56) (no grammatical corrections made to CRs cited in this book).
35. Note 33, *op. cit.*
36. Caldwell, Donald L., *JG 26 Luftwaffe Fighter Wing Diary, 1939-1942*, Vol. 1 (Mechanicsburg: Stackpole Books, 2012) (pp. 51-52, p. 54); Ramsey, Winston G. (ed.), *op. cit.* (*Luftwaffe* entry for 11 August 1940).
37. IPR, 32 Squadron, 11 August 1940 (Air 16/955 records, National Archives) (take off time *c.* 10h05).
38. Note 37, *op. cit.*; CR, F/O P. M. Gardner, 32 Squadron, 11 August 1940 (Air 50/16/8 records, National Archives).
39. Caldwell, Donald L., *op. cit.* (pp. 51-52).
40. James, T. Cecil G., *op. cit.* (p. 57).
41. Website, Wood, Tony, *op. cit.*
42. Flying logbook, *Uffz* Hans-Helmut Habermehl, *1/JG 54*, entry for 11 August 1940; copy of logbook courtesy of Peter Arnot.
43. *Lageberichte*, 20.VI.1940-10.X. 1940, *Luftflottenkommando 3*; Records of Headquarters, German Air Force High Command (*Oberkommando der Luftwaffe*-OKL), The National Archives, National Archives and Records Service, Washington, 1966; NA

Microcopy No. T-321, Record Group No. 242/1028, Item No. OKL/2308, Roll No. 88; entries for 11 August 1940.
44. James, T. Cecil G., *op. cit.* (p. 57); IPR, 1 Squadron, 11 August 1940 (Air 16/955 records, National Archives); CR, F/Lt R. G. Dutton, 145 Squadron, 11 August 1940 (Air 50 records, National Archives).
45. *Lageberichte Luftflottenkommando 3, op. cit.* (entries for 11 August 1940); Mason Francis K., *Battle over Britain* (London: McWhirter Twins, 1969) (p. 223-226); Prien, Jochen, *Pik-As: Geschichte des Jagdgeschwaders 53, Teil 1* (Illertissen: Flugzeug Publikations, 1989) (p. 175); Website, Wood, Tony, *op. cit.*
46. James, T. Cecil G., *op. cit.* (p. 58).
47. *ibid.*
48. James, T. Cecil G., *op. cit.* (pp. 58-59); IPR, 601 Squadron, 11 August 1940 (Air 16/955 records, National Archives).
49. Website, Wood, Tony, *op. cit.*
50. *ibid.*
51. Prien, Jochen, 1989, *op. cit.* (p. 175); Federl, Christian, *Jagdgeschwader 2 "Richthofen"* (Zweibrücken: VDM Heinz Nickel, 2006) (pp. 105-107).
52. James, T. Cecil G., *op. cit.* (pp. 57-59); CR, Sgt E. G. Snowden, 213 Squadron, 11 August 1940 (Air 50 records, National Archives).
53. Bungay, Stephen, *The Most Dangerous Enemy* (London: Aurum Press, 2009) (p. 183).
54. CR, Sgt E. G. Snowden, 213 Squadron, 11 August 1940 (Air 50 records, National Archives).
55. Website, Holm, Michael, *The Luftwaffe, 1933-1945*; www.ww2.dk
56. CR, F/Lt R. G. Dutton, 145 Squadron, 11 August 1940 (Air 50 records, National Archives).
57. CRs, P/Os P. L. Parrott and J. H. Harrison, 145 Squadron, 11 August 1940 (Air 50/62/12 and Air 50/62/47 records, respectively, National Archives).
58. CRs, F/Lts R. G. Dutton and A. H. Boyd, 145 Squadron, 11 August 1940 (respectively, Air 50 records, National Archives, and Air 50/62/37 records, National Archives).
59. Federl, Christian, *op. cit.* (pp. 105-107).
60. Mombeek, Eric and Roba, Jean-Louis, with Goss, Chris, *Am Himmel Frankreichs; die Geschichte des JG 2 "Richthofen", Band 2: 1940-1941* (Linkebeek: ASBL La Porte d'Hoves, 2013) (p. 39); Website, Wood, Tony, *op. cit.*
61. Ramsey, Winston G. (ed.), *op. cit.* (RAF entry for 11 August 1940).

62. Ramsey, Winston G. (ed.), *op. cit.* (*Luftwaffe* entry for 13 August 1940).
63. Townsend, Peter, *Duel of Eagles* (London: Weidenfeld and Nicolson, 1970) (pp. 300-301).
64. Note 60, *op. cit.*
65. CR, Sgt E. G. Snowden, 213 Squadron, 11 August 1940 (Air 50 records, National Archives).
66. Webpage, *213 Squadron Association*; https://213squadronassociation.homestead.com/WidgeWight/WidgePage.html
67. Website, *The Battle of Britain London Monument*, The Airmen's Stories – Sgt S. L. Butterfield; www.bbm.org.uk/airmen/Butterfield.htm
68. *Lageberichte Luftflottenkommando 3, op. cit.* (entries for 11 August 1940).
69. Website, Wood, Tony, *op. cit.* Note, however, that these *Luftwaffe* claims lists are not infallibly complete, with significant gaps especially in claims by Me 110 units.
70. *ibid.*
71. CR, Sgt E. G. Snowden, 213 Squadron, 11 August 1940 (Air 50 records, National Archives).
72. Ramsey, Winston G. (ed.), *op. cit.* (*Luftwaffe* entry for 11 August 1940).
73. Note 71, *op. cit.*
74. IPR, 145 Squadron, 11 August 1940 (Air 16/955 records, National Archives).
75. CR, F/Lt R. G. Dutton, 145 Squadron, 11 August 1940 (Air 50 records, National Archives).
76. CR, P/O P. L. Parrott, 145 Squadron, 11 August 1940 (Air 50/62/12 records, National Archives).
77. CR, F/Lt A. H. Boyd, 145 Squadron, 11 August 1940 (Air 50/62/37 records, National Archives).
78. Note 57, *op. cit.*
79. CR, P/O P. L. Parrott, 145 Squadron, 11 August 1940 (Air 50/62/12 records, National Archives).
80. CR, P/O J. H. Harrison, 145 Squadron, 11 August 1940 (Air 50/62/47 records, National Archives).
81. Note 79, *op. cit.*
82. Note 80, *op. cit.*
83. Website, *Isle of Wight Aviation, Isle of Wight Crashes*; https://wight.hampshireairfields.co.uk/iowc.html; Ramsey, Winston G. (ed.), *op. cit.* (RAF entry for 11 August 1940).

Notes

84. IPR, 145 Squadron, 11 August 1940 (Air 16/955 records, National Archives).
85. CR, F/Lt R. G. Dutton, 145 Squadron, 11 August 1940 (Air 50 records, National Archives).
86. *ibid.*
87. CR, Sgt J. Kwiecinski, 145 Squadron, 11 August 1940 (Air 50/62/49 records, National Archives).
88. CR, F/Lt R. G. Dutton, 145 Squadron, 11 August 1940 (Air 50 records, National Archives).
89. *ibid.*
90. CR, F/O W. Urbanowicz, 145 Squadron, 11 August 1940 (Air 50 records, National Archives), copy in Gretzyngier, Robert, *Poles in Defence of Britain: A day-by-day chronology of Polish day and night fighter pilot operations: July 1940 – June 1941* (London: Grub Street, 2016) (p. 13).
91. *ibid.*
92. Website, *Isle of Wight Aviation, Isle of Wight Crashes, op. cit.*; Ramsey, Winston G. (ed.), *op. cit.* (RAF entry for 11 August 1940).
93. CRs, F/Lt A. H. Boyd and P/O P. W. Dunning-White, 145 Squadron, 11 August 1940 (respectively, Air 50/62/37 records and Air 50/62/75 records, National Archives).
94. IPR, 145 Squadron, 11 August 1940 (Air 16/955 records, National Archives).
95. CR, P/O D. N. Forde, 145 Squadron, 11 August 1940 (Air 50 records, National Archives).
96. Website, Holm, Michael, *op. cit.*
97. CR, P/O P. W. Dunning-White, 145 Squadron, 11 August 1940 (Air 50/62/75 records, National Archives).
98. CR, P/O D. N. Forde, 145 Squadron, 11 August 1940 (Air 50 records, National Archives).
99. Kershaw, Robert, *Never Surrender: Lost voices of a generation at war* (London: Hodder and Stoughton, 2009) (p. 167).
100. Website, *Hampshire Airfields, Hampshire Crashes*; https://hampshire.hampshireairfields.co.uk/hancrash.html; Ramsey, Winston G. (ed.), *op. cit.* (RAF entry for 11 August 1940).
101. IPR, 145 Squadron, 11 August 1940 (Air 16/955 records, National Archives).
102. *ibid.*
103. Website, Wood, Tony, *op. cit.*; Mombeek, Eric and Roba, Jean-Louis, with Goss, Chris, *op. cit.* (p. 39); Ramsey, Winston G. (ed.), *op. cit.* (RAF entry for 11 August 1940).

104. *Lageberichte Luftflottenkommando 3, op. cit.* (entries for 11 August 1940).
105. Website, Wood, Tony, *op. cit.*
106. IPRs, 1, 145, 213, 601, 609 Squadrons, 11 August 1940 (Air 16/955 records, National Archives); CR, Sgt E. G. Snowden, 213 Squadron, 11 August 1940 (Air 50 records, National Archives).
107. Ramsey, Winston G. (ed.), *op. cit.* (*Luftwaffe* entry for 11 August 1940).
108. Mombeek, Eric and Roba, Jean-Louis, with Goss, Chris, *op. cit.* (p. 193); Ramsey, Winston G. (ed.), *op. cit.* (*Luftwaffe* entry for 11 August 1940).
109. Mombeek, Eric and Roba, Jean-Louis, with Goss, Chris, *op. cit.* (pp. 35-36).
110. Website, Wood, Tony, *op. cit.*; Mombeek, Eric and Roba, Jean-Louis, with Goss, Chris, *op. cit.* (pp. 35-36 and p. 39).
111. *ibid.*
112. Website, Wood, Tony, *op. cit.*; Mombeek, Eric and Roba, Jean-Louis, with Goss, Chris, *op. cit.* (p. 39).
113. IPR, 213 Squadron, 11 August 1940 (Air 16/955 records, National Archives); CR, F/O J. M. Strickland, 213 Squadron, 11 August 1940 (Air 50 records, National Archives); James, T. Cecil G., *op. cit.* (p. 59).
114. James, T. Cecil G., *op. cit.* (p. 59).
115. James, T. Cecil G., *op. cit.* (p. 59); IPR, 213 Squadron, 11 August 1940 (Air 16/955 records, National Archives).
116. *ibid.*
117. James, T. Cecil G., *op. cit.* (p. 59).
118. *Lageberichte Luftflottenkommando 3, op. cit.* (entries for 11 August 1940).
119. ORB, Form 541 (Records of Events), 213 Squadron, 11 August 1940 (Air 27 records, National Archives).
120. CR, S/L H. D. McGregor, 213 Squadron, 11 August 1940 (Air 50 records, National Archives); Note 119, *op. cit.*
121. CR, F/O J. M. Strickland, 213 Squadron, 11 August 1940 (Air 50 records, National Archives).
122. CR, S/L H. D. McGregor, 213 Squadron, 11 August 1940 (Air 50 records, National Archives).
123. CR, Sgt M. E. Croskell, 213 Squadron, 11 August 1940 (Air 50 records, National Archives).
124. CR, Sgt R. T. Llewellyn, 213 Squadron, 11 August 1940 (Air 50 records, National Archives).

125. CR, P/O J. A. L. Philippart, 213 Squadron, 11 August 1940 (Air 50/83/13 records, National Archives).
126. CRs, P/Os A. G. Osmand and M. S. H. C. Buchin, 213 Squadron, 11 August 1940 (respectively, Air 50/83/12 records and Air 50/83/1 records, National Archives).
127. Ramsey, Winston G. (ed.), *op. cit.* (*Luftwaffe* entry for 11 August 1940); Parker, Nigel, *Luftwaffe Crash Archive,* Vol. 1 (Walton on Thames: Red Kite Books, Air Research Publications, 2013) (entry for 11 August 1940).
128. *ibid.*
129. Ramsey, Winston G. (ed.), *op. cit.* (*Luftwaffe* entry for 11 August 1940).
130. James, T. Cecil G., *op. cit.* (p. 59).
131. CR, P/O J. A. L. Philippart, 213 Squadron, 11 August 1940 (Air 50/83/13 records, National Archives).
132. CR, P/O A. G. Osmand, 213 Squadron, 11 August 1940 (Air 50/83/12 records, National Archives); Ramsey, Winston G. (ed.), *op. cit.* (RAF entry for 11 August 1940).
133. Website, Wood, Tony, *op. cit.*
134. CR, Sgt M. E. Croskell, 213 Squadron, 11 August 1940 (Air 50 records, National Archives).
135. Ramsey, Winston G. (ed.), *op. cit.* (*Luftwaffe* entry for 11 August 1940).
136. James, T. Cecil G., *op. cit.* (p. 59).
137. *Lageberichte Luftflottenkommando 3, op. cit.* (entries for 11 August 1940).
138. James, T. Cecil G., *op. cit.* (p. 59).
139. ORB, Form 541 (Records of Events), 213 Squadron, 11 August 1940 (Air 27 records, National Archives).
140. CR, Sub Lt D. M. Jeram, 213 Squadron, 11 August 1940 (Air 50 records, National Archives); IPR, 213 Squadron, 11 August 1940 (Air 16/955 records, National Archives).
141. CR, Sub Lt D. M. Jeram, 213 Squadron, 11 August 1940 (Air 50 records, National Archives).
142. IPR, 213 Squadron, 11 August 1940 (Air 16/955 records, National Archives).
143. Air Ministry (compiled and introduced: Robson, Martin), *The Spitfire Pocket Manual; All marks in service 1939-1945* (London: Conway, 2010), specifically P/O D. M. Crook's logbook therein, pp. 65 – 75 (p. 69).
144. ORB, Form 540 (Summary of Events), 609 Squadron, 11 August 1940 (Air 27 records, National Archives).

Adlertag

145. *ibid.*
146. IPR, 609 Squadron, 11 August 1940 (Air 16/955 records, National Archives).
147. CR, F/O J. C. Dundas, 609 Squadron, 11 August 1940 (Air 50 records, National Archives).
148. CR, S/L H. S. Darley, 609 Squadron, 11 August 1940 (Air 50/171/17 records, National Archives).
149. IPR, 609 Squadron, 11 August 1940 (Air 16/955 records, National Archives).
150. *ibid.*
151. CR, P/O N. le C. Agazarian, 609 Squadron, 11 August 1940 (Air 50/171/1 records, National Archives).
152. IPR, 609 Squadron, 11 August 1940 (Air 16/955 records, National Archives).
153. Notes 151 and 152, *op. cit.*
154. CR, F/Lt J. H. G. McArthur, 609 Squadron, 11 August 1940 (Air 50 records, National Archives).
155. CR, P/O J. D. Bisdee, 609 Squadron, 11 August 1940 (Air 50/171/10 records, National Archives).
156. Notes 152 and 155, *op. cit.*
157. Note 155, *op. cit.*
158. Crook, David M., *Spitfire Pilot* (London: Grub Street, 2010) (pp. 87-89); Air Ministry (compiled and introduced: Robson, Martin), *op. cit.* (p. 69).
159. For example, CRs, F/Lt J. H. G. McArthur and F/O J. C. Dundas, 609 Squadron, 11 August 1940 (Air 50 records, National Archives).
160. Air Ministry (compiled and introduced: Robson, Martin), *op. cit.* (p. 69).
161. CR, P/O D. M. Crook, 609 Squadron, 11 August 1940 (Air 50/171/15 records, National Archives).
162. CR, F/O J. C. Dundas, 609 Squadron, 11 August 1940 (Air 50 records, National Archives); IPR, 609 Squadron, 11 August 1940 (Air 16/955 records, National Archives).
163. *ibid.*
164. CR, F/O J. C. Dundas, 609 Squadron, 11 August 1940 (Air 50 records, National Archives).
165. *ibid.*
166. IPR, 609 Squadron, 11 August 1940 (Air 16/955 records, National Archives).
167. *ibid.*
168. ORB, Form 540 (Summary of Events), 609 Squadron, 11 August 1940 (Air 27 records, National Archives).

169. CR, P/O J. D. Bisdee, 609 Squadron, 11 August 1940 (Air 50/171/10 records, National Archives).
170. CR, S/L H. S. Darley, 609 Squadron, 11 August 1940 (Air 50/171/17 records, National Archives).
171. Parker, Nigel, *op. cit.* (entry for 11 August 1940); Ramsey, Winston G. (ed.), *op. cit.* (*Luftwaffe* entry for 11 August 1940).
172. Mason Francis K., *op. cit.* (p. 129).
173. Wynn, Kenneth G., *Men of the Battle of Britain* (Barnsley: Frontline, 2015) (pp. 164-165).
174. Wynn, Kenneth G., *op. cit.* (pp. 255-256 and p. 541).
175. *ibid.*
176. Wynn, Kenneth G., *op. cit.* (p. 49).
177. IPR, 238 Squadron, 11 August 1940 (Air 16/955 records, National Archives); CR, P/O J. R. Urwin-Mann, 238 Squadron, 11 August 1940 (Air 50 records, National Archives).
178. CRs, F/Lt D. P. Hughes and P/O J. R. Urwin-Mann, 238 Squadron, 11 August 1940 (Air 50 records, National Archives); IPR, 238 Squadron, 11 August 1940 (Air 16/955 records, National Archives).
179. IPR, 238 Squadron, 11 August 1940 (Air 16/955 records, National Archives).
180. CR, F/Lt D. P. Hughes, 238 Squadron, 11 August 1940 (Air 50 records, National Archives).
181. *ibid.*
182. IPR, 238 Squadron, 11 August 1940 (Air 16/955 records, National Archives); CR, Sgt H. J. Marsh, 238 Squadron, 11 August 1940 (Air 50 records, National Archives).
183. ORB, Records of Events, 238 Squadron, 11 August 1940 (Air 27/1453/4 records, National Archives); IPR, 238 Squadron, 11 August 1940 (Air 16/955 records, National Archives).
184. CR, Sgt H. J. Marsh, 238 Squadron, 11 August 1940 (Air 50 records, National Archives).
185. *ibid.*
186. CR, Sgt E. S. Bann, 238 Squadron, 11 August 1940 (Air 50/91/32 records, National Archives).
187. IPR, 238 Squadron, 11 August 1940 (Air 16/955 records, National Archives).
188. CR, Sgt M. B. Domagala, 238 Squadron, 11 August 1940 (Air 50/91/7 records, National Archives), copy in Gretzyngier, Robert, *op. cit.* (p. 14).
189. *ibid.*
190. Ramsey, Winston G. (ed.), *op. cit.* (*Luftwaffe* entry for 11 August 1940).

191. IPR, 238 Squadron, 11 August 1940 (Air 16/955 records, National Archives); Note 188, *op. cit.*
192. IPR, 238 Squadron, 11 August 1940 (Air 16/955 records, National Archives).
193. Squadron Commander's Report on Flying Battle Casualty, P/O J. R. Cock, 87 Squadron, 11 August 1940 (Air 81/2576 records, National Archives); IPR, 87 Squadron, 11 August 1940 (Air 16/955 records, National Archives).
194. IPRs, 87, 213 and 238 Squadrons, 11 August 1940 (Air 16/955 records, National Archives).
195. IPR, 238 Squadron, 11 August 1940 (Air 16/955 records, National Archives).
196. Ramsey, Winston G. (ed.), *op. cit.* (*Luftwaffe* entry for 11 August 1940).
197. Notes 184 and 186, *op. cit.*
198. IPR, 238 Squadron, 11 August 1940 (Air 16/955 records, National Archives).
199. CR, P/O J. R. Urwin-Mann, 238 Squadron, 11 August 1940 (Air 50 records, National Archives).
200. IPR, 238 Squadron, 11 August 1940 (Air 16/955 records, National Archives).
201. CR, P/O J. R. Urwin-Mann, 238 Squadron, 11 August 1940 (Air 50 records, National Archives).
202. Ramsey, Winston G. (ed.), *op. cit.* (RAF entry for 11 August 1940).
203. CR, P/O J. R. Urwin-Mann, 238 Squadron, 11 August 1940 (Air 50 records, National Archives).
204. *ibid.*
205. IPR, 238 Squadron, 11 August 1940 (Air 16/955 records, National Archives).
206. Ramsey, Winston G. (ed.), *op. cit.* (RAF entry for 11 August 1940); Squadron Commander's Report on Flying Battle Casualty, Sgt G. Gledhill, 238 Squadron, 11 August 1940 (Air 81/1313 records, National Archives).
207. Alexander, Kristen, *Australia's Few and the Battle of Britain* (Barnsley: Pen and Sword, 2015) (pp. 191-194).
208. IPR, 238 Squadron, 11 August 1940 (Air 16/955 records, National Archives).
209. CR, Sgt L. Pidd, 238 Squadron, 11 August 1940 (Air 50/91/43 records, National Archives).
210. Website, Wood, Tony, *op. cit.*; Mombeek, Eric and Roba, Jean-Louis, with Goss, Chris, *op. cit.* (p. 39).

Notes

211. Mombeek, Eric and Roba, Jean-Louis, with Goss, Chris, *op. cit.* (p. 193).
212. ORB, Records of Events, 238 Squadron, 11 August 1940 (Air 27/1453/4 records, National Archives).
213. IPR, 87 Squadron, 11 August 1940 (Air 16/955 records, National Archives).
214. IPRs, 87 and 238 Squadrons, 11 August 1940 (Air 16/955 records, National Archives).
215. Parry, Simon, *The Reunion*, Flypast Magazine, December 1983 issue (pp. 32-34).
216. IPR, 87 Squadron, 11 August 1940 (Air 16/955 records, National Archives).
217. Notes 215 and 216, *op. cit.*; Alexander, Kristen, *op. cit.* (pp. 190-193).
218. IPR, 87 Squadron, 11 August 1940 (Air 16/955 records, National Archives).
219. *ibid.*
220. Squadron Commander's Report on Flying Battle Casualty, P/O J. R. Cock, 87 Squadron, 11 August 1940 (Air 81/2576 records, National Archives).
221. CR, P/O J. R. Cock, 87 Squadron, 11 August 1940 (Air 50/37/58 records, National Archives). Note that the relevant CR in the records is ascribed mistakenly to P/O Murdock.
222. CR, P/O W. D. David, 87 Squadron, 11 August 1940 (Air 50 records, National Archives). Given as two separate reports, numbered 1 and 2, although both reflect the same operation. No linguistic corrections made to CRs in this book.
223. IPR, 213 Squadron, 11 August 1940 (Air 16/955 records, National Archives); CR, Sub Lt D. M. Jeram, 213 Squadron, 11 August 1940 (Air 50 records, National Archives); CRs, P/Os J. R. Cock and W. D. David, 87 Squadron, 11 August 1940 (respectively, Air 50/37/58 records, National Archives and Air 50 records, National Archives).
224. Parker, Nigel, *op. cit.* (entry for 11 August 1940); Ramsey, Winston G. (ed.), *op. cit.* (*Luftwaffe* entry for 11 August 1940).
225. Ramsey, Winston G. (ed.), *op. cit.* (*Luftwaffe* entry for 11 August 1940).
226. IPR, 87 Squadron, 11 August 1940 (Air 16/955 records, National Archives).
227. *ibid.*
228. Ramsey, Winston G. (ed.), *op. cit.* (RAF entry for 11 August 1940).
229. Website Wood, Tony, *op. cit.*; Mombeek, Eric and Roba, Jean-Louis, with Goss, Chris, *op. cit.* (p. 39).

Adlertag

230. Mombeek, Eric and Roba, Jean-Louis, with Goss, Chris, *op. cit.* (p. 193).
231. IPR, 601 Squadron, 11 August 1940 (Air 16/955 records, National Archives).
232. Note 231, *op. cit.*; CR, F/Lt W. H. Rhodes-Moorhouse, 601 Squadron, 11 August 1940 (Air 50/165/35 records, National Archives); CRs, Sgt R. P. Hawkings, P/O W. M. L. Fiske, F/O M. D. Doulton, F/O C. R. Davis, F/O G. N. S. Cleaver and P/O J. K. U. B. McGrath, 601 Squadron, 11 August 1940 (Air 50 records, National Archives).
233. IPR, 601 Squadron, 11 August 1940 (Air 16/955 records, National Archives).
234. Note 233, *op. cit.*; CRs, Sgt R. P. Hawkings, P/O W. M. L. Fiske, F/O M. D. Doulton, F/O C. R. Davis, and P/O J. K. U. B. McGrath, 601 Squadron, 11 August 1940 (Air 50 records, National Archives).
235. Note 233, *op. cit.*; CRs, F/Lt W. H. Rhodes-Moorhouse and F/O G. N. S. Cleaver, 601 Squadron, 11 August 1940 (respectively, Air 50/165/35 records, National Archives and Air 50 records, National Archives).
236. CR, F/Lt W. H. Rhodes-Moorhouse, 601 Squadron, 11 August 1940 (Air 50/165/35 records, National Archives).
237. *ibid.*
238. CR, P/O W. M. L. Fiske, 601 Squadron, 11 August 1940 (Air 50 records, National Archives).
239. *ibid.*
240. *ibid.*
241. CR, Sgt R. P. Hawkings, 601 Squadron, 11 August 1940 (Air 50 records, National Archives).
242. CR, F/O C. R. Davis, 601 Squadron, 11 August 1940 (Air 50 records, National Archives).
243. Note 232, *op. cit.*
244. Ramsey, Winston G. (ed.), *op. cit.* (RAF entry for 11 August 1940).
245. Squadron Commander's Report on Flying Battle Casualty, P/O J. L. Smithers, 601 Squadron, 11 August 1940 (Air 81/1326 records, National Archives).
246. Squadron Commander's Report on Flying Battle Casualty, F/O R. S. Demetriadi, 601 Squadron, 11 August 1940 (Air 81/1320 records, National Archives).
247. Ramsey, Winston G. (ed.), *op. cit.* (p. 350).
248. For example, CRs, F/O G. N. S. Cleaver and P/O J. K. U. B. McGrath, Yellow Section, 601 Squadron, 11 August 1940 (Air 50 records, National Archives).

Notes

249. CR, F/Lt W. H. Rhodes-Moorhouse, 601 Squadron, 11 August 1940 (Air 50/165/35 records, National Archives).
250. CR, F/O M. D. Doulton, 601 Squadron, 11 August 1940 (Air 50 records, National Archives).
251. *ibid.*
252. *ibid.*
253. Times: *c.* 10h50-10h55; Ramsey, Winston G. (ed.), *op. cit.* (RAF entry for 11 August 1940).
254. Prien, Jochen, 1989, *op. cit.* (p. 175); Prien, Jochen, *Pik-As: Geschichte des Jagdgeschwaders 53, Teil 3* (Eutin: Struve-Druck, 1991) (p. 1662); Website, Wood, Tony, *op. cit.*
255. Website, Wood, Tony, *op. cit.*
256. Ramsey, Winston G. (ed.), *op. cit.* (*Luftwaffe* entry for 11 August 1940).
257. CR, F/O G. N. S. Cleaver, 601 Squadron, 11 August 1940 (Air 50 records, National Archives).
258. CR, P/O J. K. U. B. McGrath, 601 Squadron, 11 August 1940 (Air 50 records, National Archives).
259. *ibid.*
260. Wynn, Kenneth G., *op. cit.* (pp. 211-212).
261. IPR, 601 Squadron, 11 August 1940 (Air 16/955 records, National Archives).
262. ORB, Form 540 (Summary of Events), 152 Squadron, 11 August 1940 (Air 27 records, National Archives); IPR, 152 Squadron, 11 August 1940 (Air 16/955 records, National Archives).
263. IPR, 152 Squadron, 11 August 1940 (Air 16/955 records, National Archives).
264. Burt, Danny, *A Battle of Britain Spitfire Squadron: the men and machines of 152 Squadron in the summer of 1940* (Barnsley: Pen and Sword, 2018) (pp. 235-236).
265. IPR, 152 Squadron, 11 August 1940 (Air 16/955 records, National Archives).
266. *ibid.*
267. IPR, 152 Squadron, 11 August 1940 (Air 16/955 records, National Archives); Burt, Danny, *op. cit.* (pp. 150-153).
268. Note 254, *op. cit.*
269. IPR, 1 Squadron, 11 August 1940 (Air 16/955 records, National Archives). Note: this IPR is undated, and filed amongst IPRs from 12 August 1940, being numbered IMG_9598, in the relevant bound volume of IPRs at the National Archives.
270. CR, F/O J. C. Dundas, 609 Squadron, 11 August 1940 (Air 50 records, National Archives).

271. IPR, 1 Squadron, 11 August 1940 (Air 16/955 records, National Archives).
272. *ibid.*
273. IPR, 1 Squadron, 11 August 1940 (Air 16/955 records, National Archives); ORB, Records of Events, 1 Squadron, 11 August 1940 (Air 27/1/20 records, National Archives).
274. IPR, 1 Squadron, 11 August 1940 (Air 16/955 records, National Archives).
275. *ibid.*
276. Parker, Nigel, *Luftwaffe Crash Archive*, Vol. 3 (Walton on Thames: Red Kite Books, Air Research Publications, 2013) (entry for 4 September 1940, when Schäfer was shot down again and taken prisoner).
277. Website, de Zeng, Henry L. IV and Stankey, Douglas G., *Luftwaffe Officer Career Summaries* (2014 updated version), accessed via Michael Holm's website, *The Luftwaffe 1933-1945*: www.ww2.dk; this source at www.ww2.dk/lwoffz.html; comment by Peter Cornwell in a forum discussion: *forum.12oclockhigh.net/archive/index.php?t-40796.html*
278. CR, F/Lt M. H. Brown, 1 Squadron, 11 August 1940 (Air 50 records, National Archives).
279. IPR, 1 Squadron, 11 August 1940 (Air 16/955 records, National Archives).
280. Squadron Commander's Report on Flying Battle Casualty, P/O J. A. J. Davey, 1 Squadron, 11 August 1940 (Air 81/1314 records, National Archives).
281. Notes 279 and 280, *op. cit.*
282. Kimbell, Andrew, *The One History Forgot: David Alwyne Pemberton – A life story* (Independently published, 2018) (p. 42).
283. Ramsey, Winston G. (ed.), *op. cit.* (*Luftwaffe* entry for 11 August 1940).
284. Mombeek, Eric and Roba, Jean-Louis, with Goss, Chris, *op. cit.* (p. 193).
285. Note 283, *op. cit.*
286. Website, Wood, Tony, *op. cit.*
287. *ibid.*
288. *Lageberichte Luftflottenkommando 3*, *op. cit.* (entries for 11 August 1940).
289. IPR, 610 Squadron, 11 August 1940 (Air 16/955 records, National Archives); Bailey, David J., *610 (County of Chester) Auxiliary Air Force Squadron, 1936-1940* (Stroud: Fonthill, 2018) (pp. 290-296).

Notes

290. IPR, 610 Squadron, 11 August 1940 (Air 16/955 records, National Archives). Note, this includes the CR of F/Lt E. B. B. Smith.
291. *ibid.*
292. Bailey, David J., *op. cit.* (pp. 294-295).
293. Squadron Commander's Report on Flying Battle Casualty, Sgt J. H. Tanner, 610 Squadron, 11 August 1940 (Air 81/1304 records, National Archives).
294. Archives, Imperial War Museum, London: *Luftwaffe Quartermaster General Loss Returns* (a very large document). Electronic copy kindly provided by Nigel Parker, from original at the Museum.
295. Ramsey, Winston G. (ed.), *op. cit.* (*Luftwaffe* entry for 11 August 1940).
296. *ibid.*
297. Website, Wood, Tony, *op. cit.*; Barbas, Bernd, *Die Geschichte der I. Gruppe des Jagdgeschwaders 52* (Überlingen: self-published, undated) (p. 387).
298. ORB, Records of Events, 53 Squadron, 11 August 1940 (Air 27/503/22 records, National Archives); Website, Royal Air Force Commands; rafcommands.com/Ross/Coastal/53C.html
299. Steinhilper, Ulrich and Osborne, Peter, *Spitfire on my tail* (Bromley: Independent Books, 2009) (pp. 288-289).
300. Steinhilper, Ulrich and Osborne, Peter, *op. cit.* (pp. 288-289); Barbas, Bernd, *op. cit.* (p. 387).
301. James, T. Cecil G., *op. cit.* (pp. 60-61).
302. Hewitt, Nick, *Coastal Convoys 1939-1945: the indestructible highway* (Barnsley: Pen and Sword Maritime, 2019) (p. 115).
303. James, T. Cecil G., *op. cit.* (pp. 60-61); IPRs, 85 and 17 Squadrons, 11 August 1940 (Air 16/955 records, National Archives); IPR, 74 Squadron, 11 August 1940 (Air 16/955 records, National Archives) (take off time *c.* 11h45; were three other 74 Squadron IPRs this day, take off times *c.* 08h00, *c.* 09h50 and *c.* 13h56).
304. James, T. Cecil G., *op. cit.* (pp. 60-61); IPR, 64 Squadron, 11 August 1940 (Air 16/955 records, National Archives) (take off time *c.* 11h45; were two other 64 Squadron IPRs this day, take off times *c.* 07h30 and *c.* 09h32).
305. Vasco, John, *op. cit.* (p. 53).
306. Bergström, Christer, *The Battle of Britain: an epic conflict revisited* (Oxford: Casemate, 2015 and Eskilstuna: Vaktel, 2015) (pp. 96-98); Goss, Chris, *Dornier Do 17 units of World War 2* (Oxford: Osprey, 2019) (p. 51).
307. James, T. Cecil G., *op. cit.* (p. 60).

308. *ibid.*
309. Bergström, Christer, *op. cit.* (pp. 96-98).
310. James, T. Cecil G., *op. cit.* (pp. 60-61); Vasco, John, *op. cit.* (p. 53).
311. James, T. Cecil G., *op. cit.* (pp. 60-61); Hewitt, Nick, *op. cit.* (p. 115).
312. CRs, S/L P. W. Townsend and Sgt H. H. Allgood, 85 Squadron, 11 August 1940 (respectively, Air 50/36/231 records and Air 50/36/233 records, National Archives).
313. CR, S/L P. W. Townsend, 85 Squadron, 11 August 1940 (Air 50/36/231 records, National Archives).
314. *ibid.*
315. CR, Sgt C. E. Hampshire, 85 Squadron, 11 August 1940 (Air 50/36/191 records, National Archives).
316. CRs, Sgts C. E. Hampshire and H. H. Allgood, 85 Squadron, 11 August 1940 (respectively, Air 50/36/191 records and Air 50/36/233 records, National Archives).
317. CR, Sgt H. H. Allgood, 85 Squadron, 11 August 1940 (Air 50/36/233 records, National Archives).
318. CRs, F/Lt W. J. Harper, P/O L. W. Stevens and Sgt G. Griffiths, 17 Squadron, 11 August 1940 (respectively, Air 50/9/21 records, Air 50/9/39 records and Air 50/9/119 records, National Archives); IPR, 17 Squadron, 11 August 1940 (Air 16/955 records, National Archives).
319. CRs, F/Lt W. J. Harper and P/O L. W. Stevens, 17 Squadron, 11 August 1940 (respectively, Air 50/9/21 records and Air 50/9/39 records, National Archives).
320. CRs, P/O G. E. Pitman and Sgt G. Griffiths, 17 Squadron, 11 August 1940 (respectively, Air 50/9/36 records and Air 50/9/119 records, National Archives).
321. Bergström, Christer, *op. cit.* (pp. 96-98).
322. CRs, Sgts C. E. Hampshire and H. H. Allgood, 85 Squadron, 11 August 1940 (respectively, Air 50/36/191 records and Air 50/36/233 records, National Archives); CRs, F/Lt W. J. Harper, P/O L. W. Stevens, Sgt G. Griffiths, F/O D. H. W. Hanson and P/O G. E. Pitman, 17 Squadron, 11 August 1940 (respectively, Air 50/9/21 records, Air 50/9/39 records, Air 50/9/119 records, Air 50/9/20 records and Air 50/9/36 records, National Archives).
323. IPR, 74 Squadron, 11 August 1940 (Air 16/955 records, National Archives) (take off time 11h45); CRs of participating pilots of 74 Squadron, listed below (Note 338).
324. Eriksson, Patrick G., *Tally-Ho: RAF tactical leadership in the Battle of Britain July 1940* (Stroud: Amberley, 2023) (pp. 235-236).

Notes

325. CRs, Sgts C. E. Hampshire and H. H. Allgood, 85 Squadron, 11 August 1940 (respectively, Air 50/36/191 records and Air 50/36/233 records, National Archives); CRs, P/O L. W. Stevens, Sgt G. Griffiths, F/O D. H. W. Hanson and P/O G. E. Pitman, 17 Squadron, 11 August 1940 (respectively, Air 50/9/39 records, Air 50/9/119 records, Air 50/9/20 records and Air 50/9/36 records, National Archives).
326. CR, F/O D. H. W. Hanson, 17 Squadron, 11 August 1940 (Air 50/9/20 records, National Archives).
327. IPRs, 17 and 85 Squadrons, 11 August 1940 (Air 16/955 records, National Archives); Note 322, *op. cit.*
328. Website, Wood, Tony, *op. cit.*
329. Ramsey, Winston G. (ed.), *op. cit.* (RAF entry for 11 August 1940).
330. CR, P/O J. C. Freeborn, 74 Squadron, 11 August 1940 (Air 50/32/87 records, National Archives) (take off time 11h45).
331. CR, Sgt T. B. Kirk, 74 Squadron, 11 August 1940 (Air 50/32/29 records, National Archives).
332. Baker, E. C. R., *The Fighter Aces of the R.A.F.* (London: New English Library, 1974) (p. 165).
333. Eriksson, Patrick G., 2023, *op. cit.* (p. 48).
334. CR, W/O E. Mayne, 74 Squadron, 11 August 1940 (Air 50/32/31 records, National Archives).
335. Tidy, Douglas, *op. cit.* (p. 83).
336. Spurdle, Bob, *The Blue Arena* (Manchester: Goodall, Crécy, 2017) (pp. 27-28).
337. *ibid.*
338. Total claims based on: CRs, P/O J. C. Freeborn, F/O W. H. Nelson, Sgt T. B. Kirk, F/O J. C. Mungo-Park, W/O E. Mayne and Sgt W. M. Skinner, 74 Squadron, 11 August 1940 (respectively Air 50/32/87 records, Air 50/32/43 records, Air 50/32/29 records, Air 50/32/97 records, Air 50/32/31 records, Air 50/32/104 records, National Archives); account of P/O H. M. Stephen's action in Baker, E. C. R., *op. cit.* (p. 165). Note that the IPR, 74 Squadron, 11 August 1940 (Air 16/955 records, National Archives) (take off at *c.* 11h45) sums these individual claims to reflect only four damaged but one probable Me 110, and nine unconfirmed claims, plus the single confirmed one.
339. IPR, 74 Squadron, 11 August 1940 (Air 16/955 records, National Archives) (take off at *c.* 11h45).
340. Bergström, Christer, *op. cit.* (pp. 96-98); Website, Wood, Tony, *op. cit.*
341. Ramsey, Winston G. (ed.), *op. cit.* (*Luftwaffe* entry for 11 August 1940).

342. Goss, Chris, *The Luftwaffe Fighters' Battle of Britain* (Manchester: Crécy, 2010) (p. 37).
343. CR, Sgt T. B. Kirk, 74 Squadron, 11 August 1940 (Air 50/32/29 records, National Archives).
344. CRs, F/O W. H. Nelson, F/O J. C. Mungo-Park, W/O E. Mayne and Sgt W. M. Skinner, 74 Squadron, 11 August 1940 (respectively Air 50/32/43 records, Air 50/32/97 records, Air 50/32/31 records and Air 50/32/104 records, National Archives).
345. CR, S/L P. W. Townsend, 85 Squadron, 11 August 1940 (Air 50/36/231 records, National Archives).
346. *ibid.*
347. CR, P/O L. W. Stevens, 17 Squadron, 11 August 1940 (Air 50/9/39 records, National Archives).
348. Ramsey, Winston G. (ed.), *op. cit.* (*Luftwaffe* entry for 11 August 1940).
349. IPR, 64 Squadron, 11 August 1940 (Air 16/955 records, National Archives) (take off time *c.* 11h45).
350. *ibid.*
351. *ibid.*
352. *ibid.*
353. CR, Sgt J. Mann, 64 Squadron, 11 August 1940 (Air 50/24/85 records, National Archives).
354. Ramsey, Winston G. (ed.), *op. cit.* (*Luftwaffe* entry for 11 August 1940).
355. Website, Wood, Tony, *op. cit.*
356. James, T. Cecil G., *op. cit.* (p. 61).
357. *ibid.*
358. ORB, Summary of Events (Form 540), 151 Squadron, 11 August 1940 (Air 27 records, National Archives); ORB, Records of Events (Form 541), 151 Squadron, 11 August 1940 (Air 27/1018/30 records, National Archives); James, T. Cecil G., *op. cit.* (p. 61).
359. ORB, Form 540, 151 Squadron, 11 August 1940 (Air 27 records, National Archives).
360. James, T. Cecil G., *op. cit.* (p. 61).
361. Ramsey, Winston G. (ed.), *op. cit.* (*Luftwaffe* entry for 11 August 1940).
362. Short citation from: Squadron Commander's Report on Flying Battle Casualty, Sgt F. E. Baker, 56 Squadron, 11 August 1940 (Air 81/1307 records, National Archives).
363. Report by F/Lt P. S. Weaver, 56 Squadron, in Sgt F. E. Baker's casualty file, 11 August 1940 (Air 81/1307 records, National Archives).

Notes

364. Report by C/O *HMS Westminster*, and Report by F/Lt P. S. Weaver, 56 Squadron, in Sgt F. E. Baker's casualty file, 11 August 1940 (Air 81/1307 records, National Archives).
365. *ibid.*
366. ORB, Summary of Events, 604 Squadron, 11 August 1940 (Air 27/2082/21 records, National Archives); Burt, Danny, *op. cit.* (p. 223).
367. ORB, Summary of Events, 604 Squadron, 11 August 1940 (Air 27/2082/21 records, National Archives); Burt, Danny, *op. cit.* (p. 153 and p. 223).
368. Goss, Chris, 2019, *op. cit.* (p. 51); IPR, 111 Squadron, 11 August 1940 (Air 16/955 records, National Archives); CRs, F/Lt S. D. P. Connors and S/L J. M. Thompson, 111 Squadron, 11 August 1940 (respectively, Air 50/43/17 records, National Archives and Air 50 records, National Archives); Bergström, Christer, *op. cit.* (p. 98); Ramsey, Winston G. (ed.), *op. cit.* (*Luftwaffe* entry for 11 August 1940); Website, Wood, Tony, *op. cit.*
369. IPR, 74 Squadron, 11 August 1940 (Air 16/955 records, National Archives) (take off at *c.* 13h56); Bergström, Christer, *op. cit.* (p. 98); Ramsey, Winston G. (ed.), *op. cit.* (*Luftwaffe* entry for 11 August 1940); Note 30, *op. cit.*
370. CR, F/Lt S. D. P. Connors, 111 Squadron, 11 August 1940 (Air 50/43/17 records, National Archives).
371. CR, P/O J. C. Freeborn, 74 Squadron, 11 August 1940 (Air 50/32/87 records, National Archives) (take off time *c.* 13h56).
372. Report of the loss of his ship, by Lt. E. J. C. Edwards, RNVR, C/O *HMT Edwardian*; copy given on auctioneers web page, Auctioneers: Spink and Son Ltd., London; auction of war medals of Leading Seaman E. Tambling (Spink.com/lot/17003000580) who served on *HMT Edwardian*; spink.com
373. *ibid.*
374. *ibid.*
375. *ibid.*
376. Ramsey, Winston G. (ed.), *op. cit.* (*Luftwaffe* entry for 11 August 1940).
377. Prien, Jochen and Stemmer, Gerhard, 1997, *op. cit.* (p. 72 and pp. 78-79); Prien, Jochen and Stemmer, Gerhard, 1996, *op. cit.* (p. 18).
378. Prien, Jochen and Stemmer, Gerhard, 1997, *op. cit.* (p. 79).
379. IPR, 74 Squadron, 11 August 1940 (Air 16/955 records, National Archives) (take off at *c.* 13h56).
380. *ibid.*

381. Note 378, *op. cit.*
382. IPR, 111 Squadron, 11 August 1940 (Air 16/955 records, National Archives); Note 370, *op. cit.*
383. CRs, F/Lt S. D. P. Connors and S/L J. M. Thompson, 111 Squadron, 11 August 1940 (respectively, Air 50/43/17 records, National Archives and Air 50 records, National Archives).
384. Note 370, *op. cit.*
385. IPR, 111 Squadron, 11 August 1940 (Air 16/955 records, National Archives).
386. Website, Wood, Tony, *op. cit.*
387. *ibid.*
388. Note 385, *op. cit.*
389. CR, S/L J. M. Thompson, 111 Squadron, 11 August 1940 (Air 50 records, National Archives).
390. Details on 111 Squadron's losses in: Squadron Commander's Report on Flying Battle Casualty, for P/O R. R. Wilson, P/O J. H. H. Copeman, P/O J. W. McKenzie and Sgt R. B. Sim, 111 Squadron, 11 August 1940 (respectively, Air 81/1324 records, Air 81/1318 records, Air 81/1316 records and Air 81/ 1315 records, National Archives) (same collective report on all four lost pilots and on Sgt H. S. Newton's crash given in each file).
391. Eriksson, Patrick G., 2023, *op. cit.* (pp. 49-53).
392. Notes 385 and 390, *op. cit.*; ORB, Records of Events, 111 Squadron, 11 August 1940 (Air 27/866/14 records, National Archives).
393. Website, Duxford Radio Society; www.duxfordradiosociety.org/equipment/pip-squeak.html
394. *ibid.*
395. *ibid.*
396. IPR, 111 Squadron, 11 August 1940 (Air 16/955 records, National Archives).
397. Ramsey, Winston G. (ed.), *op. cit.* (*Luftwaffe* entry for 11 August 1940).
398. Note 3, *op. cit.*
399. Goss, Chris, 2019, *op. cit.* (p. 51).
400. Note 396, *op. cit.*
401. *Luftwaffe Quartermaster General Loss Returns, op. cit.*
402. IPR, 41 Squadron, 11 August 1940 (Air 16/955 records, National Archives); Note 397, *op. cit.*; Wallens, R. W. 'Wally', *Flying made my Arms ache* (Upton-upon-Severn: The Self Publishing Association Ltd., 1990) (p. 124).
403. IPR, 41 Squadron, 11 August 1940 (Air 16/955 records, National Archives).

404. *ibid.*
405. *ibid.*
406. *ibid.*

2. Second major raid, Portsmouth, radar stations and forward airfields attacked: 12 August 1940

1. James, T. Cecil G., *The Battle of Britain* (Abingdon: Routledge, 2012), (pp. 63-64).
2. *ibid.*
3. *ibid.*
4. IPR, 610 Squadron, 12 August 1940 (Air 16/955 records, National Archives).
5. IPR, 54 Squadron, 12 August 1940 (Air 16/955 records, National Archives) (take off time *c.* 07h30; was one later IPR this day, take off time *c.* 17h10; times from: Air Ministry Operational Record Books, No. 11 (Fighter) Group, Appendices, 1 September 1939 – 30 September 1940, (Air 25/197 records, National Archives).
6. Dildy, Douglas C. and Crickmore, Paul F., *To Defeat The Few: The Luftwaffe's Campaign to destroy RAF Fighter Command, August-September 1940* (Oxford: Osprey, 2020) (p. 202); Caldwell, Donald L., *JG 26 Luftwaffe Fighter Wing Diary, 1939-1942*, Vol. 1 (Mechanicsburg: Stackpole Books, 2012) (pp. 52-54); Bergström, Christer, *The Battle of Britain: an epic conflict revisited* (Oxford: Casemate, 2015 and Eskilstuna: Vaktel, 2015) (pp. 99-100); Website, Wood, Tony, *Tony Wood's Combat Claims and Casualties Lists*, website accessed via Don Caldwell's website: don-caldwell.we.bs/claims/tonywood.htm (with many succeeding repeats and relatively minor edits by fellow historians); Flying logbook, *Uffz* Hans-Helmut Habermehl, *1/JG 54*, entries for 12 August 1940, copy of logbook courtesy of Peter Arnot, operation from 12h17–13h40; Steinhilper, Ulrich and Osborne, Peter, *Spitfire on my tail* (Bromley: Independent Books, 2009) (pp. 288-289); Barbas, Bernd, *Die Geschichte der II. Gruppe des Jagdgeschwaders 52* (Überlingen: self-published, undated) (pp. 32-33).
7. IPR, 54 Squadron, 12 August 1940 (Air 16/955 records, National Archives) (take off time *c.* 07h30).
8. An idea already mooted by David Bailey in his meticulously researched squadron history: *610 (County of Chester) Auxiliary Air Force Squadron, 1936-1940* (Stroud: Fonthill, 2018) (p. 306).
9. James, T. Cecil G., *op. cit.* (pp. 63-64).

10. Excerpt from: CR, S/L J. Ellis, 610 Squadron, 12 August 1940 (Air 50/172/22 records, National Archives), copy in Bailey, David J., *op. cit.* (pp. 297-298).
11. Excerpt from: CR, Sgt H. H. Chandler, 610 Squadron, 12 August 1940 (Air 50/172/11 records, National Archives), copy in Bailey, David J., *op. cit.* (p. 300).
12. CRs, S/L J. Ellis and Sgt B. G. D. Gardner, 610 Squadron, 12 August 1940 (respectively, Air 50/172/22, copy in Bailey, David J., *op. cit.* (pp. 297-298), and Air 50/172/29, copy in Bailey, David J., *op. cit.* (p. 299)).
13. CRs, Sgt H. H. Chandler and P/O B. V. Rees, 610 Squadron, 12 August 1940 (respectively, Air 50/172/11, copy in Bailey, David J., *op. cit.* (p. 300), and Air 50/172/61, copy in Bailey, David J., *op. cit.* (pp. 300-301)).
14. *ibid.*
15. Bergström, Christer, *op. cit.* (pp. 99-100); Dildy, Douglas C. and Crickmore, Paul F., *op. cit.* (p. 202); Barbas, Bernd, *op. cit.* (pp. 32-33).
16. Barbas, Bernd, *op. cit.* (pp. 32-33); Website, Wood, Tony, *op. cit.*
17. Bailey, David J., *op. cit.* (pp. 296-307).
18. Note 12, *op. cit.*
19. Caldwell, Donald L., *op. cit.* (pp. 52-54).
20. Note 19, *op. cit.*; Website, Wood, Tony, *op. cit.*
21. Squadron Commander's Report on Flying Battle Casualty, F/Lt E. B. B. Smith, 610 Squadron, 12 August 1940 (Air 81/1337 records, National Archives).
22. Bailey, David J., *op. cit.* (pp. 296-307).
23. Caldwell, Donald L., *op. cit.* (pp. 52-54).
24. Ramsey, Winston. G. (ed.), *The Battle of Britain: then and now* (London: Battle of Britain Prints International Ltd., 1982), (RAF entry for 12 August 1940).
25. CRs, Sgt B. G. D. Gardner and Sgt H. H. Chandler, 610 Squadron, 12 August 1940 (Air 50/172/29, and Air 50/172/11 records, National Archives), copies in Bailey, David J., *op. cit.* (pp. 299-300).
26. CR, P/O C. O. J. Pegge, 610 Squadron, 12 August 1940 (Air 50/172/58 records, National Archives), copy in Bailey, David J., *op. cit.* (p. 300).
27. Ramsey, Winston. G. (ed.), *op. cit.* (*Luftwaffe* entry for 12 August 1940); Parker, Nigel, *Luftwaffe Crash Archive*, Vol. 1 (Walton on Thames: Red Kite Books, Air Research Publications, 2013) (entry for 12 August 1940).
28. Knight, Dennis, *Harvest of Messerschmitts: the chronicle of a village at war ~1940* (London: Frederick Warne, 1981) (p. 88).

29. IPR, 54 Squadron, 12 August 1940 (Air 16/955 records, National Archives) (take off time *c.* 07h30).
30. CR, P/O C. F. Gray, 54 Squadron, 12 August 1940 (Air 50/21/106 records, National Archives).
31. CR, P/O H. K. F. Matthews, 54 Squadron, 12 August 1940 (Air 50/21/53 records, National Archives).
32. *ibid.*
33. Squadron Commander's Report on Flying Battle Casualty, P/O D. R. Turley-George, 54 Squadron, 12 August 1940 (Air 81/1330 records, National Archives); Ramsey, Winston. G. (ed.), *op. cit.* (RAF entry for 12 August 1940).
34. Ramsey, Winston. G. (ed.), *op. cit.* (RAF entry for 12 August 1940); IPR, 54 Squadron, 12 August 1940 (Air 16/955 records, National Archives) (take off time *c.* 07h30).
35. Notes 30 and 31, *op. cit.*
36. Ramsey, Winston. G. (ed.), *op. cit.* (*Luftwaffe* entry for 12 August 1940); Website, de Zeng, Henry L. IV, *Luftwaffe Airfields 1935-1945*, accessed via website, Holm, Michael, *The Luftwaffe 1933-1945*; www.ww2.dk; this source at www.ww2.dk/lwairfields.html
37. Website, de Zeng, Henry L. IV, *op. cit.*
38. Website, Wood, Tony, *op. cit.*
39. Bergström, Christer, *op. cit.* (pp. 99-100); this author based this statement on *Oblt* Hans-Ekkehard Bob's logbook, and a copy of the *9/JG 54 Kriegstagebuch* (war diary) supplied by the same pilot.
40. Caldwell, Donald L., *op. cit.* (pp. 52-54).
41. Note 38, *op. cit.*
42. Notes 30 and 31, *op. cit.*
43. Dildy, Douglas C. and Crickmore, Paul F., *op. cit.* (p. 202); Knight, Dennis, *op. cit.* (p. 88).
44. Ramsey, Winston. G. (ed.), *op. cit.* (RAF entry for 12 August 1940).
45. IPR, 54 Squadron, 12 August 1940 (Air 16/955 records, National Archives) (take off time *c.* 07h30); ORB, Records of Events (Form 541), 54 Squadron, 12 August 1940 (Air 27/511/25 records, National Archives).
46. Vasco, John, *Messerschmitt Bf 110 Bombsights over England: Erprobungsgruppe 210 in the Battle of Britain* (Atglen: Schiffer, 2002) (pp. 54-56).
47. *ibid.*
48. Vasco, John, *op. cit.* (p. 168).
49. Knight, Dennis, *op. cit.* (pp. 88-89).
50. Bekker, Cajus, *The Luftwaffe War Diaries* (London: Corgi, 1969) (pp. 186-189).

51. Dildy, Douglas C. and Crickmore, Paul F., *op. cit.* (pp. 202-203).
52. *ibid.*
53. Vasco, John, *op. cit.* (pp. 54-56).
54. Wood, Derek and Dempster, Derek, *The Narrow Margin* (London: Arrow Books, 1967) (pp. 278-279).
55. *ibid.*
56. *ibid.*
57. Note 51, *op. cit.*
58. Mason, Francis K., *Battle over Britain* (London: McWhirter Twins, 1969) (p. 230-231); Bungay, Stephen, *The Most Dangerous Enemy* (London: Aurum Press, 2009) (p. 206).
59. Collier, Richard, *Eagle Day; the Battle of Britain August 6 – September 15 1940* (London: Pan, 1969) (pp. 46-49).
60. James, T. Cecil G., *op. cit.* (p. 65).
61. *ibid.*
62. *ibid.*
63. Royal National Lifeboat Institution, Archive and Library; rnliarchive.blob.core.windows.net/media/1674/1940wys.pdf
64. James, T. Cecil G., *op. cit.* (p. 65).
65. *ibid.*
66. Caldwell, Donald L., *op. cit.* (pp. 52-54).
67. *ibid.*
68. IPR, 65 Squadron, 12 August 1940 (Air 16/955 records, National Archives) (take off time *c.* 10h30 and 11h00 for the two flights; was one later IPR this day, take off time *c.* 12h30); IPR, 501 Squadron, 12 August 1940 (Air 16/955 records, National Archives) (take off time *c.* 10h30; were two later IPRs this day, take off times *c.* 12h20 and 17h25).
69. IPR, 501 Squadron, 12 August 1940 (Air 16/955 records, National Archives) (take off time *c.* 10h30); CRs, P/O P. Zenker, P/O K. N. T. Lee and S/L A. L. Holland, 501 Squadron, 12 August 1940 (respectively, Air 50/162/63, Air 50/162/36 and Air 50/162/28 records, National Archives), copy of Zenker's CR in Gretzyngier, Robert, *Poles in Defence of Britain: A day-by-day chronology of Polish day and night fighter pilot operations: July 1940–June 1941* (London: Grub Street, 2016) (p. 16), copy of Lee's CR in Darlow, Steve, *Five of the Few* (London: Grub Street, 2010) (p. 39).
70. IPR, 65 Squadron, 12 August 1940 (Air 16/955 records, National Archives) (take off time *c.* 10h30 and 11h00 for the two flights); CRs, F/Lt C. G. C. Olive, Sgt J. R. Kilner, F/O T. Smart, P/O K. G. Hart, P/O B. E. F. Finucane and F/Sgt R. R. MacPherson,

Notes

65 Squadron, 12 August 1940 (appendices to 65 Squadron ORB, Air 27/596 records, National Archives; via Nigel Parker).
71. Caldwell, Donald L., *op. cit.* (pp. 52-54); Website, Wood, Tony, *op. cit.*
72. Note 68, *op. cit.*
73. Note 71, *op. cit.*
74. Squadron Commander's Reports on Flying Battle Casualties, P/O R. W. G. Beley and F/O A. B. Tucker, 151 Squadron, 12 August 1940 (respectively, Air 81/1333 and Air 81/1334 records, National Archives).
75. Note 74, *op. cit.*; Ramsey, Winston. G. (ed.), *op. cit.* (RAF entry for 12 August 1940).
76. Website, Wood, Tony, *op. cit.*
77. ORB, Summary of Events (Form 540) and Records of Events (Form 541), 65 Squadron, 12 August 1940 (Air 27/592/5 records, National Archives); IPR, 65 Squadron, 12 August 1940 (Air 16/955 records, National Archives) (take off time *c.* 10h30 and 11h00 for the two flights); CR F/Lt C. G. C. Olive, 65 Squadron, 12 August 1940 (appendices to 65 Squadron ORB, Air 27/596 records, National Archives; via Nigel Parker).
78. IPR, 65 Squadron, 12 August 1940 (Air 16/955 records, National Archives) (take off time *c.* 10h30 and 11h00 for the two flights); CR F/Lt C. G. C. Olive, 65 Squadron, 12 August 1940 (appendices to 65 Squadron ORB, Air 27/596 records, National Archives; via Nigel Parker) (take off time *c.* 10h30-11h00).
79. ORB, Summary of Events (Form 540) and Records of Events (Form 541), 65 Squadron, 12 August 1940 (Air 27/592/5 records, National Archives); IPR, 65 Squadron, 12 August 1940 (Air 16/955 records, National Archives) (take off time *c.* 10h30 and 11h00 for the two flights).
80. CRs, F/Lt C. G. C. Olive, Sgt J. R. Kilner, F/O T. Smart, P/O K. G. Hart, P/O B. E. F. Finucane and F/Sgt R. R. MacPherson, 65 Squadron, 12 August 1940 (appendices to 65 Squadron ORB, Air 27/596 records, National Archives; via Nigel Parker) (take off time *c.* 10h30-11h00).
81. Caldwell, Donald L., *op. cit.* (pp. 52-54); Parker, Nigel, *op. cit.* (entry for 12 August 1940).
82. Website, Wood, Tony, *op. cit.*
83. IPR, 65 Squadron, 12 August 1940 (Air 16/955 records, National Archives) (take off time *c.* 10h30 and 11h00 for the two flights).
84. Caldwell, Donald L., *op. cit.* (pp. 52-54); Website, Wood, Tony, *op. cit.*

Adlertag

85. IPR, 501 Squadron, 12 August 1940 (Air 16/955 records, National Archives) (take off time *c.* 10h30).
86. Note 85, *op. cit.*; Hepper, David, *British Warship Losses in the Modern era: 1920-1982* (Barnsley: Seaforth/Pen and Sword, 2022); CRs, P/O P. Zenker and P/O K. N. T. Lee, 501 Squadron, 12 August 1940 (respectively, Air 50/162/63 and Air 50/162/36 records, National Archives), copy of Zenker's CR in Gretzyngier, Robert, *op. cit.* (p. 16), copy of Lee's CR in Darlow, Steve, *op. cit.* (p. 39).
87. Caldwell, Donald L., *op. cit.* (pp. 52-54).
88. Bickers, Richard T., *Ginger Lacey: Fighter Pilot* (London: Pan, 1969) (pp. 86-88).
89. IPR, 501 Squadron, 12 August 1940 (Air 16/955 records, National Archives) (take off time *c.* 10h30); Ramsey, Winston. G. (ed.), *op. cit.* (*Luftwaffe* entry for 12 August 1940).
90. Note 88, *op. cit.*
91. Hepper, David, *op. cit.*
92. Note 63, *op. cit.*
93. Wynn, Kenneth G., *Men of the Battle of Britain* (Barnsley: Frontline, 2015) (p. 244).
94. CR, S/L A. L. Holland, 501 Squadron, 12 August 1940 (Air 50/162/28 records, National Archives).
95. *ibid.*
96. Website, Wood, Tony, *op. cit.*
97. Note 94, *op. cit.*
98. James, T. Cecil G., *op. cit.* (pp. 65-67).
99. *ibid.*
100. *ibid.*
101. *Lageberichte*, 20.VI.1940-10.X. 1940, *Luftflottenkommando 3*; Records of Headquarters, German Air Force High Command (*Oberkommando der Luftwaffe-OKL*), The National Archives, National Archives and Records Service, Washington, 1966; NA Microcopy No. T-321, Record Group No. 242/1028, Item No. OKL/2308, Roll No. 88; entries for 12 August 1940.
102. Bungay, Stephen, *op. cit.* (p. 204); Bekker, Cajus, *op. cit.* (pp. 186-189).
103. *Lageberichte Luftflottenkommando 3, op. cit.* (entries for 12 August 1940).
104. James, T. Cecil G., *op. cit.* (pp. 65-67); IPRs, 257 and 266 Squadrons, 12 August 1940 (Air 16/955 records, National Archives).
105. James, T. Cecil G., *op. cit.* (pp. 65-67).
106. *ibid.*

Notes

107. Note 105, *op. cit.*; Air Ministry Operational Record Books, No. 11 (Fighter) Group, Appendices, 1 September 1939–30 September 1940 (Air 25/197 records, National Archives).
108. Note 107, *op. cit.*; IPR, 43 Squadron, 12 August 1940 (Air 16/955 records, National Archives); CRs, F/Lt A. H. Boyd, F/O R. M. B. Rowley and F/Lt R. G. Dutton, 145 Squadron, 12 August 1940 (respectively, Air 50/62/37 records, Air 50/62/58 records and Air 50 records, National Archives).
109. Prien, Jochen, *Pik-As: Geschichte des Jagdgeschwaders 53, Teil 1* (Illertissen: Flugzeug Publikations, 1989) (pp. 175-177).
110. Website, Wood, Tony, *op. cit.*
111. Note 109, *op. cit.*
112. Green, William, *Aircraft of the Battle of Britain* (London: MacDonald-Pan, 1969) (p. 33, p. 52).
113. Website, Holm, Michael, *op. cit.*
114. Goss, Chris, *The Luftwaffe Bombers' Battle of Britain* (Manchester: Crécy, 2000) (pp. 65-73).
115. Note 113, *op. cit.*
116. Von Eimannsberger, Ludwig, *Zerstörer Gruppe; a history of V./(Z) LG 1 – I./NJG 3 1939-1941* (Atglen: Schiffer, 1998) (pp. 94-95, p. 205, p. 208).
117. Website, Holm, Michael, *op. cit.*
118. See also: IPR, 609 Squadron, 12 August 1940 (Air 16/955 records, National Archives).
119. Dildy, Douglas C. and Crickmore, Paul F., *op. cit.* (pp. 206-208); Bungay, Stephen, *op. cit.* (p. 204); Mason, Francis K., *op. cit.* (pp. 231-233); Hough, Richard and Richards, Denis, *The Battle of Britain: The Jubilee History* (London: Penguin, 2001) (pp. 145-148).
120. Dildy, Douglas C. and Crickmore, Paul F., *op. cit.* (pp. 206-208); Bungay, Stephen, *op. cit.* (p. 204); Hough, Richard and Richards, Denis, *op. cit.*, (pp. 145-148).
121. Mason, Francis K., *op. cit.* (pp. 231-233).
122. Bungay, Stephen, *op. cit.* (p. 204).
123. James, T. Cecil G., *op. cit.* (pp. 65-67).
124. IPR, 152 Squadron, 12 August 1940 (Air 16/955 records, National Archives).
125. CRs, F/Lt F. M. Thomas, F/O E. S. Hogg and F/Lt D. P. A. Boitel-Gill, 152 Squadron, 12 August 1940 (respectively, Air 50/64/11 records, Air 50/64/87 records and Air 50 records, National Archives).
126. Bungay, Stephen, *op. cit.* (p. 204).
127. CR, P/O R. M. Hogg, 152 Squadron, 12 August 1940 (Air 50/64/88 records, National Archives).

128. Hough, Richard and Richards, Denis, *op. cit.*, (pp. 145-148).
129. *ibid.*
130. IPR, 152 Squadron, 12 August 1940 (Air 16/955 records, National Archives); Note 125, *op. cit.*; CR, P/O W. Beaumont, 152 Squadron, 12 August 1940 (Air 50/64/79 records, National Archives).
131. Note 128, *op. cit.*
132. Note 128, *op. cit.*; Goss, Chris, *op. cit.* (pp. 65-73); Ramsey, Winston. G. (ed.), *op. cit.* (*Luftwaffe* entry for 12 August 1940).
133. Ramsey, Winston. G. (ed.), *op. cit.* (*Luftwaffe* entry for 12 August 1940); Parker, Nigel, *op. cit.* (entry for 12 August 1940).
134. Air Ministry Operational Record Books, No. 11 (Fighter) Group, Appendices, 1 September 1939–30 September 1940 (Air 25/197 records, National Archives); IPR, 152 Squadron, 12 August 1940 (Air 16/955 records, National Archives); James, T. Cecil G., *op. cit.* (pp. 65-67).
135. CRs, Sgt E. E. Shepperd, F/Lt F. M. Thomas and F/O E. S. Hogg, 152 Squadron, 12 August 1940 (respectively, Air 50/64/25, Air 50/64/11 and Air 50/64/87 records, National Archives).
136. CR, P/O T. S. Wildblood, 152 Squadron, 12 August 1940 (Air 50/64/94 records, National Archives); Burt, Danny, *A Battle of Britain Spitfire Squadron: the men and machines of 152 Squadron in the summer of 1940* (Barnsley: Pen and Sword, 2018) (p. 200).
137. Ramsey, Winston. G. (ed.), *op. cit.* (RAF entry for 12 August 1940); Burt, Danny, *op. cit.* (p. 245).
138. Website, Wood, Tony, *op. cit.*
139. Goss, Chris, *op. cit.* (pp. 65-73); Ramsey, Winston. G. (ed.), *op. cit.* (*Luftwaffe* entry for 12 August 1940); Townsend, Peter, *Duel of Eagles* (London: Weidenfeld and Nicolson, 1970) (pp. 305-306); McKee, Alexander, *Strike from the Sky – The Battle of Britain Story* (London: New English Library, 1969) (pp. 75-78).
140. Goss, Chris, *op. cit.* (pp. 65-73); Ramsey, Winston. G. (ed.), *op. cit.* (*Luftwaffe* entry for 12 August 1940).
141. CR, P/O T. S. Wildblood, 152 Squadron, 12 August 1940 (Air 50/64/94 records, National Archives).
142. McKee, Alexander, *op. cit.* (pp. 75-78).
143. James, T. Cecil G., *op. cit.* (pp. 65-67).
144. Mason, Francis K., *op. cit.* (pp. 231-233).
145. Ramsey, Winston. G. (ed.), *op. cit.* (*Luftwaffe* entry for 12 August 1940); Parker, Nigel, *op. cit.* (entry for 12 August 1940).
146. Notes 142 and 144, *op. cit.*
147. Goss, Chris, *op. cit.* (pp. 65-73).

148. CR, P/O W. S. Williams, 266 Squadron, 12 August 1940 (Air 50 records, National Archives).
149. IPR, 266 Squadron, 12 August 1940 (Air 16/955 records, National Archives).
150. *Ibid.*
151. Note 149, *op. cit.*; CR, S/L R. L. Wilkinson, 266 Squadron, 12 August 1940 (Air 50 records, National Archives).
152. CR, S/L R. L. Wilkinson, 266 Squadron, 12 August 1940 (Air 50 records, National Archives).
153. CRs, Sgts R. V. Baraclough and D. E. Kingaby, 266 Squadron, 12 August 1940 (respectively, Air 50/105/5 and Air 50/105/36 records, National Archives).
154. Note 149, *op. cit.*
155. Squadron Commander's Report on Flying Battle Casualty, P/O D. G. Ashton, 266 Squadron, 12 August 1940 (Air 81/1345 records, National Archives).
156. CR, P/O N. G. Bowen, 266 Squadron, 12 August 1940 (Air 50/105/12 records, National Archives).
157. Note 148, *op. cit.*; Ramsey, Winston. G. (ed.), *op. cit.* (RAF entry for 12 August 1940).
158. ORB, Records of Events (Form 541), 609 Squadron, 12 August 1940 (Air 27/2102/16 records, National Archives); CR, P/O D. M. Crook, 609 Squadron, 12 August 1940 (Air 50/171/15 records, National Archives).
159. ORB, Records of Events (Form 541), 609 Squadron, 12 August 1940 (Air 27/2102/16 records, National Archives).
160. CR, P/O C. N. Overton, 609 Squadron, 12 August 1940 (Air 50/171/57 records, National Archives).
161. CR, F/Lt J. H. G. McArthur, 609 Squadron, 12 August 1940 (Air 50/171/41 records, National Archives).
162. CR, P/O D. M. Crook, 609 Squadron, 12 August 1940 (Air 50/171/15 records, National Archives).
163. Note 160, *op. cit.*
164. *Ibid.*
165. CR, F/O H. M. Goodwin, 609 Squadron, 12 August 1940 (Air 50/171/31 records, National Archives).
166. *Ibid.*
167. *Ibid.*
168. CR, P/O M. E. Staples, 609 Squadron, 12 August 1940 (Air 50/171/70 records, National Archives).
169. CR, F/O J. C. Dundas, 609 Squadron, 12 August 1940 (Air 50/171/24 records, National Archives).

170. ORB, Records of Events (Form 541), 609 Squadron, 12 August 1940 (Air 27/2102/16 records, National Archives).
171. CR, F/Lt J. H. G. McArthur, 609 Squadron, 12 August 1940 (Air 50/171/41 records, National Archives).
172. Ibid.
173. CR, P/O J. C. Newbery, 609 Squadron, 12 August 1940 (Air 50/171/48 records, National Archives).
174. Ibid.
175. CR, P/O R. F. G. Miller, 609 Squadron, 12 August 1940 (Air 50/171/44 records, National Archives).
176. CR, P/O N. le C. Agazarian, 609 Squadron, 12 August 1940 (Air 50/171/1 records, National Archives).
177. Ibid.
178. CR, P/O D. M. Crook, 609 Squadron, 12 August 1940 (Air 50/171/15 records, National Archives).
179. Ibid.
180. ORB, Records of Events (Form 541), 609 Squadron, 12 August 1940 (Air 27/2102/16 records, National Archives).
181. Ramsey, Winston. G. (ed.), *op. cit.* (RAF entry for 12 August 1940).
182. Bergström, Christer, *op. cit.* (pp. 100-102).
183. CR, S/L H. Harkness, 257 Squadron, 12 August 1940 (Air 50 records, National Archives).
184. CR, P/O A. C. Cochrane, 257 Squadron, 12 August 1940 (Air 50/100/18 records, National Archives).
185. IPR, 257 Squadron, 12 August 1940 (Air 16/955 records, National Archives).
186. Ibid.
187. Ibid.
188. Ibid.
189. Ibid.
190. Ibid.
191. Ibid.
192. Ibid.
193. CR, P/O C. F. A. Capon, 257 Squadron, 12 August 1940 (Air 50 records, National Archives).
194. IPR, 257 Squadron, 12 August 1940 (Air 16/955 records, National Archives).
195. Wynn, Kenneth G., *op. cit.* (p.223).
196. Ibid.
197. See for example: Willis, John, *Churchill's Few: The Battle of Britain Remembered* (London: Michael Joseph, 1985) (pp. 88-90, p. 115 etc.); Thomas, Nick, *Hurricane Squadron Ace: The Story of Battle*

Notes

of Britain Ace Air Commodore Peter 'Pete' Brothers, CBE, DSO, DFC and Bar* (Barnsley: Pen and Sword, 2014) (pp. 133-135), this book gives a much more balanced view and defends S/L Harkness in many ways, especially his courage.

198. Willis, John, 1985, *op. cit.*; Willis, John, *Secret Letters: A Battle of Britain Love Story* (London: Mensch Publishing, 2020).
199. Willis, John, 1985, *op. cit.* (p. 124); Wynn, Kenneth G., *op. cit.* (p. 41), and updates to Wynn book: https://www.battleofbritainmemorial.org/men-of-the-battle-updates-and-additions/
200. IPR, 257 Squadron, 12 August 1940 (Air 16/955 records, National Archives).
201. Willis, John, 2020, *op. cit.* (Author's Note, Kindle edition).
202. Willis, John, 1985, *op. cit.* (p. 124).
203. ORB, Summary of Events (Form 540) and Records of Events (Form 541), 257 Squadron, August - September 1940 (Air 27 records, National Archives).
204. Sarkar, Dilip, *The Few: The Story of the Battle of Britain in the Words of the Pilots* (Stroud: Amberley, 2012) (p. 33).
205. IPRs, 257 Squadron, 3 and 7 September 1940 (Air 16/955 records, National Archives).
206. Thomas, Nick, *op. cit.* (pp. 133-135).
207. This combat report is cited in: IPR, 257 Squadron, 12 August 1940 (Air 16/955 records, National Archives).
208. ORB, Summary of Events (Form 540), 145 Squadron, 12 August 1940 (Air 27 records, National Archives).
209. CRs, F/Lt R. G. Dutton, P/O J. E. Storrar and F/O R. M. B. Rowley, 145 Squadron, 12 August 1940 (Air 50 records, National Archives for Dutton and Storrar; Air 50/62/58 records, National Archives for Rowley).
210. CR, F/Lt R. G. Dutton, 145 Squadron, 12 August 1940 (Air 50 records, National Archives).
211. Note 210, *op. cit.*; CR, F/O W. Urbanowicz, 145 Squadron, 12 August 1940, copy in Gretzyngier, Robert, *op. cit.* (p. 16).
212. CR, F/O W. Urbanowicz, 145 Squadron, 12 August 1940, copy in Gretzyngier, Robert, *op. cit.* (p. 16).
213. Note 211, *op. cit.*
214. CR, P/O P. L. Parrott, 145 Squadron, 12 August 1940 (Air 50 records, National Archives).
215. CR, F/Lt A. H. Boyd, 145 Squadron, 12 August 1940 (Air 50/62/37 records, National Archives).
216. Note 215, *op. cit.*; Ramsey, Winston. G. (ed.), *op. cit.* (RAF entry for 12 August 1940).

217. CR, P/O J. E. Storrar, 145 Squadron, 12 August 1940 (Air 50 records, National Archives).
218. Notes 217 and 215, *op. cit.*; ORB, Form 540 (Summary of Events), 145 Squadron, 12 August 1940 (Air 27 records, National Archives).
219. CR, F/O R. M. B. Rowley, 145 Squadron, 12 August 1940 (Air 50/62/58 records, National Archives).
220. Ramsey, Winston. G. (ed.), *op. cit.* (RAF entry for 12 August 1940).
221. Goss, Chris, *Brothers in Arms: The Story of a British and a German Fighter Unit, August to December 1940* (Barnsley: Air World/Pen and Sword, 2020) (p. 145).
222. Prien, Jochen, *op. cit.* (pp. 175-177), *Gefechtsbericht* of *Hpt* Mayer and other related engagements.
223. Prien, Jochen, *op. cit.* (pp. 175-177); Goss, Chris, 2020, *op. cit.* (pp. 142-146).
224. Website, Wood, Tony, *op. cit.*
225. For example, Goss, Chris, 2020, *op. cit.* (p. 145).
226. ORB, Records of Events (Form 541), 145 Squadron, 12 August 1940 (Air 27/984/8 records, National Archives).
227. Goss, Chris, *The Luftwaffe Fighters' Battle of Britain: The inside story: July – October 1940* (Manchester: Crécy, 2010) (pp. 38-39).
228. Note 224, *op. cit.*
229. Prien, Jochen, *op. cit.* (p. 177); Goss, Chris, 2010, *op. cit.* (pp. 38-39).
230. A reasonably detailed analysis of the complexities and often confusion implicit in the German claims system is given in: Eriksson, Patrick G., *Alarmstart East: The German Fighter Pilot's Experience on the Eastern Front 1941-1945* (Stroud: Amberley, 2020) (pp. 233-270).
231. Website, Wood, Tony, *op. cit.*
232. Prien, Jochen, *op. cit.* (pp. 175-177); Note 231, *op. cit.*
233. ORB, Form 540 (Summary of Events), 145 Squadron, 12 August 1940 (Air 27 records, National Archives).
234. IPR, 43 Squadron, 12 August 1940 (Air 16/955 records, National Archives); CR, P/O F. R. Carey, 43 Squadron, 12 August 1940 (Air 50 records, National Archives).
235. CR, P/O F. R. Carey, 43 Squadron, 12 August 1940 (Air 50 records, National Archives).
236. *Ibid.*
237. CR, P/O C. A. Woods-Scawen, 43 Squadron, 12 August 1940 (Air 50 records, National Archives).
238. Notes 235 and 237, *op. cit.*

239. IPR, 43 Squadron, 12 August 1940 (Air 16/955 records, National Archives).
240. ORB, Form 541 (Records of Events), 213 Squadron, 12 August 1940 (Air 27 records, National Archives); CR, F/Lt J. E. J. Sing, 213 Squadron, 12 August 1940 (Air 50 records, National Archives).
241. CRs, F/Lt J. E. J. Sing, F/O J. M. Strickland, Sgt G. D. Bushell, P/O H. W. Cottam, P/O H. D. Atkinson and F/Sgt C. Grayson, 213 Squadron, 12 August 1940 (Air 50 records, National Archives for Sing, Strickland, Bushell and Cottam; Air 50/83/17 records, National Archives for Atkinson, and Air 50/83/27 records, National Archives for Grayson).
242. CR, S/L H. D. McGregor, 213 Squadron, 12 August 1940 (Air 50 records, National Archives).
243. CRs, F/Lt J. E. J. Sing and F/O J. M. Strickland, 213 Squadron, 12 August 1940 (Air 50 records, National Archives).
244. CR, F/Lt J. E. J. Sing, 213 Squadron, 12 August 1940 (Air 50 records, National Archives).
245. CR, F/O J. M. Strickland, 213 Squadron, 12 August 1940 (Air 50 records, National Archives).
246. Prien, Jochen, *op. cit.* (p. 270).
247. Prien, Jochen, *op. cit.* (p. 177, p. 270).
248. CR, Sgt G. D. Bushell, 213 Squadron, 12 August 1940 (Air 50 records, National Archives).
249. *Ibid.*
250. CR, P/O H. D. Atkinson, 213 Squadron, 12 August 1940 (Air 50/83/17 records, National Archives).
251. CR, F/Sgt C. Grayson, 213 Squadron, 12 August 1940 (Air 50/83/27 records, National Archives).
252. CR, P/O H. W. Cottam, 213 Squadron, 12 August 1940 (Air 50 records, National Archives).
253. Air Ministry Operational Record Books, No. 11 (Fighter) Group, Appendices, 1 September 1939–30 September 1940 (Air 25/197 records, National Archives). These records include the Fighter Command Aircraft Combats which list numbers of aircraft scrambled for each RAF fighter squadron, mission times, claims and losses, and approximate area of engagements, on a daily basis.
254. Squadron Commander's Reports on Flying Battle Casualty, Sgts G. N. Wilkes and S. G. Stuckey, 213 Squadron, 12 August 1940 (Respectively Air 81/1335 and Air 81/2581 records, National Archives).
255. Website, Holm, Michael, *op. cit.*

Adlertag

256. Ramsey, Winston. G. (ed.), *op. cit.* (*Luftwaffe* entry for 12 August 1940); Parker, Nigel, *op. cit.* (entry for 12 August 1940).
257. *Ibid.*
258. *Ibid.*
259. Website, Wood, Tony, *op. cit.*
260. *Lageberichte Luftflottenkommando 3, op. cit.* (entries for 12 August 1940).
261. James, T. Cecil G., *op. cit.* (pp. 70-71).
262. *Ibid.*
263. Mason, Francis K., *op. cit.* (pp. 231-233).
264. Bekker, Cajus, *op. cit.* (pp. 186-189).
265. Notes 261 and 264, *op. cit.*
266. James, T. Cecil G., *op. cit.* (pp. 67-68).
267. *Ibid.*
268. *Ibid.*
269. Note 266, *op. cit.*; Vasco, John, *op. cit.* (pp. 54-56).
270. Goss, Chris, *Dornier Do 17 Units of World War 2* (Oxford: Osprey, 2019), Combat Aircraft Series #129 (p. 51); Bergström, Christer, *op. cit.* (p. 102).
271. Barbas, Bernd, *Die Geschichte der I. Gruppe des Jagdgeschwaders 52* (Überlingen: self-published, undated) (pp. 96-97).
272. Barbas, Bernd, II/JG 52, *op. cit.* (p. 299).
273. Prien, Jochen and Stemmer, Gerhard, *Messerschmitt Bf 109 im Einsatz bei der III./Jagdgeschwader 3* (Eutin: Struve-Druck, 1995) (p. 38); Website, Wood, Tony, *op. cit.*
274. Flying logbook, *Uffz* Hans-Helmut Habermehl, *1/JG 54*, entries for 12 August 1940, copy of logbook courtesy of Peter Arnot, operation from 12h17 – 13h40.
275. James, T. Cecil G., *op. cit.* (pp. 67-68).
276. Air Ministry Operational Record Books, No. 11 (Fighter) Group, Appendices, 1 September 1939 – 30 September 1940 (Air 25/197 records, National Archives).
277. Note 275, *op. cit.*
278. ORB, Summary of Events (Form 540), 615 Squadron, 12 August 1940 (Air 27/2123/15 records, National Archives); CR, P/O P. H. Hugo, 615 Squadron, 12 August 1940 (Air 50/175/13 records, National Archives).
279. Parker, Nigel, *op. cit.* (entry for 12 August 1940).
280. James, T. Cecil G., *op. cit.* (pp. 67-68).
281. Prien, Jochen and Stemmer, Gerhard, 1995, *op. cit.* (p. 38).
282. Website, Wood, Tony, *op. cit.* Interestingly, this claim was only confirmed two years after the event!

Notes

283. James, T. Cecil G., *op. cit.* (pp. 67-68).
284. *Ibid.*
285. *Ibid.*
286. Vasco, John, *op. cit.* (pp. 54-56); Dildy, Douglas C. and Crickmore, Paul F., *op. cit.* (pp. 203-204); Goss, Chris, 2019, *op. cit.* (p. 51).
287. Note 283, *op. cit.*
288. Bekker, Cajus, *op. cit.* (p. 190).
289. Vasco, John, *op. cit.* (pp. 54-56).
290. *Ibid.*
291. *Ibid.*
292. IPR, 65 Squadron, 12 August 1940 (Air 16/955 records, National Archives) (take off time *c.* 12h30; was one earlier IPR this day, take off time *c.* 10h30/11h00).
293. Olive, Gordon and Newton, Dennis (Editor), *Spitfire Ace: My Life as a Battle of Britain Fighter Pilot* (Stroud: Amberley, 2015) (pp. 146-148); Quill, Jeffrey, *Spitfire: A Test Pilot's Story* (London: Arrow, 1985) (pp. 167-169).
294. Olive, Gordon and Newton, Dennis, *op. cit.* (pp. 146-148).
295. *Ibid.*
296. *Ibid.*
297. *Ibid.*
298. Notes 292 and 293, *op. cit.*
299. ORB, 65 Squadron, 12 August 1940, Summary of Events (includes both Summary and Records of Events for this unit) for *c.* 12h45 engagement (Air 27/592/5 records, National Archives).
300. Quill, Jeffrey, *op. cit.* (pp. 167-169).
301. Olive, Gordon and Newton, Dennis, *op. cit.* (pp. 146-148).
302. *Ibid.*
303. *Ibid.*
304. Quill, Jeffrey, *op. cit.* (pp. 167-169).
305. CRs, P/Os F. S. Gregory and B. E. F. Finucane, 65 Squadron, 12 August 1940 (appendices to 65 Squadron ORB, Air 27/956 records, courtesy of Nigel Parker) (take off time *c.* 12h30).
306. IPR, 65 Squadron, 12 August 1940 (Air 16/955 records, National Archives) (take off time *c.* 12h30).
307. *Ibid.*
308. *Ibid.*
309. *Ibid.*
310. IPR, 501 Squadron, 12 August 1940 (Air 16/955 records, National Archives) (take off time *c.* 12h20; were two other IPRs this day, take off times *c.* 10h30 and 17h25).
311. *Ibid.*

312. *Ibid.*
313. CRs, F/O S. Witorzenc and F/Lt G. E. B. Stoney, 501 Squadron, 12 August 1940 (respectively, Air 50/162/61 and Air 50/162/58 records, National Archives).
314. CR, Sgt J. H. Lacey, 501 Squadron, 12 August 1940 (Air 50/162/34 records, National Archives).
315. Squadron Commander's Report on Flying Battle Casualty, F/O K. Lukaszewicz, 501 Squadron, 12 August 1940 (Air 81/1384 records, National Archives).
316. IPR, 501 Squadron, 12 August 1940 (Air 16/955 records, National Archives) (take off time *c.* 12h20); Vasco, John, *op. cit.* (p. 159).
317. Vasco, John, *op. cit.* (pp. 54-56).
318. Barbas, Bernd, I/JG 52, *op. cit.* (pp. 96-97 and p. 352).
319. James, T. Cecil G., *op. cit.* (pp. 67-68).
320. IPR, 615 Squadron, 12 August 1940 (Air 16/955 records, National Archives).
321. CR, F/Lt L. M. Gaunce, 615 Squadron, 12 August 1940 (Air 50 records, National Archives).
322. CR, P/O P. H. Hugo, 615 Squadron, 12 August 1940 (Air 50/175/13 records, National Archives).
323. CR, P/O J. A. P. McClintock, 615 Squadron, 12 August 1940 (Air 50/175/21 records, National Archives).
324. Note 320, *op. cit.*
325. Barbas, Bernd, II/JG 52, *op. cit.* (pp. 32-33, and p. 299).
326. Website, Wood, Tony, *op. cit.*
327. Barbas, Bernd, II/JG 52, *op. cit.* (p. 327).
328. Parker, Nigel, *op. cit.* (entry for 12 August 1940).
329. CRs, F/Lt L. M. Gaunce, P/O P. H. Hugo and P/O J. A. P. McClintock, 615 Squadron, 12 August 1940 (respectively, Air 50 records, Air 50/175/13 records and Air 50/175/21 records, National Archives).
330. Note 328, *op. cit.*
331. CR, P/O J. A. P. McClintock, 615 Squadron, 12 August 1940 (Air 50/175/21 records, National Archives).
332. Wood, Derek and Dempster, Derek, *op. cit.* (p. 279).
333. James, T. Cecil G., *op. cit.* (pp. 68-70).
334. *Ibid.*
335. IPR, 54 Squadron, 12 August 1940 (Air 16/955 records, National Archives) (take off time *c.* 17h10; was one earlier IPR this day, take off time *c.* 07h30); IPR, 56 Squadron, 12 August 1940 (Air 16/955 records, National Archives); James, T. Cecil G., *op. cit.* (pp. 68-70).
336. James, T. Cecil G., *op. cit.* (pp. 68-70).

Notes

337. Dildy, Douglas C. and Crickmore, Paul F., *op. cit.* (pp. 204-206).
338. Goss, Chris, 2019, *op. cit.* (pp. 51-52).
339. James, T. Cecil G., *op. cit.* (pp. 68-70).
340. Dildy, Douglas C. and Crickmore, Paul F., *op. cit.* (pp. 204-206).
341. *Ibid.*
342. Website, Holm, Michael, *op. cit.*
343. CR, F/Lt M. N. Crossley, 32 Squadron, 12 August 1940, 17h30 (Air 50/16/31 records, National Archives; are two reports under the same reference, one timed at 17h30 and the other at 17h50).
344. Notes 336 and 337, *op. cit.*
345. *Ibid.*
346. Caldwell, Donald L., *op. cit.* (pp. 52-54).
347. For example: Wood, Derek and Dempster, Derek, *op. cit.* (p. 279); Barbas, Bernd, II/JG 52, *op. cit.* (pp. 32-33); Knight, Dennis, *op. cit.* (pp. 90-91).
348. Vasco, John, *op. cit.* (pp. 54-56).
349. Hough, Richard and Richards, Denis, *op. cit.*, (pp. 149-151).
350. *Ibid.*
351. James, T. Cecil G., *op. cit.* (pp. 68-70).
352. Ramsey, Winston. G. (ed.), *op. cit.* (p. 107, in Chapter on Hawkinge airfield).
353. Dildy, Douglas C. and Crickmore, Paul F., *op. cit.* (pp. 204-206).
354. Eriksson, Patrick G., *Tally-Ho: RAF tactical leadership in the Battle of Britain July 1940* (Stroud: Amberley, 2023) (p. 93).
355. Dildy, Douglas C. and Crickmore, Paul F., *op. cit.* (pp. 204-206).
356. Prien, Jochen and Stemmer, Gerhard, 1995, *op. cit.* (p. 38); Prien, Jochen and Stemmer, Gerhard, *Messerschmitt Bf 109 im Einsatz bei der II./Jagdgeschwader 3* (Eutin: Struve-Druck, 1996) (p. 18); Prien, Jochen and Stemmer, Gerhard, *Messerschmitt Bf 109 im Einsatz bei Stab und I./Jagdgeschwader 3* (Eutin: Struve-Druck, 1997) (p. 80).
357. James, T. Cecil G., *op. cit.* (pp. 68-70).
358. CRs, F/O P. S. Weaver, F/Sgt G. Smythe and F/Sgt F. W. Higginson, 56 Squadron, 12 August 1940 (respectively, Air 50 records, Air 50/22/52 and 50/22/29 records, National Archives).
359. CRs, P/O D. Hamilton Grice, F/Lt M. N. Crossley (17h30 report) and P/O K. Pniak, 32 Squadron, 12 August 1940 (respectively, Air 50/16/11, Air 50/16/31 and Air 50/16/20 records, National Archives).
360. CRs, F/O H. J. Woodward, Sgt P. S. Hawke and F/Lt L. F. Henstock, 64 Squadron, 12 August 1940 (respectively, Air 50 records, Air 50/24/31 and Air 50/24/33 records, National Archives).
361. Mason, Francis K., *op. cit.* (p. 234).

362. James, T. Cecil G., *op. cit.* (pp. 68-70).
363. *Fliegerblatt*, Official Publication of the *Gemeinschaft der Flieger Deutscher Streitkräfte E.V.*, No. 6 of 2008 (pp. 119-120; *Reaktionen auf Suchanzeigen: Oblt Albrecht Drehs, III/JG 54*).
364. Flying logbook, *Uffz* Hans-Helmut Habermehl, *1/JG 54*, entries for 12 August 1940, copy of logbook courtesy of Peter Arnot, operation from *c.* 17h15-18h15.
365. Bergström, Christer, *op. cit.* (p. 103).
366. Website, Wood, Tony, *op. cit.*
367. Steinhilper, Ulrich and Osborne, Peter, *op. cit.* (pp. 288-289).
368. Barbas, Bernd, II/JG 52, *op. cit.* (pp. 32-33).
369. Barbas, Bernd, II/JG 52, *op. cit.* (pp. 32-33, p. 299, p. 327).
370. Website, Wood, Tony, *op. cit.*
371. Caldwell, Donald L., *op. cit.* (pp. 52-54).
372. Note 370, *op. cit.*
373. Note 371, *op. cit.*
374. IPR, 32 Squadron, 12 August 1940 (Air 16/955 records, National Archives).
375. CR, F/Lt M. N. Crossley, 32 Squadron, 12 August 1940 (17h30 report) (Air 50/16/31 records, National Archives).
376. CRs, P/O D. Hamilton Grice, F/Lt M. N. Crossley (17h30 report), P/O K. Pniak, P/O J. E. Proctor, F/O J. B. W. Humpherson, P/O P. M. Gardner, Sgt E. R. Bayley and P/O R. F. Smythe, 32 Squadron, 12 August 1940 (respectively, Air 50/16/11, Air 50/16/31, Air 50/16/20, Air 50/16/21, Air 50/16/14, Air 50/16/8 records, and Air 50 records (Bayley, Smythe), National Archives).
377. CRs, P/O D. Hamilton Grice, F/Lt M. N. Crossley (17h30 report), P/O J. E. Proctor, Sgt E. R. Bayley and P/O R. F. Smythe, 32 Squadron, 12 August 1940 (respectively, Air 50/16/11, Air 50/16/31, Air 50/16/21, and Air 50 records (Bayley, Smythe), National Archives).
378. CRs, P/O K. Pniak, F/O J. B. W. Humpherson, P/O P. M. Gardner and Sgt W. B. Higgins, 32 Squadron, 12 August 1940 (respectively, Air 50/16/20, Air 50/16/14, Air 50/16/8 and Air 50/16/13 records, National Archives).
379. CRs, F/Lt M. N. Crossley (17h30 report) and P/O K. Pniak, 32 Squadron, 12 August 1940 (respectively, Air 50/16/31 and Air 50/16/20 records, National Archives).
380. CRs, F/Lt M. N. Crossley (17h30 report), P/O K. Pniak, F/O J. B. W. Humpherson and Sgt W. B. Higgins, 32 Squadron, 12 August 1940 (respectively, Air 50/16/31, Air 50/16/20, Air 50/16/14 and Air 50/16/13 records, National Archives).

Notes

381. Ramsey, Winston. G. (ed.), *op. cit.* (RAF entry for 12 August 1940); Thomas, Nick, *op. cit.* (p. 90).
382. CRs, F/Lt M. N. Crossley (17h50 report) and P/O J. E. Proctor, 32 Squadron, 12 August 1940 (respectively, Air 50/16/31 and Air 50/16/21 records, National Archives).
383. CR, P/O P. M. Gardner, 32 Squadron, 12 August 1940 (Air 50/16/8 records, National Archives).
384. IPR, 32 Squadron, 12 August 1940 (Air 16/955 records, National Archives).
385. CR, P/O R. F. Smythe, 32 Squadron, 12 August 1940 (Air 50 records, National Archives).
386. *Ibid.*
387. *Ibid.*
388. Vasco, John, *op. cit.* (pp. 54-56).
389. CR, Sgt E. A. Bayley, 32 Squadron, 12 August 1940 (Air 50 records, National Archives).
390. *Ibid.*
391. CR, P/O D. Hamilton Grice, 32 Squadron, 12 August 1940 (Air 50/16/11 records, National Archives). No grammatical corrections made to CRs in this volume.
392. IPR, 32 Squadron, 12 August 1940 (Air 16/955 records, National Archives).
393. ORB, Records of Events (Form 541), 64 Squadron, 12 August 1940 (Air 27/589/22 records, National Archives).
394. CR, F/Lt L. F. Henstock, 64 Squadron, 12 August 1940 (Air 50/24/33 records, National Archives).
395. ORB, Summary of Events (Form 540), 64 Squadron, 12 August 1940 (Air 27/589/21 records, National Archives).
396. Note 393, *op. cit.*
397. CR, P/O J. J. O'Meara, 64 Squadron, 12 August 1940 (Air 50/24/86 records, National Archives).
398. IPR, 64 Squadron, 12 August 1940 (Air 16/955 records, National Archives).
399. CR, Sgt J. Mann, 64 Squadron, 12 August 1940 (Air 50/24/85 records, National Archives).
400. Note 394, *op. cit.*
401. CR, F/O H. J. Woodward, 64 Squadron, 12 August 1940 (Air 50 records, National Archives).
402. Note 399, *op. cit.*
403. Notes 399 and 397, *op. cit.*
404. Note 399, *op. cit.*
405. Note 397, *op. cit.*

406. CR, F/Lt L. F. Henstock, 64 Squadron, 12 August 1940 (Air 50/24/33 records, National Archives).
407. IPR, 64 Squadron, 12 August 1940 (Air 16/955 records, National Archives).
408. Ramsey, Winston. G. (ed.), *op. cit.* (RAF entry for 12 August 1940).
409. CR, Sgt P. S. Hawke, 64 Squadron, 12 August 1940 (Air 50/24/31 records, National Archives).
410. *Ibid.*
411. Vasco, John, *op. cit.* (pp. 54-56); Goss, Chris, 2019, *op. cit.* (pp. 51-52).
412. Donahue, Arthur G., *Tally-Ho! Yankee in a Spitfire* (The War Vault, 2021) (pp. 50-54); Squadron Commander's Report on Flying Battle Casualty, P/O A. G. Donahue, 64 Squadron, 12 August 1940 (Air 81/1387 records, National Archives).
413. Ramsey, Winston. G. (ed.), *op. cit.* (RAF entry for 12 August 1940).
414. IPR, 64 Squadron, 12 August 1940 (Air 16/955 records, National Archives).
415. Barbas, Bernd, II/JG 52, *op. cit.* (pp. 32-33, p. 327).
416. Website, Wood, Tony, *op. cit.*
417. IPR, 501 Squadron, 12 August 1940 (Air 16/955 records, National Archives) (take off time *c.* 17h25; were two earlier IPRs this day, take off times *c.* 10h30 and *c.* 12h20).
418. Note 417, *op. cit.*; CR, P/O J. A. A. Gibson, 501 Squadron, 12 August 1940 (Air 50/162/21 records, National Archives).
419. Note 417, *op. cit.*
420. Chance Vought VF 156 aircraft; https://en.wikipedia.org/wiki/Vought_SB2U_Vindicator
421. Note 418, *op. cit.*
422. CR, P/O J. A. A. Gibson, 501 Squadron, 12 August 1940 (Air 50/162/21 records, National Archives).
423. IPR, 501 Squadron, 12 August 1940 (Air 16/955 records, National Archives) (take off time *c.* 17h25).
424. Note 422, *op. cit.*
425. Note 423, *op. cit.*
426. Ramsey, Winston. G. (ed.), *op. cit.* (RAF entry for 12 August 1940).
427. Notes 422 and 423, *op. cit.*
428. IPR, 56 Squadron, 12 August 1940 (Air 16/955 records, National Archives).
429. Page, Geoffrey, *Tale of a Guinea Pig* (London: Corgi, 1983) (pp. 88-98).
430. Revell, Alex, *Fighter Aces! The Constable Maxwell Brothers; Fighter Pilots in two World Wars* (Barnsley: Pen and Sword, 2010) (pp. 124-125).

Notes

431. IPR, 56 Squadron, 12 August 1940 (Air 16/955 records, National Archives); CR, F/O P. S. Weaver, 56 Squadron, 12 August 1940 (Air 50 records, National Archives); CR, F/Sgt G. Smythe, 56 Squadron, 12 August 1940 (Air 50/22/52 records, National Archives).
432. *Ibid.*
433. Note 430, *op. cit.*; McKee, Alexander, *op. cit.* (pp. 79-82).
434. *Ibid.*
435. CR, F/Sgt F. W. Higginson, 56 Squadron, 12 August 1940 (Air 50/22/29 records, National Archives).
436. McKee, Alexander, *op. cit.* (pp. 79-82).
437. Squadron Commander's Report on Flying Battle Casualty, P/O A. G. Page, 56 Squadron, 12 August 1940 (Air 81/1340 records, National Archives).
438. Page, Geoffrey, *op. cit.* (pp. 88-98).
439. Note 436, *op. cit.*
440. Notes 436 and 438, *op. cit.*
441. *Ibid.*
442. CR, F/Sgt F. W. Higginson, 56 Squadron, 12 August 1940 (Air 50/22/29 records, National Archives).
443. *Ibid.*
444. Sutton, Barry, *Fighter Boy; Life as a Battle of Britain Pilot* (Stroud: Amberley, 2010) (pp. 154-156).
445. *Ibid.*
446. *Ibid.*
447. CR, F/O P. S. Weaver, 56 Squadron, 12 August 1940 (Air 50 records, National Archives).
448. For example, Ramsey, Winston. G. (ed.), *op. cit.* (*Luftwaffe* entry for 12 August 1940).
449. Bergström, Christer, *op. cit.* (p. 103); Goss, Chris, 2019, *op. cit.* (pp. 51-52).
450. Goss, Chris, 2019, *op. cit.* (pp. 51-52).
451. Bergström, Christer, *op. cit.* (p. 103).
452. IPR, 56 Squadron, 12 August 1940 (Air 16/955 records, National Archives).
453. CRs, P/O D. Hamilton Grice, Sgt E. R. Bayley and P/O R. F. Smythe, 32 Squadron, 12 August 1940 (respectively, Air 50/16/11, and Air 50 records (Bayley, Smythe), National Archives).
454. IPR, 56 Squadron, 12 August 1940 (Air 16/955 records, National Archives); CR, F/Sgt G. Smythe, 56 Squadron, 12 August 1940 (Air 50/22/52 records, National Archives).
455. *Ibid.*

Adlertag

456. IPR, 56 Squadron, 12 August 1940 (Air 16/955 records, National Archives).
457. Ramsey, Winston. G. (ed.), *op. cit.* (*Luftwaffe* entry for 12 August 1940); Bergström, Christer, *op. cit.* (p. 103); Note 363, *op. cit.*; Website, Wood, Tony, *op. cit.*
458. IPRs, 32, 54 (take off time *c.* 17h10) and 56 Squadrons, 12 August 1940 (all Air 16/955 records, National Archives); CRs, P/O P. M. Gardner, Sgt W. B. Higgins and P/O K. Pniak, 32 Squ., 12 August 1940 (respectively Air 50/16/8, Air 50/16/13 and Air 50/16/20 records, National Archives).
459. Website, Wood, Tony, *op. cit.*
460. CR, F/Lt A. C. Deere, 54 Squadron, 12 August 1940 (Air 50 records, National Archives).
461. IPR, 54 Squadron, 12 August 1940 (Air 16/955 records, National Archives) (take off time *c.* 17h10).
462. *Ibid.*
463. Note 460, *op. cit.*
464. Notes 460 and 461, *op. cit.*
465. Note 460, *op. cit.*
466. CR, Sgt W. Klosinsky, 54 Squadron, 12 August 1940 (Air 50/21/45 records, National Archives).
467. Ramsey, Winston. G. (ed.), *op. cit.* (*Luftwaffe* entry for 12 August 1940).
468. IPR, 54 Squadron, 12 August 1940 (Air 16/955 records, National Archives) (take off time *c.* 17h10).
469. *Ibid.*
470. *Ibid.*
471. *Ibid.*
472. *Ibid.*
473. IPR, 501 Squadron, 12 August 1940 (Air 16/955 records, National Archives) (take off time *c.* 17h25).
474. Website, Wood, Tony, *op. cit.*
475. *Ibid.*
476. Ramsey, Winston. G. (ed.), *op. cit.* (RAF entry for 12 August 1940).
477. Ramsey, Winston. G. (ed.), *op. cit.* (*Luftwaffe* entry for 12 August 1940).
478. *Ibid.*
479. CR, F/Lt A. C. Deere, 54 Squadron, 12 August 1940 (Air 50 records, National Archives).
480. For example, Dildy, Douglas C. and Crickmore, Paul F., *op. cit.* (pp. 204-206).

Notes

3. Eagle Day: 13 August 1940

1. Dildy, Douglas C. and Crickmore, Paul F., *To Defeat The Few: The Luftwaffe's Campaign to Destroy RAF Fighter Command, August–September 1940* (Oxford: Osprey, 2020) (pp. 210-211).
2. Collier, Basil, *The Battle of Britain* (London: Fontana/Collins, 1969) (pp. 70-73).
3. Operational Record Books (ORBs), Summary of Events (Form 540), 19, 266, 12 and 142 Squadrons, 13 August 1940 (respectively, Air 27/252/22 records, Air 27/1558/9 records, Air 27/164/10 records and Air 27/972/3 records, National Archives).
4. ORB (Form 540), Summary of Events, 19 and 266 Squadrons, 13 August 1940 (respectively, Air 27/252/22 records and Air 27/1558/9 records, National Archives); Bishop, Patrick, *Fighter Boys; Saving Britain 1940* (London: HarperCollins, 2003) (pp. 271-273).
5. Bishop, Patrick, *op. cit.* (pp. 271-273).
6. Dildy, Douglas C. and Crickmore, Paul F., *op. cit.* (pp. 210-211); Collier, Richard, *Eagle Day: the Battle of Britain August 6–September 15 1940* (London: Pan Books, 1969) (pp. 57-64, p. 306); McKee, Alexander, *Strike from the Sky – The Battle of Britain Story* (London: New English Library, 1969) (pp. 85-88).
7. James, T. Cecil G., *The Battle of Britain* (Abingdon: Routledge, 2012) (pp. 71-73); Middleton, Drew, *The Sky Suspended; the Battle of Britain* (London: Pan Books, 1963) (pp. 62-63); McKee, Alexander, *op. cit.* (pp. 85-88); Hough, Richard and Richards, Denis, *The Battle of Britain: The Jubilee History* (London: Penguin, 2001) (pp. 154-157).
8. James, T. Cecil G., *op. cit.* (pp. 71-73).
9. Middleton, Drew, *op. cit.* (pp. 62-63); McKee, Alexander, *op. cit.* (pp. 85-88); Hough, Richard and Richards, Denis, *op. cit.* (pp. 154-157).
10. James, T. Cecil G., *op. cit.* (pp. 71-73); McKee, Alexander, *op. cit.* (pp. 85-88).
11. McKee, Alexander, *op. cit.* (pp. 85-88); Hough, Richard and Richards, Denis, *op. cit.* (pp. 154-157); Collier, Richard, *op. cit.* (pp. 57-64).
12. Note 11, *op. cit.*; Bishop, Patrick, *op. cit.* (pp. 160-163).
13. Collier, Richard, *op. cit.* (pp. 57-64).
14. Dildy, Douglas C. and Crickmore, Paul F., *op. cit.* (pp. 210-211).
15. Ramsey, Winston. G. (ed.), *The Battle of Britain: then and now* (London: Battle of Britain Prints International Ltd., 1982)

(*Luftwaffe* entry for 13 August 1940); Goss, Chris, *Dornier Do 17 units of World War 2* (Oxford: Osprey, 2019) (p. 53).
16. Goss, Chris, *The Luftwaffe Bombers' Battle of Britain* (Manchester: Crécy, 2000) (pp. 74-77); McKee, Alexander, *op. cit.* (pp. 85-88).
17. James, T. Cecil G., *op. cit.* (pp. 71-73).
18. *ibid.*
19. Note 10, *op. cit.*
20. Note 17, *op. cit.*
21. James, T. Cecil G., *op. cit.* (pp. 73-74).
22. Intelligence Patrol Report (IPR), 151Squadron, 13 August 1940 (Air 16/955 records, National Archives).
23. *ibid.*
24. *ibid.*
25. Combat Report (CR), F/Lt R. L. Smith, 151 Squadron, 13 August 1940 (Air 50/63/98 records, National Archives) (no linguistic or grammatical corrections made to CRs cited in this book).
26. Notes 22 and 25, *op. cit.*
27. Parker, Nigel, *Luftwaffe Crash Archive,* Vol. 1 (Walton on Thames: Red Kite Books, Air Research Publications, 2013) (entry for 13 August 1940, Do 17 of 7/KG 2 which crashed at Stodmarsh).
28. Note 25, *op. cit.*
29. *ibid.*
30. Website, *The Battle of Britain London Monument,* The Airmen's Stories – F/Lt. R. L. Smith; www.bbm.org.uk/airmen/SmithRL.htm
31. CR, Sgt J. E. Savill, 151 Squadron, 13 August 1940 (Air 50/63/96 records, National Archives).
32. Ramsey, Winston. G. (ed.), *op. cit.* (*Luftwaffe* entry for 13 August 1940); Parker, Nigel, *op. cit.* (entry for 13 August 1940).
33. Parker, Nigel, *op. cit.* (entry for 13 August 1940).
34. Ramsey, Winston. G. (ed.), *op. cit.* (*Luftwaffe* entry for 13 August 1940).
35. CR, F/O R. M. Milne, 151 Squadron, 13 August 1940 (Air 50/63/86 records, National Archives): there are two 'sub-reports' under this reference, reflecting the two combats he had; in his second sub-report he refers to himself flying as Yellow 1. Yellow Section was part of A Flight, while Milne belonged to B Flight, as recorded in: ORB, Records of Events, 151 Squadron, August 1940 (Air 27/1018/30 records, National Archives). Milne might thus actually have been leading Green Section, an inherent part of B Flight.
36. CR, F/O R. M. Milne, 151 Squadron, 13 August 1940 (Air 50/63/86 records, National Archives), first sub-report.

37. CR, Sgt J. E. Savill, 151 Squadron, 13 August 1940 (Air 50/63/96 records, National Archives).
38. Note 36, *op. cit.*
39. Collier, Richard, *op. cit.* (pp. 57-64).
40. CR, F/O R. M. Milne, 151 Squadron, 13 August 1940 (Air 50/63/86 records, National Archives), first sub-report.
41. Ramsey, Winston. G. (ed.), *op. cit.* (*Luftwaffe* entry for 13 August 1940); Parker, Nigel, *op. cit.* (entry for 13 August 1940); Saunders, Andy, *Finding the Foe; Outstanding Luftwaffe Mysteries of the Battle of Britain and Beyond Investigated and Solved* (London: Grub Street, 2010) (pp. 146-148).
42. *ibid.*
43. CR, Sgt W. M. Skinner, 74 Squadron, 13 August 1940 (Air 50/32/104 records, National Archives); CR, F/O H. M. Ferriss, 111 Squadron, 13 August 1940 (Air 50 records, National Archives).
44. Goss, Chris, 2000, op. cit. (pp. 74-77).
45. *ibid.*
46. IPR, 74 Squadron, 13 August 1940 (Air 16/955 records, National Archives).
47. Note 44, *op. cit.*
48. Collier, Basil, *op. cit.* (pp. 70-73); Dildy, Douglas C. and Crickmore, Paul F., *op. cit.* (pp. 210-211).
49. Note 46, *op. cit.*
50. CR, F/Lt S. Brzezina, 74 Squadron, 13 August 1940 (Air 50/32/10 records, National Archives).
51. CR, S/L A. G. Malan, 74 Squadron, 13 August 1940 (Air 50 records, National Archives).
52. Ramsey, Winston. G. (ed.), *op. cit.* (*Luftwaffe* entry for 13 August 1940).
53. Note 50, *op. cit.*
54. Squadron Commander's Report on Flying Battle Casualty, F/Lt S. Brzezina, 74 Squadron, 13 August 1940 (AIR 81/1390 records, National Archives).
55. Notes 50 and 51, op. cit.
56. IPR, 74 Squadron, 13 August 1940 (Air 16/955 records, National Archives).
57. Collier, Richard, *op. cit.* (pp. 57-64).
58. Ramsey, Winston. G. (ed.), *op. cit.* (*Luftwaffe* entry for 13 August 1940); Parker, Nigel, *op. cit.* (entry for 13 August 1940).
59. Operational Record Books (ORBs) (Form 540), Summary of Events, 12 and 142 Squadrons, 13 August 1940 (respectively, Air 27/164/10 records and Air 27/972/3 records, National Archives).

60. Operational Record Book (Form 540), Summary of Events, 266 Squadron, 13 August 1940 (Air 27/1558/9 records, National Archives).
61. Collier, Richard, *op. cit.* (pp. 57-64).
62. McKee, Alexander, *op. cit.* (pp. 85-88).
63. IPRs, 151, 74, 111 Squadrons, 13 August 1940 (Air 16/955 records, National Archives).
64. CR, S/L J. M. Thompson, 111 Squadron, 13 August 1940 (Air 50 records, National Archives).
65. Note 61, *op. cit.*
66. Ramsey, Winston. G. (ed.), *op. cit.* (*Luftwaffe* entry for 13 August 1940).
67. CR, F/O R. M. Milne, 151 Squadron, 13 August 1940 (Air 50/63/86 records, National Archives), second sub-report.
68. Darlow, Steve, *Five of the Few* (London: Grub Street, 2010) (pp. 66-67).
69. Ramsey, Winston. G. (ed.), *op. cit.* (*Luftwaffe* entry for 13 August 1940); CR, P/O J. C. Freeborn, 74 Squadron, 13 August 1940 (Air 50/32/87 records, National Archives).
70. CR, Sgt W. L. Dymond, 111 Squadron, 13 August 1940 (Air 50/43/23 records, National Archives).
71. CR, Sgt J. T. Craig, 111 Squadron, 13 August 1940 (Air 50/43/19 records, National Archives).
72. Parker, Nigel, *op. cit.* (entry for 13 August 1940).
73. CR, P/O J. C. Freeborn, 74 Squadron, 13 August 1940 (Air 50/32/87 records, National Archives).
74. Ramsey, Winston. G. (ed.), *op. cit.* (*Luftwaffe* entry for 13 August 1940); Saunders, Andy, *op. cit.* (pp. 146-148).
75. CR, F/O H. M. Ferriss, 111 Squadron, 13 August 1940 (Air 50 records, National Archives).
76. CR, P/O A. G. McIntyre, 111 Squadron, 13 August 1940 (Air 50/43/37 records, National Archives).
77. CR, F/O H. Szczesny, 74 Squadron, 13 August 1940 (Air 50/32/112 records, National Archives).
78. Ramsey, Winston. G. (ed.), *op. cit.* (RAF entry for 13 August 1940); Arthur, Max, *Last of the Few: The Battle of Britain in the Words of the Pilots Who Won It* (London: Virgin Books, 2010) (p. 149).
79. IPRs, 151, 74, 111 Squadrons, 13 August 1940 (Air 16/955 records, National Archives).
80. *ibid.*
81. Ramsey, Winston. G. (ed.), *op. cit.* (*Luftwaffe* entry for 13 August 1940).

Notes

82. CR, P/O J. A. Walker, 111 Squadron, 13 August 1940 (Air 50/43/88 records, National Archives).
83. Ramsey, Winston. G. (ed.), *op. cit.* (RAF entry for 13 August 1940).
84. Website, Wood, Tony, *Tony Wood's Combat Claims and Casualties Lists*; accessed via Don Caldwell's website: don-caldwell.we.bs/claims/tonywood.htm. These claims lists are not complete and contain gaps, some large also, especially for certain Me 110 units in 1940; however, they do reflect accredited *Luftwaffe* victory claims and not just submitted and unverified claims.
85. For example: Dildy, Douglas C. and Crickmore, Paul F., *op. cit.* (pp. 210-211) (one 266 Squadron Spitfire lost); Collier, Richard, *op. cit.* (pp. 57-64) (all 266 Squadron Spitfires lost).
86. ORB (Form 540), Summary of Events, 53 Squadron, 13 August 1940 (Air 27/503/21 records, National Archives).
87. ORBs (Form 540), Summary of Events, 19, 12 and 142 Squadrons, 13 August 1940 (respectively, Air 27/252/22 records, Air 27/164/10 records and Air 27/972/3 records, National Archives).
88. ORB (Form 540), Summary of Events, 266 Squadron, 13 August 1940 (Air 27/1558/9 records, National Archives).
89. Ramsey, Winston. G. (ed.), *op. cit.* (RAF entry for 13 August 1940).
90. Dildy, Douglas C. and Crickmore, Paul F., *op. cit.* (pp. 210-211); Collier, Richard, *op. cit.* (pp. 57-64); Bekker, Cajus, *The Luftwaffe War Diaries* (London: Corgi, 1969) (p. 195).
91. Dildy, Douglas C. and Crickmore, Paul F., *op. cit.* (pp. 210-211).
92. James, T. Cecil G., *op. cit.* (pp. 71-73).
93. *ibid.*
94. Dildy, Douglas C. and Crickmore, Paul F., *op. cit.* (p. 374).
95. Note 92, *op. cit.*
96. *ibid.*
97. Details given in: Parker, Nigel, *op. cit.*
98. Processes and methods examined in: Neitzel, Sönke and Welzer, Harald, *Soldaten: On Fighting, Killing and Dying; The Secret World War II Tapes of German POWs* (London: Simon and Schuster, 2012) (especially, pp. vii-x).
99. Transcripts of recorded conversations: File WO208/4118, SRA 111-440; copies very kindly supplied by Nigel Parker from originals held by the National Archives (WO refers to a War Office file; SRA = Special Report Air Force).
100. Transcripts of recorded conversations: File WO208/4118, SRA 382, dated 23 August 1940.
101. Neitzel, Sönke and Welzer, Harald, *op. cit.* (pp. 32-35).

102. Neitzel, Sönke and Welzer, Harald, *op. cit.* (p. 34).
103. For example: Neitzel, Sönke and Welzer, Harald, *op. cit.*
104. Transcripts of recorded conversations: File WO208/4118, SRA 359, dated 19 August 1940.
105. Transcripts of recorded conversations: File WO208/4118, SRA 364, dated 20 August 1940.
106. Transcripts of recorded conversations: File WO208/4118, SRA 382, dated 23 August 1940.
107. Transcripts of recorded conversations: File WO208/4118, SRA 393, dated 25 August 1940.
108. *Lageberichte*, 20.VI.1940-10.X. 1940, *Luftflottenkommando 3*; Records of Headquarters, German Air Force High Command (*Oberkommando der Luftwaffe-OKL*), The National Archives, National Archives and Records Service, Washington, 1966; NA Microcopy No. T-321, Record Group No. 242/1028, Item No. OKL/2308, Roll No. 88; entries for 13 August 1940.
109. *ibid.*
110. *Lageberichte Luftflottenkommando 3*, *op. cit.* (entries for 13 August 1940); Dildy, Douglas C. and Crickmore, Paul F., *op. cit.* (pp. 211-212).
111. *ibid.*
112. James, T. Cecil G., *op. cit.* (pp. 71-74).
113. James, T. Cecil G., *op. cit.* (pp. 71-74); Townsend, Peter, *Duel of Eagles* (London: Weidenfeld and Nicolson, 1970) (pp. 310-311); Dildy, Douglas C. and Crickmore, Paul F., *op. cit.* (pp. 211-212); *Luftwaffe* unit locations from: Website, Holm, Michael, *The Luftwaffe, 1933-1945*; www.ww2.dk
114. Von Eimannsberger, Ludwig, *Zerstörer Gruppe: a History of V./(Z) LG 1–I./NJG 3 1939-1941* (Atglen: Schiffer, 1998) (p. 94, p. 205, p. 208); Dildy, Douglas C. and Crickmore, Paul F., *op. cit.* (pp. 211-212).
115. Website, Holm, Michael, *op. cit.*
116. *ibid.*
117. Prien, Jochen, *Pik-As: Geschichte des Jagdgeschwaders 53, Teil 1* (Illertissen: Flugzeug Publikations, 1989) (p. 177); *Lageberichte Luftflottenkommando 3, op. cit.* (entries for 13 August 1940).
118. Website, Wood, Tony, *op. cit.*
119. James, T. Cecil G., *op. cit.* (pp. 71-74).
120. Note 115, *op. cit.*
121. Note 119, *op. cit.*
122. James, T. Cecil G., *op. cit.* (pp. 71-74); Air Ministry Operational Record Books, No. 11 (Fighter) Group, Appendices, 1 September

Notes

1939–30 September 1940 (Air 25/197 records, National Archives), specifically Fighter Command Aircraft Combats records for 13 August 1940.

123. IPR, 257 Squadron, 13 August 1940 (Air 16/955 records, National Archives).
124. Confirmed also by: CR, F/O L. R. Mitchell, 257 Squadron, 13 August 1940 (Air 50/100/124 records, National Archives).
125. IPR, 64 Squadron, 13 August 1940 (Air 16/955 records, National Archives); James, T. Cecil G., *op. cit.* (pp. 71-74).
126. James, T. Cecil G., *op. cit.* (pp. 71-74); IPR, 601 Squadron, 13 August 1940 (Air 16/955 records, National Archives) (action at *c.* 06h40-07h15; were two later actions, at c. 12h15 and at c. 16h30-17h00).
127. Air Ministry Operational Record Books, No. 11 (Fighter) Group, Appendices, 1 September 1939–30 September 1940 (Air 25/197 records, National Archives), specifically Fighter Command Aircraft Combats records for 13 August 1940; ORB (Form 540), Summary of Events, 238 Squadron, 13 August 1940 (Air 27 records, National Archives).
128. James, T. Cecil G., *op. cit.* (pp. 71-74).
129. *ibid.*
130. IPRs, 43 and 601 Squadrons, 13 August 1940 (Air 16/955 records, National Archives); CRs for both squadrons discussed subsequently.
131. IPR, 257 Squadron, 13 August 1940 (Air 16/955 records, National Archives).
132. CR, S/L J. V. C. Badger, 43 Squadron, 13 August 1940 (Air 50 records, National Archives).
133. CR, P/O H. C. Upton, 43 Squadron, 13 August 1940 (Air 50 records, National Archives).
134. IPR, 43 Squadron, 13 August 1940 (Air 16/955 records, National Archives); CR, F/Lt Sir Archibald P. Hope, 601 Squadron, 13 August 1940 (Air 50 records, National Archives) (action at *c.* 06h40-07h15).
135. For example: CR's, F/Lt T. F. Dalton-Morgan and F/Lt F. R. Carey, 43 Squadron, 13 August 1940 (Air 50 records, National Archives).
136. IPR, 257 Squadron, 13 August 1940 (Air 16/955 records, National Archives).
137. IPR, 601 Squadron, 13 August 1940 (Air 16/955 records, National Archives) (action at *c.* 06h40-07h15).
138. *Lageberichte Luftflottenkommando 3, op. cit.* (entries for 13 August 1940).

139. Wynn, Kenneth G., *Men of the Battle of Britain* (Barnsley: Frontline, 2015) (p. 216).
140. CR, Sgt H. J. L. Hallowes, 43 Squadron, 13 August 1940 (Air 50 records, National Archives).
141. *ibid.*
142. *ibid.*
143. Ramsey, Winston. G. (ed.), *op. cit.* (RAF entry for 13 August 1940).
144. Dalton-Morgan, T. with Williams, Clive, *Tommy Leader* (Wendover: Griffon International, 2007) (p. 45).
145. CR, F/Lt T. F. Dalton-Morgan, 43 Squadron, 13 August 1940 (Air 50 records, National Archives) (no grammatical corrections made to CRs cited in this book).
146. Dalton-Morgan, T. with Williams, Clive, *op. cit.* (p. 45).
147. Wynn, Kenneth G., *op. cit.* (pp. 77-78).
148. CR, F/Lt F. R. Carey, 43 Squadron, 13 August 1940 (Air 50 records, National Archives).
149. CRs, Sgt A. Deller and P/O H. C. Upton, 43 Squadron, 13 August 1940 (respectively, Air 50/19/12 records and Air 50 records, National Archives).
150. CR, Sgt J. L. Crisp, 43 Squadron, 13 August 1940 (Air 50/19/9 records, National Archives).
151. *Lageberichte Luftflottenkommando 3*, *op. cit.* (entries for 13 August 1940); Ramsey, Winston. G. (ed.), *op. cit.* (*Luftwaffe* entry for 13 August 1940); Von Eimannsberger, Ludwig, *op. cit.* (p. 94, p. 205, p. 208).
152. CR, Sgt J. P. Mills, 43 Squadron, 13 August 1940 (Air 50 records, National Archives).
153. Mombeek, Eric and Roba, Jean-Louis, with Goss, Chris, *Am Himmel Frankreichs; die Geschichte des JG 2 "Richthofen", Band 2: 1940-1941* (Linkebeek: ASBL La Porte d'Hoves, 2013) (p. 47).
154. *ibid.*
155. CR, P/O C. A. Woods-Scawen, 43 Squadron, 13 August 1940 (Air 50 records, National Archives).
156. CR, P/O R. Lane, 43 Squadron, 13 August 1940 (Air 50/19/34 records, National Archives).
157. Wynn, Kenneth G., *op. cit.* (p. 203).
158. IPR, 43 Squadron, 13 August 1940 (Air 16/955 records, National Archives).
159. Report on his being shot down and wounded, F/Lt T. F. Dalton-Morgan, 43 Squadron, 13 August 1940, in his casualty file (Air 81/2584 records, National Archives).

Notes

160. CR, P/O H. C. Upton, 43 Squadron, 13 August 1940 (Air 50 records, National Archives).
161. IPR, 601 Squadron, 13 August 1940 (Air 16/955 records, National Archives) (action at c. 06h40-07h15).
162. *ibid.*
163. James, T. Cecil G., *op. cit.* (pp. 71-74).
164. CR, Sgt A. Deller, 43 Squadron, 13 August 1940 (Air 50/19/12 records, National Archives).
165. CR, P/O C. A. Woods-Scawen, 43 Squadron, 13 August 1940 (Air 50 records, National Archives).
166. CR, P/O R. Lane, 43 Squadron, 13 August 1940 (Air 50/19/34 records, National Archives).
167. Note 161, *op. cit.*
168. CR, F/Lt Sir Archibald P. Hope, 601 Squadron, 13 August 1940 (Air 50 records, National Archives) (action at c. 06h40-07h15).
169. CR, F/O H. J. Riddle, 601 Squadron, 13 August 1940 (Air 50/165/36 records, National Archives) (action at c. 06h40-07h15).
170. CR, P/O H. C. Mayers, 601 Squadron, 13 August 1940 (Air 50 records, National Archives) (action at c. 06h40-07h15).
171. Ramsey, Winston. G. (ed.), *op. cit.* (*Luftwaffe* entry for 13 August 1940).
172. Parker, Nigel, *op. cit.* (entry for 13 August 1940).
173. CR, F/O M. D. Doulton, 601 Squadron, 13 August 1940 (Air 50 records, National Archives) (action at c. 06h40-07h15).
174. CR, F/O W. P. Clyde, 601 Squadron, 13 August 1940 (Air 50 records, National Archives) (action at c. 06h40-07h15).
175. CR, F/O C. R. Davis, 601 Squadron, 13 August 1940 (Air 50 records, National Archives) (action at c. 06h40-07h15).
176. CR, P/O J. K. U. B. McGrath, 601 Squadron, 13 August 1940 (Air 50 records, National Archives) (action at c. 06h40-07h15).
177. ORB (Form 541), Records of Events, 601 Squadron, August 1940 (Air 27/2068/16 records, National Archives).
178. CR, F/O W. P. Clyde, 601 Squadron, 13 August 1940 (Air 50 records, National Archives) (action at c. 06h40-07h15).
179. CR, P/O T. Grier, 601 Squadron, 13 August 1940 (Air 50 records, National Archives) (action at c. 06h40-07h15).
180. CR, P/O W. M. L. Fiske, 601 Squadron, 13 August 1940 (Air 50 records, National Archives) (action at c. 06h40-07h15).
181. CR, F/O M. D. Doulton, 601 Squadron, 13 August 1940 (Air 50 records, National Archives) (action at c. 06h40-07h15).

Adlertag

182. CR, Sgt R. P. Hawkings, 601 Squadron, 13 August 1940 (Air 50 records, National Archives) (action at *c.* 06h40-07h15).
183. Elston, Wolfgang E., *Berlin revisited* (2004, revised version); thought to be unpublished excerpt perhaps in a school magazine-type publication. Copy provided by Professor Elston to author.
184. Elston, Wolfgang E., *Erinnerungen an die Goldschmidt-Schule – Berlin Grunewald: 1938 bis 1939*. This is an extended German language version of an essay in English published in a book of reminiscences of the *Goldschmidt-Schule* (copy from Professor Elston direct to author): Heims, S. J., *Passages from Berlin: Recollections of former students and staff of the Goldschmidt Schule (1935-1939)* (South Berwick, Maine: Atlantic Printing, 1987).
185. Elston, Wolfgang E., *Memories of Stoatley Rough School, Haslemere, Surrey, England 1939-1945 (written in honour of Nore Astfalck's 90th birthday and dedicated to the entire staff of Stoatley Rough)* (Memoir, 1990). Manuscript supplied by Professor Elston directly to author; held as a twenty-one page memoir by several libraries and document centres, including the Wiener Library for the Study of the Holocaust and Genocide, London.
186. Website, www.exploringsurreyspast.org.uk
187. Wikipedia; https://en.wikipedia.org/wiki/Bertha_Bracey
188. IPRs, 43 and 257 Squadrons, 13 August 1940 (Air 16/955 records, National Archives); CR, F/O L. R. Mitchell, 257 Squadron, 13 August 1940 (Air 50/100/124 records, National Archives); James, T. Cecil G., *op. cit.* (pp. 71-74).
189. IPR, 257 Squadron, 13 August 1940 (Air 16/955 records, National Archives).
190. *ibid.*
191. *ibid.*
192. CR, F/O L. R. Mitchell, 257 Squadron, 13 August 1940 (Air 50/100/124 records, National Archives).
193. *ibid.*
194. Note 189, *op. cit.*
195. *Lageberichte Luftflottenkommando 3, op. cit.* (entries for 13 August 1940); James, T. Cecil G., *op. cit.* (pp. 71-74); Dildy, Douglas C. and Crickmore, Paul F., *op. cit.* (pp. 211-212).
196. ORB (Form 541), Records of Events, 238 Squadron, August 1940 (Air 27/1453/4 records, National Archives).
197. *ibid.*
198. Note 196, *op. cit.*; ORB (Form 540), Summary of Events, 238 Squadron, August 1940 (Air 27 records, National Archives).

Notes

199. Batt, L. Gordon, *Scramble! A flying memoir of one of the Few* (Gunthorpe: The Battle of Britain Historical Society, 2001) (pp. 39-42).
200. *ibid.*
201. *Lageberichte Luftflottenkommando 3, op. cit.* (entries for 13 August 1940).
202. Website, Wood, Tony, *op. cit.*
203. ORB (Form 540), Summary of Events, 238 Squadron, August 1940 (Air 27 records, National Archives).
204. Details on his being shot down and wounded, Sgt E. W. Seabourne, 238 Squadron, 13 August 1940, in his casualty file (Air 81/1377 records, National Archives); Website, *The Battle of Britain London Monument*, The Airmen's Stories – Sgt E. W. Seabourne; www.bbm.org.uk/airmen/Seabourne.htm
205. Website, *The Battle of Britain London Monument*, The Airmen's Stories – Sgt E. W. Seabourne; www.bbm.org.uk/airmen/Seabourne.htm
206. *ibid.*
207. Batt, L. Gordon, *op. cit.* (pp. 39-42).
208. *ibid.*
209. Note 207, *op. cit.*; Ramsey, Winston. G. (ed.), *op. cit.* (RAF entry for 13 August 1940).
210. Website, Wood, Tony, *op. cit.*
211. ORB (Form 540), Summary of Events, 238 Squadron, August 1940 (Air 27 records, National Archives).
212. James, T. Cecil G., *op. cit.* (pp. 71-74).
213. IPR, 64 Squadron, 13 August 1940 (Air 16/955 records, National Archives); CR, F/Sgt E. G. Gilbert, 64 Squadron, 13 August 1940 (Air 50/24/28 records, National Archives).
214. IPR, 64 Squadron, 13 August 1940 (Air 16/955 records, National Archives).
215. *ibid.*
216. CR, F/O H. J. Woodward, 64 Squadron, 13 August 1940 (Air 50 records, National Archives).
217. CR, P/O P. J. Simpson, 64 Squadron, 13 August 1940 (Air 50/24/95 records, National Archives).
218. CR, F/Sgt E. G. Gilbert, 64 Squadron, 13 August 1940 (Air 50/24/28 records, National Archives).
219. Dildy, Douglas C. and Crickmore, Paul F., *op. cit.* (pp. 211-212).
220. Ramsey, Winston. G. (ed.), *op. cit.* (RAF entry for 13 August 1940).
221. Ramsey, Winston. G. (ed.), *op. cit.* (*Luftwaffe* entry for 13 August 1940).

222. *ibid.*
223. Mombeek, Eric and Roba, Jean-Louis, with Goss, Chris, *op. cit.* (p. 47).
224. Note 220, *op. cit.*
225. *Lageberichte Luftflottenkommando 3, op. cit.* (entries for 13 August 1940).
226. Website, Wood, Tony, *op. cit.*
227. Mason, Francis K., *Battle over Britain* (London: McWhirter Twins, 1969) (p. 238); Parker, Nigel, *op. cit.* (entry for 13 August 1940); Archives, Imperial War Museum, London: *Luftwaffe Quartermaster General Loss Returns* (a very large document). Electronic copy kindly provided by Nigel Parker, from original at the Museum.
228. Mason, Francis K., *op. cit.* (p. 238); Parker, Nigel, *op. cit.* (entry for 13 August 1940).
229. CR's, S/L J. S. Dewar and P/O D. T. Jay, 87 Squadron, 13 August 1940 (respectively, Air 50/37/49 records and Air 50/37/17 records, National Archives).
230. *ibid.*
231. *ibid.*
232. Ramsey, Winston. G. (ed.), *op. cit.* (*Luftwaffe* entry for 13 August 1940).
233. James, T. Cecil G., *op. cit.* (pp. 74-75).
234. *ibid.*
235. *ibid.*
236. *Lageberichte Luftflottenkommando 3, op. cit.* (entries for 13 August 1940); Von Eimannsberger, Ludwig, *op. cit.* (pp. 94-97, p. 205, pp. 209-212).
237. *Lageberichte Luftflottenkommando 3, op. cit.* (entries for 13 August 1940).
238. Von Eimannsberger, Ludwig, *op. cit.* (pp. 94-97, p. 205, pp. 209-212).
239. Collier, Richard, *op. cit.* (pp. 66-67); Townsend, Peter, *op. cit.* (p. 311).
240. For example, Collier, Richard, *op. cit.* (pp. 66-67).
241. For example, Townsend, Peter, *op. cit.* (p. 311).
242. Bekker, Cajus, *op. cit.* (pp. 195-198).
243. Website, Wood, Tony, *op. cit.*
244. Prien, Jochen, *op. cit.*
245. Website, Wood, Tony, *op. cit.*
246. Von Eimannsberger, Ludwig, *op. cit.* (pp. 94-97).
247. James, T. Cecil G., *op. cit.* (pp. 74-75); Air Ministry Operational Record Books, No. 11 (Fighter) Group, Appendices, 1 September

Notes

1939–30 September 1940 (Air 25/197 records, National Archives), specifically Fighter Command Aircraft Combats records for 13 August 1940.

248. For example, CR's F/Lt Sir Archibald P. Hope, P/O H. C. Mayers and F/O C.R. Davis, 601 Squadron, 13 August 1940 (all Air 50 records, National Archives) (action at *c.* 12h00-13h00).
249. Von Eimannsberger, Ludwig, *op. cit.* (pp. 94-97).
250. CR's F/O D. P. Hughes, Sgt H. Marsh and P/O J. S. Wigglesworth, 238 Squadron, 13 August 1940 (respectively, Air 50 records, Air 50/91/14 records and Air 50/91/48 records, National Archives) (Hughes' claim at *c.* 12h00-13h00, and made a later claim at *c.* 16h00-17h00); ORB (Form 541), Records of Events, 238 Squadron, August 1940 (Air 27/1453/4 records, National Archives) (action at *c.* 12h00-13h00; were two other actions that day, one at *c.* 06h40-07h15 and *c.* 16h00-17h00).
251. CR's F/O D. P. Hughes, Sgt H. Marsh, P/O J. S. Wigglesworth, P/O C. T. Davis and P/O V. C. Simmonds, 238 Squadron, 13 August 1940 (respectively, Air 50 records, Air 50/91/14 records, Air 50/91/48 records, Air 50/91/38 and Air 50/91/18 records, National Archives) (all in *c.* 12h00-13h00 action; Hughes, Davis and Simmonds also in c. 16h00-17h00 action).
252. CR F/O D. P. Hughes, 238 Squadron, 13 August 1940 (Air 50 records, National Archives) (action at *c.* 12h00-13h00).
253. CR's F/O D. P. Hughes, P/O C. T. Davis and P/O V. C. Simmonds, 238 Squadron, 13 August 1940 (respectively, Air 50 records, Air 50/91/38 and Air 50/91/18 records, National Archives) (*c.* 12h00-13h00 action).
254. CR's F/O D. P. Hughes and P/O V. C. Simmonds, 238 Squadron, 13 August 1940 (respectively, Air 50 records and Air 50/91/18 records, National Archives) (*c.* 12h00-13h00 action).
255. CR P/O C. T. Davis, 238 Squadron, 13 August 1940 (Air 50/91/38 records, National Archives) (*c.* 12h00-13h00 action).
256. CR's F/O D. P. Hughes and P/O C. T. Davis, 238 Squadron, 13 August 1940 (respectively, Air 50 records and Air 50/91/38 records, National Archives) (*c.* 12h00-13h00 action).
257. CR, F/Lt Sir Archibald P. Hope, 601 Squadron, 13 August 1940 (Air 50 records, National Archives) (action at *c.* 12h00-13h00).
258. Bekker, Cajus, *op. cit.* (pp. 195-198).
259. CR P/O V. C. Simmonds, 238 Squadron, 13 August 1940 (Air 50/91/18 records, National Archives) (*c.* 12h00-13h00 action).
260. Note 252, *op. cit.*
261. Note 258, *op. cit.*

262. Note 255, *op. cit.*
263. CR Sgt H. Marsh, 238 Squadron, 13 August 1940 (Air 50/91/14 records, National Archives).
264. Ramsey, Winston. G. (ed.), *op. cit.* (*Luftwaffe* entry for 13 August 1940).
265. CR P/O J. S. Wigglesworth, 238 Squadron, 13 August 1940 (Air 50/91/48 records, National Archives).
266. ORB (Form 541), Records of Events, 238 Squadron, August 1940 (Air 27/1453/4 records, National Archives).
267. IPR, 601 Squadron, 13 August 1940 (Air 16/955 records, National Archives) (action at *c.* 12h15); CR, F/Lt Sir Archibald P. Hope, 601 Squadron, 13 August 1940 (Air 50 records, National Archives) (action at *c.* 12h00-13h00).
268. *ibid.*
269. Note 257, *op. cit.*
270. CR, P/O H. C. Mayers, 601 Squadron, 13 August 1940 (Air 50 records, National Archives) (action at *c.* 12h00-13h00).
271. CRs, F/Lt Sir Archibald P. Hope and P/O H. C. Mayers, 601 Squadron, 13 August 1940 (Air 50 records, National Archives) (action at *c.* 12h00-13h00).
272. Dildy, Douglas C. and Crickmore, Paul F., *op. cit.* (p. 176).
273. For example, Eriksson, Patrick G., *Tally-Ho: RAF Tactical Leadership in the Battle of Britain, July 1940* (Stroud: Amberley, 2023) (p. 33).
274. Website, *RNLI (Royal National Lifeboat Institution) Archive*, Accounts of Services by Life-boats, p. 94; rnliarchive.blob.core.windows.net/media/1674/1940wys.pdf
275. Ramsey, Winston. G. (ed.), *op. cit.* (RAF entry for 13 August 1940).
276. Website, *RNLI (Royal National Lifeboat Institution) Archive*, Accounts of Services by Life-boats, p. 12; rnliarchive.blob.core.windows.net/media/1674/1940wys.pdf
277. Note 274, *op. cit.*
278. CR, F/O C. R. Davis, 601 Squadron, 13 August 1940 (Air 50 records, National Archives) (action at *c.* 12h00-13h00). Note that no linguistic corrections are made to citations from original documents in this book.
279. CR, F/Sgt A. H. D. Pond, 601 Squadron, 13 August 1940 (Air 50/163/34 records, National Archives) (action at *c.* 12h00-13h00).
280. *ibid.*
281. ORB (Form 541), Records of Events, 601 Squadron, August 1940 (Air 27/2068/16 records, National Archives).

Notes

282. CRs, F/O W. P. Clyde and P/O W. M. L. Fiske, 601 Squadron, 13 August 1940 (Air 50 records, National Archives) (action at *c.* 12h00-13h00).
283. CR, F/O W. P. Clyde, 601 Squadron, 13 August 1940 (Air 50 records, National Archives) (action at *c.* 12h00-13h00).
284. CR, P/O T. Grier, 601 Squadron, 13 August 1940 (Air 50 records, National Archives) (action at *c.* 12h00-13h00).
285. CRs, F/O W. P. Clyde and P/O T. Grier, 601 Squadron, 13 August 1940 (Air 50 records, National Archives) (action at *c.* 12h00-13h00).
286. CR, P/O W. M. L. Fiske, 601 Squadron, 13 August 1940 (Air 50 records, National Archives) (action at *c.* 12h00-13h00).
287. CR, F/O M. D. Doulton, 601 Squadron, 13 August 1940 (Air 50 records, National Archives) (action at *c.* 12h00-13h00).
288. Unless otherwise noted, loss data discussed here from: Ramsey, Winston. G. (ed.), *op. cit.* (*Luftwaffe* entry for 13 August 1940); Parker, Nigel, *op. cit.* (entry for 13 August 1940); *Luftwaffe Quartermaster General Loss Returns, op. cit.*; Von Eimannsberger, Ludwig, *op. cit.* (pp. 94-97, pp. 209-212, p. 205).
289. Collier, Richard, *op. cit.* (pp. 66-67).
290. Note 288, *op. cit.*
291. Parker, Nigel, *op. cit.* (entry for 13 August 1940).
292. CR Sgt H. Marsh, 238 Squadron, 13 August 1940 (Air 50/91/14 records, National Archives).
293. Note 288, *op. cit.*
294. Website, de Zeng, Henry L. IV and Stankey, Douglas G., *Luftwaffe Officer Career Summaries* (2014 updated version), accessed via Michael Holm's website, *The Luftwaffe 1933-1945*, www.ww2.dk; this source at www.ww2.dk/lwoffz.html: Oblt Michel Junge; Website, Kracker, Tom, *Aircrew Remembered 2012-2024 – the Kracker Luftwaffe Archive: Axis Powers Pilots and Crew:* Oblt Michel Junge, aircrewremembered.com/KrackerDatabase/?q=Haas+&qand=Alfred
295. *ibid.*
296. Recorded as such in the *Luftwaffe Quartermaster General Loss Returns, op. cit.*
297. Note 288, *op. cit.*
298. Von Eimannsberger, Ludwig, *op. cit.* (pp. 94-97).
299. Website, Wood, Tony, *op. cit.*
300. IPR, 213 Squadron, 13 August 1940 (Air 16/955 records, National Archives) (action at *c.* 12h30-13h00; squadron had another IPR for engagement at *c.* 16h00-17h00); Air Ministry Operational

Adlertag

Record Books, No. 11 (Fighter) Group, Appendices, 1 September 1939–30 September 1940 (Air 25/197 records, National Archives), specifically Fighter Command Aircraft Combats records for 13 August 1940.

301. IPR, 213 Squadron, 13 August 1940 (Air 16/955 records, National Archives) (action at *c.* 12h30-13h00).
302. CR, F/Lt J. M. Strickland, 213 Squadron, 13 August 1940 (Air 50/83/43 records, National Archives).
303. Note 301, *op. cit.*
304. CR, P/O J. E. P. Laricheliere, 213 Squadron, 13 August 1940 (Air 50/83/34 records, National Archives) (action at *c.* 12h30-13h00; pilot had another CR for action at *c.* 16h00-17h00).
305. *ibid.*
306. *ibid.*
307. *Lageberichte Luftflottenkommando 3, op. cit.* (entries for 13 August 1940); Ramsey, Winston. G. (ed.), *op. cit.* (*Luftwaffe* entry for 13 August 1940).
308. James, T. Cecil G., *op. cit.* (pp. 74-75).
309. Brown, Peter, *Honour Restored: The Battle of Britain, Dowding and the Fight for Freedom* (Stroud: The History Press, 2010) (pp. 82-89).
310. *ibid.*
311. *Lageberichte Luftflottenkommando 3, op. cit.* (entries for 13 August 1940).
312. James, T. Cecil G., *op. cit.* (p. 76); Bungay, Stephen, *The Most Dangerous Enemy* (London: Aurum Press, 2009) (pp. 209-210); Note 311, *op. cit.*
313. Note 311, *op. cit.*
314. Dierich, Wolfgang, *Die Verbände der Luftwaffe 1935-1945: Gliederungen und Kurzchroniken – eine Dokumentation* (Stuttgart: Motorbuch Verlag, 1976) (pp. 219-226).
315. *Lageberichte Luftflottenkommando 3, op. cit.* (entries for 13 August 1940).
316. *ibid.*
317. Prien, Jochen, *op. cit.* (pp. 177-178).
318. Website, Wood, Tony, *op. cit.*
319. ORB (Form 540), Summary of Events, 152 Squadron, August 1940 (Air 27/1025/1 records, National Archives).
320. Bishop, Patrick, *Battle of Britain* (London: Quercus, 2010) (pp. 166-167).
321. Prien, Jochen, *op. cit.* (pp. 177-178).
322. Bekker, Cajus, *op. cit.* (p. 198).
323. Mason, Francis K., *op. cit.* (pp. 239-240).

Notes

324. IPRs, 213 and 238 Squadrons, 13 August 1940 (Air 16/955 records, National Archives) (action at *c.* 16h00-17h00); Wood, Derek and Dempster, Derek, *The Narrow Margin* (London: Arrow Books, 1967) (pp. 282-283).
325. IPR, 609 Squadron, 13 August 1940 (Air 16/955 records, National Archives).
326. Bungay, Stephen, *op. cit.* (p. 210).
327. Ramsey, Winston. G. (ed.), *op. cit.* (*Luftwaffe* entry for 13 August 1940).
328. *Lageberichte Luftflottenkommando 3, op. cit.* (entries for 13 August 1940).
329. Note 328, *op. cit.*; Website, Holm, Michael, *op. cit.*
330. Bungay, Stephen, *op. cit.* (pp. 209-210).
331. Website, Wood, Tony, *op. cit.*
332. Note 330, *op. cit.*
333. James, T. Cecil G., *op. cit.* (p. 76).
334. Parker, Nigel, *Luftwaffe Crash Archive,* Vol. 4 (Walton on Thames: Red Kite Books, Air Research Publications, 2014) (entry for 17 September 1940).
335. Ramsey, Winston. G. (ed.), *op. cit.* (*Luftwaffe* entry for 13 August 1940).
336. Note 329, *op. cit.*
337. Note 330, *op. cit.*
338. *Lageberichte Luftflottenkommando 3, op. cit.* (entries for 13 August 1940).
339. James, T. Cecil G., *op. cit.* (pp. 75-77).
340. *ibid.*
341. Bekker, Cajus, *op. cit.* (p. 198).
342. Note 331, *op. cit.*
343. Bungay, Stephen, *op. cit.* (pp. 209-210).
344. Note 338, *op. cit.*
345. Note 338, *op. cit.*; Dildy, Douglas C. and Crickmore, Paul F., *op. cit.* (p. 114); RAF Casualty File, RAF Andover: Squadron Leader L. de L. Leder and Pilot Officer A. D. Mountstephen: report of deaths. Flight Lieutenant A. E. Dark: injured in an enemy bombing raid on RAF Andover, Hampshire, 13 August 1940 (Air 81/1366 records, National Archives).
346. Mason, Francis K., *op. cit.* (pp. 239-240).
347. Green, William, *Aircraft of the Battle of Britain* (London: MacDonald/Pan, 1969) (p. 52).
348. Wikipedia history of RAF Andover; https://en.wikipedia.org/wiki/RAF_Andover; time of raid on Andover confirmed in Air 81/1366 file – see Note 345 above.

Adlertag

349. Parker, Nigel, 2013, *op. cit.* (entry for 13 August 1940).
350. Bungay, Stephen, *op. cit.* (pp. 209-210); Ramsey, Winston. G. (ed.), *op. cit.* (*Luftwaffe* entry for 13 August 1940).
351. Mason, Francis K., *op. cit.* (pp. 239-240).
352. Note 351, *op. cit.*; Bungay, Stephen, *op. cit.* (pp. 209-210).
353. CR, F/Lt D. P. A. Boitel-Gill, 152 Squadron, 13 August 1940 (Air 50 records, National Archives).
354. Saunders, Andy, *Stuka Attack! The Dive-Bombing Assault on England during the Battle of Britain* (London: Grub Street, 2013) (pp. 87-90).
355. Holland, James, *The Battle of Britain: Five months that changed history May–October 1940* (London: Corgi Books, 2011) (p. 618).
356. Prien, Jochen, *op. cit.* (pp. 177-178).
357. Website, Wood, Tony, *op. cit.*; Ramsey, Winston. G. (ed.), *op. cit.* (*Luftwaffe* entry for 13 August 1940).
358. Air Ministry Operational Record Books, No. 11 (Fighter) Group, Appendices, 1 September 1939–30 September 1940 (Air 25/197 records, National Archives), specifically Fighter Command Aircraft Combats records for 13 August 1940; James, T. Cecil G., *op. cit.* (pp. 75-77); Mason, Francis K., *op. cit.* (pp. 239-240); Holland, James, *op. cit.* (pp. 166-167); Wood, Derek and Dempster, Derek, *op. cit.* (pp. 282-283); Note 353, *op. cit.*
359. CRs, P/O W. D. Williams and P/O G. J. Cox, 152 Squadron, 13 August 1940 (respectively, Air 50/64/95 records and Air 50/64/7 records, National Archives).
360. CR, F/Lt D. P. A. Boitel-Gill, 152 Squadron, 13 August 1940 (Air 50 records, National Archives).
361. For example: CR, F/O R. F. Inness, 152 Squadron, 13 August 1940 (Air 50 records, National Archives).
362. CR's, F/O R. F. Inness and P/O W. D. Williams, 152 Squadron, 13 August 1940 (respectively, Air 50 records and Air 50/64/95 records, National Archives).
363. Prien, Jochen, *op. cit.* (pp. 177-178); Website, Wood, Tony, *op. cit.*
364. Website, Wood, Tony, *op. cit.*
365. CR, F/O R. F. Inness, 152 Squadron, 13 August 1940 (Air 50 records, National Archives); Burt, Danny, *A Battle of Britain Spitfire Squadron: the Men and Machines of 152 Squadron in the Summer of 1940* (Barnsley: Frontline, 2018) (p. 139).
366. Ramsey, Winston. G. (ed.), *op. cit.* (RAF entry for 13 August 1940); Burt, Danny, *op. cit.* (p. 139).

Notes

367. CRs, F/O R. F. Inness, P/O I. N. Bayles and P/O G. J. Cox, 152 Squadron, 13 August 1940 (respectively, Air 50 records, Air 50/64/3 records and Air 50/64/7 records, National Archives).
368. Ramsey, Winston. G. (ed.), *op. cit.* (*Luftwaffe* entry for 13 August 1940).
369. CR, P/O W. D. Williams, 152 Squadron, 13 August 1940 (Air 50/64/95 records, National Archives).
370. CRs, P/Os J. R. Urwin-Mann and C. T. Davis, 238 Squadron, 13 August 1940 (respectively, Air 50/91/42 and Air 50/91/38 records, National Archives) (action at *c.* 16h00-17h00).
371. IPRs, 213 and 238 Squadrons, 13 August 1940 (Air 16/955 records, National Archives); various CRs for both units, detailed in succeeding paragraphs (action at *c.* 16h00-17h00).
372. IPR, 609 Squadron, 13 August 1940 (Air 16/955 records, National Archives).
373. James, T. Cecil G., *op. cit.* (pp. 75-77).
374. Note 373, *op. cit.*; IPR, 213 Squadron, 13 August 1940 (Air 16/955 records, National Archives) (action at *c.* 16h00-17h00).
375. Note 372, *op. cit.*
376. CR, F/Lt J. E. J. Sing, 213 Squadron, 13 August 1940 (Air 50 records, National Archives).
377. ORB (Form 541), Records of Events, 213 Squadron, August 1940 (Air 27/1315/20 records, National Archives); Note 376, *op. cit.*
378. CR, P/O A. G. Osmand, 213 Squadron, 13 August 1940 (Air 50/83/12 records, National Archives).
379. CRs, Sgt G. D. Bushell and P/O H. D. Atkinson, 213 Squadron, 13 August 1940 (respectively, Air 50/83/22 records and Air 50/83/17 records, National Archives).
380. CR, P/O J. E. P. Laricheliere, 213 Squadron, 13 August 1940 (Air 50/83/34 records, National Archives) (action at *c.* 16h00-17h00).
381. *ibid.*
382. Wynn, Kenneth G., *op. cit.* (p. 310).
383. Eriksson, Patrick G., *op. cit.* (pp. 118-119).
384. IPR, 213 Squadron, 13 August 1940 (Air 16/955 records, National Archives) (action at *c.* 16h00-17h00).
385. Squadron Commander's Report on Flying Battle Casualty, Sgt P. P. Norris, 213 Squadron, 13 August 1940 (Air 81/1382 records, National Archives).
386. Air 81 casualty file, Sgt P. P. Norris, 213 Squadron, 13 August 1940 (Air 81/1382 records, National Archives).

387. Reynaud, J-Y., Teyssier, B., Auffret, J. P., Berne, S., De Batist, M., Marsset, T. and Walker, P., *The offshore sedimentary cover of the English Channel and its northern and western Approaches* (Journal of Quaternary Science, 18(3-4), pp. 361-371).
388. Ramsey, Winston. G. (ed.), *op. cit.* (*Luftwaffe* entry for 13 August 1940).
389. Website, *The Battle of Britain London Monument,* The Airmen's Stories – F/Lt D. P. Hughes; www.bbm.org.uk/airmen/HughesDP.htm
390. ORB (Form 540), Summary of Events, 238 Squadron, August 1940 (Air 27 records, National Archives).
391. CR, F/O D. P. Hughes, 238 Squadron, 13 August 1940 (Air 50 records, National Archives) (action at *c.* 16h00-17h00).
392. IPR, 238 Squadron, 13 August 1940 (Air 16/955 records, National Archives) (action at *c.* 16h00-17h00); CR, P/O V. C. Simmonds, 238 Squadron, 13 August 1940 (Air 50/91/18 records, National Archives) (action at *c.* 16h00-17h00).
393. CR, P/O C. T. Davis, 238 Squadron, 13 August 1940 (Air 50/91/38 records, National Archives) (action at *c.* 16h00-17h00).
394. CR, P/O V. C. Simmonds, 238 Squadron, 13 August 1940 (Air 50/91/18 records, National Archives) (action at *c.* 16h00-17h00).
395. CR, P/O J. R. Urwin-Mann, 238 Squadron, 13 August 1940 (Air 50/91/42 records, National Archives).
396. IPR, 238 Squadron, 13 August 1940 (Air 16/955 records, National Archives) (action at *c.* 16h00-17h00).
397. Ramsey, Winston. G. (ed.), *op. cit.* (*Luftwaffe* entry for 13 August 1940); Parker, Nigel, 2013, *op. cit.* (entry for 13 August 1940).
398. *Lageberichte Luftflottenkommando 3, op. cit.* (entries for 13 August 1940).
399. Ramsey, Winston. G. (ed.), *op. cit.* (p. 374).
400. Air 81 casualty file, Sgt R. Little, 238 Squadron, 13 August 1940 (Air 81/1424 records, National Archives); Ramsey, Winston. G. (ed.), *op. cit.* (RAF entry for 13 August 1940).
401. Air 81 casualty file, Sgt R. Little, 238 Squadron, 13 August 1940 (Air 81/1424 records, National Archives).
402. Ramsey, Winston. G. (ed.), *op. cit.* (RAF entry for 13 August 1940).
403. Website, Wood, Tony, *op. cit.*
404. *ibid.*
405. IPR, 609 Squadron, 13 August 1940 (Air 16/955 records, National Archives); CR's, S/L H. S. Darley and F/Lt F. J. Howell, 609 Squadron, 13 August 1940 (respectively, Air 50/171/17 and Air 50/171/36 records, National Archives).

Adlertag

425. CR, F/O H. M. Goodwin, 609 Squadron, 13 August 1940 (Air 50/171/31 records, National Archives).
426. For example: CR P/O C. N. Overton, 609 Squadron, 13 August 1940 (Air 50/171/57 records, National Archives).
427. Ramsey, Winston. G. (ed.), *op. cit.* (*Luftwaffe* entry for 13 August 1940); Parker, Nigel, 2013, *op. cit.* (entry for 13 August 1940).
428. *ibid.*
429. Claims totals derived from: 609 Squadron combat reports; Crook, David M., *op. cit.* (pp. 94-114).
430. CR, F/O W.P. Clyde, 601 Squadron, 13 August 1940 (Air 50 records, National Archives) (action at *c.* 16h00-17h00).
431. IPR, 601 Squadron, 13 August 1940 (Air 16/955 records, National Archives) (action at *c.* 16h00-17h00).
432. ORB (Form 541), Records of Events, 601 Squadron, August 1940 (Air 27/2068/16 records, National Archives).
433. CR, F/Lt Sir Archibald P. Hope, 601 Squadron, 13 August 1940 (Air 50 records, National Archives) (action at *c.* 16h00-17h00).
434. Wynn, Kenneth G., *op. cit.* (pp. 545-546).
435. Note 431, *op. cit.*
436. CR, F/O C. R. Davis, 601 Squadron, 13 August 1940 (Air 50 records, National Archives) (action at *c.* 16h00-17h00).
437. Note 431, *op. cit.*
438. Note 436, *op. cit.*
439. CRs, F/O W. P. Clyde, P/O J. K. U. B. McGrath, F/Sgt A. H. D. Pond and Sgt L. N. Guy, 601 Squadron, 13 August 1940 (respectively, Air 50 records for Clyde and McGrath, Air 50/165/34 and Air 50/165/1 records, National Archives) (action at *c.* 16h00-17h00).
440. Note 433, *op. cit.*
441. CR, Sgt L. N. Guy, 601 Squadron, 13 August 1940 (Air 50/165/1 records, National Archives).
442. CR, F/O G. N. S. Cleaver, 601 Squadron, 13 August 1940 (Air 50/165/5 records, National Archives).
443. Note 436, *op. cit.*
444. CR, P/O J. K. U. B. McGrath, 601 Squadron, 13 August 1940 (Air 50 records, National Archives) (action at *c.* 16h00-17h00).
445. *ibid.*
446. CR, F/Sgt A. H. D. Pond, 601 Squadron, 13 August 1940 (Air 50/165/34 records, National Archives) (action at *c.* 16h00-17h00).
447. *ibid.*
448. CR, F/O W.P. Clyde, 601 Squadron, 13 August 1940 (Air 50 records, National Archives) (action at *c.* 16h00-17h00).

Notes

449. *ibid.*
450. CR, P/O T. Grier, 601 Squadron, 13 August 1940 (Air 50 records, National Archives) (action at *c.* 16h00-17h00).
451. CR, Sgt A. S. MacDonald, 601 Squadron, 13 August 1940 (Air 50/165/23 records, National Archives).
452. CR, F/O C. Riddle, 601 Squadron, 13 August 1940 (Air 50/165/36 records, National Archives).
453. CR, F/O C. R. Davis, 601 Squadron, 13 August 1940 (Air 50 records, National Archives) (action at *c.* 16h00-17h00).
454. CR, F/Sgt A. H. D. Pond, 601 Squadron, 13 August 1940 (Air 50/165/34 records, National Archives) (action at *c.* 16h00-17h00).
455. *ibid.*
456. CR, Sgt L. N. Guy, 601 Squadron, 13 August 1940 (Air 50/165/1 records, National Archives).
457. Ramsey, Winston. G. (ed.), *op. cit.* (*Luftwaffe* entry for 13 August 1940); Parker, Nigel, 2013, *op. cit.* (entry for 13 August 1940).
458. Website, de Zeng, Henry L. IV and Stankey, Douglas G., *op. cit.*
459. James, T. Cecil G., *op. cit.* (p. 76); Bungay, Stephen, *op. cit.* (pp. 209-210); *Lageberichte Luftflottenkommando 3, op. cit.* (entries for 13 August 1940).
460. Ramsey, Winston. G. (ed.), *op. cit.* (*Luftwaffe* entry for 13 August 1940); Goss, Chris, *The Luftwaffe Fighters' Battle of Britain* (Manchester: Crécy, 2010) (pp. 45-47).
461. *ibid.*
462. Bergström, Christer, *op. cit.* (pp. 106-110).
463. Ramsey, Winston. G. (ed.), *op. cit.* (*Luftwaffe* entry for 13 August 1940).
464. IPR, 257 Squadron, 13 August 1940 (Air 16/955 records, National Archives) (action at *c.* 16h00-17h00).
465. CR, S/L H. Harkness, 257 Squadron, 13 August 1940 (Air 50/100/12 records, National Archives).
466. CR, P/O C. F. A. Capon, 257 Squadron, 13 August 1940 (Air 50/100/99 records, National Archives) (no grammatical corrections made to CRs cited in this book).
467. Note 464, *op. cit.*
468. *ibid.*
469. Ramsey, Winston. G. (ed.), *op. cit.* (*Luftwaffe* entry for 13 August 1940).
470. CR, F/Lt R. R. S. Tuck, 92 Squadron, 13 August 1940 (Air 50/40/51 records, National Archives).
471. IPR, 43 Squadron, 13 August 1940 (Air 16/955 records, National Archives) (action at *c.* 16h00-17h00).

472. Note 471, *op. cit.*; IPR, 92 Squadron, 13 August 1940 (Air 16/955 records, National Archives).
473. Note 471, *op. cit.*
474. Note 471, *op. cit.*; Townsend, Peter, *op. cit.* (p. 312); Bowyer, Chaz, *Fighter Pilots of the RAF 1939-1945* (London: William Kimber, 1984) (p. 133).
475. IPR, 43 Squadron, 13 August 1940 (Air 16/955 records, National Archives) (action at *c.* 16h00-17h00).
476. *ibid.*
477. *ibid.*
478. *ibid.*
479. *ibid.*
480. ORB (Form 541), Records of Events, 145 Squadron, August 1940 (Air 27/984/8 records, National Archives); ORB (Form 540), Summary of Events, 145 Squadron, August 1940 (Air 27/984/7 records, National Archives).
481. ORB (Form 540), Summary of Events, 145 Squadron, August 1940 (Air 27/984/7 records, National Archives).
482. James, T. Cecil G., *op. cit.* (pp. 75-79).
483. Von Eimannsberger, Ludwig, *op. cit.* (p. 56); Ramsey, Winston. G. (ed.), *op. cit.* (*Luftwaffe* entry for 13 August 1940); Website, Holm, Michael, *op. cit.*
484. Website, Holm, Michael, *op. cit.*
485. James, T. Cecil G., *op. cit.* (pp. 75-79).
486. *ibid.*
487. *ibid.*
488. *ibid.*
489. James, T. Cecil G., *op. cit.* (pp. 75-79); Von Eimannsberger, Ludwig, *op. cit.* (p. 56); IPR, 56 Squadron, 13 August 1940 (Air 16/955 records, National Archives).
490. James, T. Cecil G., *op. cit.* (pp. 75-79).
491. Aders, Gebhard and Held, Werner, *Jagdgeschwader 51 'Mölders'* (Stuttgart: Motorbuch, 1985) (p. 64).
492. Note 490, *op. cit.*
493. Note 490, *op. cit.*; CR, P/O B. E. F. Finucane, 65 Squadron, 13 August 1940 (Air 50/25/87 records, National Archives).
494. James, T. Cecil G., *op. cit.* (pp. 75-79).
495. *ibid.*
496. *ibid.*
497. Dildy, Douglas C. and Crickmore, Paul F., *op. cit.* (p. 214); Saunders, Andy, 2013, *op. cit.* (pp. 80-86); Nowarra, Heinz J., *Luftschlacht*

Notes

um England: Verlorener Sieg (Friedberg: Podzun-Pallas-Verlag, 1978) (pp. 36-37); Bekker, Cajus, *op. cit.* (pp. 198-199).
498. For example: Bungay, Stephen, *op. cit.* (p. 210); Mason, Francis K., *op. cit.* (p. 240).
499. Prien, Jochen, *Geschichte des Jagdgeschwaders 77, Teil 1, 1934-1941* (Eutin: Struve-Druck, 1992) (p. 347).
500. Bungay, Stephen, *op. cit.* (p. 210).
501. Bishop, Patrick, 2010, *op. cit.* (pp. 167-168).
502. Ramsey, Winston. G. (ed.), *op. cit.* (*Luftwaffe* entry for 13 August 1940); IPR, 65 Squadron, 13 August 1940 (Air 16/955 records, National Archives).
503. Prien, Jochen, 1992, *op. cit.* (p. 347).
504. Saunders, Andy, 2013, *op. cit.* (pp. 80-86).
505. Bungay, Stephen, *op. cit.* (p. 210).
506. Hough, Richard and Richards, Denis, *op. cit.* (pp. 161-162).
507. James, T. Cecil G., *op. cit.* (pp. 75-79); Bishop, Patrick, 2010, *op. cit.* (pp. 167-168); ORB (Form 540), Summary of Events, 53 Squadron, August 1940 (Air 27/503/21 records, National Archives).
508. Note 506, *op. cit.*
509. Eriksson, Patrick G., *Alarmstart* (Stroud: Amberley, 2017) (p. 85, pp. 88-89).
510. Note 506, *op. cit.*
511. ORB (Form 540), Summary of Events, 53 Squadron, August 1940 (Air 27/503/21 records, National Archives).
512. Prien, Jochen, 1992, *op. cit.* (p. 347); Prien, Jochen, *Geschichte des Jagdgeschwaders 77, Teil 4, 1944-1945* (Eutin: Struve-Druck, undated) (p. 2382).
513. Website, Wood, Tony, *op. cit.*
514. Dildy, Douglas C. and Crickmore, Paul F., *op. cit.* (p. 214); Saunders, Andy, 2013, *op. cit.* (pp. 80-86); Hunt, Leslie, *Twenty-One Squadrons; The History of the Royal Auxiliary Air Force: 1925-1957* (London: Garnstone Press, 1972) (p. 317).
515. Hough, Richard and Richards, Denis, *op. cit.* (pp. 161-162).
516. Saunders, Andy, 2013, *op. cit.* (pp. 80-86).
517. Hough, Richard and Richards, Denis, *op. cit.* (pp. 161-162); Air 81 casualty file, RAF Detling, 13 August 1940 (Air 81/1471 records, National Archives) (one of several such files).
518. Air 81 casualty file, RAF Detling, 13 August 1940 (Air 81/1471 records, National Archives) (one of several such files).
519. ORB (Form 541), Records of Events, 53 Squadron, August 1940 (Air 27/503/22 records, National Archives).

520. Note 518, *op. cit.*
521. Website, *South-East History Boards*; sussexhistoryforum.co.uk/index.php?topic=3177.0
522. Knight, Dennis, *Harvest of Messerschmitts: the chronicle of a village at war 1940* (London: Frederick Warne, 1981) (p. 92).
523. ORB (Form 540), Summary of Events, 53 Squadron, August 1940 (Air 27/503/21 records, National Archives); ORB (Form 540), Summary of Events, 500 Squadron, August 1940 (Air 27/1941/23 records, National Archives).
524. Saunders, Andy, 2013, *op. cit.* (pp. 80-86).
525. ORB (Form 541), Records of Events, 53 Squadron, August 1940 (Air 27/503/22 records, National Archives).
526. For example: Caldwell, Donald L., *JG 26 Luftwaffe Fighter Wing Diary, 1939-1942*, Vol. 1 (Mechanicsburg: Stackpole Books, 2012) (pp. 55-56); Bishop, Patrick, 2010, *op. cit.* (pp. 167-168); Mason, Francis K., *op. cit.* (p. 240).
527. Priller, Josef, *J.G. 26: Geschichte eines Jagdgeschwaders* (Stuttgart: Motorbuch Verlag, 1980) (pp. 79-80).
528. Saunders, Andy, 2013, *op. cit.* (pp. 80-86).
529. James, T. Cecil G., *op. cit.* (pp. 75-79).
530. Ramsey, Winston. G. (ed.), *op. cit.* (*Luftwaffe* entry for 13 August 1940).
531. IPR, 65 Squadron, 13 August 1940 (Air 16/955 records, National Archives).
532. Barbas, Bernd, *Die Geschichte der I. Gruppe des Jagdgeschwaders 52* (Überlingen: self-published, undated) (p. 97).
533. Flying logbook, *Uffz* Hans-Helmut Habermehl, *1/JG 54*, entry for 13 August 1940; copy of logbook courtesy of Peter Arnot.
534. Prien, Jochen and Stemmer, Gerhard, *Messerschmitt Bf 109 im Einsatz bei Stab und I./Jagdgeschwader 3* (Eutin: Struve-Druck, 1997) (p. 80); Prien, Jochen and Stemmer, Gerhard, *Messerschmitt Bf 109 im Einsatz bei der II./Jagdgeschwader 3, 1940-1945* (Eutin: Struve-Druck, 1996) (p. 19).
535. James, T. Cecil G., *op. cit.* (pp. 75-79).
536. IPR, 65 Squadron, 13 August 1940 (Air 16/955 records, National Archives).
537. CR, Sgt J. R. Kilner, 65 Squadron, 13 August 1940 (Air 50/25/99 records, National Archives).
538. CR, F/Lt C. G. C. Olive, 65 Squadron, 13 August 1940 (Air 50/25/110 records, National Archives).
539. Note 536, *op. cit.*

Notes

540. Ramsey, Winston. G. (ed.), *op. cit.* (*Luftwaffe* entry for 13 August 1940).
541. *ibid.*
542. Website, Wood, Tony, *op. cit.*; Aders, Gebhard and Held, Werner, *op. cit.* (p. 64).
543. Note 536, *op. cit.*
544. IPR, 56 Squadron, 13 August 1940 (Air 16/955 records, National Archives).
545. CR, F/Lt E. J. Gracie, 56 Squadron, 13 August 1940 (Air 50 records, National Archives).
546. Ramsey, Winston. G. (ed.), *op. cit.* (*Luftwaffe* and RAF entries for 13 August 1940).
547. CR, F/Lt P. S. Weaver, 56 Squadron, 13 August 1940 (Air 50 records, National Archives).
548. IPR, 56 Squadron, 13 August 1940 (Air 16/955 records, National Archives); Ramsey, Winston. G. (ed.), *op. cit.* (RAF entry for 13 August 1940).
549. CR, P/O C. C. O. Joubert, 56 Squadron, 13 August 1940 (Air 50/22/36 records, National Archives).
550. Ramsey, Winston. G. (ed.), *op. cit.* (RAF entry for 13 August 1940); Collier, Richard, *op. cit.* (pp. 68-75).
551. IPR, 56 Squadron, 13 August 1940 (Air 16/955 records, National Archives).
552. Ramsey, Winston. G. (ed.), *op. cit.* (*Luftwaffe* entry for 13 August 1940); Parker, Nigel, 2013, *op. cit.* (entry for 13 August 1940).
553. Ramsey, Winston. G. (ed.), *op. cit.* (*Luftwaffe* entry for 13 August 1940).
554. *ibid.*
555. James, T. Cecil G., *op. cit.* (pp. 75-79).
556. Ramsey, Winston. G. (ed.), *op. cit.* (RAF entry for 13 August 1940).
557. McKee, Alexander, *op. cit.* (pp. 90-91).
558. Caldwell, Donald L., *op. cit.* (pp. 55-56); Nowarra, Heinz J., *op. cit.* (pp. 36-37).
559. *ibid.*
560. Nowarra, Heinz J., *op. cit.* (pp. 36-37).
561. Website, Wood, Tony, *op. cit.*
562. Ramsey, Winston. G. (ed.), *op. cit.* (*Luftwaffe* entry for 13 August 1940); Knight, Dennis, *op. cit.* (p. 92).
563. Parker, Nigel, 2013, *op. cit.* (entry for 13 August 1940).
564. CR, F/Lt C. G. C. Olive, 65 Squadron, 13 August 1940 (Air 50/25/110 records, National Archives).

565. CR, F/Lt E. J. Gracie, 56 Squadron, 13 August 1940 (Air 50 records, National Archives).
566. Ramsey, Winston. G. (ed.), *op. cit.* (*Luftwaffe* entry for 13 August 1940); Website, Holm, Michael, *op. cit.*

4. Conclusions

1. Dildy, Douglas C. and Crickmore, Paul F., *To Defeat The Few: The Luftwaffe's Campaign to destroy RAF Fighter Command, August-September 1940* (Oxford: Osprey, 2020) (pp. 264-265).
2. Aders, Gebhard and Held, Werner, *Jagdgeschwader 51 'Mölders'* (Stuttgart: Motorbuch, 1985) (pp. 62-63, p. 247).
3. Nowarra, Heinz J., *Luftschlacht um England: Verlorener Sieg* (Friedberg: Podzun-Pallas-Verlag, 1978) (p. 21).
4. Eriksson, Patrick G., *Tally-Ho: RAF Tactical Leadership in the Battle of Britain, July 1940* (Stroud: Amberley, 2023) (pp. 193-194).
5. Osterkamp, Theo, *Durch Höhen und Tiefen jagd ein Herz* (Heidelberg: Kurt Vowinckel Verlag, 1952) (pp. 360-363).
6. *ibid.*
7. *ibid.*
8. *ibid.*
9. *ibid.*
10. Osterkamp, Theo, *op. cit.* (pp. 318-323).
11. Price, Alfred, *Battle of Britain Day; 15 September 1940* (London: Sidgwick and Jackson, 1990) (pp. 143-144).

Bibliography

Aders, Gebhard and Held, Werner, *Jagdgeschwader 51 'Mölders'* (Stuttgart: Motorbuch, 1985)
Air Ministry (compiled and introduced: Robson, Martin), *The Spitfire Pocket Manual; All marks in service 1939-1945* (London: Conway, 2010)
Alexander, Kristen, *Australia's Few and the Battle of Britain* (Barnsley: Pen and Sword, 2015)
Arthur, Max, *Last of the Few: The Battle of Britain in the Words of the Pilots Who Won It* (London: Virgin Books, 2010)
Bailey, David J., *610 (County of Chester) Auxiliary Air Force Squadron, 1936-1940* (Stroud: Fonthill, 2018)
Baker, E. C. R., *The Fighter Aces of the R.A.F.* (London: New English Library, 1974)
Barbas, Bernd, *Die Geschichte der I. Gruppe des Jagdgeschwaders 52* (Überlingen: self-published, undated)
Barbas, Bernd, *Die Geschichte der II. Gruppe des Jagdgeschwaders 52* (Überlingen: self-published, undated)
Batt, L. Gordon, *Scramble! A flying memoir of one of the Few* (Gunthorpe: The Battle of Britain Historical Society, 2001)
Bekker, Cajus, *The Luftwaffe War Diaries* (London: Corgi, 1969)
Bergström, Christer, *The Battle of Britain: an epic conflict revisited* (Oxford: Casemate, 2015 and Eskilstuna: Vaktel, 2015)
Bickers, Richard T., *Ginger Lacey: Fighter Pilot* (London: Pan, 1969)
Bishop, Patrick, *Fighter Boys; Saving Britain 1940* (London: Harper Collins, 2003)
Bishop, Patrick, *Battle of Britain* (London: Quercus, 2010)
Bowyer, Chaz, *Fighter Pilots of the RAF 1939–1945* (London: William Kimber, 1984)

Brown, Peter, *Honour Restored: The Battle of Britain, Dowding and the Fight for Freedom* (Stroud: The History Press, 2010)

Bungay, Stephen, *The Most Dangerous Enemy* (London: Aurum Press, 2009)

Burt, Danny, *A Battle of Britain Spitfire Squadron: the men and machines of 152 Squadron in the summer of 1940* (Barnsley: Frontline, 2018)

Caldwell, Donald L., *JG 26 Luftwaffe Fighter Wing Diary, 1939-1942*, Vol. 1 (Mechanicsburg: Stackpole Books, 2012)

Collier, Basil, *The Battle of Britain* (London: Fontana/Collins, 1969)

Collier, Richard, *Eagle Day: the Battle of Britain August 6–September 15 1940* (London: Pan, 1969)

Crook, David M., *Spitfire Pilot* (London: Grub Street, 2010)

Dalton-Morgan, T. with Williams, Clive, *Tommy Leader* (Wendover: Griffon International, 2007)

Darlow, Steve, *Five of the Few* (London: Grub Street, 2010)

Dierich, Wolfgang, *Die Verbände der Luftwaffe 1935-1945: Gliederungen und Kurzchroniken – eine Dokumentation* (Stuttgart: Motorbuch, 1976)

Dildy, Douglas C. and Crickmore, Paul F., *To Defeat The Few: The Luftwaffe's Campaign to destroy RAF Fighter Command, August-September 1940* (Oxford: Osprey, 2020)

Donahue, Arthur G., *Tally-Ho! Yankee in a Spitfire* (The War Vault, 2021)

Eriksson, Patrick G., *Alarmstart* (Stroud: Amberley, 2017)

Eriksson, Patrick G., *Alarmstart East: The German Fighter Pilot's Experience on the Eastern Front 1941–1945* (Stroud: Amberley, 2020)

Eriksson, Patrick G., *Tally-Ho: RAF Tactical Leadership in the Battle of Britain, July 1940* (Stroud: Amberley, 2023)

Federl, Christian, *Jagdgeschwader 2 "Richthofen"* (Zweibrücken: VDM Heinz Nickel, 2006)

Goss, Chris, *The Luftwaffe Bombers' Battle of Britain* (Manchester: Crécy, 2000)

Goss, Chris, *Luftwaffe Fighters' Battle of Britain: The inside story: July–October 1940* (Manchester: Crécy, 2010)

Goss, Chris, *Dornier Do 17 units of World War 2* (Oxford: Osprey, 2019)

Goss, Chris, *Brothers in Arms: The Story of a British and a German Fighter Unit, August to December 1940* (Barnsley: Air World/Pen and Sword, 2020)

Green, William, *Aircraft of the Battle of Britain* (London: MacDonald-Pan, 1969)

Bibliography

Steinhilper, Ulrich and Osborne, Peter, *Spitfire on my tail* (Bromley: Independent Books, 2009)

Sutton, Barry, *Fighter Boy: Life as a Battle of Britain pilot* (Stroud: Amberley, 2010)

Thomas, Nick, *Hurricane Squadron Ace: The Story of Battle of Britain Ace Air Commodore Peter 'Pete' Brothers, CBE, DSO, DFC and Bar* (Barnsley: Pen and Sword, 2014)

Tidy, Douglas, *I fear no Man; the Story of No 74 (Fighter) Squadron Royal Flying Corps and Royal Air Force* (Cape Town: Purnell, 1972)

Townsend, Peter, *Duel of Eagles* (London: Weidenfeld and Nicolson, 1970)

Vasco, John, *Messerschmitt Bf 110 Bombsights over England: Erprobungsgruppe 210 in the Battle of Britain* (Atglen: Schiffer, 2002)

Von Eimannsberger, Ludwig, *Zerstörer Gruppe: a History of V./(Z) LG 1 – I./NJG 3 1939-1941* (Atglen: Schiffer, 1998)

Wallens, R. W. 'Wally', *Flying made my Arms ache* (Upton-upon-Severn: The Self Publishing Association Ltd., 1990)

Willis, John, *Churchill's Few: The Battle of Britain remembered* (London: Michael Joseph, 1985)

Willis, John, *Secret Letters: A Battle of Britain Love Story* (London: Mensch Publishing, 2020) (also, Author's Note, Kindle edition)

Wood, Derek and Dempster, Derek, *The Narrow Margin* (London: Arrow Books, 1967)

Wynn, Kenneth G., *Men of the Battle of Britain: a biographical directory of the Few* (Barnsley: Frontline, 2015; West Malling: The Battle of Britain Memorial Trust, 2015) and updates to this book: https://www.battleofbritainmemorial.org/men-of-the-battle-updates-and-additions/

Websites

De Zeng, Henry L. IV, *Luftwaffe Airfields 1935-1945*, www.ww2.dk/lwairfields.html

De Zeng, Henry L. IV and Stankey, Douglas G., *Luftwaffe Officer Career Summaries* (2014 updated version), www.ww2.dk/lwoffz.html

Duxford Radio Society, www.duxfordradiosociety.org/equipment/pip-squeak.html

Hampshire Airfields, Hampshire Crashes, https://hampshire.hampshireairfields.co.uk/hancrash.html

Holm, Michael, *The Luftwaffe, 1933-1945*, www.ww2.dk

Isle of Wight Aviation, Isle of Wight Crashes, https://wight.hampshireairfields.co.uk/iowc.html

Adlertag

Kracker, Tom, *Aircrew Remembered 2012-2024 – the Kracker Luftwaffe Archive: Axis Powers Pilots and Crew:* Oblt Michel Junge, aircrewremembered.com/KrackerDatabase/?q=Haas+&qand=Alfred

Royal Air Force Commands, rafcommands.com/Ross/Coastal/53C.html

Royal National Lifeboat Institution, Archive and Library; Accounts of Services by Life-boats, p. 12, p. 94, rnliarchive.blob.core.windows.net/media/1674/1940wys.pdf

South-East History Boards, sussexhistoryforum.co.uk/index.php?topic=3177.0

Spink and Son Ltd., Auctioneers, London, catalogue, auction of war medals of Leading Seaman E. Tambling (Spink.com/lot/17003000580) who served on *HMT Edwardian*: copy of Report of the loss of his ship, by Lt. E. J .C. Edwards, RNVR, C/O *HMT Edwardian,* spink.com

Surrey Heritage (Surrey Country Council), *Exploring Surrey's Past,* www.exploringsurreyspast.org.uk

The Battle of Britain London Monument, *The Airmen's Stories –*
Sgt S. L. Butterfield, www.bbm.org.uk/airmen/Butterfield.htm
Sgt E. W. Seabourne, www.bbm.org.uk/airmen/Seabourne.htm
F/Lt D. P. Hughes, www.bbm.org.uk/airmen/HughesDP.htm
F/Lt R. L. Smith, www.bbm.org.uk/airmen/SmithRL.htm

Wood, Tony, *Tony Wood's Combat Claims and Casualties Lists,* doncaldwell.we.bs/claims/tonywood.htm

213 Squadron Association, https://213squadronassociation.homestead.com/WidgeWight/WidgePage.html

Archives

UK National Archives, AIR set of records

Air 16/955: Fighter Command Combat Reports (also called Form 'F', often sub-headed as Intelligence Patrol Report; one for each action by each squadron, per day). Termed Intelligence Patrol Reports, abbreviated to IPRs, in this volume. Authored mainly by the Squadron Intelligence Officer, and sometimes by the Sector Intelligence Officer.

Air 25/197: Air Ministry Operational Record Books, No. 11 (Fighter) Group, Appendices, 1 September 1939-30 September 1940, National Archives, these records include the Fighter Command Aircraft Combats which list numbers of aircraft scrambled per mission for each RAF fighter squadron, mission times, claims and losses, and approximate area of engagements, on a daily basis.

Air 27: Operations Record Books (also known as Form 540 and Form 541); abbreviated to ORB in this volume. One for each squadron,

Bibliography

comprises daily record of aircraft and pilots in action; authored mainly by Squadron Adjutant with input from Intelligence Officer. If detailed National Archives number is not given, and instead only 'Air 27 records', this refers to hard copies of these reports obtained by the author 1960–1980, when they were still kept by the Public Records Office. The two components thereof, Forms 540 and 541, refer respectively to Summary of Events and Records of Events; the first speaks for itself, and the second lists individual aircraft and pilot take-offs and landing times for each day, sometimes with some additional notes.

Air 50: Combat Reports (abbreviated to CR in this volume; CRs are generally headed Form 'F', as are IPRs but they are distinct documents). One for each pilot making a claim, in each squadron action. Collected by Squadron Intelligence Officer. If detailed National Archives number is not given, and instead only 'Air 50 records', this refers to hard copies of these reports obtained by the author. For some squadrons, CRs are also given in appendices to the Squadron ORB, and these sources are shown with Air 27/x reference numbers from the National Archives and identified as from such an appendix in the Notes.

Air 81: RAF Casualty Files; include Squadron Commander's Reports on Flying Battle Casualties. One for each personnel or aircraft casualty; also such reports for each bombing raid on an RAF facility.

UK National Archives, WO set of records

Transcripts of recorded (POW) conversations: File WO208/4118, SRA 111-440, National Archives. (WO refers to a War Office file; SRA = Special Report Air Force)

Imperial War Museum

Archives, Imperial War Museum, London: *Luftwaffe Quartermaster General Loss Returns*

USA Archives

National Archives and Records Service, Washington: *Lageberichte*, 20.VI.1940-10.X. 1940, *Luftflottenkommando 3*; Records of Headquarters, German Air Force High Command, (*Oberkommando der Luftwaffe-OKL*), The National Archives, 1966; NA Microcopy No. T-321, Record Group No. 242/1028, Item No. OKL/2308, Roll No. 88; entries for 11–13 August 1940

Private Archives

Archive of Elston, Wolfgang E.: Elston, Wolfgang E., *Berlin revisited* (2004, revised version), thought to be unpublished excerpt perhaps in a school magazine-type publication, copy provided by Professor Elston to author; Elston, Wolfgang E., *Erinnerungen an die Goldschmidt-Schule – Berlin Grunewald: 1938 bis 1939*, this is an extended German language version (copy from Professor Elston to author) of an essay in English published in a book of reminiscences of the *Goldschmidt-Schule*: Heims, S. J., *Passages from Berlin: Recollections of former students and staff of the Goldschmidt Schule (1935-1939)* (South Berwick, Maine: Atlantic Printing, 1987); Elston, Wolfgang E., *Memories of Stoatley Rough School, Haslemere, Surrey, England 1939-1945 (written in honour of Nore Astfalck's 90th birthday and dedicated to the entire staff of Stoatley Rough)* (Memoir, 1990), manuscript supplied by Professor Elston to author, held as a twenty-one page memoir by several libraries and document centres, including the Wiener Library for the Study of the Holocaust and Genocide, London.

Archive of Arnot, Peter: Flying logbook, *Uffz* Hans-Helmut Habermehl, *1/JG 54*, entries for 11–13 August 1940; copy of logbook courtesy of Peter Arnot.

Scientific Journal and Magazine Articles

Fliegerblatt, Official Publication of the *Gemeinschaft der Flieger Deutscher Streitkräfte E.V.*, No. 6 of 2008 (pp. 119-120; *Reaktionen auf Suchanzeigen: Oblt Albrecht Drehs, III/JG 54*)

Parry, Simon, *The Reunion* (Flypast Magazine, December 1983 issue, p. 32-34)

Reynaud, J-Y., Teyssier, B., Auffret, J.P., Berne, S., De Batist, M., Marsset, T. and Walker, P., *The offshore sedimentary cover of the English Channel and its northern and western Approaches* (Journal of Quaternary Science, 18(3-4), pp. 361-371)

Forum

Cornwell, Peter, comment in a forum discussion, *forum.12oclockhigh. net/archive/index.php?t-40796.html*

Citations from Documents held by National Archives, UK

A fairly large number of short citations from documents held in the UK National Archives appear in this book. They are drawn mainly from the following RAF document sets held in the National Archives:

Bibliography

Intelligence Patrol Reports/Fighter Command Combat Reports; Air 16/955 (per squadron)
Operational Record Books; Air 27 (per squadron)
Combat Reports; Air 50 (per pilot)
RAF Casualty Files; Air 81 (per pilot or RAF station)
Air Ministry Operational Record Books; Air 25.

The book thus contains public sector information licensed under the Open Government License v.3.0 (http://www.nationalarchives.gov.uk/information-management/re-using-public-sector-information/uk-government-licensing-framework/).

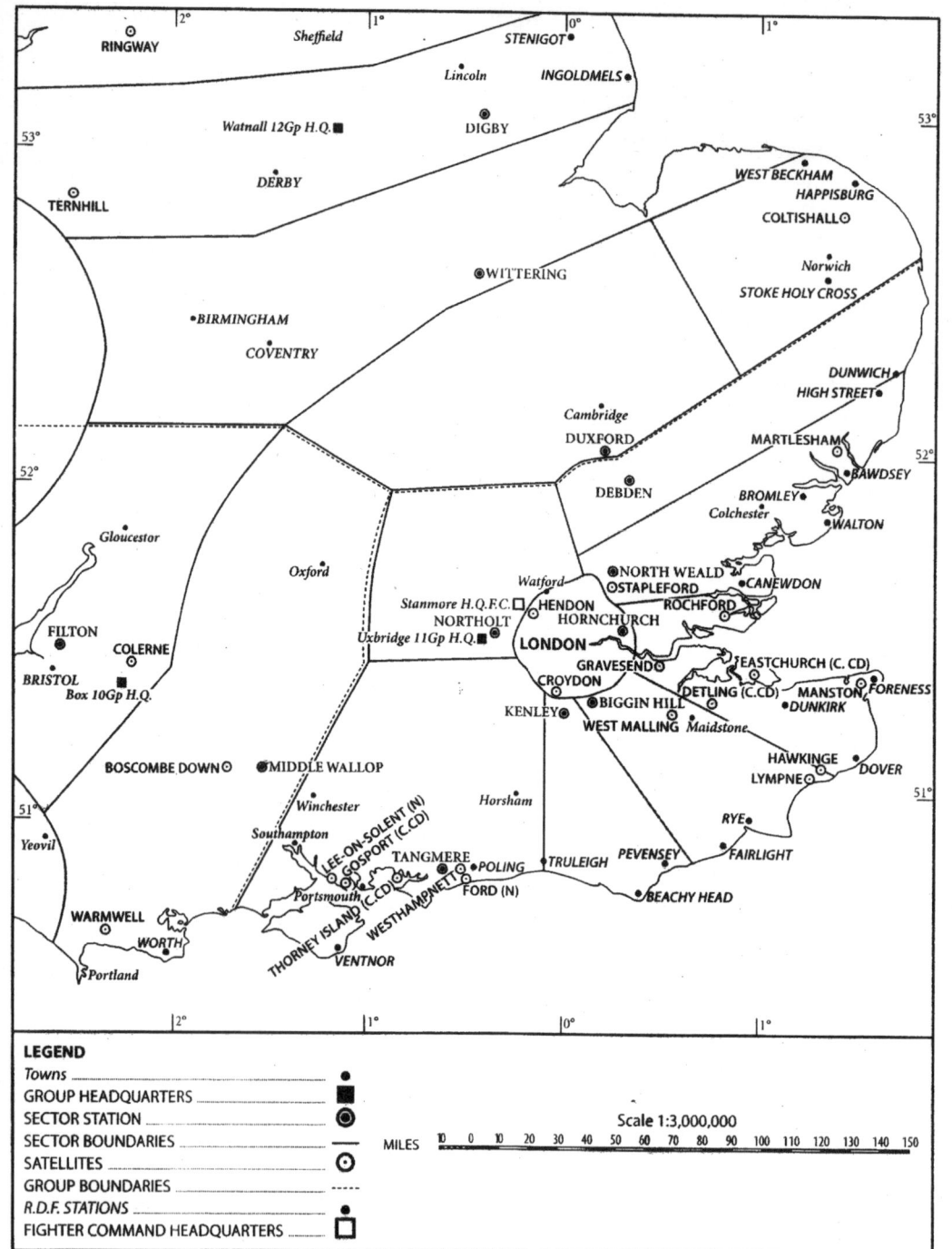

Map of 11 Group and more important parts of 10 and 12 Groups of Fighter Command; shows sector stations, sector boundaries and satellite airfields (N = naval, and C.CD = Coastal Command airfields) and radar (RDF) stations. Redrafted and simplified from an original in James, T. Cecil G., *The Battle of Britain* (Abingdon: Routledge, 2012) which is itself a reproduction of an original, Sheet 1 of Map 115, compiled and drawn at the Air Historical Branch of the RAF.

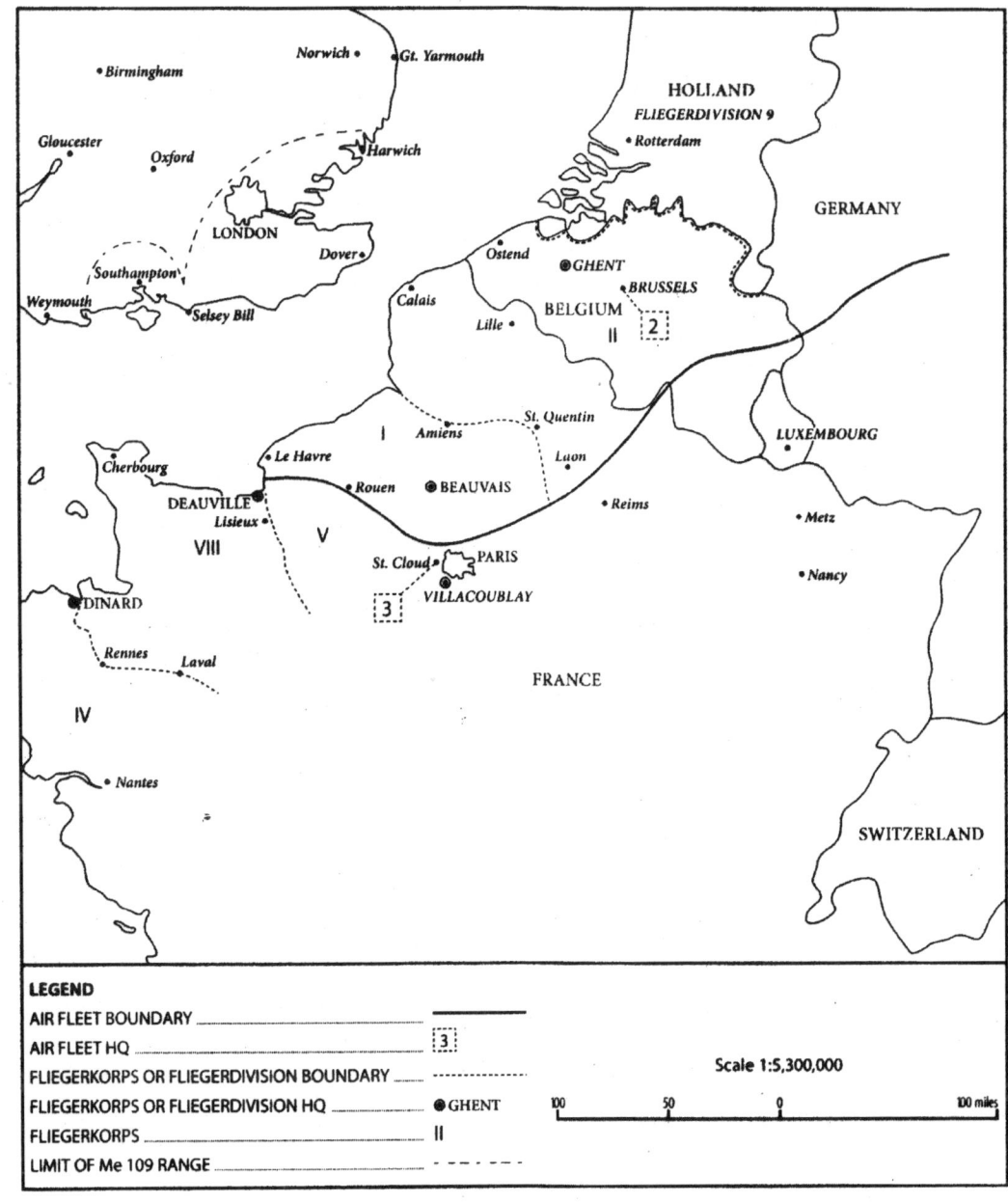

Luftflotten 2 and 3 base areas in Northern France, their component subdivisions into *Fliegerkorps* or *Fliegerdivisionen*, and the limit of the range of the Me 109 fighter, for the general Southampton area and for the London region. For the former area, note the very limited penetration possible. Simplified and redrafted from a map headed 'German Forces in the Battle of Britain', in Overy, Richard, *The Battle of Britain: the myth and the reality* (New York: W. W. Norton, 2002) (pp. 166-167).

Index

Badger, S/L John 'Tubby' 170–2, 174, 191
Bann, Sgt Eric 49, 51, 220
Boitel-Gill, F/Lt Derek 58, 93, 213
Boyd, F/Lt Adrian 32, 34, 104, 105, 112, 113
Brand, Air Vice Marshal Sir Quintin 10, 12, 14, 258
Bushell, Sgt Gordon 109, 110, 217

Carey, P/O Frank 106–7, 173–4, 176
Clyde, F/O William 181–3, 203, 227, 228
Connors, F/Lt Stanley 72, 73–4, 76
Crook, P/O David 45, 96, 97, 99, 222–4
Crossley, F/Lt Michael 22, 128–30, 140, 144

Dalton-Morgan, F/Lt Tom 172–3, 174, 176, 192
Darley, S/L H. S. 'George' 42–3, 46, 55, 60, 67, 97, 98, 221–2, 224

Davis, F/O Carl 55–6, 61, 182, 183, 191, 202–3, 204, 227, 228, 229
Deere, F/Lt Alan 78, 82, 84, 140–1, 143, 144
Domagala, Sgt Marian 49, 51, 53
Doulton, F/O Michael 56, 60, 181, 184, 204
Dowding, Air Chief Marshal Sir Hugh 10, 11, 14, 222, 246, 258
Dundas, F/O John 42, 45–6, 60, 98, 225–6
Dutton, F/Lt Roy 32–3, 60, 103–4, 234

Edelstein, Wolfgang 14, 180, 184–8
Ellis, S/L John 62, 79–80, 83, 84

Ferriss, F/O Henry 155, 159, 162–3, 164
Fighter Command (Royal Air Force)
  attacks on German bombers astern 38–9, 41, 48, 60, 75, 77, 96, 101, 103, 107, 125,

Index

126, 128–9, 134, 137, 138–9, 144, 146, 153–4, 156–7, 159, 171–2, 173, 176, 177, 183, 191
  beam 38–9, 60, 76–7, 96, 104, 107, 126–7, 134, 156–7, 179, 180, 181, 183, 191
  head on 69, 75–6, 125–6, 127, 131, 144, 146, 154–5, 158–9, 161–3, 164, 172, 173–4, 182
  quarter 38, 77, 100, 125, 164, 172, 183
  formations
  pairs 57, 68, 156
Fink, Oberst Johannes 11, 12, 19, 122–3, 124, 125, 128, 144, 149–52, 154–8, 164, 165, 246
Fiske, P/O W. M. L. 'Billy' 54–5, 60, 182, 183, 204
Freeborn, P/O John 25–6, 67, 72, 162

Gracie, F/Lt E. J. 'Jumbo' 136–8, 144, 242, 245
Göring, Reichsmarschall Hermann 9, 10–11, 13, 150, 194, 245, 255, 256, 257
Grice, P/O Douglas Hamilton 126, 130–1, 146
Grier, P/O Thomas 183, 184, 203, 228
Guy, Sgt Leonard 57, 227, 229, 231

Hallowes, Sgt Herbert 172, 176, 233–4
Harrison, P/O John 32, 105, 106
Harkness, S/L Hill 15, 100, 101–3, 113, 188, 192, 230
Henstock, F/Lt Lawrence 131–2, 133, 134, 143, 144

Hope, F/Lt Sir Archibald 180, 182, 184, 191, 199–202, 203, 227
Hughes, F/O David 47, 51, 189, 196–8, 199, 218, 219

Jeram, Sub Lt Dennis 41, 48, 52, 53

Kesselring, Feldmarschall Albert 10–12, 13, 14, 245–7, 249–50, 251, 252, 256–7, 258–9

Luftflotte 3 9-10, 14, 26, 90, 112, 147–148, 168–9, 194–5, 209, 211, 236, 245–8, 251–3, 255
Luftflotte 5 9
Luftwaffe (German Air Force)
  bomber formations 125–6, 137, 144, 147, 151–2, 171, 179, 247, 255–6
  fighter (Me 110) circles 27–33, 35, 36, 37, 42–6, 50, 54–6, 58, 60–1, 67–9, 92–4, 96–100, 104–5, 106, 108–9, 110, 111–13, 114, 146–7, 195–201, 203–5, 213, 216, 218, 227–9, 247–8, 251–2

Malan, F/Lt A. G. 'Sailor' 22–4, 25–6, 67, 68, 73, 156–7
Mann, Sgt Jack 70, 131, 132, 133
Marsh, Sgt H. J. 'Tony' 48–9, 51, 199, 205, 220
Mayers, P/O Clive 180–1, 184, 200–2, 206
McArthur, F/Lt James 44, 60, 97–8, 113, 223, 224
McGrath, P/O John 57, 182–3, 192, 227, 228
McGregor, S/L Hector 37–8, 39, 40, 60, 108

Milne, F/O Richard 153–5, 159–60, 168

Olive, F/Lt Gordon 87, 117–18, 240–1, 245
Osmand, P/O Alexander 39, 40, 216
Osterkamp, Generalmajor Theo (Jagdfliegerführer Luftflotte 2) 11–12, 13, 14, 16, 124, 145, 250, 256–7, 258–9
Overton, P/O Charles 97, 113, 114

Park, Air Vice Marshal Keith 10, 11, 12, 14, 258
Pond, F/Sgt Arthur 183, 203, 227–9

Royal National Lifeboat Institution (RNLI) 16, 202
  Margate Lifeboat 86, 89
  Weymouth RNLI Station 202

Saunders, F/Lt Gerald 87–8, 89, 117–18
Sing, F/Lt John 108, 216, 217
Smith, F/Lt Brian 62, 63, 80–1, 83
Smythe, F/Sgt George 139, 140, 143

Sperrle, Feldmarschall Hugo 10, 12–14, 245–6, 249, 251, 252, 254, 255, 257
Strickland, F/O James 37–8, 39, 60, 108–9, 207
Sutton, P/O Barry 138, 139, 142

Temme, Oberleutnant Paul 28, 175, 192, 193
Thompson, S/L John 73, 74–6, 158–9
Townsend, S/L Peter 64, 66, 69, 76
Trübenbach, Hauptmann Hanns 15, 16, 20, 237–8

Urwin-Mann, P/O John 50, 51, 189, 219

Ventnor 89–90, 92–4, 97–8, 110, 112, 114, 121, 145–7, 194, 196, 210, 233, 247, 253

Weaver, F/Lt Percy 71, 136, 138–9, 242–3
Woods-Scawen, P/O Tony 107, 172, 175, 178
Woodward, F/O Herbert 131, 132–3, 190, 191

Also available from Amberley Publishing

Available from all good bookshops or to order direct
Please call **01453-847-800**
www.amberley-books.com

Also available from Amberley Publishing

Available from all good bookshops or to order direct
Please call **01453-847-800**
www.amberley-books.com

Also available from Amberley Publishing

Available from all good bookshops or to order direct
Please call **01453-847-800**
www.amberley-books.com

Also available from Amberley Publishing

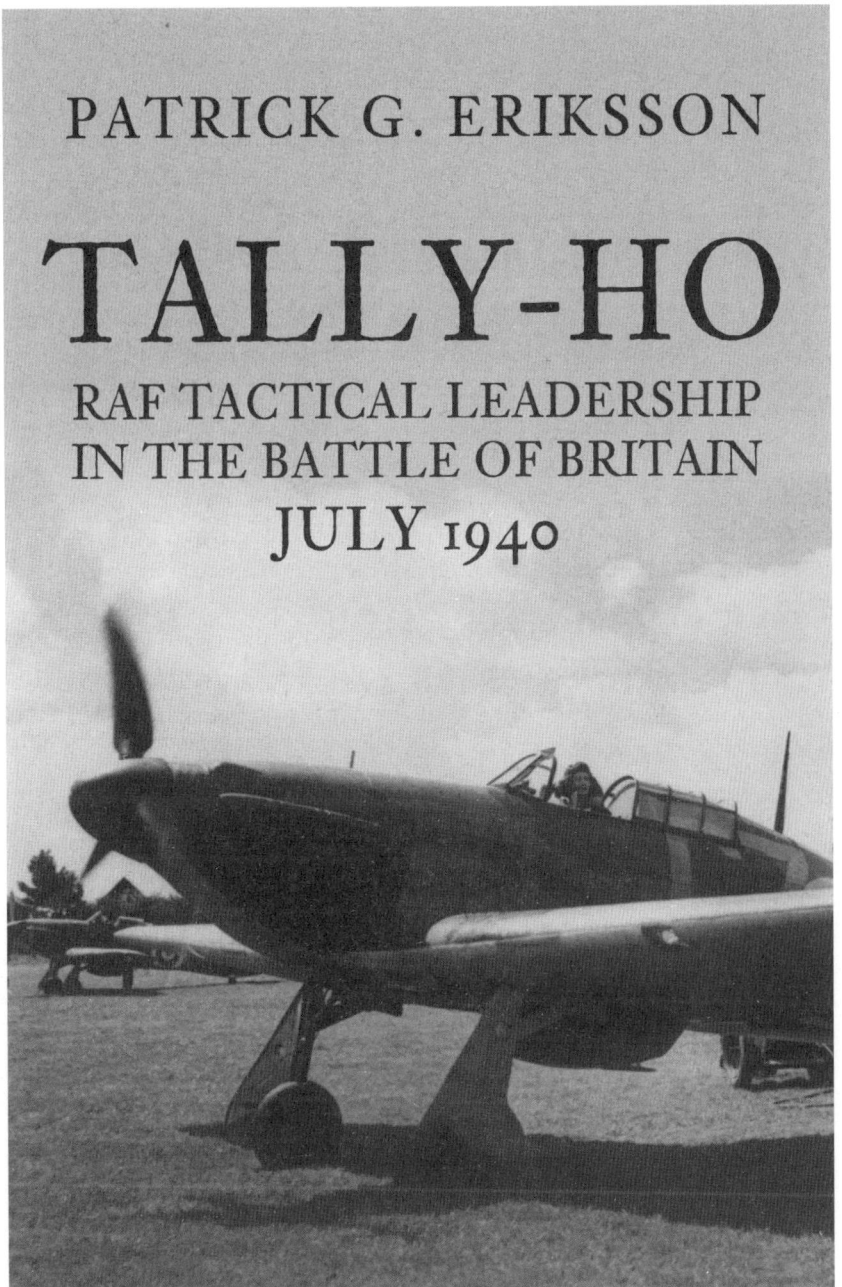

PATRICK G. ERIKSSON

TALLY-HO

RAF TACTICAL LEADERSHIP IN THE BATTLE OF BRITAIN JULY 1940

Available from all good bookshops or to order direct
Please call **01453-847-800**
www.amberley-books.com

Also available from Amberley Publishing

Available from all good bookshops or to order direct
Please call **01453-847-800**
www.amberley-books.com

Also available from Amberley Publishing

Available from all good bookshops or to order direct
Please call **01453-847-800**
www.amberley-books.com